About the author

Catharina Day comes from a long-established Irish family. She was born in Kenya but moved to County Donegal as a small child. She was married in County Donegal, and visits frequently with her husband and four children from her home in Scotland. She has compiled an anthology of Irish literature.

About the updaters of this edition

Nicky Swallow grew up in Belfast. Although she now lives in Italy, she returns to Ireland frequently to visit family and friends and has travelled extensively in the country. Connemara is her favourite place on earth.

Noelle Houston grew up in County Down and, after many travels, has returned there to live. Her life-long connection with Mayo makes it her home from home.

Vivien Stone is a writer and editorial consultant specialising in travel and culture. For the last ten years she has been getting to know southern Ireland and lives in rural County Cork for part of the year.

Mary-Ann Gallagher is a full-time travel writer, author of the Cadogan guide to Dublin.

Thanks also to **Vanessa Letts**.

Cadogan Guides
Highlands House, 165 The Broadway,
London SW19 1NE, UK
info@cadoganguides.co.uk
www.cadoganguides.com

The Globe Pequot Press
246 Goose Lane, PO Box 480, Guilford,
Connecticut 06437–0480, USA

Copyright © Catharina Day 2004

Cover design by Sarah Gardner
Cover photographs by CORBIS, Tim Mitchell and
 Alex Robinson
Maps © Cadogan Guides, drawn by Map Creation
 Ltd. Based on Ordnance Survey Ireland permit
 No.7739 © Ordnance Survey Ireland and
 Government of Ireland
Series Editor: Linda McQueen
Design: Sarah Gardner
Proofreading: Catherine Bradley
Indexing: Isobel McLean
Production: Navigator Guides Ltd

Printed in the United States by Versa Press Inc
A catalogue record for this book is available
 from the British Library
ISBN 1-86011-138-6

08

Maps

09

**Old Gods, Heroes
and Saints 229**

Reference

Introduction

Ireland is the perfect place to take a holiday. This lovely island has physical and spiritual qualities that are seldom found in the Western world. The pace of life is relaxing, the scenery beautiful and varied, with the sea never far from sight. Dublin, the capital, is cultured, attractive and easy to explore. The people of the country are easy to meet and invariably courteous and friendly. The climate is good and, though it's often damp, when the sunshine comes in soft shards it intensifies the already beautiful colours of the landscape. Forget sun culture and all its paraphernalia; travel with stout shoes and a warm jersey.

There is no such thing as a tiresome, hot journey in Ireland. Country roads are usually empty, and traffic jams are still an exception in most places. Some visitors bent on 'doing' Ireland get from one end of the country to the other in a day's drive, but this is not the way to travel at all. If you rush, the charm of the country and the people will pass you by – and the Irish do not approve of rushing.

Whatever direction you decide to go in, it is possible to stay in tranquil country houses, where the proportions and furnishings of the rooms are redolent of a more gracious age. Not only is the food delicious – fresh seafood, local meats, game and vegetables – you can also taste well-chosen wines and, of course, decent whiskey and beer. You will find the owners and staff of these places keen to help with any request you have, whether it's finding the origins of your great-granny, or directing you to the best fishing, golf, beaches, crafts and sites of historical interest.

It is so easy to travel in a country where you can explain your needs in English, and find yourself understood. Dry archaeological and historical facts suddenly become much more fascinating when you can ask for the local version of events, and hear for yourself the wonderful stories that make up history. Hearing the sound of spoken Irish is another pleasure that's in store. You'll discover a race who can express themselves with great character, humour and precision.

Ireland remains largely agricultural, with relatively few areas of industrial development. There are few huge motorways, endless suburbs, belching factories, marching powerlines, and little of the ugly side-effects of industry. Hopefully, the Irish will ensure things stay that way. Its population is relatively small, at about five million, and the Six Counties which form part of the United Kingdom make up 1,556,000 of that total. For years there has been a commonly held misconception that it was dangerous to travel in the North. Violence was confined to very small areas and no tourist has even been harmed by the Troubles within Ireland. Sensible, unprejudiced travellers will soon discover that, with the exception of a few well-known areas, the North is a quiet, unspoilt and attractive region. If your sympathy for the ordinary people of the province and your admiration for their courage and forbearance has been stirred by their problems, one of the most positive things you can do is visit the province itself.

Both North and South share a fascinating past; as Yeats wrote, 'Behind all Irish history hangs a great tapestry even Christianity had to accept, and be itself pictured there.' The Irish race has a long memory and a poetic imagination, which gives each hill, lough and pile of stones a background or story. The history of Ireland has been turbulent, and its telling fraught with prejudice and misunderstandings. But it is

A Note on Names

You will find that there are occasions when place names vary in spelling from those in this guide book. This is because different translations from the Gaelic exist, and there is no completely standardized map to follow. Bartholomews, Ordnance Survey, the RAC and the AA produce very good and detailed maps.

The Gaeltacht

This is the name given to several areas in Ireland where (Irish) Gaelic is spoken as the everyday language. These areas are mainly in the West, in Counties Donegal, Mayo, Galway and Kerry. You can expect all the signposts to be in Irish.

fascinating to approach it through its literary tradition. Ireland had its Golden Age of learning roughly between the 6th and 11th centuries; Frank O'Connor described it as the civilization of 'the little monasteries'. Monks transcribed the Celtic oral culture, wrote poetry and honoured God during the Dark Ages, when the rest of the Continent was in the hands of the barbarians. Ireland also had a strict bardic tradition, according to which members of the poets' guild had to study for up to 12 years before they were qualified. From that disciplined environment came mature poetry as evocative and delicate as poetry from China: stirring epics such as *The Tain*, which chronicles the wars of a heroic race, and moving love laments. Most of us can only read these poems in translation from the Gaelic, but luckily the translators, often present-day Irish poets, bring them close to us. From the 18th century, the ability of the Irish to express themselves in the language of the Saxon is apparent from the works of Jonathan Swift through to W. B. Yeats and the marvellous poets of today, such as Seamus Heaney. Poetry, theatre and the novel have continued to thrive since the heady days of Ireland's cultural renaissance and the uprising against the British in 1916; arts and music festivals flourish throughout the country today. Go if you can to the Abbey Theatre in Dublin or the Druid Theatre in Galway to see a play by Sean O'Casey or Brian Friel.

Modern Ireland conjures up a romantic idyll of whitewashed cottages set against a mountain landscape, and in places, this is still possible to find. But much has changed; many technological companies have been attracted to the country's highly educated young population, and have brought wealth, prosperity and transformation to the land. As a traveller in Ireland you will be able to enjoy all the conveniences of modern-day Europe and still lose yourself in its wilderness and beauty. By the end of your holiday, you may feel tuned in to the country and its people to the point where that famous saying can be aired yet again: that (the English) are more Irish than the Irish themselves: *Ipsis Hibernis hiberniores*.

A Guide to the Guide

Flying Visits is a series aimed at time-pressed short-break travellers wishing to take advantage of the wide choice of competitive direct flights to cities and towns, from

What to Go For...

	Art City	Architecture	Museums	Culture	Shopping	Gastronomy / Pubs	Houses / Gardens	Ancient Sites	Landscapes	Beaches / Coast	Mountains	Equestrian Events
Belfast	●	●	●	●	●	●	★	★	★	★	★	
Cork	●	●		●	●	●/★	●/★	★	★	★		
Derry City	●	●	●	●	●	●	★	★	★	★	★	
Dublin	●	●	●/★	●	●/★	●	●/★	★		★	★	●/★
Galway City			●	●	●	●/★		★	★	★	★	●
Killarney				●		★	★	★	★	★	★	
Limerick	●		●		●			★	★	★		
Westport				●		★	●	★	★	★	★	
Wexford			★	●				★	★	★	★	

● In the gateway city itself   ★ Within easy reach of the gateway city

Culture = theatre, cinema, opera, festivals.

mainland UK or North America, that access so effectively the heart of Ireland. *Flying Visits* caters for those who enjoy a city break, but who also may want to spend anything from a day to a week getting off the beaten track and seeing more of the countryside around – visitors, also, who may return many times for holidays by air or ferry, and who need some fresh ideas.

The four main chapters of this guide are centred on the destinations that are easy to reach directly from mainland UK: **Belfast** and **Derry City** in the north, **Westport** and **Galway City** in the northwest, **Dublin** and **Wexford** in the southeast, and **Cork**, **Killarney** and **Limerick** in the southwest. Some of these cities merit a whole trip in themselves; other smaller towns are compact enough to see in a day, and you will want to use them mainly as a base for visiting the surrounding glorious countryside, coastline and islands, for touring castles, gardens and big houses, and for experiencing the timeless quiet of Ireland's early Christian and ancient sites.

After each city come suggestions for **day trips and/or overnight stays**, all of which are perfectly easy to do by public transport, no more than an hour or two from your city base. But if you have a week to spare, and are willing to hire a car (listings are given in each city section), try following one of the suggested **five-night itineraries** from each city, and head deep into regional Ireland with all its charms. These itineraries take you by the hand day by day, with a few alternatives for wet weather, and drop you back near to your starting point ready to catch your plane or ferry home. You would be best advised, in high season at least, to book up each night's accommodation in advance using our carefully hand-picked suggestions.

Whether you have two days or a fortnight to spend exploring, *Flying Visits Ireland* helps you tailor your trip to see all that's unmissable and to add a few surprises, too.

Travel

02

Who Goes Where?

	page	Ryanair	easyJet	bmiBaby	British Midland	British European	MyTravelLite	British Airways	Aer Lingus	Aer Arann	Jet2	Air Wales	Cityjet	Delta (USA)	Aer Lingus (USA)	Other USA	Ferry (see p.11)
Belfast	34				●	●	●	●	●	●		●					●
Cork	171	●		●	●			●	●	●		●					●
Derry	63	●															
Dublin	111	●		●	●	●	●	●	●	●	●	●	●	●	●	●	●
Galway City	99									●							
Kerry (Killarney)	196	●															
Knock (Westport)	81	●	●					●	●								
Shannon (Limerick)	213	●				●			●	●		●	●	●	●	●	●	
Rosslare (Wexford)	162																●

Getting There

By Air: the Lowdown on Low-cost Flights

In the last few years the airline industry has undergone a revolution. Inspired by the success of Stelios Haji-Ioannou's 'upstart' easyJet company, other airlines – Ryanair, bmiBaby, MyTravelLite – flocked to join him in breaking all the conventions of air travel to offer fares at rock-bottom prices. After September 11th 2001, while long-haul carriers hit the ropes in a big way, these budget airlines experienced unprecedented sales, and responded by expanding their list of destinations throughout Europe.

Whereas in their first years no-frills airlines had an undoubted 'backpackerish' feel, this has become an increasingly mainstream way to travel. New airlines are still starting up all the time with an eye on expanding the no-frills cake, and larger national airlines have got in on the act, copying some of the more attractive aspects of budget travel, such as internet booking with discounts, and one-way fares. At the same time, other airlines go under or are subsumed by one another; routes are added, tested and dropped, and in 2004 the EU began looking at banning the regional airport subsidies on which some of the airlines, Ryanair in particular, rely to keep their prices down.

No Frills, No Thrills

The ways in which low prices are achieved can sometimes have a negative effect on the experience of travellers, but can sometimes be a bonus too. First, these airlines often use **smaller regional airports**, where landing fees and tarmac-time charges are at a minimum. In the UK this means you may be able to find a flight from nearer your home town: easyJet flies out of Luton and Liverpool, as well as Gatwick; British European from Exeter; bmiBaby from East Midlands; and Ryanair from Stansted and many other British cities, and so on. At the other end, you are taken direct to small, uncongested airports that are right in the heart of the countryside, not just the capital cities.

The **planes** tend to be all one-class only and with the maximum seating configuration.

Fares are one-way – so there is no need to stay over on a Saturday night to qualify for the lowest fares – and can vary enormously on the same route, according to when you travel and how far in advance you book: the most widely advertised, rock-bottom deals are generally for seats on very early-morning, early-in-the-week flights; on the most popular routes, while you might get a price of £40 for a 6am Monday flight, the same route can cost you £140 on a Friday evening. Because of this constantly changing price system it is important to note that **no-frills airlines are not always the cheapest**, above all on the very popular routes at peak times. One of the benefits of the no-frills revolution that is not always appreciated is not as much in their own prices as in the concessions they have forced on the older, mainstream carriers. It is **always** worth comparing no-frills prices with those of the main airlines, and checking out what special offers are going.

No-frills airline tickets are only sold direct, by phone or online, not through travel agents. To get the lowest prices you must book online, not by phone. You will not be issued with an actual **ticket** when you book, but given a reference number to show with your ID at check-in (some form of photographic ID, such as a driving licence, is now required even for UK domestic flights where no passport is needed). With some airlines you are not issued with an **assigned seat** at check-in either, but will board on a first-come, first-served basis. There are no 'air miles' schemes, and no **meal** will be included, though there will be (fairly expensive) snacks for sale onboard. There are no **refunds** if you miss your flight for any reason, although some of the airlines will allow you to **change** your destination, date of travel or the named traveller for a fee of around £15. There are also charges for any **excess baggage**.

Airlines

Aer Arann, Irish Republic t 0818 210 210, UK t 0800 587 2324, *www.aerarann.com*. Ireland's leading regional airline. Cork from Bristol, Southampton, Birmingham and Edinburgh. Galway from Edinburgh, Manchester, Birmingham and London Luton. Dublin six times a week from Isle of Man. Dublin to Cork, Galway, Kerry and Knock, and Cork to Belfast.

Aer Lingus, t (Irish Republic) 0818 365 000, (UK) 0845 084 4444, *www.aerlingus.com*. Dublin from Bristol, Manchester, Edinburgh, Birmingham, Glasgow, Heathrow and Jersey. Cork and Shannon from Heathrow.

Air Wales, t 0870 777 3131, *www.airwales.com*. Dublin and Cork from Swansea, Cardiff and Plymouth.

bmiBaby, t 0870 264 2229, *www.flybmi.com*. Cork from Gatwick, East Midlands, Cardiff and Manchester. Dublin from East Midlands. Belfast from Cardiff, East Midlands, Manchester and Teeside. Knock from Manchester.

British Airways, t 0845850 9850, *www.ba.com*. Dublin from Heathrow, Gatwick, Birmingham, Bristol, Edinburgh, Glasgow, Isle of Man and Manchester. Cork from Glasgow, Heathrow and Manchester. Flies to Shannon from Heathrow and Manchester. Belfast from Edinburgh, Glasgow and Manchester. Knock from Manchester.

British Midland, t 0870 607 0555, *www.flybmi. com*. Belfast and Dublin from Heathrow. Cork from Leeds Bradford.

Cityjet, t (Irish Republic) (01) 870 0100, *www.cityjet.com*. Dublin from London City.

easyJet, t 08717 500 100, *www.easyjet.com*. Belfast from Luton, Gatwick, Stansted, Bristol, Liverpool and Newcastle. Guarantees to price-match equivalent lowest fares on any rival low-cost airline.

Flybe (British European), t 0871 700 0123 (10p/min), *www.flybe.com*. Belfast from Birmingham, Edinburgh, Bristol, Exeter, Glasgow, Isle of Man, Jersey, Leeds Bradford, London City, Gatwick, Newcastle and Southampton. Dublin from Exeter, Guernsey, Jersey and Southampton. Cork and Shannon from Birmingham.

Jet2, t 0870 737 8282, *www.jet2.com*. Flies to Belfast from Leeds Bradford.

MyTravelLite, Irish Republic t 0818 300 012, UK t 08701 564 564, *www.mytravellite.com*. Dublin, Belfast and Knock from Birmingham.

Ryanair, Irish Republic t 0818 30 30 30, UK t 0871 246 0000 (10p/min), *www.ryanair. com*. Dublin from Stansted, Luton, Gatwick, Bristol, Cardiff, Bournemouth, Liverpool, Manchester, Birmingham, Leeds Bradford, Teeside, Newcastle, Blackpool, Glasgow, Edinburgh and Aberdeen. Shannon from Stansted and Glasgow. Cork, Derry, Knock and Kerry from Stansted.

Making it Work for You: 10 Tips to Remember

1 Whichever airline you travel with, the earlier you book, the cheaper seats will be.

2 Book on-line for the best prices, as there are often discounts of £2.50 to £5 per journey for on-line sales. Always compare the no-frills lines' prices with those of main carriers on the route you want to travel.

3 Be ready to travel at less convenient times. Very early morning and late night flights, and those early in the week (Mon–Wed), will always be the cheapest. But be sure to check there is a means of getting from your destination airport if you arrive at night, allowing for at least an hour's delay – if you have to fork out for a taxi rather than a shuttle bus or local bus service, this could eat up the saving you make by travelling late.

4 Think hard whether you want to book by credit card. You will have the consumer protection that that offers, but there is likely to be a supplement of anything up to £5. Consider using a debit card instead.

5 If you intend to travel often and can go at short notice, sign up for airlines' e-mail mailing lists to hear news of special offers.

6 Check whether airport taxes are included in the quoted price; they are usually extra.

7 Check the baggage allowance and don't take any excess. If you can travel light, take hand baggage only, as at some airports your airline will be low priority for the baggage handlers and there can be a long wait.

8 Take your own food and drink, allowing for possible delays, to avoid paying for over-priced airport food or on-board snacks.

9 Make sure you take your booking reference and confirmation with you to check in (this will have been emailed or posted to you). You must of course also show your passport for international flights.

10 Never ignore the advised check-in times, which are generally two hours. Don't be tempted to cut it fine, as check-in takes longer with budget airlines than with traditional carriers, and at the same time the airlines try to keep boarding times short to meet their fast turn-around times. If you care where you sit, for example if you are tall and want an aisle seat, or are travelling in a group, check in even earlier or, if the airline doesn't give assigned seats, get to the departure gate as early as possible to be ahead of the bunch.

Another way in which prices are kept down is by keeping **staffing levels** very low, especially on the ground. This means that check-in can take a lot longer than for main-carrier flights, especially for the most popular routes and at peak times. Be warned.

What's the Worst that Can Happen?

From time to time the press ripples with stories of 'holiday hell' in low-cost air travel, from people ending up a four-hour journey from their destination, to lost baggage and no one to look for it, queues, cancellations, and the danger of so many hidden extras – taxes, expensive food, travel to and from outlying airports, wheelchairs – that any old main-carrier flight could have been better value. Essentially, with no-frills flights, you're supposed to get what you pay for. If you pay a really low fare and get to your destination without a hitch, you think, hey, this is great. It's when a problem does arise, though, that you start to notice the downside of no-frills operations. Since every plane is used to the limit, there are no 'spare' aircraft, so if one has a technical problem somewhere the day's schedules can collapse like a house of cards; since there are so few ground staff, when bags gets lost there's scarcely anyone available to look for them, or even show an interest. And all the budget operators accept far fewer obligations towards customers in the event of lost bags, delays and so on than main carriers traditionally have; this is stated in the small

Comparison Websites

www.whichbudget.com
www.flights4less.co.uk
www.cheapflights.co.uk
www.opodo.co.uk
www.skyscanner.net
www.majortravel.co.uk
www.ebookers.com, t 0870 010 7000
www.cheaponlineflights.com, t 01482 326911

Getting to Ireland Cheaply from North America

It is also possible for North Americans to take advantage of the explosion of cheap inter-European flights, by taking a charter to London, and booking a UK–Ireland budget flight in advance on a budget airline's website (see p.7). This will need careful planning: you're looking at an 8–14hr flight followed by a 3hr journey across London and another 2hr hop to Ireland; it can certainly be done, especially if you are a person who is able to sleep on a night flight, but you may prefer to spend a night or two in London.

Direct to Ireland

The main airports for transatlantic flights are **Dublin** and **Shannon**, and the main carriers flying direct to Ireland are Delta Airlines and Aer Lingus.

Since **prices** are constantly changing and there are numerous kinds of deals on offer, the first thing to do is find yourself a travel agent who is capable of laying the current options before you. The time of year can make a great difference to the price and availability; prices can range from around $500 for the best bargain deals to well over $1,000.

A number of companies offer cheaper charter flights to Ireland – look in the Sunday travel sections of *The New York Times*, *Los Angeles Times*, *Chicago Tribune*, *Toronto Star* or other big-city papers.

Aer Lingus, t 1 800 IRISH AIR, *www.aerlingus.com*. Non-stop to Dublin from Los Angeles, Boston, Chicago and New York; to Shannon from Chicago, Boston and New York.

American Airlines, t 1 800 433 7300, hearing- or speech-impaired TTD t 1 800 543 1586, *www.aa.com*. Runs Aer Lingus-operated flights to Dublin from Chicago, LA or New York, and to Shannon from Baltimore/ Washington, Boston, Chicago and New York.

Continental Airlines, USA t 1 800 231 0856, hearing impaired (TTD/TT) t 1 800 343 9195, *www.continental.com*. Dublin and Shannon from New York (Newark).

Delta Airlines, t 1 800 241 4141, *www.delta.com*. Dublin and Shannon from Atlanta (with connections from New York and Chicago).

Via London

Start by finding a cheap charter flight or discounted scheduled flight to London: try the main airlines, but also check the Sunday-paper travel sections for the latest deals, and if possble research your fare initially on some of the US cheap-flight websites: *www.priceline.com*, *www.expedia.com*, *www.hotwire.com*, *www.bestfares.com*, *www.eurovacations.com*, *www.cheap trips.com*, *www.orbitz.com*, *www.cheaptickets.com*, *www.onetravel.com*.

British Airways, t 1 800 AIRWAYS, *www.ba.com*. Dublin, Cork, Shannon, Belfast via London.

United Airlines, t 1 800 538 2929, *www.united.com*. Major US centres to London.

Virgin Atlantic Airways, t 1 800 862 8621, *www.virgin-atlantic.com*. Manchester from Orlando, and London from Las Vegas, LA, Washington, New York, San Francisco and Orlando.

When you have the availability and arrival times for London flights, match up a convenient flight time on the website of the budget airline that flies to your chosen Irish city. *Be careful to choose only flights from the airports near London: Luton, Gatwick, Heathrow, London City and Stansted. Regional UK airports will not be practical options.*

You will most likely be arriving at Heathrow terminals 3 or 4 (possibly Gatwick), and may be flying out from Stansted, Luton, London City or Gatwick, all of which are in different directions and will mean travelling through central London, so leaving enough time is essential. Add together the journey times and prices for Heathrow into central London and back out again to your departure airport. You could mix and match – the Tube to Victoria and the Gatwick Express, or a taxi from Heathrow to King's Cross Thameslink and a train to Luton – but don't even think of using a bus or taxi at rush hours (7–10am and 4–7pm); train and/or Underground (Tube) are the only sensible choices. Always add on waiting times and delays in London's notoriously creaky transport system; and finally, although the cheapest budget airline fares are early morning and late at night, make sure your chosen transport is still operating.

For train, bus and tube information within London, call t 020 7222 1234, *www.transportforlondon.gov.uk*.

Airport to Airport Taxis

A taxi directly between airports might avoid central London but is an expensive option:
Heathrow–Gatwick: 1hr 30mins, £85–£100.
Heathrow–Stansted: 2hrs 15mins, £140–£160.
Heathrow–Luton: 1hr 15mins, £80–£90.

Heathrow

Heathrow is about 15 miles west of the centre. **Airport information: t** 0870 0000 123.
By Tube: Heathrow is on the Piccadilly Line. Tube trains depart every 5–9 minutes from 6am to midnight and the journey time to the centre is 55mins. Single fare £3.80.
By bus: The Airbus A2 (**t** 08705 80 80 80, *www.nationalexpress.com*) departs from all terminals every 30mins and makes several stops before terminating at King's Cross or Russell Square; the National Express 403 or 500 terminates at Victoria. £10, £15 return. It's a long ride: at least 1hr 45mins.
By train: The Heathrow Express (**t** 0845 600 1515) is the fastest option: trains every 15mins between 5.10am and 11.40pm to Paddington Station, which is on the Tube's Bakerloo, Circle and District Lines, taking 15mins. £13 single or £25 return.
By taxi: There are taxi ranks at all terminals. Fares into central London are about £35–£50.

Gatwick

Gatwick is about 20 miles south of London. There are two terminals, North and South, linked by a shuttle service. **Airport information: t** 0870 000 2468.
By train: The fastest service is the Gatwick Express (**t** 08457 48 49 50), which runs from Victoria Station to the South Terminal every 15 minutes and takes about 30mins. £11 single, £21.50 return. There are two other slower train services: another from Victoria, and one from London Bridge.
By taxi: Fares from central London with a black cab are about £40–£60.

Luton

30 miles north of London. **Airport information: t** (01582) 405 100.
By bus: Greenline bus 757 (**t** 0870 608 7261) runs roughly every half-hour between Luton Airport and stop 6 in Buckingham Palace Road, Victoria, via Finchley Rd, Baker St and Marble Arch. £8.50 single. The journey takes 1hr 15mins.
By train: Between 8am and 10pm, Thameslink (**t** 08457 48 49 50) run frequent trains from King's Cross Thameslink Station (10mins' walk from the King's Cross Station), via Blackfriars, London Bridge and Farringdon, to Luton Airport Parkway. Tickets cost £10.40 single. At Luton a free shuttle bus takes you on to the airport; the journey takes 55mins.
By taxi: A black cab will cost you around £40–£60 from central London.

Stansted

Stansted is the furthest from London, about 35 miles to the northeast. **Airport information: t** 0870 000 0303.
By bus: Airbus A6 (**t** 08705 757 747) runs every 30mins from Victoria Station, Marble Arch and Hyde Park Corner, taking 1hr 30mins or more in traffic. There are less frequent services through the night. Tickets cost £10 single or £16 return.
By train: The Stansted Express (**t** 08457 48 49 50) runs every 30mins (15mins during peak times) between 5am and 11pm to and from Liverpool Street Station, in the City, taking 45mins. Tickets cost £13.80 single.
By taxi: A black cab from central London will cost £45–£65.

Sample Journeys

Heathrow–Luton: get to Heathrow Express from terminal 15mins; wait for train 10mins; journey 15mins; go from Paddington Station down into Tube 10mins; Tube to Farringdon 15mins; go up and buy Thameslink ticket 10mins including queueing; train and shuttle to Luton 55mins. **Total journey time** 2hrs 10mins, plus 45mins for delays and hitches, so 3hrs would be safest.
Heathrow–Stansted: get to Tube station from terminal 10mins, wait for Tube 5mins, Piccadilly Line to King's Cross 1hr 10mins, change to Circle Line and continue to Liverpool Street Tube Station 15mins, up into main line station and buy Stansted Express ticket 10mins, wait for train 20mins, train journey 45mins. **Total journey time** 2hrs 55mins, plus 45mins for delays and hitches, so 3hrs 40mins would be safest.

print of their terms and conditions (all there, on the websites), but many people don't read this until after their problem has come up. The companies' explanation is always that this is what 'no-frills' is all about.

Disasters, of course, can always happen, but an awareness of the way the system works and why fares are cheap can go a good way to avoiding being caught out – *see* the tips in the box on p.8. Finally, while corners are cut in many ways, there has been no evidence that those corners involve safety issues.

Cheap Flights from Ireland to Europe

One of the big advantages to Irish and Northern Irish residents of the budget flight explosion, and of the success of Ryanair in particular, has been that Irish domestic travel, and cheap flights to European holiday destinations, have become very easy to find, without the hassle of going via London.

The main centre for a huge choice of flights out of Ireland is Dublin, with a few international flights also from Cork, Kerry, Shannon and Belfast.

From **Dublin**, Aer Lingus will take you to: Alicante, Amsterdam, Barcelona, Berlin, Bilbao, Bologna, Brussels, Copenhagen, Dubrovnik, Dusseldorf, Faro, Frankfurt, Geneva, Lisbon, Madrid, Malaga, Milan, Munich, Nice, Palma, Paris, Prague, Rome, Tenerife, Toulouse, Valencia, Venice, Vienna, Warsaw and Zurich from as little as €19. Ryanair goes to Brussels, Faro, Girona (for Barcelona), Malaga and Paris; Flybe (aka British European) to Geneva, Guernsey and Jersey; Cityjet to Malaga; Snowflake (*www.flysnowflake.com*) to Stockholm; Basiq Air (*www.basiqair.com*) to Rotterdam; Germanwings (*www.germanwings.com*) to Cologne, and Hapag-Lloyd Express (*www.hlx.com*) to Hamburg and Stuttgart.

From **Belfast**, Flybe (aka British European) flies to Toulouse, and BMI flies to Alicante, Madrid, Nice and Tenerife. From **Cork**, you can get to Paris, Amsterdam, Milan, Malaga, Barcelona or Alicante with Aer Lingus, or to Amsterdam, Paris, Milan, Malaga, Barcelona and Alicante with Ryanair; from **Shannon** Ryanair flies to Brussels, Frankfurt and Paris; and from **Kerry** Ryanair takes you to Frankfurt.

By Sea

The **ferries** from the British west coast cross the Irish Sea at the shortest possible crossing points. Which port and crossing you choose will depend on where you are starting from, and where you wish to go in Ireland – which is not as obvious as it may seem. The Irish Sea is notoriously rough, and some crossings may be cancelled owing to gales in winter.

The main crossings are as follows:

Rosslare Harbour (near Wexford) and southeast Ireland is served by Fishguard and Pembroke in South Wales.

Dublin Harbour and **Dun Laoghaire** are served by Holyhead, in North Wales, Mostyn and Liverpool. There is also a seasonal service to the Isle of Man.

Belfast and nearby **Larne**, in the North, are served by ferries and catamarans taking the short crossing from Cairnryan, Stranraer and Troon in Scotland, and by ferries taking the longer journey from Liverpool. There is also a seasonal service to the Isle of Man.

Cork, the port for the southern Republic, is reached via Swansea, in South Wales.

All the ferry ports are well connected to rail and coach transport, and all the ferry services have drive-on/drive-off facilities for cars. **Prices** depend on time of year and length of crossing, how long you intend to stay in Ireland and, if you are taking your car, the number of passengers, car size and so on. Schedules can be complex too. Find a good travel agent and let them explore the options.

Note that at some peak times of the year – Easter, Christmas and especially around spring and autumn bank holidays – and on all sailings from Liverpool, the number of passengers on certain ferry crossings is controlled. All non-motorist passengers must have a 'sailing control ticket' to board the ship at these times. These can be obtained when you book your crossing, or if you change your booking or have an open ticket, from the ferry offices. It is worth checking whether you need a control ticket before you start your journey.

Otherwise, crossings are easygoing. Unless they are packed, there is usually no problem if you miss a boat, even if you have a car. They'll just put you on the next one – but do ring ahead and let them know if you are delayed.

Ferry Companies

Irish Ferries, Dublin t 0181 300 400, Liverpool t 08705 17 17 17, *www.irishferries.com*. Holyhead–Dublin, up to 5 sailings daily; 3hrs or 1hr 49min by catamaran. Pembroke–Rosslare, 2 sailings daily all year, 3hrs 45mins.

Isle of Man Steam Packet Company/Sea Cat, Isle of Man t 08705 523 523, Dublin t 1 800 551 743, *www.steam-packet.com*. Isle of Man–Dublin, up to 4 sailings per week Mar–Oct; 4½hrs; 2hrs 50mins by fastcraft. Isle of Man–Belfast, up to 4 sailings per week, Mar–Oct; 2hrs 45mins by fastcraft. Liverpool–Dublin, Feb–Nov daily; 3hrs 55mins by fastcraft. Belfast–Troon, daily; 3½hrs by fastcraft.

Norse Merchant Ferries, Irish Republic t (01) 819 2999, UK t 0870 600 4321, *www.norsemerchant.com*. Liverpool–Belfast, day and night sailings 1–2 times daily, all year, 8hrs. Liverpool–Dublin, 1 daily, all year, 8hrs.

P&O Irish Sea, UK t 0870 2424 777, Irish Republic t 1800 409049, *www.poirishsea.com*. Five routes to Ireland: Liverpool–Dublin, 1-2 times daily, Cairnryan–Larne, 3 sailings daily, all year, 1hr 45mins; 5 catamaran sailings daily April–mid Oct, 1hr; Fleetwood–Larne, 3 times per week, 8hrs; Troon–Larne, 2 sailings daily April–Sept, 1hr 50mins; Mostyn–Dublin, 2 sailings daily, 6hrs/7½hrs.

Stena Line, reservations in the UK t 08704 00 67 98, Dublin t (01) 204 7777, *www.stenaline. ie*. Holyhead–Dun Laoghaire, 3 sailings daily all year, 3½ hrs; 3 catamaran sailings, 1½ hrs. Fishguard–Rosslare, up to 5 sailings daily all year, 3½hrs; by catamaran 1hr 50mins. Stranraer–Belfast, 2 ferry sailings daily, 1hr 45mins or 3hrs 15mins; 5 catamaran sailings daily, 1hr 45mins.

Swansea Cork Ferries, Swansea, UK t (01792) 456116, 52 South Mall, Cork City, County Cork t (021) 427 1166, *www.swanseacorkferries. com*. Swansea–Cork, 10hrs (overnight from Swansea, on alternate days, and every day except Tuesday in July and Aug).

Entry Formalities

Passports and Visas

British citizens do not require a passport to enter the **Republic**. All the same, it can be useful to take a passport or some form of identification with you for completing formalities such as hiring a car. Citizens of the USA and Canada must have a valid passport to enter the Republic, but no visa is required.

For **Northern Ireland**, entry formalities are exactly as they are for entry to the United Kingdom. US and Canadian citizens require a passport but no visa. UK citizens do not need any form of identity documents, but it's as well to carry some in case you are stopped in a security check.

Citizens (other than UK citizens) of the European Union, Australia and New Zealand need a full passport or identity card for entry into both the Republic and Northern Ireland. Passports are also required for visitors from other countries, and citizens of some may need visas too.

Customs

There is no customs inspection for travellers between the Republic and Northern Ireland or mainland Britain. Travellers do not have to pay tax or duty in the UK or Ireland on goods bought in other EU countries, as long as they are for personal use. This includes gifts, but the resale of goods may be illegal. Guidelines are issued for quantities of tobacco and alcohol regarded as reasonable for personal use; if you bring more than these amounts you must be able to satisfy customs officers that they are genuinely for your own use. The limits are: 800 cigarettes, 400 cigarillos, 200 cigars, 1kg of smoking tobacco, 10 litres of spirits, 20 litres of fortified wine, 90 litres of wine and 110 litres of beer. Under-17-year-olds cannot import tobacco or alcohol.

Duty-free no longer exists within the EU borders. If arriving from outside the EU, however, duty-free remains, as do customs

Customs Information
Irish Republic: t (01) 877 6200, *www.revenue.ie*.
UK: t 0845 010 9000, international callers t (00 44 20) 8929 0152, *www.hmce.gov.uk*.
USA: t (001 202) 354 1000 *www.customs. ustreas.gov*.
Canada: t 800 461 9999, *www.cbsa-asfc.gc.ca*, t 1 800 461 9999, (international callers t (001 204) 938 3500).

allowances, which are: 220 cigarettes or 100 cigarillos or 50 cigars or 250 grams of tobacco; 2 litres of still table wine; 1 litre of spirits or strong liqueurs over 22% alcohol, or 2 litres of fortified wine, sparkling wine or other liqueurs. The limit on all other goods including gifts and souvenirs is £145 for Northern Ireland, €92 for the Republic. Anything above these limits must be declared and tax paid.

Residents of the USA may each take home $400-worth of foreign goods without paying duty, including tobacco and alcohol allowances. Canadians can take home $500 worth of goods in a year, plus their tobacco and alcohol allowances.

Dog- and cat-owners can bring their pet to Ireland, as long as it comes directly from mainland Britain, the Channel Islands or the Isle of Man.

VAT Refunds

Any non-EU visitor can claim back the **VAT** (Value Added Tax) on goods bought in Ireland. To claim a tax refund, you must complete a form provided by the shop and present the form and goods to Customs when you leave. You must take your purchases home with you, within three months of purchase.

Getting Around

By Air

It is possible to fly from one city to another in Ireland. However, this is a small island and the main destinations are well covered by rail and bus.

By Train

In the Republic, trains are operated by **Iarnród Eireann** ('Iron Road Irish Rail'). Routes radiate out from Dublin and take you through sleepy little stations and green countryside. The system is rather like the British system of 50 or 60 years ago, with old signal boxes which still need people to operate them and keep an eye on things. People are always friendly on trains, and the ticket inspectors are far from officious. Services are reliable, and the fares are reasonable. All the same, the network is not extensive, and especially

> ### Railway Companies
> **Iarnród Eireann, t** 1850 366 222 or **t** (01) 703 4070, *www.irishrail.ie*. For information, timetables and tickets in the Republic. **NIR Travel Shop**, Great Victoria Street Station, Belfast, **t** (028) 9023 0671; NIR enquiries **t** (028) 9089 9411; reservations **t** (028) 9089 9409. For rail travel in Northern Ireland.

lacking in the west and north; you will find trains useful mostly for getting to and from Dublin. Fares are nearly always more than those of buses, especially for one-way trips.

Rail travel in Northern Ireland is run by **Northern Ireland Railways** (NIR), with services connecting Belfast to Coleraine and Derry and the ports. This system is fully integrated with Iarnród Eireann, and lines between Belfast and Dublin are operated jointly by Iarnród Eireann and NIR. It takes two hours to reach Dublin on the Belfast–Dublin non-stop express, and there are eight trains a day (five on Sundays).

Discounts and Passes

If you are planning an itinerary with lots of train trips in a short time, ask about the special rail cards, allowing unlimited travel over a given period of time. There's **Faircard** deals for under 26s, especially on return trips to or from Dublin (one of these even includes a free laundry service) as well as various discount tickets such as the **Weekender**, valid for outward travel on Fri, Sat or Sun, returning any time up to Tues. The **Irish Explorer** ticket can be used for five days out of 15, is valid on the Republic's entire intercity and suburban rail network and costs €105. The **Irish Rover** has similar conditions and can also be used in Northern Ireland (€130). Valid in the Republic only, the **Irish Explorer Rail and Bus** also includes travel on Bus Eireann, gives 8 days' travel out of 15 consecutive days and costs €160. At the top of the range is the **Emerald Card**, used for 15 days out of 30 and valid for both trains and buses in both countries; it costs €310, or €180 for 8 days out of 15.

Ireland is now part of the **Eurail Pass** and **Interail Pass** networks, which allow unlimited rail travel on European railways, including the Republic of Ireland but excluding the UK, and free ferry crossings from France to Ireland. To obtain the Eurail Pass you must be resident of a non-European country and buy it outside

Bus Companies

Bus Éireann/Busáras, Store Street, Dublin,
t (01) 836 6111, *www.buseireann.ie.*
Citybus, Belfast, t (028) 90 66 66 30,
www.translink.co.uk.
Dublin Bus, t (01) 873 4222, *www.dublinbus.ie.*
Nestor Bus, Galway, t (091) 797 144,
www.busnestor.galway.net.
Ulsterbus, Europa Buscentre, Great Victoria
Street, Belfast, t (028) 9066 6630,
www.translink.co.uk.

Europe. The Interail Pass is on sale to European residents, and is available in the UK from Rail Europe. There are also discounts for under-26s.
Rail Europe (UK), 178 Piccadilly, London W1V OBA, t 08705 848 848, *www.raileurope.co.uk.*
Rail Europe (USA/Canada), t 877 257 2887 (USA) or t 1 800 361 RAIL (Canada), *www.raileurope.com.*

By Bus

The bus service throughout Ireland is efficient and goes to the most remote places. The main companies are **Bus Eireann/Busáras** in the Republic and **Ulsterbus** in Northern Ireland. Prices are reasonable, although on Bus Eireann they can be irrational, with a 20-mile journey sometimes costing as much as one of 100 miles. The best deals are with mid-week return tickets between the principal cities. The most convenient and reliable source for bus information is always the local tourist office.

Bus Eireann offers discount **Irish Rambler** tickets for 3, 8 or 15 days costing €53, €116 and €168, respectively. There's a similar **Irish Rover** ticket, which is also good on Ulsterbus; again, the options are 3, 8 or 15 days and the respective prices are €68, €152 and €226. They also operate chatty one-day and half-day tours throughout the Republic from many cities; ask for details at any of their Travel Centres, located in the bus company offices in Cork and Dublin, or buy tickets online from the the website tours section (*www.buseirann.ie/asp/tourlist.asp*).

By Car

In this guide, the day trips and overnighters we propose from the main cities are accessible by public transport. But if you plan to follow any of the touring itineraries, a car will be necessary. And you will be rewarded: it is along these little lanes that the secret life of Ireland continues undisturbed. The black and red-brown cows still chew by the wayside while the herdsman, usually an old man or a child, salutes you with an upward nod.

Once upon a time, one of the best things about driving in Ireland was the lack of other cars, and the absence of ugly, if efficient, motorways with their obligatory motor inns and petrol stations. With the Republic's new prosperity, this has changed in many places. Traffic around the towns, especially Dublin, can be ferocious, while the government is committed to a big programme of new roads and road-widenings that are guaranteed to make the problem worse, while eroding the country's natural beauty and its way of life.

Watch out for the country driver who tends to drive right in the middle of the road, never looks in his mirror to see if anyone is behind, and probably won't indicate if he suddenly decides to turn left or right. The ones wearing old tweed caps are usually the worst offenders. There is also the other extreme: people who drive at crazy speeds on narrow roads. Cars frequently pull out of a side road in front of you and, just as you are getting up enough steam to pass, suddenly decide to turn off down another side road. Don't be alarmed by the sheepdogs which appear from cottage doorways to chase your car – they are well skilled at avoiding you.

If your car **breaks down** in any part of Ireland you will always be able to find a mechanic to give you a hand; whether it's late at night or on a Sunday, just ask someone. He or she will sweep you up in a wave of sympathy and send messengers off in all directions to find you someone with a reputation for mechanical genius. If it is some small and common part that has let you down, he will either have it or do something that will get you by until you come to a proper garage. One thing you will notice is that the Irish have a completely different attitude to machinery from most nationalities. In England, if you break down, it is an occasion for embarrassment; everybody rushes by hardly noticing you or pretending not to. In Ireland, if your car has broken down the next passing car will probably stop, and the problem will be readily taken on and discussed with great enjoyment.

In Ireland you **drive on the left** (when you are not driving in the middle of the road); the government has installed signs in seemingly random places around the country to remind us: *Conduire à gauche! Links fahren!* **Petrol stations** stay open until around 8pm, and the village ones are open after Mass on Sundays. If you are desperate for petrol and every station seems closed, you can usually knock on the door and ask somebody to start the pumps for you. Prices are roughly the same as in Britain, three or four times as much as in the US.

The **speed limit in the Republic** is 60mph (100kph) on ordinary roads, 70mph (113kph) on motorways and 30–45mph (48–69kph) through the villages and towns, as posted. Note that speed limit signs in the Republic are always given in miles. Road signs showing distances to the next towns are charmingly given in either miles or kilometres, usually without telling you which one (the older, white signs with black borders are in miles; newer, enamelled aluminium signs in green or white are usually in kilometres). Otherwise, directional signs are mainly notable for their absence; out in the country you will get lost, and probably stay lost. Some signs, especially in Gaeltacht areas, will be written in Irish; of these, the most important to know is *Go Mall* – slow down. *An Lar* is the city centre, while *Gach treo eile* signifies 'all routes'.

The **speed limit in Northern Ireland** is 70mph (112kph) on dual carriageways, 60mph (96kph) on country roads, 40mph (64kph) in built-up areas and 30mph (48kph) in towns.

Drivers and front-seat passengers must always wear a **seat belt** – it is illegal not to. Children under 12 should travel in the back. There are strict drink-driving laws in the Republic as in the North, and the police will use a breathalyser test if they suspect that you 'have drink taken'; the legal limit is roughly two pints of Guinness.

There are some excellent **motoring maps**: Bartholomew's quarter inch, obtainable from the AA and Bord Fáilte, gives good details of minor roads. The principal roads in Northern Ireland are marked A, lesser roads B; in the Republic they are N (national) and R (regional). Scenic routes are signposted and marked on the Bord Fáilte map. Place names on signposts in the Republic are usually given in English and in Irish; in the places where Irish only is used a good map will be useful.

Residents of the Republic of Ireland, Northern Ireland and Great Britain using private cars and motorcycles may cross the borders with very little formality. A **full, up-to-date licence** is all you need. Under EU regulations, private motor insurers will provide the minimum legal cover required in all EU countries, although they may need to be told before you travel. Always carry the **vehicle log book**. If you have hired a car, be sure to tell the rental company that you plan to cross borders, and confirm that you have all the necessary papers; the rental company should also deal with all the insurance headaches.

The rules governing border crossings and approved roads change often. You should use an approved road to cross the border, or you may incur penalties. If in doubt, anyone in the border regions will know whether a back road is approved. The army checkpoints have decreased considerably, but it is as well to carry your licence or some means of identification and slow down. Surprisingly, you are more likely to encounter a Garda checkpoint coming south than a British checkpoint going north.

AA (Automobile Association) or, in the North, **RAC** (Royal Automobile Club) offices will give you all the details of necessary formalities if you are not clear about anything. The **AAA** in the USA will be able to help with licence and insurance questions before you set off.

AA, t 0870 600 0371, international **t** 44 191 223 7071, *www.theaa.com.*

RAC, t 0800 550 550, *www.rac.co.uk.*

AAA, USA **t** 1 800 AAA HELP, New York branch **t** 212 468 2600, *www.aaa.com.*

Parking meters are used to control car parking in the central zones of Dublin. The meters are in operation during specific hours from Mondays to Saturdays, when street parking is prohibited at non-metered sites. Yellow lines along the kerbside or edge of the roadway indicate waiting restrictions. In some large towns a **disc system** is used to control parking in the centre. Parking discs can be bought, usually in books of ten, at shops and garages near the car parks. Unexpired time on a parking disc can be used at another parking place. In **Belfast** it's best to head for a car park; in Northern Ireland, for security reasons, parking is not permitted in central city areas marked off as 'Control Zones', which are clearly indicated by yellow signs saying 'Control Zone. No Unattended Parking'.

Car Hire

All of the big chains will meet you at the airports and the ferry ports of the Republic, but you can do better to wait and get a cheaper deal with a city centre branch, or even better, with one of the **local budget firms**. If you can book in advance you can get a car for as little as €150 (UK £110) a week subject to availability. Otherwise, rates for the smallest cars can go as high as €311 (UK £500) or more.

In Northern Ireland, the story is much the same. The chains all operate from both of Belfast's airports, but it's much less expensive to hire a car from their city centre branches. Local firms can offer even better deals. Look out also for fly-drive or rail-sail-drive **packages** offered by some of the airlines and ferry companies: these usually represent major savings. Note that to hire a car you should normally be over 23 and in possession of a licence which you have held for at least two years without endorsement. The car hire company will organize **insurance**, but do check this. If you do not take extra collision-damage waiver insurance you can be liable to damage up to €1,714 (UK £2,790). Check that your contract covers both the North and the Republic if you plan to drive in both areas.
Rent-a-car Ireland, t 0800 018 6682, *www. rentacar-ireland.com*. Discount rates with the leading car hire companies.

By Bicycle

Ireland is one of the most pleasant countries in which to cycle. Once you escape the highways the roads are quiet, there are still many birds and animals that live around the hedgerows, and in many places there is no pollution to spoil the air. This means, of course, that you'll encounter all the whiffs and pongs of the countryside, and in between the delicious gorse and honeysuckle perfumes will waft the strong, healthy smell of manure.

You can take your own bike onto the ferry for free, or you can rent one when you arrive. In the Republic the **Raleigh Rent-A-Bike** network connects some 70 centres throughout the country, with tandems, racing bikes and ordinary touring bikes available for hire. For full details get the *Cycling Ireland* leaflet from the nearest Bord Fáilte office. This gives details of the main hire companies, lists Irish cycling holiday specialists, and also describes 23 suggested routes. Raleigh network members and other bike hire shops are listed within the 'Getting Around' sections in each chapter.

For information on cycling in the Republic *see www.cyclingireland.ie* or contact the **Irish Cycling Federation,***www.icf.ie*.

The Northern Ireland Tourist Board produces a leaflet on cycling which lists tours, routes and events for cyclists, plus a number of cycle hire companies. Rental rates are comparable to those in the Republic. Note that bicycles hired in the Republic cannot be taken into Northern Ireland, and vice versa. Irish Cycling Safaris run well-organized and enjoyable holidays bicycling through scenic country.
Irish Cycling Safaris, Belfield Bike Shop, University College Dublin, Dublin 4, **t** (01) 260 0749, *www.cyclingsafaris.com*.
Sustrans, t 0845 113 0065, *www.sustrans.org. uk*. Information on national cycle network.

On Foot

If you enjoy **walking** in the countryside, Bord Fáilte and the Northern Ireland Tourist Board produce useful leaflets on public footpaths. The website *www.irishwaymarkedways.ie* is a mine of information for those wanting to walk in the Republic of Ireland.

From all accounts, **hitch-hiking** in the countryside seems to be a fairly safe but rather slow method of transport round the South. In the North you might find that people will not pick you up because years of the Troubles have made them cautious. It would be unwise to hitch around border areas anyway, and there are plenty of buses that will take you through. On major roads write your destination on a bit of cardboard and hold it up. You will find you have to compete with local people who hitch regularly from town to town.

Practical A–Z

Calendar of Events

www.festivals.ireland.ie; www.discover northernireland.com.

March

Dublin Film Festival, t (01) 872 1122, *www. dubliniff.com.*

St Patrick's Week, Irish Republic, **t** (01) 676 3205, *www. stpatricksday.ie;* Northern Ireland, **t** (028) 4461 0800, *www.st-patricksdayfestival.com.* Events around St Patrick's Day (17 March), with parades, music, theatre; especially in Dublin, Cork, Galway, Limerick.

World Irish Dancing Championships, *www. clrg.ie,* **t** (028) 9027 0222/**t** (01) 475 2220.

July

Galway Arts Festival, t (091) 509700, *www. galwayartsfestival.ie, info@gaf.iol.ie.* One of the biggest: theatre, arts and music.

August

Fleadh Cheoil na hÉireann. Up to 5,000 traditional musicians play impromptu sessions; usually held in summer (changes venues). Contact Bernard O'Sullivan, 32 Belgrave Square, Monkstown, Co. Dublin, **t** (01) 280 0295, *www.comhaltas.com.*

Dublin Horse Show, RDS, Ballsbridge, Dublin 4, *www.rds.ie,* **t** (01) 668 0866.

September

Waterford International Festival of Light Opera, t (051) 872639, **f** (051) 876002, *www.waterfordfestival.com.* A dozen light operas, one after the other, performed in Waterford's lovely old Theatre Royal.

Dublin Theatre Festival (late Sept–Oct), 44 East Essex Street, Temple Bar, Dublin 2, **t** (01) 679 2320, *www.dublintheatrefestival.com.* Ireland's premier theatrical event.

Galway International Oyster Festival, t (091) 587992, *www.galwayoysterfestival.ie.*

October

Wexford Opera Festival, Theatre Royal, High St, Wexford, **t** (053) 22400, **f** (053) 24289, *www.wexfordopera.com.*

Cork Film Festival, 10 Washington St, Cork, **t** (021) 427 1711, *www.corkfiilmfest.org.* Feature films, documentaries and shorts.

November

Belfast Festival at Queens, t (028) 9027 2600, *www.belfastfestival.com.* World-class classical and jazz concerts, films, opera, visual arts, literature and theatre.

Climate

Ireland lies on the Gulf Stream, which makes the climate mild, equable and moist. No temperature of over 90°F or below 0°F has ever been recorded.

Rain is Ireland's blessing, yet, from the reputation it has in its own country and abroad, you might imagine it was a curse. It keeps the fields and trees that famous lush green, and the high level of water vapour in the air gives it a sleepy quality and softens the colours of the landscape. Nearly every drizzly day has this gleam of sunshine, which is why the Irish are always very optimistic about the weather.

Snow is rare. Spring tends to be drier, especially after the blustery winds of March, and the crisp colours and freshness of autumn only degenerate into the cold and damp of winter in late December. You can hope for at least 6 hours of sunshine a day over most of the country during May, June, July and August.

Disabled Travellers

Tourism Ireland produces useful booklets advising travellers with disabilities. Particularly commended is *Accessible Accommodation in Northern Ireland.*

The tourist board also publishes a comprehensive list of accommodation with access in its annual guides, available from its offices. In Dublin the National Rehabilitation Board can offer you information and assistance.

Specialist Organizations in Ireland

Comhairle, 44 North Great George's Street, Dublin 1, **t** (01) 874 7503, *www.comhairle.ie.*

Disability Action, 189 Airport Rd West, Belfast BT3 9ED, **t** (028) 9029 7880, *www.disability action.org.*

Irish Wheelchair Association, Blackheath Drive, Clontarf, Dublin 3, **t** (01) 8186 400, *www.iwa.ie/.* Services for disabled travellers; also guides for disabled holidaymakers

National Disability Authority, Dublin,
t (01) 608 0400, *www.nda.ie.*

Specialist Organizations in Britain

Access Ability, *www.access-ability.co.uk.*
Information on travel agencies catering
specifically for disabled people.

Emerging Horizons, *www.emerginghorizons.
com.* International on-line travel newsletter.

Holiday Care Service, Imperial Building,
Victoria Rd, Horley, Surrey, RH6 7PZ, t (01293)
774 535, f 784647, Minicom t (01293) 776943,
*holiday.care@virgin.net, www.holidaycare.
org.uk.* Up-to-date information on destinations, transport and helpful tour operators.

RADAR (Royal Association for Disability and
Rehabilitation), 12 City Forum, 250 City Road,
London EC1V 8AF, t (020) 7250 3222, f 7250
0212, Minicom t (020) 7250 4119, *www.radar.
org.uk; radar@radar.org.uk.* Information and
books on travel.

RNIB (Royal National Institute for the Blind),
105 Judd St, London WC1H 9NE, t (020) 7388
1266, *www.rnib.org.uk.*

Specialist Organizations in the USA

American Foundation for the Blind, 11 Penn
Plaza, Suite 300, New York, NY 10001, t (212)
502 7600 or t 800 AFB LINE, *www.afb.org*
The best source of information in the USA
for visually impaired travellers.

Mobility International USA, PO Box 10767,
Eugene, OR 97440, USA, t/TTY (541) 343 1284,
f 343 6812, *www.miusa.org.* Information on
international educational exchange
programmes and volunteer service overseas.

SATH (Society for Accessible Travel and
Hospitality), 347 5th Avenue, Suite 610, New
York, NY 10016, t (212) 447 7284, f 725 8253,
www.sath.org, sathtravel@aol.com. Travel
and access information; also details other
access resources on the web.

Eating Out

You will normally find service in Ireland
friendly. A variety of good eating places are
listed under 'Eating Out' in each chapter; in
the various culinary deserts, those listed are
the best of an indifferent lot. Restaurants are
categorized in the price ranges above. Also *see*
Food and Drink, pp.25–30.

> **Restaurant Price Categories**
> *Prices are per head, for dinner, excluding wine.*
>
> | | | |
> |---|---|---|
> | *luxury* | over €100 | over £65 |
> | *expensive* | €65–100 | £40–65 |
> | *moderate* | €32–65 | £20–40 |
> | *inexpensive* | under €32 | under £20 |

Electricity

The current is 220 volts AC, so you should
bring a converter if you have any American
appliances or computers. Wall sockets take the
standard British-style three-pin (flat) fused
plugs, so Americans and other Europeans will
need a plug adaptor too.

Embassies and Consulates

British Embassy, 31 Merrion Road, Dublin 4,
t (01) 269 5211, *www.britishembassy.ie.*
Canadian Chancery and Consulate, 65 St
Stephen's Green, Dublin 2, t (01) 417 4100.
US Embassy, 42 Elgin Road, Dublin 4,
t (01) 668 8777.
US Consulate, 14 Queen's Street, Belfast
BT1 6EG, t (028) 9032 8239.

Emergencies and Hazards

The **emergency telephone number** (to call
any of the emergency services) in both the
Republic and the North is t 999. In the
Republic you can also call t 112.

Health and Insurance

If you need **medical** or **dental** treatment in
the Republic, you will be expected to pay for
the treatment then claim back the costs from
your insurance company. *In extremis* the international emergency services offered by
companies such as Europ Assistance or Travel
Assistance International, which are often
incorporated into travel insurance packages,
demonstrate their blessings.

For all kinds of medical care, citizens of EU
countries can benefit from the mutual agree-
ments that exist between EU member
countries. British citizens travelling to the
Republic can make use of any GP who has an
agreement with the Health Board, but to

benefit from this you should take **Form E111** with you, available from post offices and health centres in the UK in advance of your departure. The same scheme also applies to dentists and to hospitals.

To make a **claim** for loss or theft of baggage, you will need evidence that you have reported the incident to the police.

Heritage Centres

In the last few years there has been a huge increase in these centres all over Ireland. The larger ones incorporate local history, flora and fauna, using audiovisuals or lifesize models and actors dressed in period costume. The Office of Public Works have purpose-built a few Interpretative Centres in places of great natural beauty and fragile ecology. Inevitably such places destroy some of the beauty and peace with huge car parks, WCs, craft centres, etc., however sympathetic the architecture and landscaping may be. Many of the small heritage centres double as genealogical centres and are situated in fine old buildings (mainly in towns) which have been restored by the efforts of the local people.

Money

The official currency of the **Republic of Ireland** is the **euro (€)**. In **Northern Ireland** the currency is still the **UK pound sterling (£)**.

Euro notes come in denominations of 5, 10, 20, 50, 100, 200 and 500, with coins for €1 and €2. Each single euro consists of 100 cents; coins are used for 1, 2, 5, 10, 20 and 50 cents.

As everywhere, the best exchange rates are available at banks, and the worst at hotels. Rates will also be less good at *bureaux de change*, though these are useful when banks are closed.

You can obtain **cash** in local currencies from bank ATMs, usually sited in airports as well as towns and cities. Check with your bank or building society as to whether charges will be applied to your withdrawals, and which ATMs you may use. Leading **credit** and **debit cards** (Visa, Mastercard/Access, American Express and Diner's Club) are widely accepted in major hotels, restaurants and shops.

The main brands of **traveller's cheques** (American Express, Visa and Thomas Cook) are accepted by banks throughout the Republic of Ireland and Northern Ireland.

Small towns have at least one **bank**. They are open Mon–Fri 10am–12.30pm and 1.30–4pm in the Republic. Banks in larger towns usually have one day each week – normally market day or Thursday – when they will stay open until 5pm. Larger branches do not close for lunch. In the North banks also open at 10am and close at 4pm, but in Belfast and Derry they do not close for lunch. The bank usually occupies the grandest building in town.

Tipping

Tipping is not really a general habit in Ireland, except in taxis and in eating places where there is table service. Taxi-drivers will expect to be tipped at a rate of about 10% of the fare; porters and doormen 50 cents or so. There is no tipping in pubs, but in hotel bars where you are served by a waiter it is usual to leave a small tip. A service charge of 12%, sometimes 15%, is usually raised automatically on hotel and restaurant bills. Where this is not the case, a tip of this magnitude would be in order, if the service merits it.

Post Offices

Letterboxes are green in the Republic and red in the North. As you would expect, you have to put British stamps on letters posted in the North. **Post offices** are open 9am–5.30pm on weekdays, 9am–1pm on Saturdays, and closed on Sundays and public holidays. Sub-post offices often close on one day a week at 1pm. The GPO in O'Connell Street, Dublin, is open 8am–11pm, and in the mornings on Sundays and bank holidays.

Shopping

Shopping in Ireland is the most relaxing pastime. High-quality design and craftsman-ship make for goods which will last you a lifetime. You can find them easily in the craft centres which have been set up all over the country. The **Crafts Council of Ireland**, based at Castle Yard, Kilkenny, **t** (056) 776 1804, **f** (056) 776 3754, *www.ccoi.ie*, has given a great boost

Public Holidays

January: New Year's Day (1st).
March: St Patrick's Day, Republic only (17th).
March/April: Good Friday, widely observed as a holiday, but not official; Easter Monday.
May: May Day (1st or early May); Spring Holiday, N. Ireland only (end May).
June: June Holiday, Republic only (first Mon).
July: Orange Parades, N. Ireland only (12th).
August: August Holiday Republic only (first Monday in Aug). Summer Holiday, N. Ireland only (end Aug).
October: October Holiday, Republic only (last Mon).
December: Christmas Day (25th); Boxing Day/ St Stephen's Day (26th)

to many talented craft workers and helped them to market their wares and join forces in studios and workshops. Crafts are not cheap, because of the artistry and labour involved, but you can find bargains at china, crystal and linen factory shops if you are prepared to seek them out. Grinning leprechauns, colleen dolls, Guinness slogan T-shirts and shamrock mugs are stacked high in most gift shops if you want something cheerful and cheap, but do not ignore the real products from Ireland.

Opening Hours

Shops are usually open Mon–Sat from 9 or 9.30am to 5.30 or 6pm. Craft shops in scenic areas are usually open on Sundays as well, especially if they have a tea room.

You shouldn't have much trouble finding food or petrol on Sundays; most supermarkets are open at least in the morning.

Irish Specialities

Connemara marble: a natural green stone, found in the west, which ranges from bright field-green through to jade and oak-leaf colour, sometimes with stripes of brown. It is worked into jewellery and sold with other locally made objects, such as paperweights.

Food and drink: Soda, wheaten and potato breads are found everywhere in Ireland – McCambridge's brown bread is even available in airport shops. Smoked salmon and farmhouse cheese is sold in every shape, size and texture. Irish whiskey (note the 'e' in the Irish spelling) is slightly sweeter than Scotch; try Bushmills, Paddy's, Power's and Jameson's.

Cork gin is considered to have a delicious tang of juniper. Popular liqueurs are Irish Mist, which contains whiskey and honey, Tullamore Dew and Bailey's Irish Cream.

Glass: Waterford Crystal is world-famous for its quality and design. The hand-blown glass from the Jerpoint Glassworks in Co. Kilkenny is worth collecting.

Hand-knits and Aran sweaters: Connacht, Donegal and the coastal stretches of Munster have the greatest variety. In the Clifden/ Leenane region of Connemara, you can buy soft, striped wool rugs and cured sheepskins, which make good bedside rugs. Aran sweaters are made from tough wool, and are lightly coated in animal oils so that they are water-resistant. They have differing patterns; in the past there were family patterns so that drowned fishermen could be recognized. Make sure you buy one which has the hand-knitted label – it makes all the difference.

Jewellery, silver and antiques: Claddagh rings are still the nicest of all love tokens, and are very evocative of the west. Antiques are now highly prized and expensive.

Lace: Irish lace is one of the lightest and most precious of all the specialities to take home. It is fun if you can visit the convents and co-operatives where the lace is made. Try the Lace Cooperative, Carrickmacross, *see* p.154; or the Good Shepherd Convent, Limerick, pp.216 and 218.

Linen: you can buy excellent Irish linen teacloths and fine linen sheets in Belfast. Hand-embroidered handkerchiefs and table-cloths are for sale in Co. Donegal.

Pottery and china: talented potters work in rural communities all over Ireland, and the best places to find their work for sale is at IDA centres and craft shops. Look out for Roundstone in Connemara, Co. Galway, Arklow in Co. Wicklow, and the work of Nicholas Mosse, sold at the Kilkenny Design Centre.

Tweed: hand-woven from wool, tweed keeps you warm, but also lets your skin 'breathe'. Donegal tweed is particularly attractive, with its subtle shades. In Ardara and its environs you will still find thick, naturally dyed tweed.

Woven baskets: you can buy baskets made of willow or rush all over Ireland: bread baskets, turfholders, place mats and St Brigid Crosses – charms against evil.

Telephones and Internet

The **country code** for the Republic is **t 353**; for Northern Ireland **t 44**, if calling from outside the UK. However, if you are calling Northern Ireland from the Republic of Ireland, all 8-digit numbers can be prefixed with just **t 048**.

Ireland shares the same **time zone** as Great Britain, and follows the same pattern of seasonal adjustment in the summer (i.e. Greenwich Mean Time plus one hour, from the end of March to the end of October).

The **Internet** has a wealth of information to help you prepare all the practical details for your holiday, such as accommodation, especially in the busy summer months, when festivals make rooms hard to come by in even the smallest of towns. Internet cafés are blossoming in Ireland; airports and libraries also usually provide access points and local tourist offices can direct you to the nearest ones.

Irish Tourist Offices Abroad

UK: Tourism Ireland, Nations House, 103 Wigmore St, London W1U 1QS, UK only **t** 0800 039 7000, or **t** (020) 7518 0800, *www.tourismireland.com*; 98 West George Street, 7th Floor, Glasgow G2 1PJ, **t** (0141) 572 4030.

USA: 345 Park Avenue, 17th floor, New York, NY 10154, **t** 1 800 223 6470 / (212) 418 0800, **f** (212) 371 9052, *www.shamrock.org*, *www.tourismireland.com*.

Canada: 2 Bloor Street West, Suite 1501, Toronto, M4W 3E2, **t** (416) 925 6368. **f** (416) 925 6033.

off Grafton Street, from Ireland **t** (01) 605 7700 for information, for reservations **t** (01) 602 4000, *see www.visitdublin.com* and *www.ireland.travel.ie*. Tourism Ireland in the North is through the NITB, 59 North St, Belfast BT1 1NB, on **t** (028) 9023 1221, **f** (028) 9024 0960, *www.discovernorthernireland.com*.

Toilets

Public loos – *leithreas* – are often labelled in Irish: *Fir* (men) and *Mná* (women). They're usually pretty grim. Nobody minds if you slip into a lounge bar to use the loo, though it's a good excuse to stop for a drink as well.

Tourist Boards

Ireland was until recently served by two separate tourist boards: *Bord Fáilte* (or the Irish Tourist Board) in the Republic, and the Northern Ireland Tourist Board (NITB) . The new **Tourism Ireland** has now amalgamated these two tourism services. Their offices will do literally anything to help and organize whatever is practical. They can supply you with a wealth of beautifully presented maps and leaflets, most of which are free, and they also publish fuller booklets on, for example, accommodation, for which there are modest charges. They can also find a hotel or B&B in your price range and book it for you.

The head office for the Irish Tourist Board in Dublin is Faílte Ireland, Baggot St Bridge, Dublin 2, **t** (01) 602 4000, although it serves mainly for administration. A more useful office if you are in Dublin is the capacious Dublin Tourism Centre on Suffolk Street, just

Where to Stay

Whether you are a traveller with plenty of loot to spend, or one who is intent on lodging as cheaply as possible, Ireland offers plenty of choice. Places to stay range from romantic castles, graceful country mansions, cosy farmhouses, smart city hotels and hostels which, though spartan, are clean and well-run.

Prices

Tourism Ireland registers and grades hotels and guest houses, and divides the many B&B businesses into Farm, Town and Country Houses. All of this is very useful, but you really do not get much idea of the atmosphere and style of the place. The establishments listed in this book are described and categorized according to price, and include a variety of lodgings ranging from a luxurious castle to a simple farmhouse. The price categories are of necessity quite loosely based, and some of the more expensive establishments do weekend deals which are very good value. Always check prices and terms when making a booking.

Luxury

Expect top-quality rooms with style and opulence. Furnishings will include priceless antiques, whilst the facilities and service provide every modern convenience.

Expensive

All bedrooms have their own bathroom, direct-dial telephone, central heating, TV and the other mod cons, but many have something else as well – charm, eccentricity, and a feeling of mellow comfort.

Moderate

Not as luxurious, but most of these places have private bathrooms and extremely good cooking and service. Again, some of them have a wonderful atmosphere combined with attractive décor, which is sometimes more atmospheric for its touch of age.

Inexpensive

Whitewashed farmhouses, Georgian manses, rectories, old manor houses, modern bungalows and fine town houses come under this heading, along with the increasing numbers of holiday hostels. They are all very good value and good 'craic', and you will often get marvellous, simple cooking. Not all of the bedrooms will have central heating or en suite facilities, but there will be perfectly good bathrooms close by.

Reservations

Make sure that you book early for the peak months of June, July and August. At other times of the year it is usually quite all right to book on the morning of the day you wish to stay (except in Dublin, which can be crowded in any season).

Hotels

The tourist boards register and grade hotels into five categories: **Four-star** stands for the most luxuriously equipped bedrooms and public rooms with night service, a very high standard of food and plenty of choice. Most bedrooms have their own bath and suites are available – the sort of place where delicious snacks are automatically served with your cocktails. This grading includes baronial mansions set in exquisite grounds or the rather plush anonymity of some Dublin hotels. **Three-star** grade stands for a luxury hotel which doesn't have quite so many items on

Accommodation Price Ranges

Note: *Prices listed here and elsewhere in the book are for bed and breakfast per person.*

luxury	over €115	over £70
expensive	€80–115	£50–70
moderate	€40–80	£25–50
inexpensive	under €40	under £25

the *table d'hôte*, nor does it have night service; but the food is just as good and the atmosphere probably less restrained. **Two-star** and **one-star** grades are clean, comfortable but limited, two-star offering more in the line of bathrooms and food.

All Tourism Ireland graded hotels have heating and hot and cold water in the bedrooms. If you come across a hotel that is ungraded, it is because its grading is under review or because it has just opened, or does not comply with Tourism Ireland's requirements. The prices of hotels vary enormously, no matter what grade they are, and the grading takes no account of charm.

Guest Houses

These are usually houses which have become too large and expensive to maintain as private houses. The minimum number of bedrooms is five. The top grade **four-star** houses are just as good as their hotel equivalent, as are those graded lower down the scale, although the atmosphere is different. Some of the best places to stay are guest houses, particularly in Dublin.

If you are on holiday to avoid people, a guest house is the last place you should book into. It is impossible not to be drawn into a conversation, whether about fishing or politics. You will get a large, thoroughly uncontinental breakfast, and delicious evening meals with a choice within a set meal. Dinner is usually very punctual, at eight, after everyone has sat around by the fire over very large drinks. Lunch or a packed lunch can be arranged.

All grades of guest house have hot and cold water, and heating in the bedrooms. Four-star guest house rooms have private bathrooms, but their reputation is based on scrumptious food and comfortable surroundings. Sometimes the owners provide high tea; sometimes the only meal they do is breakfast.

Farmhouses, Town and Country Houses

Often these family homes complete your stay in Ireland, for you meet Irish people who are kind, generous and intelligent. This is also the most economical way to stay in Ireland if you don't want to stay in a tent or in a youth hostel. If you are not going to a place that is recommended, it is largely a matter of luck whether you hit an attractive or a mediocre set-up, but always watch out for the shamrock sign, Tourism Ireland's sign of approval.

Wherever you go, you should have a comfortable bed (if you are tall, make sure it is long enough; sometimes Irish beds can be on the small side) and an enormous breakfast: orange juice, cereal, eggs, bacon, sausages, toast, marmalade and a pot of tea or coffee. You can get much cheaper weekly rates, with partial or full board. Very often you can eat your evening meal in the dining room of the B&B. Again, there will be masses to eat and it will be piping hot. There is often great flexibility about breakfast and other meals: they happen when it suits you.

Some houses serve **dinner** at around €12–30 (UK£7–18), and some offer 'high tea', which is less costly (between €8–12, UK£5–7). '**High tea**' is a very sensible meal which has evolved for the working man who begins to feel hungry at about 6pm. You get a plate of something hot, perhaps chicken and chips, followed by fresh soda bread, jam and cakes and a pot of tea. Some houses provide tea and biscuits as a nightcap for nibblers at around 10pm.

For people who are hitch-hiking or using public transport, the town houses are the easiest to get to and find; but the real favourites are farmhouses and country houses. The farms concentrate on dairy, sheep, crop farming or beef cattle and often a mixture of everything. Tucked away in lovely countryside, they may be traditional or modern. The farmer's wife, helped by her children, usually makes life very comfortable and is often ready to have a chat. Some of the town and country houses are on fairly main roads, but they are generally not too noisy as there is so little traffic about.

Youth Hostels

The Irish YHA is called *An Oige*, and has 44 hostels. These are distributed all over the Republic; there are a few in the Six Counties, often in wild and remote places, which are doubly attractive to the enterprising traveller. Members of the International Youth Hostel Federation can use all of these hostels in Ireland. There is no age limit, and your card can be used worldwide.

Youth hostels are sometimes superb houses, and range from cottages to castles. They are great centres for climbers, walkers and fishers, and not too spartan; many have a comfortable laxity when it comes to the rules. You must provide your own sheet and sleeping bag. A flap or pocket to cover the pillows can be bought at the *An Oige* office, and the hostel provides blankets or sheet bags. All the hostels have fully equipped kitchens, and most also provide breakfast, packed lunches and an evening meal on request.

Charges vary according to age, month and location; during July and August it is slightly more expensive, and it is vital to book. This applies also to weekends. All *An Oige* and YHANI (Youth Hostel Association of Northern Ireland) hostels may be booked from one hostel to another, or centrally by contacting the head office listed below. Most of the hostels are open all year round.

All information, an essential handbook and an excellent map can be obtained from the *An Oige* Office, 61 Mountjoy Street, Dublin 7, **t** (01) 830 4555, **f** (01) 830 5808, *www.ireland yha.org*, *mailbox@anoige.ie*. For Northern Ireland, contact Hostelling International Northern Ireland, 22 Donegall Road, Belfast, BT12 5JN, **t** (028) 9032 4733, *www.hini.org.uk*.

Besides the youth hostels, a large number of **independent hostels** have appeared in recent years. These are friendly, open to everyone (children are welcome in most hostels), and most have double and family rooms; some even have single rooms. They are also less likely than the youth hostels to have bothersome rules, such as curfews and no access to rooms during daytime. All hostels will rent you sheets and all hostels provide duvets and blankets. These hostels are listed in Tourism Ireland's *Accommodation Guide*, or you can get a list from Independent Holiday Hostels (IHH), **t** (01) 836 4700, **f** (01) 836 4700, *www.hostels-ireland.com*.

Food and Drink

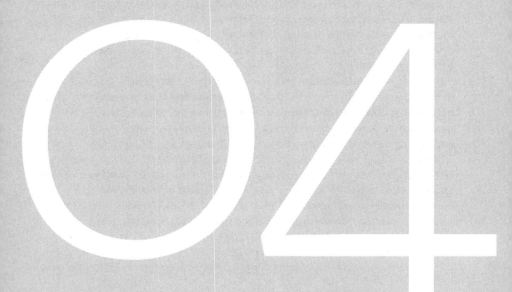

Beyond the Potato

Eating out in Ireland can be a memorable experience, if the chef gets it right. The basic ingredients are the best in the world: succulent beef, lamb, salmon, seafood, ham, butter, cream, eggs and wonderful **bread** – which is often homemade, and varies from crumbly, nutty-tasting wheaten bread to moist white soda bread, crispy scones, potato bread and barm brack, a rich fruity loaf which is traditionally eaten at Hallowe'en. Irish **potatoes** are light and floury and best when just off the stalk, and crispy carrots and cabbages are sold in every grocery shop, often bought in from the local farms. If you stay in a country house hotel, the walled garden will probably produce rare and exotic vegetables and fruit.

The history of Ireland has quite a lot to do with the down-side of cooking: over-cooked food, few vegetables, and too many synthetic cakes. The landless peasants had little to survive off except potatoes, milk and the occasional bit of bacon, so there is little traditional 'cuisine'. **Fish** was until recently regarded as 'penance food', to be eaten only on Fridays. Local people talk with amusement of those who eat oysters or mussels, and most of the fine seafood harvested from the seaweed-fringed loughs and the open sea goes straight to France, where it appears on the starched linen tablecloths of the best restaurants. But do not despair if you love fat oysters or fresh salmon, because they can always be got, either in the bars, the new-style restaurants which are really excellent, or straight from the fisherman. Remember, everything in Ireland works on a personal basis. Start your enquiries for any sort of local delicacy at the local post office, grocer or butcher, or in the pub.

Having got over the trauma of the famine, and since the relative prosperity of the 1960s, many people in Ireland like to eat **meat**: you cannot fail to notice the number of butchers or 'fleshers' in every town. Steak appears on every menu, and, if you are staying in a simple Irish farmhouse, huge lamb chops with a minty sauce, Irish stew made from the best end of mutton neck, onions and potatoes, and bacon and cabbage casserole baked in the oven are delicious possibilities. Fish, however, is becoming more and more readily available.

The standard of **restaurants** in Ireland is getting much better. This is especially true of those that are run by people from other European countries, many of whom set up here because of the beauty of the country and the raw ingredients. There are Irish cooks, too, who combine the local specialities and traditional recipes with ingredients and cooking methods from other cultures. Ballymaloe House in County Cork springs to mind (*see* p.195). Serious cooking is still a recent phenomenon, and many places will be trying to impress you (and the restaurant guides) with showy creativity – so expect to come across some bizarre sauces and combinations of ingredients. Eating out can be a massive disappointment. Too many restaurants still serve up musty and watery vegetables, overcooked meat, frozen fish, and salads of the limp lettuce and coleslaw variety. Also, eating out is not cheap, unless you have a pub lunch. To compete with the pubs, many restaurants do charge considerably less for lunch than dinner, so if it is convenient you can save a lot by having your main meal of the day in the afternoon.

To get around the serious problem of eating cheaply in Ireland, fill up on the huge **breakfasts** provided by the bed and breakfast places. If the lady of the house also cooks high tea or supper for her guests, take advantage of that as well. The food she produces is usually delicious and very good value. Irish people love their food, and are generous with it: huge portions are normal in the home and often in restaurants. It is a sign of inhospitality to give a poor meal. (They say, 'It was but a daisy in a bull's mouth'.) Bakeries usually sell tea, coffee and soft drinks along with fresh apple pie, doughnuts, cakes and sausage rolls. Roadside cafés serve the usual menu of burgers, chicken 'n' chips and so on. In the North they do a roaring trade in takeaway foods. Most of the big towns have Chinese restaurants, pizza places and fish and chip shops.

Vegetarians will find an increasing number of restaurants in Dublin and the larger towns that cater specifically for their needs. Also, vegetarians will find that even where no special menu exists, people are generally keen to provide suitable fare. If you are staying in a country house, you should telephone in advance to let them know you are vegetarian. You can sample the many delicious cheeses of Ireland by finding a good deli or wholefood shop, buying some bread and salad and taking yourself off to eat a picnic in some wonderfully scenic place. If it is drizzling, warm yourself up afterwards with a glass of Irish coffee in the local pub.

Eating Out

Restaurant Listings

You will normally find the service in Ireland friendly and helpful. A variety of good eating places are listed for each city, day trip, overnighter and touring day; in the various culinary deserts which exist, those listed are the best of an indifferent lot. The establishments are categorized in brackets (*see* p.19 for price ranges). Do bear in mind that proprietors and places change, so it is always best to phone.

Luxury

Cost is no object – these restaurants serve creative and delicious food, cooked with fine ingredients. They are often in the dining-rooms of stately country houses or castles, where the silver and crystal sparkle and you are surrounded by fine pictures and furniture. Or they may be smart, fashionable places in the cities.

Expensive

Many country-house hotels come under this category, as do seafood restaurants around the coast and city establishments. Lunch in expensive places is often a very reasonably priced set meal, so ask about this if you do not want to fork out for dinner.

Moderate

The quality of the food may be as good as the more expensive places, but the atmosphere is informal and, perhaps, less stylish.

Inexpensive

This category includes bar food, lunchtime places and cafés. You can usually be sure of good home-made soup and one simple course.

Eating Hours and Etiquette

Most restaurants offer lunch and dinner, but do check before you go. A few do only dinner and Sunday lunches. Some country places open only for the weekend during the winter months. Service is usually included in the bill at all restaurants. In the country towns and sometimes even in Dublin you may find it difficult to pay by credit card. Check this out before you order your meal. If there is no liquor licence of any sort, the manager is usually quite happy to let you bring in your own wine or beer, if you ask. (The publicans – pub landlords – have a monopoly on licences, and many restaurants cannot get them without having to fulfil ludicrous requirements.)

Legal and Illicit Drinks

'The only cure for drinking is to drink more,' so goes the Irish proverb. Organizations such as the Pioneers exist to wean the masses off 'the drink' – alcohol costs an arm and a leg, what with the taxes and the publican's cut; yet, nevertheless, an Irish bar can be one of the most convivial places in the world. The delicious liquor, the cosy snugs and the general hubbub of excited conversation, which in the evening might easily spark into a piece of impromptu singing, makes the business of taking a drink very pleasant. Pubs can also be as quiet as a grave, especially in the late afternoon when a few men nod over their pints and an air of contemplation pervades.

You are bound to have been lured into trying **Guinness** by the persuasive advertisements you see all over the world (Guinness got to be what it is by the same sort of massive and diabolically clever advertising that made an institution of Coca-Cola). Stout, or porter, is a beer made by drying the malt at a high temperature, browning it in effect, and providing the characteristic colour and taste, though there's considerably more to the art than just that. The export trade is thriving; but the place to get a real taste of the creamy dark liquor is in an Irish bar. It is at its most delicious when it is draught and drunk in a bar around Dublin, where it is made. Guinness does not travel well, especially on Irish roads. It is said to get its special flavour from the murky waters of the River Liffey, and you can go and find out for yourself if this is so by visiting the Brewery at St James Gate. The quality of taste once it has left the brewery depends on how well the publican looks after it and cleans the pipe from the barrel, so it varies greatly from bar to bar.

If it's obvious that you are a tourist, your Guinness may be decorated with a shamrock drawn on its frothy head. They've finally managed to get Guinness into a can, though it's only a pale reflection of the real thing. If you are feeling adventurous, try something called black velvet – a mixture of Guinness and champagne. And note that it isn't just Guinness. Down in Cork, Murphy's and Beamish make stout that's just as good, and available everywhere.

Whiskey has been drunk in Ireland for more than 500 years; the word itself is derived from *uisge beatha*, the Irish for water of life. It is made from malted barley with a small proportion of wheat, oats and occasionally a pinch of rye – so it's a blended whiskey, though without the distinctive taste of blended Scotch. On the whole Irish is better than American blended, and as good as Canadian. There are several brands: Jameson's, Paddy, Power, and Bushmill's (from the North) are all good.

Irish coffee is a wonderful combination of contrasts: hot and cold, black and white, and very intoxicating. It was first dreamed up in County Limerick in the 1940s. It's made with a double measure of Irish whiskey, one tablespoon of double cream, one cup of strong, hot black coffee, and a heaped tablespoon of sugar. To make it, first warm a stemmed whiskey glass. Put in the sugar and enough hot coffee to dissolve the sugar. Stir well. Add the Irish whiskey and then pour the cream slowly over the back of a spoon. Do not stir the cream into the coffee; it should float on top. The hot, whiskey-laced coffee is drunk through the cold cream.

Poteen (pronounced 'pot-cheen') is illicit whiskey, traditionally made from potatoes, although nowadays it is often made from grain. Tucked away in the countryside are stills which no longer bubble away over a turf fire, but on a Calor gas stove. Poteen is pretty disgusting stuff unless you get a very good brew, and it probably kills off a lot of brain cells, so it's much better to stick to the legal liquid.

Bars

The old-fashioned serious drinking bar with high counter and engraved glass window, frosted so that the outside world couldn't intrude, is gradually changing. It used to be a male preserve. Farmers on a trip into town can be heard bewailing the weather, recounting the latest in cattle or land prices, or gossiping. What the inns have lost in character they compensate for, to a degree, with comfort. The bar of the local hotel is the place to find the priest when he is off-duty. My own favourite drinking establishment is the grocery shop which is also a bar, where you ask for a taxi/plumber/undertaker, only to find that the publican or his brother combine all these talents with great panache.

Licensing Hours

In the Republic, public houses are officially open Mon–Wed 10.30am–11.30pm, Thurs–Sat 10.30–12.30am, and on Sundays and St Patrick's Day from 12.30–11pm. In winter they close half an hour earlier. Plenty of places stay open later, although you'll have to get in before closing time, since they lock the doors and then carry on. The *Garda* don't seem to mind. There is no service on Christmas Day or Good Friday.

In Northern Ireland, public houses are open Mon–Sat 11am–11pm, and 12.30–10pm on Sundays. Also, you can always get a drink on Sundays at a hotel, though you are supposed to justify it by having a meal as well if you are not staying there. In the Republic, children are nearly always allowed to sit in the lounge bar with packets of crisps and fizzy orange to keep them happy, and they often appear in the evenings too when there's music.

If you do get into a conversation in a bar, a certain etiquette is followed: men always buy everybody in your group a drink, taking it in turn to buy a round; women will find they are seldom allowed to. Both sexes offer their cigarettes around when having one. If there are ten in your group, you will find yourself drunk from social necessity, and probably out of pocket as well. The price in the Republic for wine, whiskey and beer is much higher than in the UK. A bottle of whiskey is about €18. If you are bringing a car from France or the UK, it might be as well to bring some booze in with you, or you could stock up in Northern Ireland. The customs allowance is 1½ litres of distilled beverages or spirits, 12 litres of beer and (if the alcohol is bought duty-paid) 4 litres of wine per person. Customs enforcement is not systematic.

The North of Ireland

05

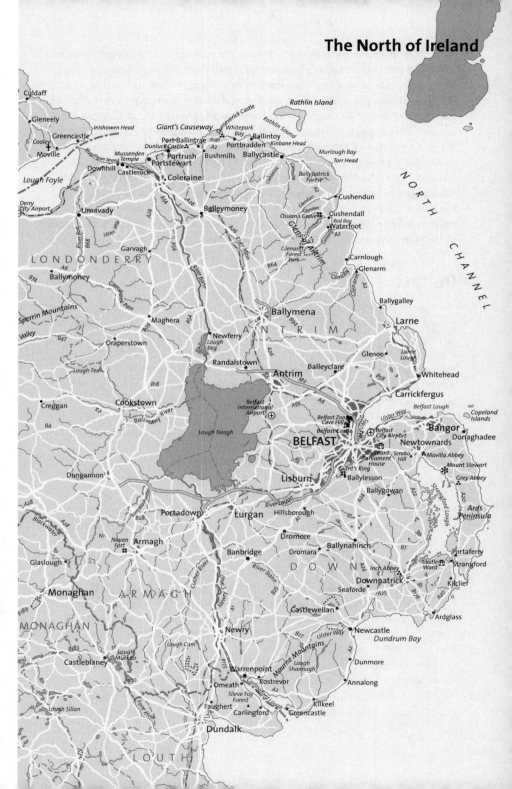

The North of Ireland

The Ulster border has meant much through the ages: Irish archaeologists have just concluded that a great earthen wall was built two thousand years ago to separate Ulster (*Ulaidhstr*: Land of the Ulstermen) from much of the South of Ireland. The Northern Ireland you will see today has suffered most in the towns from the last 40 years of the Troubles – though this has paradoxically brought about some planned and attractive public housing and buildings. It was also more industrialized during the 19th century than the South. But the visitor should not ignore Northern Ireland, thinking it is a foreign and probably dangerous country within Ireland – because it certainly is not. The countryside is just as beautiful, and has been made accessible through the development of forest parks and the guardianship of bodies such as the British National Trust; and the North is teeming with lakes and rivers – coarse fishermen find nothing like it anywhere else in the British Isles. And the vast majority of Northern Irish people are friendly, hard-working, witty and kind.

Belfast

Belfast (*Beal Feirst*: 'Mouth of the Sandy Ford') is the administrative centre of the six counties that make up Northern Ireland. It has one of the most beautiful natural settings of any city, ringed by hills which are visible from most parts of the town, and hugging the shores of the lough. It has been a city officially only since 1888; in the 19th century it grew from an insignificant town by a river ford into a prosperous commercial centre and port, with great linen mills and the famous shipyards of Harland & Wolff, which built the *Titanic*.

Architecturally, Belfast is made up of some grand Victorian public buildings and the red-brick streets which characterize many British towns. The prosperous-looking houses which make up the smart Malone Road area and which line the lough on both its sides were built by the wealthy middle class who had benefited from the linen industry. The workers in the factories and shipyards divided themselves between the Catholic Falls Road area and the Protestant Shankill Road. Unemployment became worse as the linen and ship-building industries declined, nurturing the conditions in which the terrorist armies could thrive. The division of these working class areas from the city centre was made explicit by the north–south Westlink motorway.

Belfast is probably known to most people through the exposure brought by the Troubles. Press and television news reports have recorded the bombings, the military involvement and the sectarian murders, giving the impression of a war-torn city, constantly in a state of unrest and dangerous to visit. This is simply not the case. For visitors it is surprising how normal the streets are, full of people shopping at Marks & Spencer and other proliferous British chain stores. Military patrols and armoured police vehicles are now a rare sight, where once they were an everyday part of the city's life. Belfast people share a cautious optimism about the peace process and, while old sectarian divisions die hard, there is almost unanimous support for a permanent political resolution to the violence. There are many opportunities to see good theatre, art shows and concerts, whilst the strong intellectual and historical

Getting There

Belfast has one of the biggest choices of airlines flying from the UK; *see* **Travel**, pp.6–7. You can also reach Belfast by ferry from Liverpool and Stranraer in southwest Scotland, or sail to nearby Larne north of Belfast from Cairnryan or Troon, *see* **Travel**, p.11.

Getting from the Airport

Belfast International Airport, t (028) 9442 2888. 19 miles (30km) from the city centre, at Aldergrove. The airport coach leaves every half-hour to and from the Europa Bus Centre. A taxi will cost around £22.

Belfast City Airport, t (028) 9093 9093. 4 miles (7km) from the city, served by local and UK airlines only. You can take a train from nearby Sydenham Halt to either of the city's railway stations, or the Airbus (£5), or a taxi (around £7) to Donegall Square.

Getting Around

By Train

From **Belfast Central Station**, East Bridge Street, or **Great Victoria Street Station**, trains go to all destinations. Note there are **no left luggage facilities** in any Northern Ireland railway station.

Translink, t (028) 9066 6630, *www.translink. co.uk*. For all enquiries.

By Bus

The **Europa Centre** on Great Victoria Street serves destinations in Counties Armagh, Tyrone, Londonderry, Fermanagh and West Down, the Republic, and the port for ferry services to the UK. Go to the **Laganside Bus Centre** on Donegall Quay (east of the Albert Clock) for all destinations in eastern County Antrim and North Down.

Ulsterbus operates within the city suburbs and throughout the province; coaches also go to the Republic and mainland UK.

City buses are red or red and white, and cover most routes. **City Stopper** buses nos.523–538 also serve the Falls Road and Lisburn Road.

Ulsterbus, Europa Centre, Great Victoria Street, t (028) 9066 6630. Enquiries and timetables.

There are no left luggage facilities. *Open daily 7.30am–8.30pm.*

Citybus Enquiries, t (028) 9066 6630.

By Taxi

Taxi ranks can be found at City Hall in Donegall Square, Upper Queen Street, Wellington Place and Castle Street.

City Cab, t (028) 9024 2000.
FonaCab, t (028) 9033 3333.

By Car

Parking is forbidden in the centre of Belfast. Excellent car parks and pay-and-display areas ring the centre of the city; the tourist office has a list and map.

AA, 108–110 Great Victoria Street, t 08705 989 989; 24-hour rescue service t 0800 887766.

RAC, 14 Wellington Place, t 08705 722722; 24-hour rescue service t 0800 828282.

Car Hire

Avis, 69–71 Gt Victoria St, t (028) 9024 0404.
Budget, 96–102 Great Victoria Street, t (028) 9023 0700.
Dan Dooley, 175B Airport Road, Aldergrove, t (028) 9445 2522.
Europcar, City Airport, t (028) 9045 0904; International Airport, t (028) 9442 3444.
Hertz, International Airport, t (028) 9442 2533.
McCausland Car Hire, 21–31 Grosvenor Road, t (028) 9033 3777.

Bike Hire

Life Cycles, 25 Smithfield Market, t (028) 9043 9959.
McConvey Cycles, 183 Ormeau Road, t (028) 9033 0322, *www.mcconvey.com*; also at 467 Ormeau Road, t (028) 9049 1163.
Recycle, 1–5 Albert Square, t (028) 9031 3115.

Guided Tours

Guided **walking tours** include those of pubs, historic Belfast, the university area and Laganside; **bus tours** are also available. The Belfast Welcome Centre distributes a free leaflet, called 'Walk this Way', about the tours.

Citybus, t (028) 9045 8484. Tours taking in all the main sights of Belfast, including Stormont and Belfast Castle, plus a 'Living History Tour', around the areas of Belfast associated with the Troubles.

Festivals

March: Draoicht Children's Festival, West Belfast.
April: Easter Celebrations, at Ulster Folk and Transport Museum, Cultra, Holywood, t (028) 9042 8428.
May: Belfast City Summer Festival, including the **Lord Mayor's Show,** May–June, t (028) 9032 0202; **Cathedral Quarter Arts Festival,** t (028) 9023 2403, *www.cqaf.com, cqaf@ hotmail.com*; **The Best of Ireland,** Ulster Folk and Transport Museum, t (028) 9042 8428, *www.index.com/uftm,* traditional music and crafts; **Ulster Drama Festival,** Lyric Theatre, t (028) 9038 1081, *www.lyrictheatre.co.uk.*
June: Shankill Festival. Social, cultural and recreational events, t (028) 9031 1333.
July: Story-telling Weekend, at Ulster Folk and Transport Museum, t (028) 9042 8428, story-telling and traditional music; **Orange Order Parades** (12th).
August: Ardoyne *Fleadh,* t (028) 9075 1056; *Feile an Phobail,* t (028) 9031 3440, annual festival with music, drama, Irish language events, carnival, parade; **Rare Breeds Show and Sale,** Ulster Folk and Transport Museum, t (028) 9042 8428, *www.index.com/uftm,* Ireland's largest, with rare, minority and re-established farm breeds.
September: Belfast Film Festival, t (028) 9032 5913, *www.belfastfilmfestival.org.*
November: Belfast Festival at Queen's, Queen's University. Box office, t (028) 9066 7687 for information, t (028) 9066 5577 for bookings, *www.belfastfestival.com, festival@qub.ac.uk.* Three weeks of music events, films, plays, poetry and art exhibitions, fringe shows from Edinburgh and internationally known stars. Events take place mainly around the university area.

Tourist Information

Belfast Welcome Centre, Donegall Place, t (028) 9024 6609.
Tourism Ireland Information Centre, 59 North Street, t 0800 039 7000, f (028) 9024 0960, *www.discovernorthernireland.com, www.ireland-travel.ie, visitorservices@nitb. com; open Mon–Sat 9–5.15. Extended opening hours in summer.*

Belfast Visitor and Convention Bureau, 73–5 Great Victoria Street, t (028) 9023 9026, *www.gotobelfast.com.*

Useful Contacts

Emergency services, t 999.
Belfast City Hospital, Lisburn Road, t (028) 9032 9241.
General post office, at Castle Place and Shaftesbury Square. *Open Mon–Fri 9–5.30, Sat 9–9.*

Internet Access

Revelations Café, Bradbury Place, t (028) 9032 0337, *www.revelations.co.uk, info@ revelations.co.uk.*

Shopping

The centre of Belfast is full of shopping arcades and pedestrian malls, and all the British high street stores are well-represented. Shuttle buses can take you to and from the car parks, and a large number of city buses stop at the City Hall, which is very central. The more unusual shops are situated in **Bedford Street, Dublin Road** and **Donegall Pass,** where you will find design outlets, antiques and bric-a-brac. Expensive women's clothes shops are to be found amongst the cafés and food stores on the increasingly trendy Lisburn Road.

Antiques

Alexander the Grate, Donegall Pass, t (028) 9023 2041.
Blue Cat, 42 Bedford Street, t (028) 9023 5204.
Oakland Antiques, 135–43 Donegall Pass, t (028) 9023 0176.
Past and Present, 60 Donegall Pass, t (028) 9033 3137.

Art Galleries

The Troubles seem to have generated a creative urge amongst Ulster artists which is both exploratory and introspective. Artists such as Tom Carr, T. P. Flanagan, Brian Ferran, Basil Blackshaw and Brian Ballard have produced excellent works. Entry to all the private, commercial galleries is free.

The **Northern Ireland Visual Arts Forum,** t (028) 9092 6062, *www.visualartsforumni.*

com, is a useful point of reference for anyone interested in visual arts in Northern Ireland.
Bell Gallery, 13 Adelaide Park, **t** (028) 9066 2998.
Crescent Arts Centre, 2–4 University Road, **t** (028) 9024 2338. Also includes the **Fenderesky Gallery**, *open Tues–Sat*.
Eakin Gallery, 237 Lisburn Road, **t** (028) 9066 8522.
Old Museum Arts Centre, 7 College Square North, **t** (028) 9023 5053.
Ormeau Baths Gallery, 18 Ormeau Avenue, **t** (028) 9032 1402. Worth visiting for the shows, which are usually by Irish and Ulster artists. *Open Tues–Sat 9–5*.
Tom Caldwell Gallery, 40 Bradbury Place, **t** (028) 9032 3226.
Townhouse Gallery, 125 Great Victoria Street, **t** (028) 9031 1798. Prints and etchings.
Ulster Museum, Botanic Gardens (off Stranmillis Road), **t** (028) 9038 3000.

Books

Bookfinders, 47 University Road, **t** (028) 9032 8269.
University Bookshop, 91 University Terrace, opposite Queens College, **t** (028) 9066 6302.
Waterstone's, 8 Royal Avenue, **t** (028) 9024 7355; also 44 Fountain St, **t** (028) 9024 0159.

Clothes

House of de Courcy, 487 Lisburn Road, **t** (028) 9020 0205. International designer clothes.
BT9, 45 Bradbury Place, **t** (028) 9023 9496. Stocks Irish designers.
Smyth and Gibson, Bedford Street, **t** (028) 9023 0388, *www.smythandgibson.co.uk*, *shirts@smythandgibson.co.uk*. Top-quality Irish shirts made in Derry.

Crafts

Craftworks, Bedford Street, **t** (028) 9024 4465.
The Wicker Man, 12 Donegall Arcade, Castle Place, **t** (028) 9024 3550, *www.thewickerman.co.uk*.

Delicacies

French Village Bakery, 70 Stranmillis Road, **t** (028) 9038 1671. Traditional wheaten bannock, wheaten loaf and 'Belfast Baps', as well as enormous croissants and baguettes.

Swanton's, 639 Lisburn Road. Excellent cheeses, meats, olives and pâtés plus delicious sandwiches and a few hot and cold dishes to eat in or take away.
The Yellow Door, 427 Lisburn Road, **t** (028) 9038 1961. Prepared and cooked dishes to take away plus cheeses, pastas, excellent breads and other goodies.

Irish Linen

Irish Linen Stores, Fountain Centre, College Street, **t** (028) 9032 2727.
Smyth's Irish Linens, 65 Royal Avenue, **t** (028) 9024 2232.

Markets

St George's Market, at the end of May Street, **t** (028) 9043 5704. Fresh fruit, vegetables, fish, crafts, new and vintage clothes and other wares. Held in the 19th-century 'Variety Market' building. *Tuesdays and Fridays from 7am–1pm; farmer's market Saturday mornings*.

Musical Instruments

Matchetts Ltd, Wellington Place, **t** (028) 9032 6695, **f** (028) 9057 2133, *www.matchettsmusic.com*. Chain of shops selling traditional instruments, sheet music and accessories made in Ireland.

Sports and Activities

Golf

Balmoral Golf Club, Lisburn Road, **t** (028) 9038 1514. 18 holes.
Blackwood Golf Centre, Crawfordsburn Road, Clandeboye, **t** (028) 9185 2706.
Carrickfergus Golf Club, 7 miles (12km) northeast of Belfast on the A2, **t** (028) 9336 3713. 18-hole course.
Rockmount Golf Club, Carryduff, **t** (028) 9081 2279.
Royal Belfast Golf Club, Station Road, Craigavad, **t** (028) 9042 8165. The oldest of the only four 'Royal' clubs in Ireland.

Indoor Leisure Centres

Maysfield Leisure Centre, East Bridge Street, **t** (028) 9024 1633. Central, and has a pool, gym, squash and sauna.

Where to Stay

Note that most hotels in the city cost around 20 per cent less at weekends.

Luxury

Culloden Hotel, 142 Bangor Road, Craigavad, t/f (028) 9042 5223, or f 9042 6777. One of the nicest hotels, on the northeast side of Belfast Lough. Very plush with lovely grounds and luxurious old-style furnishings.

Europa Hotel, Great Victoria Street, t/f (028) 9032 7000. Very central, modern hotel which in the past was bombed so many times that everybody lost count. Recently redecorated.

TENsquare, 10 Donegal Square South. t (028) 9024 1001, f 028 9024 3210, *www.tensquare. co.uk*. Belfast's first boutique hotel, housed in a listed Victorian building, enjoys a very central position just behind the city hall. Its restaurant, **Porcelain**, serves good fusion food (*see* below right).

Expensive

Belfast Hilton, 4 Lanyon Place, t (028) 9027 7000. New, modern hotel, right up close to the Waterfront Hall, with wonderful views.

McCausland, 34–38 Victoria Street, t (028) 9022 0200. Stylish hotel geared to business clientèle occupying an ex-grain warehouse. Bar and smart restaurant; the top floor bedrooms have great views over the city..

Moderate

Ash-Rowan Town House, 12 Windsor Avenue, t (028) 9066 1758/1983/3227. Ten minutes from the city centre; cosy and attractive.

Camera Guest House, 44 Wellington Park, t (028) 9066 0026, f (028) 9066 7856. Comfortable Victorian terraced house.

Clandeboye Lodge Hotel, 10 Estate Road, Clandeboye, t (028) 9185 2500. Luxurious hotel adjoining Blackwood Golf Course.

Dukes Hotel, 65–67 University Street, t/f (028) 9023 6666. Quiet and central.

Greenwood Guest House, 25 Park Road, t (028) 9020 2525, f (028) 9020 2530, *www.green woodhouse.co.uk*. Jason and Mary Harris offer excellent full Irish breakfasts at their imaginatively furnished Victorian town house. The house overlooks Ormeau Park. *Children welcome, babysitting available.*

Lisdara Town House, 23 Derryvolgie Avenue, Malone Road, t (028) 9068 1549, *elisabeth@ lisdara.freeserve.co.uk*. 1870s town house in quiet residential avenue, within easy reach of the city centre.

Ramada Hotel, 117 Milltown Road, Shaw's Bridge, t (028) 9092 3500, f (028) 9092 3600, *www.ramadabelfast.com*. A bit soulless, but this full service hotel has all mod cons and is conveniently located for drivers, on the ring road, 5 miles from the city centre.

Inexpensive

All of these offer good value B&B in the quiet, leafy streets of the university district. They are often busy in summer, so book ahead.

Eglantine Guest House, 21 Eglantine Avenue, t (028) 9066 7585.

The George, 9 Eglantine Ave, t (028) 9068 3212.

Liserin Guest House, 17 Eglantine Avenue, t (028) 9066 0769.

Queen's University Common Room, College Gardens, University Road, t (028) 9066 5938, f (028) 9066 4501.

Windermere Guest House, 60 Wellington Park, t (028) 9066 2693.

YWCA Hostel, Kent Street, t (028) 9024 0439.

Eating Out

Expensive

Belle Epoque, 61 Dublin Road, t (028) 9032 3244. French food in traditional style.

Deane's, 36–40 Howard Street, t (028) 9056 0000. Successful, well-run restaurant with a more affordable *brasserie* (*moderate*) in the basement, which also serves excellent food.

Porcelain, 10 Donegall Square South, t (028) 9024 1001. Part of TENsquare hotel and fast gaining the reputation as being one of Northern Ireland's most exciting eateries, Porcelain serves excellent fusion food in an appropriately stylish, contemporary ambience. Lunch is much cheaper than dinner.

Moderate

Alden's, 229 Upper Newtownards Road, t (028) 9065 0079. Excellent modern Irish and Mediterranean cooking in a lovely room. Lunch is particularly good value.

Belfast Bar & Grill, The Ramada Hotel, Shaw's Bridge, t (028) 9092 3500. Classic Irish food with a contemporary twist from Paul Rankin (*see* Cayenne) at this hotel in South Belfast.

Belfast Castle, Antrim Road, t (028) 9077 6925. Lovely city views.

Cayenne, Lesley House, 7 Shaftesbury Square, t (028) 9033 1532. Imaginative menu and reasonable set lunches. *Book ahead, closed Sun.*

Chokdee, 44 Bedford Street, t (028) 9024 8800. This brand new restaurant with super-cool contemporary décor serves exciting pan-Asian food such as sweet and sour monkfish and green chicken curry.

Nick's Warehouse, 35 Hill Street, Cathedral Quarter, t (028) 9043 9690. Popular, modern restaurant, highly recommended for its freshly prepared gourmet dishes. *Open Mon 10–5, Tues–Fri 10–10, Sat 6–10, closed Sun.*

Sun Kee, 28 Donegall Pass, t (028) 9031 2016. The best Chinese restaurant in Belfast – fabulous Cantonese roast duck. BYOB.

The Watermargin, 159–61 Donegall Pass, t (028) 9032 6888. Occupying a converted church, this huge, noisy, colourful and very popular Chinese restaurant serves all sorts of weird and wonderful specialities (ox tripe with turnip, marinated duck feet).

Moderate–Inexpensive

Rain City, 33–5 Malone Road, t (028) 0968 2929. Another of local chef Paul Rankin's projects, Rain City offers excellent Peking ribs, steak, fish cakes, chowder, Caesar salad and other classics in an informal, vibrant atmosphere. Good cocktails too.

Inexpensive

Fitzy's, 25–7 University Road, t (028) 9024 7725. Studenty bistro and pizzeria. *Open Mon–Sat 12–2.30 and 5pm–late, Sun 5–9.30.*

Maggie May's, 50 Botanic Avenue, t (028) 9032 2662. Big servings, good value veggie meals.

The Other Place, 79 Botanic Avenue, t (028) 9020 7200. Burgers, chips and Ulster fry.

Scarletts, 423 Lisburn Road, t (028) 9068 3102. Snack menu and bistro.

Speranza, 16 Shaftesbury Square, t (028) 9023 0213. Pizzas, pasta.

Villa Italia, 37–41 University Road, t (028) 9032 8356. Lively and popular. *Evenings only.*

Cafés

Belfast has some good cafés serving exotic, well-prepared food or simple, affordable meals, yet few have effective non-smoking areas and some have yet to master the art of the cappuccino.

Bewleys Oriental Café, Donegall Arcade, t (028) 9023 4955.

Bookfinders Café, 47 University Road, t (028) 9032 8269. In a bookshop; vegetarian meals.

Café Paul Rankin, 27 Fountain Street, t (028) 9031 5090. Great for breakfasts and snacks; also at 12–14 Arthur Street, t (028) 9031 0108, with a takeaway and a more relaxed area.

Cargoes, 613 Lisburn Road, t (028) 9066 5451. Mediterranean salads, café in delicatessen.

Conor, 11a Stranmillis Road, t (028) 9066 3266. Good café-cum-bar-cum-restaurant for coffees, teas and snacks opposite the Ulster Museum. Also lunch and dinner.

Equinox, 32 Howard Street, t (028) 9023 0089. Café in a sophisticated interior design and gift shop. Excellent salad, coffee, milkshakes.

Smyth & Gibson, Bedford Street, t (028) 9023 0388. Famous Derry shirtmakers with coffee outlet upstairs that does try for decent latte and cappuccino; non-smoking.

Entertainment and Nightlife

Pubs and Bars

The atmosphere in the bars mentioned below is friendly and warm. Traditional, folk and popular music is played in some places, while specialities such as champ (mashed potato with onion or leek) and stew are served in others. The best sources of information for music events are the *Belfast Telegraph* or *That's Entertainment* and *Artslink*, available from tourist offices and hotels.

Apartment, 2 Donegall Square, t (028) 9050 9777. Coffee and cocktails, meals and snacks in this hip and stylish bar in the city centre.

Crown Liquor Saloon, 46 Great Victoria Street, t (028) 9027 9901. A Victorian extravagance. Irish stew and oysters at lunchtime.

Lavery's Bar and Gin Palace, 12 Bradbury Place, t (028) 9087 1106. An old favourite for a wide range of age groups. Pub grub.

McHugh's, 29–31 Queen's Square, t (028) 9050 9990. A charming bar and restaurant in Belfast's oldest building, popular with tourists and young professionals.

The Morning Star, 17 Pottinger's Entry, t (028) 9032 3976. Attractive old pub which serves excellent meals.

Morrison's, 21 Bedford St, t (028) 9032 0030. Cleverly decorated bar – good food, cocktails, live music.

TaTu Bar and Grill, 701 Lisburn Rd, t (028) 9038 0818. Minimalist, new-age bar frequented by Belfast's bright young things. Serves drinks (great cocktails) and good food.

White's Tavern, 2–4 Winecellar Entry, t (028) 9024 3080. Founded in 1630, one of the city's original historic pubs. Live music on Thursday nights.

Live Music

Front Page, 108 Donegall Street, t (028) 9032 4924. Food and live music.

Kitchen Bar, 16–18 Victoria Square, t (028) 9032 4901. Traditional Irish bar with real ale and Ulster food, and Irish and Scottish traditional music on Friday nights.

The Rotterdam, 54 Pilot Street, t (028) 9074 6021. Folk and traditional music.

Nightclubs

The Limelight, 17 Ormeau Avenue, t (028) 9032 5968. Promotes new bands, attracts a young crowd. U2 and Oasis have played here.

M Club, 23–31 Bradbury Place, t (028) 9023 3131.

Robinson's Bar, 38–42 Great Victoria Street, t (028) 9024 7447. Has some truly awful duos and bands, but also the occasional gem.

Milk, 13–15 Tomb Street, t (028) 90278 876. Belfast's hottest club venue is tucked away on a back street near the docks. The sleek décor and cool sounds attract a hip crowd for dancing and drinking.

The Edge, Laganbank Road, t (028) 9032 2000. This riverside venue is a bar by day and popular club by night.

Arts Centres

Cultúrlann Macadam O'Fiach, 216 Falls Road, t (028) 9096 4180, *diane@culturlann.org*. Irish-language arts centre, with performance and different forms of media.

Cinema

The Movie House, Yorkgate Centre, York Road, t (028) 9075 5000.

Queen's University Film Theatre, 7 University Square, t 0800 328 2811/t (028) 9024 4857. Avant-garde, art house films are shown here in a narrow lane off Botanic Avenue.

Strand Cinema, 152–4 Holywood Road, t (028) 9067 3500.

UGC, 4 Dublin Road, t 0870 155 5176. Big multiplex.

Warner Village, Odyssey Arena, 2 Queen's Way, t 0870 240 6020.

Poetry

Ulster has also produced poets of international renown; Seamus Heaney started writing here when he was at Queen's University in the 1960s, as did Paul Muldoon at a later date. During the **Belfast Arts Festival** in November you could be lucky and hear them and other talented poets reading their work (*see* under 'Festivals').

Theatres and Concert Halls

Belfast Waterfront Hall, 2 Lanyon Place, t (028) 9033 4455/t (028) 9033 4400, *www.waterfront.co.uk*. Concert hall which accommodates about 2,200 people. Major stars from the classical and pop music world perform here.

The Grand Opera House, Great Victoria Street, t (028) 9024 1919/t (028) 9024 0411.

Lyric Theatre, 55 Ridgeway Street, off Stranmillis Road, t (028) 9038 1081. Serious Irish, European and American drama.

The Old Museum Arts Centre, 7 College Square North, t (028) 9023 5053. Avant-garde dance, theatre, comedy.

St Anne's Cathedral, Donegall Street, t (028) 9032 8332. Venue for occasional lunchtime recitals; wonderful sung services on Sunday.

The Ulster Hall, Bedford Street, t (028) 9032 3900. Another venue for concerts and comedy shows. The hall has a wonderful organ; there is a series of subscription concerts and lunchtime recitals in the summer months.

Whitla Hall, Queen's University, t (028) 9027 3075. Classical music concerts throughout the year, particularly during the Arts Festival.

atmosphere makes for good conversation and well-stocked bookshops. The well-educated young are still leaving for opportunities abroad, but many are coming back with a wealth of experience. Belfast is losing its parochial image and becoming more European-minded, and the bars and cafés more sophisticated. The new Waterfront Hall and Hilton seem to be new symbols for Belfast, just as the Europa Hotel and the Opera House became symbols of surviving the bomb and bullet during the worst of the Troubles in the 1970s.

Central Belfast

The city centre is pedestrianized, for security reasons, but you will see nothing else out of the ordinary unless you are extraordinarily unlucky. It has been spoiled by awful shopping arcades and the usual range of British high street shops, which, on the upside, does mean that shopping is convenient and there are decent cafés. There are also a few specialist interior décor, furniture and Irish design shops worth looking out for (see 'Shopping', pp.37–8). The city centre is quite compact and is easy to walk around, and the area is often lively long after nightfall.

Belfast is a 19th-century town and lacks Dublin's grace; some say this is owing to the plutocratic city fathers. Two of the more attractive buildings are on Great Victoria Street: the **Grand Opera House** and the **Crown Liquor Saloon**, the latter a gas-lit High-Victorian pub decorated with richly coloured tiles. It has been preserved by the National Trust, but has not been gentrified, and its old clientele still drink there (at night it can be noisy and a bit rough). The Opera House was also designed in High-Victorian style (by Robert Matcham, the famous theatre architect) with rich, intricate decorative detail, including carved elephants. It was restored in the 1970s by the architect Robert McKinstry, and painted on the ceiling is a fine fresco by Cherith McKinstry. Even if you don't have an evening to spare, both buildings are worth a quick look around, and the Crown is generally good for a quiet pint with lunch.

Although many of the splendours of Belfast date from its period of mercantile importance, there was a great quickening of spirit here in the 18th century. United Irishman Henry Joy McCracken, whose family first published *The Belfast Newsletter* in 1737 (the longest-running newspaper in the world), was a son of the city. Other 18th-century personalities include William Drennan, who coined the phrase 'the Emerald Isle' and founded the **Royal Academical Institution**. This distinguished building lies between College Square East and Durham Street, and was designed by Sir John Soane, the eminent London architect, classical scholar and collector. It was built between 1808 and 1810 in a style that is classical in proportion. The institution is now a school, but it is possible to look around it. The prospect is a little spoiled by the great College of Technology, built on the corner of the lawn.

The **City Hall** (*guided tours available; adm free*) in Donegall Square, built between 1896 and 1906 in Portland stone, is a grand composition with a central dome and corner towers borrowed from Wren's St Paul's Cathedral in London. Unfortunately the 18th-century Donegall Square has been replaced with a medley of different styles since the 19th century. The **Linen Hall Library** (*open Mon–Fri 9.30–5.30, Sat 9.30–4; www.linenhall.com, info@linenhall.com*) is one of the last survivors in the British Isles of the subscription library movement, so important to civilized Europe in the late 18th/early 19th century. Still a rich storehouse of books of Irish interest, it also has a comfortable room where you can sample periodicals, magazines and the day's flurry of newspapers. The librarians are polite and helpful, and the prints which line the walls echo the feeling of an earlier age.

Just along the way is the Robinson Cleaver Building, overlooking Donegall Place. This flamboyantly Victorian department store now houses a mixture of boutiques. The **Customs House** and **Courts of Justice** in Custom House Square and the **Ulster Hall** in Bedford Street with its impressive organ are all rather grey, self-important buildings in heavy Victorian style. In Corporation Square is the **Sinclair Seamen's Church**, designed by Charles Lanyon and built in 1853. The pulpit incorporates the bows, bowsprit and figurehead of a ship, the organ displays starboard and port lights, and the font is a binnacle. **St Anne's Cathedral** in Donegall Street was built in 1899 in Romanesque style, of the Basilican type. It is very imposing inside, with some fine stained-glass windows and mosaics. In the nave is the tomb of Lord Carson, the Northern Unionist leader, who died in 1935.

On the eastern bank of the River Lagan at Queen's Quay you'll find the **Odyssey Centre**. Inside there is a new interactive children's museum, **whowhatwherewhen why – W5** (*open all year Mon–Sat 10–6, Sun 12–6; adm, www. w5online.co.uk*). Kids can have great fun making giant cloud rings, playing the Laser Harp and watching the Fire Tornado. Farther upstream, at the **Lagan Weir and Lookout Centre** on Donegall Quay (*open April–Sept Mon–Fri 10–5, Sat 12–5, Sun 2–5; Oct–Mar Tues–Fri 11–3.30 Sat 1–4.30, Sun 2–4.30, closed Mon; adm*), you can take a platform view of the busy Lagan waterway, and find out about local industrial and folk history. South of here, following the Lagan, is the newly built and prestigious **Belfast Waterfront Hall**, a large concert hall and conference centre.

About 10 minutes' walk away from Donegall Square, going south down Great Victoria Street, is the leafy **university area**. This neighbourhood best reflects the character of the city, and is by far the most pleasant part of town in which to stay. Lisburn Road, in particular, has seen dozens of new cafés and art galleries spring up in the wake of the ceasefire, and the student population ensures the area's vitality.

You pass the imposing Tudor-style red-brick Queen's University building to go into the **Botanic Gardens** (*gardens open from 8 to sunset; Palm House Mon–Fri 10–5, weekends 2–4*). The gardens are small but beautifully laid out, with formal flowerbeds. The restored Victorian Palm House is a splendid combination of graceful design and clever construction. Richard Turner, the Dubliner whose ironworks produced it, was also responsible for its design. It is made of sections which comprise the earliest surviving cast-iron and curvilinear glass architecture in the world. Inside the newly restored Palm House are tender and exotic plants. Another building within the grounds worth visiting is the Tropical Ravine, which houses a large collection of tropical plants.

Inside the Botanical Gardens is the **Ulster Museum** (*www.ulstermuseum.org.uk; open Mon–Fri 10–5, Sat 1–5, Sun 2–5; adm free except for special exhibitions*). It has a variety of well-displayed and informative collections ranging from giant elk antlers to patchwork, jewellery and Irish antiquities. Of special interest is the outstanding modern art collection, with a good representation of Irish artists including Sir James Lavery, whose wife was the Irish *cailín* (colleen) on the old Irish pound notes. The museum also has a unique collection of treasure from the wreck of the Spanish Armada vessel, the *Girona*. In 1588 Philip II of Spain ordered the greatest invasion fleet ever assembled to put an end to the growing power of England. Of the 130 ships that set sail, 26 were lost on, or just off, the coast of Ireland. In 1968 a fabulous hoard of gold and silver coins, heavy gold chains, rings, ornamented crosses, a beautiful gold salamander pendant set with rubies and a filigree brooch were all recovered off the coast of Antrim. As recently as 1999 a set of delicate gold and jewelled cameos was made complete by the addition of the tweflth cameo. The temporary exhibitions are invariably excellent, and there is a programme of lectures, art films, talks and children's weekend activities. It also has a café overlooking the gardens.

The streets around and leading away from the university are attractive and tree-lined with some good restaurants and cafés, small art galleries and design shops – all a far cry from the wastelands of the 'other' Belfast, beyond the Westlink motorway.

If you want to see the **Republican enclaves** in west Belfast, which are brightened by gaudy wall paintings and political slogans, take a black taxi. These run like miniature buses and serve areas such as the Falls Road, which you can also visit by open-trip bus tour. Unemployment and poverty are obvious in the streets here, and although tourists are generally welcome they do stand out, despite efforts to provide visitor facilities. These neighbourhoods are economically and socially depressed, and visitors should exercise caution, as they might in parts of London or New York. The communities are closed to strangers and it would not be wise to go drinking in the pubs or illegal clubs, nor to walk about these parts at night. The **Unionist** working-class area in west Belfast lies beside the Falls, in the notorious Shankill Road, which has political murals of its own. The so-called 'peace line', a high barrier, divides the two communities. **Sandy Row**, a short distance from Great Victoria Street and Shaftesbury Square, is another working-class Unionist area. It seems less threatening to walk around, and there are plenty of little bakeries and small shops which gives it a bustling air. The bulk of the enclaves where the kerbstones are painted red, white and blue are over the river to the east, along Newtownards Road.

Suburbs of Belfast: South

Parliament House and Stormont Castle

Parliament House, Stormont, can be seen from the Newtownards Road (A20) about 2 miles (4km) east from the city centre. It is a very imposing Portland stone building in English Palladian style, with a floor space covering 5 acres (2ha) and it stands in a park of 300 acres (121ha). Next door is **Stormont Castle** (*grounds open daily 10–dusk; Great Hall open Mon–Fri 10–4*), built in Scottish baronial style, which houses government departments.

Parks and Gardens

There are many fine parks around Belfast. In south Belfast, in the Upper Malone Road (B103) area, is **Barnett's Park**. Within the attractive parkland is an early 19th-century house (*open all year, Mon–Sat 10–4.30; adm free*) with an art gallery, a permanent exhibition on Belfast parks and a restaurant.

Nearby is **Dixon Park** (*Ulsterbus no.24, peak time service only; open daily till dusk; adm free*), where rose-fanciers will get a chance to view the Belfast International Rose Trials, the finals of which take place in the third week of July. The park borders the River Lagan, and in summer about 100,000 roses are in bloom.

Giant's Ring and Shaw's Bridge

City bus no.13; both always accessible.

Those interested in Neolithic sites should visit the **Giant's Ring**, near Ballylesson, about a mile south of Shaw's Bridge. The Giant's Ring is a circular grassy embanked enclosure over 600ft in diameter, with a chamber tomb in the centre. The dolmen in the centre is called Druid's Dolmen. The original purpose of the site is disputed but it was probably ritualistic; its date is unknown. The giant it is named after is possibly Fionn MacCumhaill, a favourite to tag on to such places. In old times, farmers used to stage horse-races in this huge circle.

Shaw's Bridge itself is very picturesque and spans the River Lagan. It was originally built *c.* 1650, and is to be found off the B23. You can walk for 10 miles along the towpath of the River Lagan, past the public parks. Start at the Belfast Boat Club, Loughview Road, Stranmillis, and end at Moore's Bridge, Hillsborough Road, Lisburn.

Suburbs of Belfast: North

Belfast Castle and Cave Hill

*City bus nos.45, 46, 47, 48, 49, 50 or 51 to the Antrim road and then walk; call **t** (028) 9077 6925 for opening hours; adm free.*

On the northern side of the city, on the Antrim road (A6), the baronial-style Belfast Castle appears unexpectedly from the wooded slopes of Cave Hill. It was built by the third Marquess of Donegall in 1870. His family, the Chichesters, were granted the forfeited lands of Belfast and the surrounding area in 1603; the Gaelic lords of the area, the O'Neills, lost everything and fled to the Continent. The planted grounds of the castle are open to the public, and always accessible.

There is a pleasant restaurant open for full meals or snacks in the castle itself, and a heritage centre with exhibits on the flora and fauna of Cave Hill. An easy climb to the summit of Cave Hill (1,182ft) gives stunning views over the city and Belfast Lough. There are five caves and the earthworks of MacArts Fort, named after a local Gaelic chieftain of the Iron Age. It was here that the United Irishmen Wolfe Tone and his followers took their oaths of fidelity in 1798.

Belfast Zoo

Cty bus routes nos.8, 10, 45–51; www.belfastzoo.co.uk. Open April–Sept daily 10–6, Oct–Mar 10–3; adm.

Belfast Zoo, on the slopes below Cave Hill, is beautifully planted with flowers, shrubs and trees. The zoo has won awards for its emphasis on large enclosures, its breeding programme, and its mainly small-animal collection. It is great fun to view the penguins and sealions from underwater, and there is a rare opportunity to see a bespectacled bear and a red panda.

Ulster Folk and Transport Museum

Trains from central Belfast stop at Cultra station, in the grounds of the museum; t (028) 9042 8428. Open July–Sept Mon–Sat 10–6, Sun 11–6; Mar–June Mon–Fri 10–5, Sat 10–6, Sun 11–6; Oct–Feb Mon–Fri 10–4, Sat 10–5, Sun 11–5; adm.

In a parkland of nearly 200 acres, the Ulster Folk and Transport Museum, technically in County Down, provides a unique opportunity for visitors to explore Ulster's past. It is the best museum of its type in Ireland, and gives a wonderful insight into what life in the countryside was like all over Ireland until 60 years ago. It is open-air, with representative buildings of rural Ulster: a linen scutch mill, a blacksmith's forge, a spade mill and farmhouses built in different regional styles. These are all furnished appropriately, with real fires burning in the grates.

Day Trips and Overnighters from Belfast

Bangor, Donaghadee and the Copeland Islands

Bangor was a seaside resort popular with the Edwardians, as you will see from the architecture. But in the 6th and 7th centuries it was a famous centre of learning, and from here Saints Columbanus and Gall set off to found Luxeuil Monastery in Burgundy and St Gall Monastery in Switzerland. St Comgall, who founded this monastery in the middle of the 6th century, trained men like Columbanus and Gall to spread the word of Christ. The plundering Norsemen in the 9th century ravaged the town. All that remains from these times is the tower of the **Abbey Church** (*open to the public Tues–Thurs am*) opposite Bangor railway station. The church has a pretty painted ceiling and ancient settler gravestones. An interlude can be spent in the Victorian castle, which houses the town hall and **North Down Heritage Centre** (*open all year during normal working hours*), with a permanent display on Bangor as an ancient place of learning. The main attractions today are the Edwardian seafront, which has a great many B&Bs and small hotels, and a fine marina for yachtsmen; there is also a lively market in the square on Wednesdays.

Nearby **Donaghadee**, a pretty seaside town with an attractive 19th-century harbour and a good number of pubs, used to be linked with Portpatrick in Scotland by a regular sailing boat. It has the feeling of an old port where generations of men and

Getting There

Ulsterbus B1 or B2 from Belfast's Laganside bus station takes you to Bangor in 45mins, or take a **train** from Great Victoria Street or Central or Botanic stations for a shorter journey. **Ulsterbus** no.7 (the Millisle bus) goes from Laganside bus station to Donaghadee in 55mins.

Pleasure Cruises

Weather permitting, cruise boats leave from **Bangor** and **Donaghadee** in summer at 10.30, 2.30 and 7.30pm for short cruises. Information is posted on the piers, or call Bangor tourist centre on **t** (028) 9127 0069. For trips to the **Copeland Islands**, call **t** (028) 9188 3403.

Tourist Information

Bangor: **t** (028) 9127 0069; *open all year*.

Eating Out

Bangor

Shanks Restaurant, Blackwood Golf Club, 150 Crawfordsburn Road, **t** (028) 9185 3313

(*expensive*). Rich, varied menu; reputedly one of the best restaurants in the area.

Heatherlea Tea Rooms, 94 Main Street, **t** (028) 9145 3157 (*inexpensive*). Good quiche, pies and salads.

The Bangor Fish Company, 20 High Street, **t** (028) 9147 2172 (inexpensive). Great fish and chips to complete the seaside experience.

Donaghadee

Grace Neill's Bar and Restaurant, 33 High Street, **t** (028) 9188 2553 (*moderate*). Said to be one of the oldest pubs in Ireland. Adventurous food with generous portions. *Lunch 12.30–2.30, dinner from 6pm, lunch only on Sun.*

Bistro Bistro, 33 High Street, **t** (028) 9188 4595 (*moderate*). Interesting, well-cooked food plus a great Sunday brunch with live jazz.

Pier 36, 36 The Parade, **t** (028) 9188 4466 (*moderate*). Good seafood is on offer at this harbourside pub. Both traditional and more exotic dishes (like wild boar) feature on the menu. Grilled local lobster is a house speciality; there are good salads and vegetarian options. There is also a cheaper bar menu.

women have waited for the wind and the tide to change. The poet John Keats stayed at Grace Neill's Bar on the High Street, as did Peter the Great of Russia. ('Gracie's' is the oldest pub in Ireland, established in 1611, and is still one of the most attractive pubs in the town, *see* above.) You can go stream-fishing at night in the summer with a white feather as a lure. Or go out to the **Copeland Islands** – long, low islands covered with spring turf and rabbit's trails, enchanting in spring and summer. It is possible to reach them and also to go out stream-fishing on a regular boat.

Hillsborough

This is the town where the Anglo-Irish Agreement was reached in 1985. It is one of the most English-looking villages in Ulster, with fine Georgian architecture, several excellent antiques shops in the Main Street, tasteful craft shops and numerous restaurants and pubs. To the south of the town in parkland is a massive **fort** built by Sir Arthur Hill, an English settler, in the 17th century (*open summer Mon–Sat 10–7, Sun 2–7; winter Tues–Sat 10–4, Sun 2–4, closed Mon*). **Hillsborough Castle**, which was the official residence of the Governor of Northern Ireland until 1973 and which mostly houses various officials, stands in the parkland, too. The wrought-iron gates which bar one's approach from the town are exquisite. **St Malachy's**, the Church of Ireland parish church, is in handsome planter's-style Gothic and was built by the Hill family in

Getting There

Ulsterbus nos.238 and 38 from Great Victoria Street bus station in Belfast take about 40mins to Hillsborough.

Tourist Information

Hillsborough: t (028) 9268 9717; *open all year.*

Eating Out

Hillside Restaurant and Bar, 21 Main Street, t (028) 9268 2765 (*moderate–inexpensive*). Salad bar, soups, plus oysters in season. Has a good reputation. *Open 12–2.30 and 5–9.*
The Plough Inn, The Square, t (028) 9268 2985 (*inexpensive*). Recommended by locals, pub grub and upstairs seafood bistro. *Pub open daily 12–2.15 and 6–9.30; bistro open daily 12–2.15 and 5–8.*

1774. If you are lucky enough to get inside, you'll see that it is typical of the cool, unadorned churches of that style, with box pews and 18th- and 19th-century wall tablets. It has a well-cared-for atmosphere; very different from the fate of so many Church of Ireland buildings in the Republic, which have become redundant because of dwindling congregations. Just outside the town there is a very pretty lake which is good for a tramp around.

Mount Stewart

Approximately 15 miles (24km) east of Belfast, on the A20 to Newtownards, the demesne wall of **Mount Stewart**, the boyhood home of Robert Stewart, Lord Castlereagh, appears (*house open for guided tours only, mid-Mar–April and Oct Sat and Sun 12–6; May, June and Sept Wed–Mon 1–6pm; July and Aug daily 12–6; gardens open Mar and Oct–Dec weekends only 10–4; April daily 10–6; May–Sept daily 10–8; t (028) 4278 8387/ t (028) 4278 8487*). The 18th-century house and grounds are now in the care of the National Trust. Edith, Lady Londonderry, 7th Marchioness (1879–1959) and one of the foremost political hostesses of her generation, created the wonderful gardens some 70 years ago for her children. There are some lovely topiary animals, colourful parterres and wonderful trees. If you ever come across her children's story *The Magic Inkpot*, you will recognize some of the place names from around here.

Also in the grounds is the **Temple of the Winds**, inspired by the building in Athens and built in 1780 for picnicking in style. In the Mount Stewart schoolhouse you can buy patchwork and handmade cottage furniture. The tea-room in the house itself is painted beautifully with the animals from Noah's Ark. Lady Londonderry nicknamed all the famous men and women who were her friends after animals in the Ark – it is fun to guess who was who.

Getting There

Ulsterbus nos.9, 9A and 19 go from Laganside bus station in Belfast to Portaferry. It passes Mount Stewart after about 50mins.

Eating Out

Mount Stewart House Tearooms, t (028) 4278 8387 (*inexpensive*). The recently refurbished, light and airy tea rooms serve wholesome fresh produce including stews, sausages and mash, fish, soups and salads. *Open Mar–Sept daily 10–5; Oct daily 11–4; Nov–Feb Wed–Sun 11–3.*

Downpatrick

This is an attractive Georgian town built on an old hill-fort which reputedly belonged to one of the Red Branch Knights. It is sited at the natural meeting-point of several river valleys, and so has been occupied for a long time, both suffering and benefiting from the waves of settlers and invaders: missionaries, monks, Norsemen, Normans and Scots (the army of Edward Bruce). **St Patrick's gravestone**, a large lump of granite, may be seen in the Church of Ireland Cathedral graveyard, although this is not the reason why the town carries his name; the association was made by the Norman John de Courcy, a Cheshire knight who was granted the counties of Antrim and Down by Henry II in 1176, and who established himself here at this centre of St Patrick's veneration by promoting the Irish saint. De Courcy donated some relics of Saints Patrick, Columba and Brigid to his Foundation and gave the town its name, adding Patrick to *Dundalethglas*, as it was previously called.

During the Middle Ages Downpatrick suffered at the hands of the Scots: in 1316 it was burnt by Edward Bruce, and later it was destroyed by the English during the Tudor wars. In the early 18th century, stability returned to the town under the influence of an English family called Southwell, who acquired the Manor of Downpatrick through marriage. They built a quay on the River Quoile and encouraged markets and building. The **cathedral**, which had lain in ruins between 1538 and 1790, reopened in 1818. It is very fine inside, with impressive stained-glass windows. The **Saint Patrick Centre**, on Market Street (*www.saintpatrickcentre.com; open Oct–Mar Mon–Sat 10–5, Sun by request; 17 Mar 9.30–7; April–May and Sept Mon–Sat 9.30–5.30, Sun 1–5.30; June–Aug Mon–Sat 9.30–6, Sun 10–6; last adm 1½hrs before close; adm*), uses the saint's own words to tell the story of his life and work in the context of the period in which he lived. The **Southwell Charity School and Almshouse** in English Street near Down Cathedral is a handsome early-Georgian building in the Irish Palladian style, and is now a home for the elderly. Nearby, in the old county jail in the Mall, is the **Down County Museum** (*open all year Mon–Fri 10–5 Sat–Sun 1–5*), which contains very interesting exhibits of Stone Age artefacts and local history. There are also useful starting points for leads on relics associated with St Patrick, which you might come across elsewhere in the county, and there's a nice bright café.

Getting There

Take the **Ulsterbus** from Great Victoria Street bus station in Belfast. The journey to Downpatrick takes 45mins to an hour.

Tourist Information

Downpatrick: t (028) 4461 2233; *open all year.*

Festivals

17 March: St Patrick's Day, t (028) 4461 2233, *events@downdc.gov.uk.*

Eating Out

Denvir's Pub, 14 English Street, t (028) 4461 2012 *(inexpensive)*. An ancient gem of a pub with a genuine 'olde-worlde' atmosphere and an open fire. Good wholesome food.

St Patrick's Visitor Centre, Market Street, t (028) 4461 9000 *(inexpensive)*. The café here serves snacks all day *(closes at 4.30pm)* plus hot food between noon and 2.30. There is a roof terrace for warm weather.

Justine's, 19 English Street, t (028) 4461 7886 *(inexpensive)*. Another old pub serving a range of hot and cold snacks.

Armagh

Armagh (*Ard Macha*), now sprawled over seven hills, was a centre of Christian learning and tranquillity when Rome was in ruins and London glowed with endless fires started by the barbarians. Today there is little to show of the ancient city – its appearance is distinctly Georgian – yet it is still the ecclesiastical centre of Ireland. Armagh is a lovely city to walk around with its fine buildings, especially in the Mall and in Beresford Row. The **Courthouse** dates from 1809 and is the work of Francis Johnston, as are many buildings here; he was a local architect who later achieved fame in Dublin. It was bombed in 1993, but has since been completely restored. Many of the most interesting places to visit are just a brisk walk away.

A visit to the **Armagh County Museum** in the Mall East (*open Mon–Fri 10–5, Sat 10–1 and 2–5; adm free*) helps to fill in the city's background. Here, a 17th-century painting shows the old wide streets, space for markets and the prominence of the early hilltop cathedral of St Patrick. There is also a wide range of regional archaeological exhibits, a local natural history section, and an art gallery which has works by the Irish mystic poet and artist George Russell (1867–1935), better known as A. E. Russell. The **Royal Irish Fusiliers Museum** (*open Mon–Fri 10–12.30 and 1–4; adm*), with displays of old uniforms, weapons and medals, is also in the Mall.

The two cathedral churches are unmistakable features of the city's skyline, for they each crown neighbouring hills. Founded by St Patrick, the ancient **Church of Ireland Cathedral** (*open April–Oct, 9.30–5, Nov–Mar, 9.30–4; adm free*) is in the perpendicular style with a massive central tower. Its present appearance dates mainly from the 18th century, but its core is medieval. Before medieval times the city suffered terribly from the Viking raids, and the cathedral and town were sacked at least twenty times in five hundred years. Inside the cathedral is a memorial to Brian Boru, the most famous high king of all Ireland, who visited Armagh in 1004 and was received with great state. The precious *Book of Armagh* (*c*. AD 807), which is now in Trinity College, Dublin, was placed in his hands and his visit noted in the book. He presented 20 ounces of pure gold to the church. Ten years later he hammered the Vikings at the Battle of Clontarf in 1014, which put a stop to their encroachment into inland areas, but Brian Boru was killed in his tent after the battle was won. His body and that of his son were brought back to be buried here and the memorial to them is in the west wall.

The other heirloom of those ancient days is St Patrick's Bell, which is enclosed in a cover dating from the 12th century; it can also be seen at the National Museum in Dublin. The moulding on the west door is very fine, and there is a good stained-glass window in the choir. Notice the carved medieval stone heads high up on the cathedral's exterior and the mysterious statues in the crypt. The surrounding streets run true to the rings of the Celtic *rath* or fort in which St Patrick built his church – directed, it is said, by a flight of angels.

On the corner of Abbey Street is **Armagh Public Library**, also known as Robinson's Library, which contains some rare books, maps and a first edition of *Gulliver's Travels*, annotated by Jonathan Swift himself. Richard Robinson, Archbishop of Armagh, was a very influential figure in the building of the 18th-century city. There is an exhibition

Getting There

Ulsterbus Express buses run from Belfast to Armagh, Mon–Fri every hour 6.30am–6.30pm; on Sundays there are only two. Armagh City Bus Station, **t** (028) 3752 2266.

Tourist Information

Armagh: St Patrick's Trian Centre, 40 English Street, **t** (028) 3752 1800, **f** (028) 3752 8329, *www.armagh-visit.com; open all year.*

Festivals

17 March: St Patrick's Day. Parade in Armagh City, with a concert in St Patrick's Hall.
May: Apple Blossom Festival, Armagh City, **t** (028) 3752 2282.

Shopping

Cloud Cuckoo, Ogle Street, Armagh, **t** (028) 3751 0771. Crafts.
Quinn's Antiquities, 27 Dobbin Street, Armagh, **t** (028) 3751 0947. Antiques and bric-a-brac.
St Patrick's Trian, 40 English Street, Armagh, **t** (028) 3752 1801. Crafts.

Markets

Shambles Market, Cathedral Road. *Tuesday and Friday, 9–5.*
Variety Market, Market Street. *Tuesday and Friday 9–5.*

Where to Stay

The Charlemont Arms Hotel, 63 English Street, **t** (028) 3752 2028, **f** 3752 6979 (*expensive*).
De Averell Guest House, 3 Seven Houses, English Street, **t** (028) 3751 1213, **f** 3751 1221 (*moderate*). Georgian town house with a good basement restaurant.
Drumsill House Hotel, 35 Moy Road, **t** (028) 3752 2009, **f** 3752 5624 (*moderate*). Modern and bland but comfortable.
Deans Hill, t (028) 3752 4923, **f** 3752 2186 (*moderate*). Pretty 18th-century house with lovely gardens, close to the Observatory. Two en suite rooms, one with a four-poster.

Hillview Lodge, 33 Newtownhamilton Road, **t** (028) 3752 2000, **f** 3752 8276 (*moderate*). Reliable B&B with six en suite rooms.

Eating Out

D'Arby Byrne Restaurant, Palace Demesne, **t** (028) 3752 9634 (*moderate*). Set in beautiful grounds, serves coffee, lunch, afternoon tea. *Open Mon–Sat 10–4.30, Sun 12.30–2.30.*
Rainbow, 13 Upper English Street, **t** (028) 3752 5391 (*moderate–inexpensive*). Morning coffee, lunch and afternoon tea; bistro menu in the evenings. *Open Mon–Sat 9–5.30, Fri–Sat 7.30pm–9.30pm.*
Calvert Tavern, 3 Scotch Street, **t** (028) 3752 4186 (*inexpensive*). Good pub grub: open sandwiches and grills. *Food served till 10pm.*
Hester's Place, 12 English Street, **t** (028) 3752 2374 (*inexpensive*). Irish stew, great Ulster fry. *Open Mon–Sat 9–5.30.*
Jodie's, 37a Scotch St, **t** (028) 3752 7577 (*inexpensive*). Cheerful surrounds, usually has some vegetarian options. *Open weekdays (exc Wed) for lunch; weekends for dinner.*
Navan Centre, 81 Killylea Road, **t** (028) 3752 5550 (*inexpensive*). Hot meals, snacks and coffee.
The Pilgrim's Table, 38 English Street (inside St Patrick's Trian complex), **t** (028) 3752 1801 (*inexpensive*). Reputedly the best lunch in town, with pleasant surroundings.

Entertainment and Nightlife

Theatre and Cinema

Armagh City Filmhouse, Market Street, **t** (028) 3751 1033. Four-screen cinema complex.
Market Place Theatre and Arts Centre, t (028) 3752 1821. New arts centre, with drama, music and dance, two theatres, a gallery and restaurants and bars.

Traditional Music

Charlemont Arms, Armagh, **t** (028) 3752 2928. One Thurs per month.
Palace Stables Heritage Centre, t (028) 3751 1248. Armagh Pipers Club once a month.

and historical centre in English Street, **St Patrick's Trian**; it derives this name from an ancient division of the city (*open all year; adm for exhibitions*). Inside, the story of Armagh through the ages is illustrated by an audiovisual show; there is also an exhibition on the life and work of St Patrick, and his connections with Armagh. The 'Land of Lilliput' is a child-orientated exhibition, which has a giant model of Gulliver as the centrepiece. The centre also has art exhibitions, tourist information, and is home to **Armagh Ancestry** (*open Mon–Sat 9–5*), a central source for chasing up ancestors in Armagh county.

Across the valley are the twin spires of the Catholic **Cathedral of St Patrick**. This is a complete contrast to its more sombre Protestant neighbour, with its profusion of magnificent internal gilding, marbles, mosaics and stained glass. The building was started in 1849 and finished in 1873; the passing of the years is marked by a collection of cardinals' red hats suspended in the Lady Chapel.

Armagh has the most advanced facilities for astronomical studies in the British Isles. The institution owes its pre-eminence to Archbishop Richard Robinson, who endowed the **Armagh Observatory** in 1790. It is complemented by the **Armagh Planetarium and Hall of Astronomy** on College Hill (*www.armagh-planetarium.co.uk; open all year, Mon–Fri 10–4, Sat–Sun 1.15–4; adm for shows and exhibition; observatory dome and grounds free*), which has Ireland's largest public telescope and hosts presentations in its star theatre. (Star shows are put on more frequently in summer; ring and book for these.) In the grounds you'll find the Astropark, which is a scale model of the universe. The Observatory was designed by Francis Johnston, who is also responsible for the Georgian terrace on the east side of the Mall.

On the south side of the city is the palace demesne. The **Palace Stables Heritage Centre** (*open all year, daily; adm*) is a restored 18th-century building in the demesne of the Bishop's Palace. The 'Day in the Life' exhibition features typical scenes of life here in 1776 in the time of Archbishop Robinson. Craft exhibitions, fairs, lectures, art shows, music, dance and storytelling events are all held here.

Navan Fort

The ancient fort of *Emain Macha*, now called **Navan Fort**, dates from 600 BC and is about 2 miles (3km) west of Armagh City on the A28. The fort was a centre of pagan power and culture, and is famous for its association with the Red Branch Knights. When Fergus was King of Ulster in the 4th century, *Emain Macha* was burned, its timber structures completely destroyed. By the time St Patrick came to *Ard Macha* (Armagh), this Bronze Age centre of power had lain in ruins for over a hundred years. Today, the grassy *rath* extends over about 12 acres (5ha). It is easy to walk or take a bus there from town, and you are rewarded with a pleasant view over the city when you arrive. Once in danger of being destroyed to make way for a quarry, the site has become a chief tourist attraction. An excellent interpretative centre, the **Navan Centre** (*open all year, Mon–Sat 10–5, Sun 12–5; adm; t (028) 3752 5550, www.navan.com, navan@enterprise.net*) has opened close by with a restaurant and shop. The centre is in the shape of a Bronze Age fort, and very unobtrusive; it is definitely worth a detour. The no.73 bus from Mall West in Armagh will drop you outside.

Touring from Belfast 1: South

Day 1: Down the Ards Peninsula

Morning: Drive east from Belfast on the A20 to **Newtownards**, with its impressive town square, 17th-century market cross and fine town hall. On the outskirts of town are the 13th–15th-century **Movilla Abbey**, and **Scrabo Hill**, with its prominent lookout tower (*open Easter and June–Sept Sat–Thurs 10.30–6; free access to park*). Continue on the A20 to **Mount Stewart**, the 18th-century boyhood home of Robert Stewart, Lord Castlereagh (*see p.48*). Edith, Lady Londonderry, created its wonderful gardens some 70 years ago for her children, with topiary animals, colourful parterres and wonderful trees, and a Temple of the Winds.

Lunch: A light lunch at Mount Stewart Tearooms, *see below.*

Afternoon: Head south to **Grey Abbey**, one of the most complete Cistercian abbeys in Ireland (*open April–Sept Tues–Sat 10–6, Sun 2–6; Oct–Mar Tues–Sat 10–4, Sun 2–4; adm*), on the northern edge of the pretty village of Greyabbey. Then on to **Portaferry**, the most picturesque town on the peninsula, situated where the tip of the peninsula forms a narrow strait with the mainland of Down, with a view across to Strangford. The main street is wide, with brightly painted old houses. In Castle Street is the Exploris Aquarium (*open Mon–Fri 10–6, Sat 11–6, Sun 1–6; Sept–Mar closes 5pm; adm*). On summer evenings you might be lucky and hear some open-air music.

Dinner and Sleeping: In Portaferry or Strangford, *see below.*

Day 1

Lunch at Mount Stewart
Mount Stewart House, National Trust Tearooms, t (028) 4278 8387 (*inexpensive*). See p.48.

Dinner in Portaferry
Portaferry Hotel, 10 The Strand, t (028) 4272 8231 (*moderate*). Seafood, delivered straight from the fishing boats of Portavogie.
The Narrows, 8 Shore Road, t (028) 4272 8148 (*moderate*). Excellent locally sourced dishes prepared with flair and served in lovely bright surroundings.

Dinner in Strangford
A ferry runs between Portaferry and Strangford every half-hour, and the journey of five minutes is well worth it for the view up Strangford Lough. Check the last return time if you are sleeping back in Portaferry – the last ferry Strangford–Portaferry leaves at 10.30pm, and Portaferry–Strangford at 10.15pm.

The Lobster Pot, 9–11 The Square, t (028) 4488 1288 (*moderate*). Very good set meals and pub grub. Oysters and other shellfish a speciality.
Cuan Bar and Restaurant, 6 The Square, t (028) 4488 1222 (*moderate*). Venison, quail, plus hot & cold buffet.

Sleeping in Portaferry
Portaferry Hotel, 10 The Strand, t (028) 4272 8231, f (028) 4272 8999, *www.portaferry hotel.com* (*expensive–mod-erate*). Old-fashioned, yet well-appointed, in a lovely situation; excellent food, too.
The Narrows, 8 Shore Road, t (028) 4272 8148, f 4272 8105, *www.narrows. co.uk* (*moderate*). A recent development with sea views, restaurant and a walled garden.
Adair's, 22 The Square, t (028) 4272 8412 (*inexpensive*). A very simple and clean place to stay.
Barholm, 11 The Strand, t (028) 4272 9598, *barholm@dial.pipex.com* (*inexpensive*). Youth hostel.

Day 2: South Down: Castles, Wells and Abbeys

Morning: Take the car ferry over to **Strangford**. No less than five small castles lie within reach of the village: **Kilclief Castle** (*open July–Aug Tues–Sat 10–6 Sun 2–6; adm*) is easy to find on the A2 between Strangford and Ardglass, and is very well preserved. One mile west of Strangford on the A25, you will pass by **Castle Ward** (*open June–Aug 12–6; May Wed–Mon 12–6; April, Sept and Oct Sat and Sun 12–6; grounds open Oct–April daily 10–4; May–Sept daily 10–8; adm*). Built in the 1760s by Bernard Ward, afterwards Lord Bangor, and his wife Lady Anne, the house has a neoclassical façade and a Gothic castellated garden front.

Lunch: In Downpatrick or Seaforde, *see* below.

Afternoon: Spend the afternoon in the Georgian town of **Downpatrick** (*see* p.49), or pick a couple of nearby sights. **St Patrick's Church** in Saul, 1½ miles northeast, is on the spot where St Patrick founded his first church after deciding to return to Ireland to convert the people. To the east of Downpatrick, off the B1, are the **Struell Wells** (*always accessible; adm free*). There must have been worshippers at this pagan shrine, a group of holy wells, long before the arrival of St Patrick; the waters are still known for their curative properties. To the west of Downpatrick, on the A24, is the little village of **Seaforde**; in the grounds of the Big House here is an attractive butterfly house (*open April–Sept Mon–Sat 10–5, Sun 1–6; adm*). **Inch Abbey**, off the A7 (*always open; adm*), is a ruined Cistercian abbey on an island in the Quoile Marshes.

Dinner and Sleeping: Take the A25 then A2 to **Newcastle**, *see* below.

Day 2

Lunch in Downpatrick

Denvir's Pub, 14 English Street, **t** (028) 4461 2012 (*inexpensive*). Ancient gem of a pub with a genuine 'olde-worlde' atmosphere.

Lunch in Seaforde

Seaforde Inn, 24 Main Street, **t** (028) 4481 1232 (*moderate*). Venison sausages and mussels.

Dinner in Newcastle

Stone Boat, 4 South Promenade, **t** (028) 4372 3445 (*moderate*). Inn overlooking harbour with a restaurant serving locally caught seafood and bar food (*inexpensive*).

Sea Salt Bistro, 51 Central Promenade, **t** (028) 4372 5027 (*moderate–inexpensive*). Modern bistro under a retro pink neon sign serving daytime snacks and more substantial fare in the evenings; Thai-style mussels, seafood chowder, steak and chips and veggie options. *Open lunch daily, dinner Wed–Sun.*

Sleeping in Newcastle

Hastings Slieve Donard Hotel, Downs Road, Newcastle, **t** (028) 4372 3681, **f** (028) 4372 4830, *www.hastingshotels.com* (*expensive*). Set in six acres of private grounds, with a health spa, pool, and decent restaurant (*moderate*). Close to golf links.

Burrendale Hotel, 49 Castlewellan Road, Newcastle, **t** (028) 4372 2599, **f** (028) 4372 2328, *www.burrendale.com* (*expensive–moderate*). Modern, popular with bus tours. Good restaurant and bistro; pool, sauna and health suite.

Newcastle Youth Hostel, 30 Downs Road, Newcastle, **t/f** (028) 4372 2133, *www.hini. org.uk* (*inexpensive*). Centrally heated apartment and family rooms beside the sea, at the foot of the mountains.

The Briers Country House, 39 Middle Tollymore Road, **t** (028) 4372 4347 (*moderate*). 18th-century house set in two acres of garden with spacious rooms, near the entrance to Tollymore Forest Park. Good restaurant, also open to non-residents (*moderate*).

Day 3: The Mountains of Mourne

Morning: Take the A2 along the coast from Newcastle. From here there's a fine view of the Mournes. As you head south out of Newcastle, past the now quiet harbour, you come to the **National Trust Mourne Coastal Path**, which runs for 4 miles (6km) from the very popular Bloody Bridge picnic site, along the rocky shoreline to Dunmore Head. The mountain path beside the Bloody Bridge River is a starting point for hill-walks into the Mournes. Here are the splendid mountains of Slieve Donard (2,796ft) and Slieve Commedagh. A network of by-roads runs deep into the foothills behind **Annalong**, with its old harbour and corn mill, and **Kilkeel**, where you'll find the unspoilt, undisturbed Mourne way of life.

Lunch: In Annalong or Kilkeel, *see* below.

Afternoon: Continuing on round the coast, the land levels out quite a bit. Leave the A2 and explore **Greencastle**, ancient capital of the 9th-century Kingdom of Mourne, and its fort (*keep open April–Sept Tues–Sat 10–7, Sun 2–7; grounds accessible at all times*). The road swings round still more, ever twisting and turning as it makes its way along the indented coast. The town of **Rostrevor** is a quiet place to use as a base for walking in the Mourne Mountains or in the pine-scented Rostrevor Forest. Not far from Rostrevor is **Warrenpoint**, a lively and popular resort, spacious and well planned, with a very big square and a promenade over half a mile (800m) long, the town being bounded by the sea on two sides. From here you soon reach **Newry**.

Dinner and Sleeping: In Warrenpoint or Newry, *see* below.

Day 3

Lunch in Annalong
Harbour Inn, 6 Harbour View, **t** (028) 4376 8678 (*inexpensive*). Reasonable lunches and bar food in a pleasant setting.

Lunch in Kilkeel
The Fisherman, 68 Greencastle Street, **t** (028) 4176 2130 (*moderate*). A favourite with the locals, serves lobster stuffed with prawns, mixed seafood creole, local lamb and steak.
Kilmorey Arms Hotel, 41 Greencastle Street, **t** (028) 4176 2220 (*inexpensive*). Cosy revamped bar in a historic hotel serving good pub grub.

Dinner in Warrenpoint
Aylesforte House, 44 Newry Road, **t** (028) 4177 2255 (*moderate*). Exotic eastern-style menu; also bistro-type snacks served in the bar.
The Duke Restaurant, Duke Street, **t** (028) 4175 2084 (*moderate*). Above Duke's pub, this excellent and popular restaurant offers menus based on fish straight from Kilkeel harbour. The midweek set menu is particularly good value. Ambitious and creative dishes rub elbows with classics.

Dinner in Newry
I Sapori Italiani, 16 The Mall, **t** (028) 3025 2086 (*moderate*). This deservedly popular restaurant serves authentic Italian food in an appropriately rustic setting. *Closed Mon.*

Sleeping in Warrenpoint
Ryan B&B, 19 Milltown Street, Burren, **t/f** (028) 4177 2506 (*moderate*). Three en suite rooms.

Sleeping in Newry
Bellmont Hall, 18 Downshire Road, **t** (028) 3026 2163, *www.belmont-hall.co.uk* (*expensive*). An elegant Georgian house with ten rooms offering luxurious B&B accommodation. Library, bar and lots of antiques.
Mourne Country Hotel, 52 Belfast Rd, **t** (028) 3026 7922 (*moderate*). Modern building set in private grounds. Decent rooms and food.

Day 4: The Cooley Peninsula

Morning: Head down the west side of Carlingford Lough. The Cooley Peninsula, in the extreme north of County Louth (you'll need some euros as you are now in Eire) is one of the most beautiful, untouched places in Ireland. You can have a marvellous walk across the **Cooley Mountains** along the slopes of Slieve Foye (2 miles northeast of Carlingford, on the R173) and Ravensdale Forest. Seek out **Faughart Hill**, which is just north of Dundalk, signposted a few miles off the Dundalk to Newry Road on the left. From here, the whole of Leinster spreads out below you. This is where Edward Bruce was killed in battle in 1318. You can see the Wicklow Hills rippling across the plain to join the Slieve Bloom and the Cooley Hills behind. In Faughart graveyard, there is a shrine to St Brigid, patroness of Ireland.

Lunch: In Carlingford, *see* below.

Afternoon: Spend the afternoon in **Carlingford**, which looks across its lough to the Mourne Mountains. This town is full of castellated buildings; it is said to have possessed 32 'castles' in the days of the Pale, when almost every house on the border was fortified in some way. The ruins of the Anglo-Norman King John's Castle, built in 1210 by John de Courcy, with arrow slits in the outer walls, are impressive, and you can see that the town was a place of great strategic importance in medieval times. Nowadays, it is nothing more than a little village with a 16th-century arched Tholsel, a Mint, and Taaffe's Castle, which is multi-storeyed and attached to a modern house.

Dinner and Sleeping: In Carlingford, *see* below.

Day 4

Lunch in Carlingford

The Anchor Bar (aka **PJ's**). Old grocery store and bar near the Mint, serving pub grub and oysters in season.

Jordan's Town House & Restaurant, Newry Street, t (042) 937 3223 (*expensive–moderate*). Good, simple cooking using the best of local ingredients, including pig's trotters. An 'early bird' menu is also available.

Dinner in Carlingford

Captain Corelli's, Newry Street, t (042)938 3848 (*moderate–inexpensive*). This cheerful restaurant serves excellent Italian food (the chef is from Rome) at very reasonable prices. Delicious pastas (tagliatelle and ravioli are home-made), plus good fish and meat. Also local oysters and smoked salmon.

Dinner and Sleeping in Carlingford

Ghan House, t (042) 957 3682, *www.ghan house.com* (*expensive*). This elegant Georgian house just outside the town is set between the mountains and the sea, with views over the lough and the Mournes. The luxurious rooms are filled with antiques while the restaurant serves gourmet food featuring local fish and lamb, vegetables and herbs from the garden and home-baked bread. The hotel also runs cookery courses with big-name chefs.

Oyster Catcher Lodge and Bistro, t (042) 937 3922 (*moderate*). This striking blue-painted house in the heart of town has a handful of comfortable and spacious sunny rooms and an excellent informal bistro serving local produce from sea and land, such as oysters, crab, lobster plus organically-reared lamb. Influences of North Africa and the Middle East.

Beaufort Guest House, Ghan Road, t (042) 937 3879 (*moderate*). Home to the Carlingford sailing club, this yellow-painted award-winning house is superbly situated right on the lough.

Day 5: Townscapes of the North

Morning: Head northwest through Dundalk to **Castleblaney**, with its plain Georgian Court House and, nearby, the wooded demesne of Hope Castle with nature trails and picnic sites. Then continue north to busy, prosperous **Monaghan**. Built on an old monastic site, this market town has some very fine urban architecture, especially round the market square, called the Diamond. The large Market House dates from 1792. There is also a surprising amount of red brick in the smaller streets off the square. The small Monaghan County Museum, founded in 1974 (*open Tues–Sat 11–1 and 2–5*), on Hill Street on the west side of Market Street, won the EEC museum award in 1980. The museum has amongst its treasures the Clogher Cross, a fine example of Early Christian metalwork, with its highly decorative detail. The 1860s Roman Catholic St Macartan's Cathedral, on the N2 to Dundalk, was designed by J. J. McCarthy, whose work is in the Gothic Revival style of Pugin – although sadly a modern 'improvement' has been to remove the original altarpiece. The St Louis Convent Heritage Centre (*open Thurs–Tues 10–12 and 2.30–4.30, Sat–Sun 2.30–4.30*) traces the fascinating history of this order throughout the world. The building itself is beautiful, and there is a *crannog* (artificial island in a lake) in the grounds..

Lunch: In Monaghan, *see* below, or, for something special, in nearby Glaslough.

Afternoon: From Monaghan head back towards Belfast and compare the fine buildings of **Armagh** (*see* pp.50–52).

Dinner and Sleeping: In Armagh, *see* below.

Day 5

Lunch in Monaghan
The Hillgrove Hotel, Old Armagh Road, t (047) 81288 (*moderate*). Traditional food and carvery.

Andy's Restaurant, 12 Market St, t (047) 82250 (*moderate–inexpensive*). All manner of very well-cooked foods, including ostrich.

Squealing Pig Bar and Restaurant, The Diamond, t (047) 84562 (*moderate–inexpensive*). Has a very good reputation locally.

Lunch in Glaslough
Castle Leslie, t (047) 88109 (*expensive*). An old-world dining experience in truly opulent surrounds. *Advance booking only*.

Dinner in Armagh
Jodie's, 37a Scotch St, t (028) 3752 7577 (*inexpensive*). Cheerful surroundings, and usually has some vegetarian options. *Open weekends only for dinner*.

Rainbow, 13 Upper English Street, t (028) 3752 5391 (*moderate–inexpensive*). Bistro menu on Friday and Saturday evenings.

Calvert Tavern, 3 Scotch Street, t (028) 3752 4186 (*inexpensive*). Good pub grub: open sandwiches and grills. *Food served till 10pm*.

Sleeping in Armagh
The Charlemont Arms Hotel, 63 English Street, t (028) 3752 2028, f 3752 6979 (*expensive*).

De Averell Guest House, 3 Seven Houses, English Street, t (028) 3751 1213, f 3751 1221 (*moderate*). Georgian town house with a good basement restaurant.

Drumsill House Hotel, 35 Moy Road, t (028) 3752 2009, f 3752 5624 (*moderate*). Modern and bland but comfortable.

Deans Hill, t (028) 3752 4923, f 3752 2186 (*moderate*). Pretty 18th-century house with lovely gardens, close to the Observatory. Two en suite rooms, one with a four-poster.

Hillview Lodge, 33 Newtownhamilton Road, t (028) 3752 2000, f 3752 8276 (*moderate*). Reliable B&B with six en suite rooms.

Touring from Belfast 2: North

Day 1: Up the Antrim Coast

Morning: The Antrim coast has a well-deserved reputation for being one of the most spectacular in Europe. Take the M5 then the M2 or A2 loughside road north from Belfast to the oldest town in Northern Ireland, **Carrickfergus**. The town takes its name from one of the Dalriadic kings, Fergus; the kings of Scotland were descended from his line and, therefore, the kings and queens of England. The town is lovely, very well kept and pedestrianized in parts with some good craft shops. Carrickfergus Castle (*open April–Sept Mon–Sat 10–6, Sun 2–6; Oct–Mar Mon–Sat 10–4, Sun 2–4; adm*) is the most prominent sight in the town, and there is an old parish church.

Lunch: In Carrickfergus, *see* below.

Afternoon: On your way north out of Carrickfergus you pass **Kilroot**. Here, in its ruined Church of Ireland church, Dean Jonathan Swift (1667–1745), best remembered for his satirical book *Gulliver's Travels*, began his clerical life. The road north takes you along by the lough, and you will pass one of the glens (*see* Day 2) that break through the Antrim plateau – **Glenoe**, with four waterfalls. **Larne** is an important port, but there isn't much else to see and you should head on up the A2 to Carnlough Bay. **Glenarm** is one of the oldest of the glen villages, dating from the 13th century. **Carnlough**, the town at the foot of Glencloy, has a lovely sandy beach.

Dinner and Sleeping: In Glenarm or Ballygalley, *see* below.

Day 1

Lunch in Carrickfergus

The Windrose, Rodgers Quay, t (028) 9335 1164 (*moderate–inexpensive*). Certainly the most attractive place to eat in town, this large pub/bistro overlooks the new marina (southwest of town) and has a big, sunny deck for warmer weather.

Northgate Restaurant, 59 North Street, t (028) 9336 4136 (*inexpensive*). Choose between grills, fries and other pub food at this dark-wood-panelled restaurant.

O'Neill's Coffee Shop, 27 North Street, t (028) 9335 1546 (*inexpensive*). Home-made cakes, pies and the odd hot dish.

Le Petit Café, 14 North Street, t (028) 9336 0643 (*inexpensive*). Filled baguettes, baked potatoes, soups and pasta in this modern café with a nautical theme.

Dinner and Sleeping in Ballygalley

Hastings Ballygalley Castle Hotel, Coast Road, t (028) 2858 3212, f (028) 2858 3681, *www.*

hastingshotels.com (*expensive*). One of the excellent Hastings Hotels chain, this added-to 17th-century castle is now a luxurious waterfront hotel. The Garden Restaurant serves up good, classic dishes, or you can eat in the atmospheric dungeon by an open fire.

Dinner in Glenarm

Charlie's, Altmore Street, t (028) 2884 1276 (*moderate–inexpensive*). Ann Reid cooks according to seasonal availability (you might be able to sample locally smoked or wild salmon) and serves meals in what feels like her cosy living room.

Sleeping in Glenarm

Riverside House, 13 Toberwine Street, t (028) 2884 1474 (*inexpensive*). Elaine Boyle runs this well-kept house with colourful window boxes. Several of the bright, sunny en suite rooms have balconies overlooking the river.

Take-A-Break studios, Altmore Street, t (028) 841582 (*inexpensive*). Basic but perfectly clean self-catering accommodation.

Day 2: The Glens of Antrim

Morning: Beyond Larne, still on the A2 coast road, 60 miles of wonderful maritime scenery stretches ahead of you. After the Ice Age, the **Glens of Antrim** were formed by the movement of the glaciers which gouged out the nine short steep valleys running out towards the sea. The coast road links all nine: from south to north, Glenarm, Glencloy, Glenariff, Glenballyeamon, Glenaan, Glencorp, Glendun, Glenshesk and Glentaisie. **Glenariff** is the largest and most popular of the glens, with its big waterfalls. Head for **Waterfoot** at the foot of the Glenariff River, by the lovely Red Bay, so called because of the reddish sand washed by the streams from the sandstone. This area is perfect for nature rambles, with **Glenariff Forest Park** (*open daily 10–dusk*) inland. There is a beautiful walk beside the waterfalls and cascades of the glen. You can spend the whole day hiking here; wear boots.

Lunch: In Waterfoot, *see* below, or the café in Glenariff Forest Park, or take a picnic.

Afternoon: Continuing on the coast road, you reach delightfully situated **Cushendall**, called the capital of the glens. **Oísín's Grave**, a megalithic tomb and stone circle, is at the end of a path on the lower slopes of Tieve Bulliagh about 2 miles west of Cushendall, in Glenaan. A mile out of the village, on the way to Cushendun and by the sea, are the ruins of **Layde Church**, in use up to 1790. **Cushendun** village and its beach are in the care of the National Trust; Clough Williams-Ellis, who designed the pretty cottages here, also designed the seaside village of Portmeirion in Wales.

Dinner and Sleeping: In Cushendall or Cushendun, *see* below.

Day 2

Lunch in Waterfoot
Ruairi's, 9 Main Street, t (028) 2177 2910 (*inexpensive*). Bright, modern restaurant serving light lunches: burgers, fish and chips.

Dinner in Cushendall
Glens Hotel, 6 Coast Road, t (028) 2177 1223. Bar food (*inexpensive*) served until 9.30pm, or you can eat steaks, lamb or locally caught salmon, sea bass and mussels in the restaurant (*moderate–inexpensive*).
Harry's Restaurant, 10 Mill Street, t (028) 2177 2022 (*inexpensive*). Good bar snacks plus a full restaurant menu.

Dinner in Cushendun
Mary McBride's, 2 Main Street, t (028) 2176 1511 (*moderate–inexpensive*. This characterful pub serves meals featuring local ingredients; Torr Head lobster, Cushendun salmon, fish chowder, steaks and more.

Sleeping in Cushendall
The Meadows, 81 Coast Road, t (028) 2177 2020 (*low moderate*). Anne Carey's neat house has comfortable and spacious en suite rooms and lovely coastal views. She will arrange meals at the private boat club over the road.

Sleeping in Cushendun
Drumkeerin, 201a Torr Road, t (028) 2176 1554, *www.drumkeerinbedandbreakfast.co.uk* (*low moderate*) Mary McFadden was voted the AA Landlady of the year in 2002; she and husband Joe (both artists) run this delightful B&B with a lovely garden and fabulous views just above the village. Breakfasts – with home-made breads, cakes and jams – are exceptional. There is also a hostel-style self-catering annexe in the garden.
The Villa Farmhouse, 185 Torr Road, t (028) 2176 1252 (*inexpensive*). Comfortable Victorian villa in nice gardens, close to the beach. Three well-furnished en suite rooms and inexpensive evening meals. If you want seafood, contact Catherine Scally in advance.

Day 3: Sea Views and Island Birds

Morning: If it's sunny and you're going to Rathlin, get a very early start. If you are staying on the mainland, have a lie-in. Whichever, stock up on picnic food first in Cushendun, then head northwards along the spectacular coast road to **Torr Head**, from where you can see the Mull of Kintyre, only about 15 miles away on the Scottish coast. Then either drive down to lovely **Murlough Bay** for a walk and a picnic or, if the weather is good (or you may get stuck there!), drive straight on to **Ballycastle** and catch the 10.30 ferry (Caledonian MacBrayne ferries, **t** (028) 2076 9299, *www.calmac.co. uk*; 45mins) to **Rathlin Island**, only 14 miles from the Mull of Kintyre. Sea birds nest all over the island, which is starred with wild orchids, bogs and little lakes; its 70 inhabitants farm and fish, and the roads are blessedly silent.

Lunch: Picnic in Murlough Bay, or on Rathlin Island.

Afternoon: If you are on Rathlin, you could stay all afternoon and maybe even sleep there. If not, then visit **Ballycastle**, a particularly attractive resort town, divided into the market end and the harbour end. The town is famous for its tennis tournament on the grass courts which overlook the sea; there is a fine beach, friendly pubs, and plenty of old-fashioned shops where you can find seaside essentials like film, shrimping nets, buckets and spades. The harbour has a memorial to Count Marconi and his assistant, George Kemp, who in 1898 established radio contact between Ballycastle and Rathlin Island.

Dinner and Sleeping: On Rathlin Island or in Ballycastle, *see* below.

Day 3

Lunch on Rathlin
McCuaig's Bar, The Quay, Rathlin Island, **t** (028) 2076 3974 (*inexpensive*). Pub grub.

Dinner and Sleeping on Rathlin
National Trust Manor House, **t** (028) 2076 3964, *www.ntni.org.uk* (*moderate*). Comfortable guest house on the harbour-front overlooking Church Bay. Evening meal on request (*inexpensive*). The Brockley Tea Rooms serve refreshments during the day. **Rathlin Guest House**, The Quay, **t** (028) 2076 3917 (*inexpensive*). If you want to stay at this friendly B&B over a summer weekend, book well in advance. Meals served.

Dinner in Ballycastle
Cellar Restaurant, The Diamond, **t** (028) 2076 3037 (*moderate–inexpensive*). You can eat fish, seafood, lamb, steak and surf'n'turf in this brick-vaulted basement restaurant which also puts on live music nights.

Wysner's Restaurant, 16 Ann Street, **t** (028) 2076 2372 (*moderate–inexpensive*). A small, friendly, family-run restaurant with quite a sophisticated and regularly changing menu featuring salmon caught from Carrick-a-Rede, Singapore noodles, chicken fajitas and a delicious Bushmills Malt cheesecake.

Dinner and Sleeping in Ballycastle
Glenmore House and Restaurant, Whitepark Bay Road, **t** (028) 2076 3584 (*moderate*). On the B15 coast road with spectacular views, this new farmhouse has 7 well-equipped rooms, some of which even have jacuzzis. The 90 acre-grounds include a lake. Evening meal provided (*inexpensive*). **Colliers Hall**, 50 Cushendall Road, **t** (028) 2076 2531, *www.colliershall.com* (*inexpensive*). An old working farm with 3 comfortable en suite bedrooms and a log fire. **Hilsea**, North Street, **t** (028) 2076 2385 (*inexpensive*). Large Victorian villa overlooking Rathlin Island and just a few minutes from the ferry with 15 rooms (mostly en suite).

Day 4: Rope Bridges and Rock Columns

Morning: A short distance northwest from Ballycastle is **Kinbane Head**, and a mile on is the famous swinging **Carrick-a-rede Rope Bridge** (*open April–Sept daily 10–6, July–Aug daily 10–8; tearoom; adm*). The bridge is narrow, bouncy and made of planks with wire handrails, and it is thrilling to cross. The views are tremendous, and a small salmon fishery still operates on the ocean side. Nearby **Ballintoy** is one of the prettiest towns on the coast: if you catch it on a good day it looks like a Mediterranean fishing village with its white church and buildings. You can walk west from here to **Whitepark Bay**, a great curve of beach with sand dunes. On the edge of the cliffs is Dunseverick Castle, of which only one massive wall remains. In under the cliffs is the little hamlet of **Portbraddan** , where you will get a good close-up view of traditional salmon netting. Beachcombers can find fossils, and flower enthusiasts can examine the dunes.

Lunch: In Ballintoy or at the Giant's Causeway, *see* below.

Afternoon: Head off the A2 on the B146 to wonder at the **Giant's Causeway** (*see* also pp.70–71), a World Heritage Site, famous for its spectacular polygonal black basalt columns set among white chalk (*car parking is provided, and a shuttle bus goes to the Causeway*). There's a Visitors' Centre (*open July–Aug daily 10–7; Sept–June 10–5; guided tours June–Sept*), and next to the Centre is the Causeway School Museum (*open July–Aug, 11–4.30*), which takes you back to a small country school of 1920.

Dinner and Sleeping: Near the Causeway at Port Ballintrae or Bushmills, *see* below.

Day 4

Lunch in Ballintoy
Fullerton Arms, Main Street, **t** (028) 2070 9613 (*inexpensive*). This pleasant guest house, bar and restaurant is one of the very few places to eat in the village; luckily, the food is good. You can choose from the bistro menu (soups, spicy chicken wings, steak, pork, tuna, scampi) or eat a light lunch in the bar.
O'Rourke's Kitchen. This restored stone cottage enjoys an enviable position right on the harbour wall; views of the Atlantic and simple, traditional dishes and home baking.

Lunch at the Giant's Causeway
Giant's Pantry Café, in the visitor centre, **t** (028) 2073 1582. Coffees, teas, cakes, sand-wiches, soups and other snacks.

Dinner in Port Ballintrae
Sweeney's Wine Bar, Seaport Avenue, Port Ballintrae, **t** (028) 2073 2404 (*inexpensive*). Grilled meats and vegetarian meals.

Dinner in Bushmills
Bushmills Inn, Dunluce Road, **t** (028) 2073 2339 (*expensive–moderate*). Delicious cold salmon and salads in an excellent bistro-style restaurant.
Distiller's Arms, 140 Main Street, **t** (028) 2073 2843 (*moderate*). This 18th-century building was once the property of the distillery owners. Nowadays, it houses a stylish modern restaurant and bar. The excellent cooking (Mediterranean with the odd oriental twist) features lots of fish; try the salmon fillet cured with Bushmills whiskey.

Sleeping in Bushmills
Bushmills Inn, Main Street, **t** (028) 2073 2339, **f** (028) 2073 2048 (*expensive*). Comfortable, good service, excellent food.
Causeway Hotel, 40 Causeway Road, **t** (028) 2073 1226/2073 1210, **f** (028) 2073 2552 (*moderate*). Delightful family-run hotel.
Craig Park, 24 Carnbore Road, **t** (028) 2073 2496, **f** (028) 2073 2479 (*moderate*). Country house near the causeway.

Day 5: Whiskey and Farmlands

Morning: Tour the **Bushmills Distillery** (*open April–Oct Mon–Sat 9.30–5.30, Sun 12–5.30; rest of year Mon–Fri only; a tour takes about one hour; adm*), which produces the area's famous Coleraine whiskey. Then move on via the A2 to **Dunluce Castle**, sometimes translated as Mermaid's Fort (*open April–Sept Mon–Sat 10–6, Sun 2–6; Oct–Mar Tues–Sat 10–4, Sun 2–4; adm*), whose bold ruins keep watch over the magnificent coastline. The next town is Northern Ireland's biggest seaside resort, **Portrush**, a rather uninspiring mecca of amusement arcades and fish and chips.

Lunch: Some of the better restaurants in Portrush or Portstewart, *see* below.

Afternoon: Just west is the more personable resort of **Portstewart**. Inland is **Coleraine**, alleged to have been founded by St Patrick; most of what you see here was developed by the Irish Society of London. A fantastic final afternoon can be spent at the **Downhill Estate** and **Mussenden Temple** (*open mid Mar–May and Sept Sat–Sun 11–6, June–Aug and Easter daily 11–7.30; glen and grounds always open; adm free*). This ruined palace, just off the A2 at Downhill village, was built in the late 18th century by the famous Earl-Bishop, Frederick Augustus Hervey (1730–1803). The landscaped estate which still remains includes the Mussenden Temple perched on a cliff overlooking the sea, the ruins of the palace, family memorials, gardens, a fishpond and woodland and cliff walks (also *see* pp.69–70). Then head south on the A26, through some of the richest farmland in the North, to prosperous **Ballymena**.

Dinner and Sleeping: In Ballymena, *see* below.

Day 5

Lunch in Portrush

Ramore Wine Bar, The Harbour, **t** (028) 7082 4313 (*moderate–inexpensive*). Laid-back, popular eatery with a buzzy atmosphere. Background jazz, harbour views and delicious creative modern food.

Magheraboy House Hotel, 41 Magheraboy Road, **t** (028) 7082 3507 (*moderate*). Hearty meals for hungry people.

Harbour Bar, Harbour Road, **t** (028) 7082 2430 (*moderate*). Great atmosphere and excellent food.

Lunch in Portstewart

Smyth's, The Diamond, 2–4 Lever Road, **t** (028) 7083 3564 (*inexpensive*). Excellent, stylish restaurant in Aylmer Smyth's old home, serving creative food using local ingredients.

Dinner in Ballymena

Water Margin Restaurant, 8 Cullybackey Road, **t** (028) 2564 8368 (*moderate*). Cantonese.

Manley Restaurant, State Shopping Centre, 70a Ballymoney Road, **t** (028) 2564 9360 (*moderate*). Cantonese and Peking cooking.

Dinner and Sleeping in Ballymena

Galgorm Manor, **t** (028) 2588 1001, **f** 2588 0080, *www.galgorm.com* (*luxury*). A spectacular 17th-century castle with lovely lawns transformed into a plush hotel. Self-catering cottages in grounds. Has an elegant restaurant serving high quality dishes based on local produce, or the rustic Gillie's bar serving traditional hot and cold bar food. Live music in the latter Fri and Sat eves.

Adair Arms Hotel, Ballymoney Road, **t** (028) 2565 3674, **f** 2564 0436 (*moderate*). Attractive old 23-room hotel, and two restaurants.

Leighinmohr House Hotel, Leighinmohr Avenue, **t** (028) 2565 2313, **f** 2565 6669, *www.leighinmohrhotel.com* (*moderate*). Elegant and comfortable country house set in extensive grounds on the outskirts of town with a good restaurant and a cosy bar.

Derry City

Derry (*Doire*: 'Oak Grove') is a symbolic city situated on the River Foyle. Before the 1960s it was probably best known for its association with the pretty 'Londonderry Air' (better known as 'Danny Boy'), but it has until recently been one of Northern Ireland's trouble-spots. The strife is not unprecedented, for it has survived three sieges.

The city is a place well worth visiting. On most of the approaches to its centre you will see its image across the water: a fine walled city, built around the curve of the Foyle. Some ugly buildings have been allowed to mar its elegant profile, but not as yet too many, and the docks are no longer crowded with thousands of folk sailing to a brand new world, as they were in the 19th century. A walk around the historic walls gives you a good view of the docks and the wide River Foyle. Big ships still harbour in the port, located three miles downstream of Derry, although in the days of the British Empire they carried exotic cargo such as silk from Bombay. To the northwest of the old city walls is the historic Republican Bogside, with its much-repainted and photo-graphed 'Free Derry' monument and murals. Irish nationalists and Catholics usually call the city 'Derry'; for Northern Irish Protestants it's 'Londonderry' (although in general both county and city are known as 'Derry'). One solution among the politically correct has been to write 'London/Derry', leading local jokers to label it 'Stroke City'.

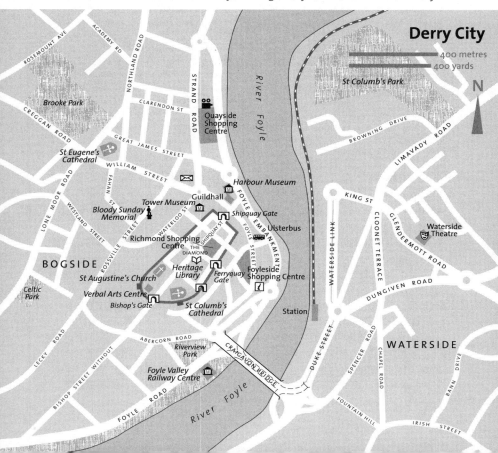

Getting There

Ryanair flies to Derry from London's Stansted airport; *see* Travel, p.7.

Getting from the Airport

City of Derry Airport, t (028) 7181 0784, *www.derry.net/airport/*. For flights to Manchester, Glasgow, Dublin and London Stansted. There is no shuttle and the bus service is irregular; a taxi costs £10.

Getting Around

By Rail

Translink, t (028) 9066 6630. Mainline services from Belfast to Derry link several coastal towns along the way.

By Bus

Ulsterbus, t (028) 7126 2261. To Belfast.
Londonderry and Lough Swilly Bus Company, t (028) 7126 2017. Goes into County Donegal too.

Car Hire

Desmond Motors, 173 Strand Road, t (028) 7136 7137.
Hertz, Derry Airport, t (028) 7181 1994.

Bike Hire

Happy Days Cycle Hire, 245 Lone Moor Road, t (028) 7128 7128.

Festivals

March: St Patrick's Day, t (028) 7137 6545, March 17th; City of Drama Festival, t (028) 7136 5151; *Buth an Earraigh*, t (028) 7126 4132, Irish language festival.
July–August: Maiden City Festival, t (028) 7134 6677, or look in local newspapers – *The Derry Journal* or *The Sentinel*; Orange Order Parades, 12th July; Gasyard Wall *Feile*, t (028) 7126 2812, events in the city, including music, workshops and exhibitions; Walled City Cultural Trail, t (028) 7126 7284.
October: Banks of the Foyle Hallowe'en Carnival, t (028) 7126 7284, *www.derrycity. gov.uk/halloween*; 17–31 October.
November: Foyle Film Festival, t (028) 7126 7432; Craft Fair, t (028) 7136 5151, ext. 6911.
December: Ferryquay Gate. Anniversary of the shutting of Derry's gates during the siege of 1689, on the Saturday nearest the 18th.

Tourist Information

Derry: 44 Foyle Street, t (028) 7126 7284, f (028) 7137 7992, t/f (028) 7136 9501, *www.derry visitor.com*, *www.discovernorthernireland. com*; *open all year*.

Guided Walking Tours

City Tours, 11 Carlisle Road, t (028) 7127 1997.
McNamara's Famous Guided Walking Tours, t/f (028) 7134 5335. Tours of the city.
Northern Ireland Tours and Guides Ltd, 70 Marlborough Street, t (028) 7128 9051.
Top Dog Tours, Tirmacool, Buncrana, Co. Donegal, t 0868 046134. Tours of Derry City.

Shopping

Antiques

The Whatnot, 22 Bishop St, t (028) 7128 8333.

Derry is the most complete walled city in Ireland, with early 17th-century walls about a mile in circumference, pierced by seven gates, six bastions and many cannon. It was first besieged during the rebellion of 1641, then during the Cromwellian wars of 1649, and finally there was an historic siege in 1689. This siege still plays a very important part in the mind of the Ulster Unionist, for it sums up the courage of the Protestant settlers who resisted with the cry, 'No surrender.' The city was being assailed by James II, who had lost his throne in England and was trying to repair his fortunes in Ireland with the help of Louis XIV of France. Thirteen apprentice boys rushed to the gates of the city and shut them in the face of his approaching army. This secured Londonderry for William III, who had been invited to take over from

Art Galleries

The McGilloway Gallery, 6 Shipquay Street,
t (028) 7136 6011. Irish paintings, mainly
landscape.
The Orchard Gallery, Orchard Street,
t (028) 7126 9675. Contemporary Irish art.

Books

Bookworm, 18–20 Bishop Street, t (028)
7128 2727. Terrific section of books of
Irish interest.
Foyle Books, Craft Village, 12a Magazine
Street, t (028) 7137 2530. Second-hand
bookseller.

Crafts

The Donegal Shop, 8 Shipquay Street, t (028)
7126 6928.
Tower Museum Gift Shop, Union Hall Place,
t (028) 7137 4404.

Sports and Activities

Golf

City of Derry Golf Club, 49 Victoria Road,
t (028) 7134 6369.
Foyle International Golf Centre, 12 Alder Road,
t (028) 7135 2222.

Indoor Leisure Centres

Brooke Park Leisure Centre, Rosemount
Avenue, t (028) 7126 2637.
Lisnagelvin Leisure Centre, Ritchill Park,
Waterside, t (028) 7134 7695.
St Columb's Park Leisure Centre, Limavady
Road, t (028) 7134 3941.
Templemore Sports Complex, Buncrana Road,
t (028) 7128 9200.

Where to Stay

City Hotel, Queen's Quay, t (028) 7136 5800
(*expensive*). Grand new hotel overlooking
the River Foyle.
Tower Hotel, Butcher Street, t (028) 7137 1000
(*expensive*). Stylish new hotel within the
city walls.
Beech Hill Country House Hotel, 32 Ardmore
Road, t (028) 7134 9279, f (028) 7134 5366,
www.beech-hill.com, *info@beech-hill.com*
(*expensive*). Lovely grounds and well-known
for good cuisine.
Quality Hotel Da Vinci's, 15 Culmore Rd,
t (028) 7127 9111, f (028) 7127 9222,
www.derryhotels.com, *info@davincishotel.*
com (*expensive*). 70-room hotel complex,
10mins' walk from the city.
Hastings Everglades Hotel, Prehen Road,
t (028) 7134 6722, f (028) 7134 9200, *res@egh.*
hastingshotels.com (*moderate*). Overlooking
the River Foyle. Bland but comfortable.
The Saddler's House, 36 Great James Street,
t (028) 7126 9691 (*inexpensive*). Central 19th-
century townhouse. Contact Joan Pyne.
Manor House, 15 Main Street, Eglinton, (near
Derry City Airport), t (028) 7181 0222 (*inex-*
pensive). Attractive manor house; contact
Mrs Davidson.

Eating Out

Ardmore Restaurant, Beech Hill Country
House, 32 Ardmore Road, t (028) 7134 9279
(*expensive*). Delicious, imaginative food, such
as home-made tagliatelle and sumptuous
puddings.
Linenhall Bar, 3 Market Street, t (028) 7137 1665
(*expensive–moderate*). Lunches.

James II by the English parliament. The siege that followed resulted in many deaths,
for the city had no stores of food. Citizens ate rats, dogs and even the starch for laun-
dering linen. Every year now the anniversary of the shutting of the gates is celebrated
on the Saturday nearest 18 December, and the Raising of the Siege on 12 August.

The City Walls and City Centre

Derry has many attractions to offer the visitor, with interesting museums and
charming old streets. Great efforts have been made to improve the cultural life of the
city, and its own spontaneous creativity in theatre, poetry and the arts has brought a
welcome energy. One of the greatest changes has been the development of three

Fitzroy's, 2–4 Bridge Street and 3 Carlisle Road, t 7126 6211. A busy city centre brasserie.

India House, 51 Carlisle Road, t (028) 7126 0532 (*moderate*). Spicy, well-cooked and reasonably priced food.

Spice Restaurant, 162 Spencer Road, Waterside, t (028) 7134 4875 (*inexpensive*). Lunch and dinner available in this restaurant, recommended for its warmth, good service and excellent cosmopolitan menu. *Closed Mon, and Sat lunch.*

Browns Restaurant, 1 Bonds Hill, t (028) 7134 5180 (*moderate*). Diverse menu based on good quality lamb, fish and vegetables.

La Sosta Ristorante, 45a Carlisle Road, Derry, t (028) 7137 4817 (*moderate*). Popular Italian.

Badger's, 16 Orchard Street, t (028) 7136 0736/7136 3306 (*inexpensive*). Grills, salads; lively bar and restaurant. *Open Mon–Thurs 12–7, Fri–Sat 12–9.30pm, Sun 12–5.*

Beckett's Bar, 44 Foyle Street, t (028) 7136 0066 (*inexpensive*). Recommended for its good pub lunches.

Dungloe Bar, 41 Waterloo Street, t (028) 7126 7716 (*inexpensive*). Pub grub and traditional music.

The Exchange, Exchange House, Queen's Quay, t (028) 7127 3990 (*inexpensive*). Fashionable restaurant and wine bar.

Metro Bar, 3 Bank Place, t (028) 7126 7401 (*inexpensive*). Soups and stews.

Entertainment and Nightlife

You'll find live traditional music in the pubs around Waterloo Street.

Pubs and Clubs

Linenhall Bar, 3 Market St, t (028) 7137 1665.

Grand Central, 27 Strand Road, t (028) 7126 7826.

The Metro, 3 Bank Place, t (028) 7126 7401.

River Inn Bar, 36 Shipquay St, t (028) 7137 1965.

Badgers, 16 Orchard Street, t (028) 7136 0736. Award-winning pub.

Monico Lounge, 4–6 Custom House Street, t (028) 7126 3121. One of Derry's oldest pubs, just beside the Derry Walls.

Theatre and Cinema

The Playhouse, 5–7 Artillery Street, Derry, t (028) 7126 8027, *thederryplayhouse@hotmail.com*. Non-sectarian community arts centre with performances and workshops.

Orchard Street Cinema, Derry, t (028) 7126 2845. Shows mainly art-house films.

Strand Multiplex Cinema, Strand Road, Derry, t (028) 7126 0494. Seven-screen cinema for new release movies.

Millennium Forum, Newmarket Street, t (028) 7126 4455. New theatre offering a wide-ranging programme.

Arts Centres

Comhaltas Ceoltoiri Eireann, 15 Crawford Square, t (028) 7128 6359, *www.comhaltas.com*. Traditional Irish culture, with music, singing, *ceilidh* and set-dancing.

Verbal Arts Centre, Mall Wall and Stable Lane, Bishop Street Within, t (028) 7126 6946, *info@verbalartscentre.co.uk*. Northern Ireland's only centre devoted to literature and the storytelling tradition.

The Nerve Centre, 7–8 Magazine Street, t (028) 7126 0562. Multimedia centre with in-house cinema.

huge retail complexes – Quayside, Foyleside and the Richmond Centre – which are a fair indicator of a new-found commercial confidence in a stable future for the city. Another major development is the relocation of the **Verbal Arts Centre** to a building beside the city walls. The centre supports all forms of written and spoken expression.

The walls of Derry have been restored, making for a very interesting walk around the old part. They are entered by seven gates, and all along the circuit are views towards the Foyle, or into the Bogside and beyond to the hills. Information plaques mark every structure of note along the walls – accompanied by unofficial graffiti. If you start at **Shipquay Gate** opposite the Guildhall, you will see some of the cannon used in the siege of 1689. Walking on in a westward direction you come to **Ferryquay Gate**, where the gates were slammed and locked by the determined apprentice boys in the face of James II's troops. Moving on, you soon come to the long low plantation Church of Ireland **Cathedral of St Columb** (*chapter house museum open summer Mon–Sat 9–5, winter Mon–Sat 9–1 and 2–4; adm; t (028) 7126 7313*), which lies between Fountain Street and Bishop Street on Clooney Terrace, and is an example of Planters' Gothic. The building was founded by the Corporation of London in 1633, and restored in 1886, and was the first specifically Protestant cathedral to be built in the British Isles after the Reformation. The roof rests on stone corbels carved into heads which represent past bishops of Derry. The philosopher George Berkeley (1685–1753) was Dean here between 1724 and 1732, and the well-known cleric the Earl of Bristol was bishop between 1768 and 1803. He was extremely rich and cultured, favoured Catholic emancipation and opposed the tithe system (*see* p.69). The bishop's throne incorporates the chair used at the consecration of the cathedral in 1633. There are a number of exhibits illustrating the spirit of the 17th-century siege; and the stained glass windows depict incidents from it. The small museum inside is worth visiting for its relics of the siege and mementoes of Cecil Frances Alexander, composer of such famous hymns as 'Once in Royal David's City' and 'There is a Green Hill Far Away'.

Bishop's Gate, nearby, has fine stone carvings. It actually dates from 1789 when the original was replaced with this triumphal arch. The terraced housing area behind the walls here is the Fountain, a dwindling Protestant preserve, the only one this side of the city. Now, as you turn the corner, you can see the Double Bastion with its cannons which still point out over the **Bogside**, where the Jacobite army was camped. There is a wonderful view from here, and you can clearly see the Bogside's large wall murals. (The area immediately below the walls is a football pitch, well-used by the youngsters from the area.) If you continue, you will come to **St Augustine's Church**, set amongst mature trees; somewhere here is the site of St Columba's (St Colmcille's) monastery, which, as the plaque proudly says, marks 1,400 years of continuous Christian settlement. On the corner opposite is the Apprentice Boys' Hall; along the walls here are plane trees, planted to commemorate the apprentice boys. Overlooking the Bogside is the base of a monument to the Reverend George Walker, who rallied the dispirited Derry people to continue their defiance. The original statue was destroyed by an IRA bomb in 1973, and when a replacement was commissioned the IRA vowed they would blow that one up as well (it now resides safely behind a high fence, a few metres along the street past the Apprentice Boys' Hall). The rest of the wall brings you back down Magazine Street, with its attractive 18th-century houses, to Shipquay Gate again; notice the fine **Presbyterian Church** in Upper Magazine Street, with its classical lines. This area has been much rebuilt, since hardly a single building was left undamaged in the ceaseless IRA bombing campaign of the 1970s. The **Craft Village**, off Shipquay Street (*contact Inner City Trust for information, t (028) 7126 0329*), a representation of Derry between the 16th and 19th centuries, is worth a look, not least for a coffee break in one of the cafés – or a browse amongst the craft shops. The **Courthouse** (1813), in Bishop Street, is a good example of Greek Revival architecture; as the city's main symbol of British justice, it received a great deal of IRA attention, and the scars of numerous car-bombs are still evident.

To visit the **Bloody Sunday Memorial** pass through the Butcher's Gate. It is down to the right, close by the road. This commemorates 30 January 1972, when a civil rights march ended in 13 deaths after the Parachute Regiment opened fire on the marchers – government inquiries into the incident are continuing even now in the Guildhall. Close by, just outside the city walls, is the 18th-century **church of St Columba**, also called Long Tower Church. It is built on the site of a 12th-century monastery called Templemore. St Columba is further commemorated in a boys' school of that name further down the street.

St Eugene's Roman Catholic Cathedral, off Infirmary Road and Great James Street, has a fine east window and high altar. It was built in Gothic style in 1873.

The **Tower Museum** (*open July–Aug Mon–Sat 10–5, Sun 2–5; Sept–June Tues–Sat and bank hols 10–5; adm; t (028) 7137 2411, towermuseum@derrycity.gov.uk*) in O'Doherty Tower, Union Hall Place, preserves the treasures of the Corporation of London, including a two-handed sword said to belong to Sir Caher O'Doherty, who raided Derry in 1608. This is an outstanding museum, the winner of several awards, and it does help you to grasp both the complex history of ancient Derry and the effects of the Troubles. Artefacts from the Spanish Armada ships wrecked off the coast in 1588 are also on display. Leave time to go to the less fashionable but enthralling **Harbour Museum** in Harbour Square (*open Mon–Fri, 10–1 and 2–4.30; t (028) 7137 7331*), where ship models in glass cases, a replica of a 30ft curragh in which St Colmcille (Columba) would have sailed to Iona and other examples of Derry's maritime history are on view.

Within the walls you will notice some attractive Georgian houses, some with medieval foundations. At the top of the hill on the Diamond, the central square of the old town, excavations were undertaken to try to uncover an early settlement, possibly the Columban foundation. However, they only revealed domestic material from the early 17th-century settler population. The old workhouse is now the **Workhouse Museum**, 23 Glendermott Road (*open July–Aug Mon–Sat 10–4.30; Sept–June Mon–Thurs and Sat 10–4.30; adm free; t (028) 7131 8328*), with exhibits on the famine; upstairs is the original workhouse dormitory in the same condition as it was for the poor souls who were sent there. In another room is the 'Atlantic Memorial Exhibition', which explains the importance of the Foyle and Derry during the Second World War; Britain, Canada and the USA all had navy bases here.

Southeast across the Craigavon Bridge is the largely Protestant **Waterside** area.

Museums Outside the Centre

Rail enthusiasts might enjoy the **Foyle Valley Railway Centre** on Foyle Road, close to Craigavon Bridge (*open Tues–Sat, 10–4.30; adm free, charge for train ride; t (028) 7126 5234*), where you can take a trip in a 1934 diesel railcar on the 3-mile track beside the Foyle. At the **Amelia Earhart Centre**, at Ballyarnet Country Park (*adm by appt, t (028) 7137 7331, t/f (028) 7135 4040, ameliaearhart@compuserve.com*), is a museum commemorating the first woman pilot to fly solo across the Atlantic, who accidentally landed nearby in 1932 after mistaking the city for Paris. You may wish to trace your family history at the **Heritage Library** (*open Mon–Fri 9–5; 14 Bishop Street, t (028) 7126 9792*), which holds all of County Londonderry's genealogical records.

Day Trips and Overnighters from Derry

Limavady

About 12 miles east of Derry City, **Limavady** is beautifully situated in the Roe Valley with fine mountain scenery to the north and southeast. Before the Fishermongers Company arrived, Limavady was an important centre of the territory of the O'Cahans, a *sept* under the lordship of the O'Neills, although no trace remains of their castle now. The town is associated with the famous 'Londonderry Air', noted down by Miss Jane Ross in 1851 from the playing of an itinerant piper. Three miles out of town (take a taxi) is the **Roe Valley Country Park**, with a visitors' centre (*open Easter–Sept 9–5.45; Oct–Mar 10–5*) and Weaving Shed Museum (*open June daily 1–5, May Sat and Sun 1–5*).

Downhill

A really worthwhile expedition can be made to the **Downhill Estate** (*t (028) 7084 8728, www.nationaltrust.co.uk; open mid- Mar–May and Sept Sat–Sun 11–6, June–Aug and Easter daily 11–7.30; glen and grounds always open; adm free*). The Estate's best known features are the **Mussendun Temple**, perched on the top of the cliff, and the ruined **palace** of the old Earl-Bishop of Derry. Entry into the demesne is by three gates, one at the bottom of the hill at Castlerock and two (Lion's and Bishop's Gates) on the road sloping up from Downhill. From Castlerock you pass the lakes and climb up the Black Glen, a carpet of bluebells in spring, to the gardens at Bishop's Gate. The estate was laid out in the late 18th century by the eccentric Earl-Bishop, Frederick Augustus Hervey (1730–1803), one of the most interesting and enlightened Church of Ireland bishops. The palace itself is sited on a windswept hill with wonderful views of the Inishowen hills and the Antrim headlands. Hervey was extravagant and well-travelled. He built up a great art collection with the episcopal revenues from his Derry bishopric (which in the 18th century was the second-richest in Ireland), and had a second residence at Ballyscullion near Bellaghy, which is totally ruined. The bishop was a great advocate of toleration, contributing both to Catholic and Presbyterian churches. One of his amusements was party-giving. If you go down to the Temple, the

Getting There

Bus 143 leaves Derry (Foyle Street bus station) for **Limavady** around every hour, taking between 30 and 50mins.

From Limavady you can take the 134 bus to Coleraine for the **Downhill Estate**; to visit direct from Derry it's best to take the train to Castlerock, a scenic 35min journey followed by a ½mile walk.

Tourist Information

Limavady: 7 Connell Street, t (028) 7776 0307, *www.discovernorthernireland.comr.*

Eating Out

The Lime Tree, 60 Catherine Street, Limavady, t (028) 7776 4300 (*moderate–inexpensive*). Fresh local produce with a modern twist. *Closed Sat, Mon and Tues.*

Lucille's Kitchen, 17 Catherine Street, Limavady, t (028) 7776 8180 (*inexpensive*). Sandwiches and hot snacks on offer.

The Spinning Wheel, Roe Valley Country Park, 41 Dogleap Road, t (028) 7772 2920 (*inexpensive*). Traditional home-made lunches. There's no café on the Estate; take a picnic.

Getting There

Regular **buses** go to Greencastle from Derry.

Eating Out

Kealy's Seafood Bar, Greencastle, t (074) 93 81010 (*moderate–inexpensive*). Popular and award-winning seafood restaurant, where lunches are a bargain. *Open 12.30–3 and 7–9.30, Sun till 8.30; closed Mon.*
The Castle Inn, Greencastle, t (074) 938 1426, (*inexpensive*). Traditional home cooking. *Open 1–3.*
The Ferryport, Greencastle (*inexpensive*). Soup and toasties served all day.

story of the great race he organized between the Church of Ireland and the Presbyterian ministers is told. There was suspicion that he was more of a Classicist than a Christian: his temple, on a cliff edge, is modelled on the Roman Temple of Vesta, and suggests a somewhat independent interpretation of religion.

In Castlerock village, **Hezlett House**, 107 Sea Road (*open June–end Aug Wed–Mon 12–6pm;Mar–May and Sept Sat and Sun 12–6*) is one of the few surviving buildings in Northern Ireland from before the 18th century. The 17th-century thatched cottage is simply furnished in late Victorian style. The house is accessible directly from Castlerock (¾m) or from Bishop's Gate, along the road to Coleraine (½m).

Moville and Greencastle

The scenic route up the Inishowen coast takes you to the picturesque village of Moville, formerly a point of departure for emigrants to the New World, and on to Greencastle, a beach resort with the remains of a 14th-century castle. The **Inishowen Maritime Museum and Planetarium** (*open Mon–Sat 10–6, Sun 12–6*) in the old coast-guard station displays a wide variety of marine history from the emigration story to local fishing boats. The new planetarium gives star shows that relate to seafaring.

The Giant's Causeway

The Giant's Causeway is a UNESCO World Heritage Site (the only one in Ireland), and the mix of black basalt columns, white chalk, sea, moorland and sandy beaches makes for a spectacular coastline. About 60 million years ago there was great volcanic activity, and basalt lavas poured out to cover the existing chalk limestone landscape. It actually baked the chalk into a hard rock – very unlike the soft chalk of southern England. These lava flows and eruptions were separated by several million years, allowing tropical vegetation and soils to accumulate. The cooling of the basalt lavas was very variable. When exposed to the air or water, they cooled rapidly and formed skins like that on the top of custard. If they cooled slowly at depth, they shrank to form even polygonal columns like the Giant's Causeway. Here the Ice Ages eroded the cliffs, and graceful arches have been formed by the action of the sea and weather.

Irish myths are very clear with their version of how the Causeway was created. It was built by the great hero, Fionn MacCumhaill (Finn McCool), a warrior, magician and poet who was over 52 ft tall. Fionn had a feud with a Scottish giant called Benandonner, who lived on the Scottish island of Staffa. They challenged each other to a fight, and Fionn began to build the Causeway to get to his rival. He was so tired

Getting There

Take the scenic **train** to Portrush or Coleraine and then a **bus** to the Causeway; it takes up to three hours each way from Derry.

Tourist Information

Giant's Causeway: Visitor Centre, 44 Causeway Road, Bushmills, **t** (028) 2073 1855.

Portrush: Dunluce Centre, Sandhill Drive, **t** (028) 7082 3333; *open April–Sept.*

Where to Stay and Eat

The longish journey from Derry makes an overnight stay a good idea. *See* Belfast tour, Day 4, p.61, for lunch, dinner and overnight suggestions.

by this great labour, however, that he fell asleep as soon as he was finished. The next day Fionn's wife, the giantess Oonagh, saw the massive Benandonner pounding towards them down the Causeway, demanding to know where Fionn was. Quick-thinking Oonagh covered Fionn over and, pointing to his still sleeping form, told the Scot to stop being so noisy before he woke the baby. Benandonner, unable to imagine how big Fionn had to be if this was the size of his child, turned tail and ran back to Staffa, tearing up most of the Causeway behind him.

There is a two-mile circular walk past the strange formations. The National Trust, which manages the Causeway, has made great efforts to make the site accessible to the thousands who visit each year, yet retain the beauty and natural habitat of the area. No souvenir shops and ice-cream vans mar the scenery here. The Trust now owns 104 acres (42ha) of the North Antrim cliff path between the causeway itself and the ruins of Dunseverick Castle beside Whitepark Bay. You will find the Giant's Causeway on the B146, a looproad off the A2 between Ballycastle and Bushmills. Car parking is provided, and a shuttle bus covers the one kilometre from there to the Causeway itself; otherwise access is on foot only. The **Visitors' Centre** (*t (028) 2073 1855; open July–Aug daily 10–7; earlier closing time during the rest of the year; guided tours June–Sept, by appointment only at other times; adm for car park*) at the entrance includes a tea room, shop and information on the geology and history of the area. Next to the Centre is the **Causeway School Museum** (*t (028) 2073 1777; open July–Aug only, daily 11–4.30*), which takes you back to a small country school circa 1920.

You can walk a couple of miles north along another coastal path to **Port Ballintrae**, a picturesque fishing village, and past a huge strand with strong Atlantic rollers, called **Runkerry**. Here, a Spanish galleon, the *Girona*, was sunk off the Giant's Causeway. It contained the most valuable cargo yet found (now in the Ulster Museum, Belfast).

Omagh

Omagh, the capital of County Tyrone, is separated from the other large town of the county, Cookstown, by the Black Bog. This accounts for the turfcraft souvenirs you may find – which make a change from the more usual Irish linen hankies or crochet. Some people tell you that there is something French about this town, with its twin-spired church and its reputation for liveliness. Brian Friel, the playwright, is a native. (Any of his plays are worth making a special effort to see; he gives a profound and

Getting There

Bus 273 from Derry to Omagh (1¼hrs), which stops at the Folk Park (55mins) on request.

Tourist Information

Omagh: 1 Market Street, **t** (028) 8224 7831; *open all year.*

Internet Access

Omagh Library, 1 Spillar's Place (off Dublin Road), **t** (028) 8224 4821.
Also at the tourist office.

Where to Stay and Eat

Hawthorn House, 72 Old Mountfield Road, **t** (028) 8225 2005 (*moderate*). Open daily for breakfast, lunch and dinner. Recommended for its excellent gourmet food. Rooms also.
Clanabogan House, 85 Clanabogan Rd, **t** (028) 8224 1171 (*inexpensive*). Contact Robert and Mary Montgomery for B&B.

Golden Hill, 32 Tattykeel Road, **t** (028) 8225 1257, *goldenhill@sperrins.com* (*inexpensive*). Lovely scenic location where visitors are especially welcome.
Mellon Country Inn, 134 Beltany Road, **t** (028) 8166 1224 (*moderate*). Good steaks.
Coach Inn, 1 Railway Terrace, **t** (028) 8224 3330 (*inexpensive*). Good pub food.
Coffee@Grinders, Market Street, **t** (028) 8224 3390 (inexpensive). Soup and snacks 9–5.

Entertainment and Nightlife

Traditional Music

Teach Ceoil in Rousky, **t** (028) 8164 8882, and *Dun Uladh,* Ballinamullan. Evenings of *craic*, traditional music, dance, stories and poetry. Enquire at the Omagh tourist office or *Commhaltas Ceoltoiri Eireann* in Omagh, **t** (028) 8224 2777, **f** (028) 8225 2162.
An Creagan **Visitor Centre, t** (028) 8076 1112. *Open weekends only.*

lyrical insight into Irish culture.) Other writers from this area are Benedict Kiely, Alice Milligan and William Forbes Marshall. The town is a good spot for fishing on the Camowen and Owenreagh Rivers. Those wanting to hear musical talent should time their visit to coincide with the West Tyrone Feis in May, also known as the Omagh Feis, which has plenty of Irish music and dancing. Since 15 August 1998, Omagh has been known as the site of the most devastating single act of violence in the history of the Troubles: 29 people were killed by a bomb that day in the city centre. There is now a small memorial garden at the site, on Drumragh Avenue beside Strule Bridge, where one may spend some time in quiet reflection.

You might base yourself here for a night if you want to make a special trip to the **Ulster Amercan Folk Park** (*t (028) 8224 3292, www.folkpark.com; open Easter–Sept Mon–Sat 10.30–6, Sun 11–6.30, rest of year Mon–Fri 10.30–5; last entry 4.30; adm*) in Castletown, a fascinating reconstruction of the life that emigrants left behind in Ireland and that which they encountered in their new land, that has deservedly won tourism awards. The nearby **Ulster History Park** at Cullion (*t (028) 8164 8188, www. omagh.gov.uk/historypark.htm; open July and Aug 10–6.30; April–June and Sept 10–5.30; Oct–Mar Mon–Fri 10–5; last entry 1hr before close; adm; joint ticket with Folk Park available*) traces human settlemet and society from 8000 BC to the 17th century.

East of Omagh, at Creggan, you will find the **An Creagán Visitor Centre** (*open daily April–Sept, 11–6.30, Oct–Mar, 11–4.30; adm; t (028) 8076 1112, f 8076 1116*) with bog trails, archaeological exhibits and a restaurant. Archaeological walks and events are held throughout the year here.

Touring from Derry

Day 1: Around Lough Eske to Donegal

Morning: Take the A5 south out of Derry to **Strabane**, birthplace of John Dunlap, printer of the American Declaration of Independence, and then turn northwest four miles to **Raphoe**, an ancient town with a venerable cathedral, ruined Bishop's Palace and pretty village green. Seventh-century St Adomnan founded a monastery here; he was an O'Donnell like his ancestor St Columba, and wrote a Life of the great missionary abbot which reveals much about early Christian society. At nearby **Beltany** you can wonder at a stone circle with a mystical alignment. Then head southwest via Ballybofey to lovely **Lough Eske** which you can drive around in 40 minutes; in summer, view the rhododendron garden at Ardnamona House (*adm*).

Lunch: By Lough Eske, or in Donegal Town, *see* below.

Afternoon: Take the N13 south to **Donegal Town**. Situated on the River Eske, it is a crowded, busy place even without the tourist buses which congregate near the hotels on the Diamond. A diamond – or 'square' to most visitors – is an area where fairs and gatherings were held, and in the Plantation period it was placed in the shadow of the castle (*open May–Oct, daily 9.30–5.45; adm*) so as to guard against the fighting. The town is nowadays one of the best places to buy Donegal tweed. You might also be interested in the Donegal Railway Heritage Centre.

Dinner and Sleeping: In Donegal Town, *see* below.

Day 1

Lunch by Lough Eske

Harvey's Point Restaurant and Country Hotel, Lough Eske, **t** (074) 9722208 (*moderate*). Continental food in beautiful surroundings.

Lunch in Donegal Town

See Dinner, below.

Dinner near Donegal Town

Coxtown Manor, Laghey, **t** (074) 97 34575 (*moderate*). Irish/Belgian menu using seasonal fish and game.
Harbour Restaurant Quay, Quay Street, **t** (074) 97 21702 (*moderate*). Seafood and lasagne.
McGroarty's Pub, The Diamond, **t** (074) 97 22519 (*inexpensive*). Good pub food.

Sleeping in Donegal Town

St Ernans House Hotel, St Ernans Island, Donegal Town, **t** (074) 97 21067, *www.sain-ternans.com* (*luxury*). A gracious house on a wooded tidal island accessed by a causeway.

The décor is rather too colour co-ordinated, but it is still a lovely place to stay.
Central Hotel, The Diamond, Donegal, **t** (074) 97 21027 (*moderate*). Comfortable hotel with good views over Donegal Bay.
Quiet Water, Muckross, St Ernans, **t** (074) 97 23313 (*inexpensive*). Quiet, convenient B&B. *Open all year.*

Dinner and Sleeping around Lough Eske

Ardnamona House, Lough Eske, near Donegal Town, **t** (074) 97 22650 (*moderate*). Magical views over landscaped gardens, with wonderful food and hospitality from the Clarks. Famous for its rhododendrons, and for originally being the family home of the 20th century poet Rupert Brooke.
Rhu Gorse, Lough Eske, 6 miles from Donegal Town, **t** (074) 97 21685 (*inexpensive*). A modern, family-run country house, overlooking the Blue Stack Mountains. *Closed Sept–Easter.*

Day 2: Into the Gaeltacht

Morning: Donegal Town is a few miles away from the **Gaeltacht**, the officially recognized Irish-speaking area. The area begins at **Killybegs**; in the summer, bordering hedgerows bloom with honeysuckle and fuchsia, and as you get further west the sweet, acrid smell of peat hangs on the damp air. This prosperous place is the most important fishing port in Ireland. In the Catholic church there is the fine sculpted medieval grave slab of Noall Mór MacSwyne, which was found near St John's Point. The famous **Donegal Carpet Factory** on the Kilcar road out of Killybegs started up here in the 1890s, headed by a Scots weaver, Alexander Morton; the hand-knotted carpets were often designed for palaces and embassies all over the world.

Lunch: In Killybegs or Teelin, or Glencolmcille, *see* below.

Afternoon: Beyond Killybegs you encounter some of the grandest scenery in Donegal; the cliffs of Bunglass, Scregeigther and Slieve League are among the highest in Europe. To detour to Bunglass, turn south in the centre of Carrick village towards Teelin. **Glencolmcille** should be visited next; there is a craft shop where you can buy handmade products such as jams, soaps and wines made from gorse or bluebells, and the village has also become one of the most important centres for Irish culture and music. Glencolmcille Folk Village and Museum (*open Easter–Sept Mon–Fri 10–6, Sun 12–6; adm*) constitutes three cottages, representing different periods of Irish life. There is also a 3½mile pilgrimage walk along the valley. Take the signposted road to **Ardara**, a vibrant centre for Donegal tweed and Aran sweaters.

Dinner and Sleeping: In Ardara, *see* below.

Day 2

Lunch in Killybegs
Bay View Hotel, Killybegs, t (074) 97 31950, *bvhotel@iol.ie* (*moderate*). Mainly a seafood restaurant.

The Fleet Inn, Bridge Street, t (074) 97 32848 (*moderate*). More seafood specialities.

Lunch in Teelin
Cul a Quin, t (074) 97 39101. Soup and sandwiches in a cosy pub.

Lunch in Glencolmcille
An Chistin, Ulster Cultural Foundation, Glencolmcille, t (074) 97 30213/97 30248 (*inexpensive*). Specializes in seafood, salads, soups. *Open for lunch and dinner Mar–Oct*.

Glencolmcille Folk Village Tearoom, t (074) 97 30017 (*inexpensive*). Home-made scones, bread and soups. *Open Easter–Sept*.

Glencolmcille Hotel, t (074) 97 30003 (*inexpensive*). Simple food in a bright restaurant overlooking the sea.

Dinner in Ardara
Nancy's Bar, t (074) 95 41187 (*inexpensive*). Delicious oysters and burgers. *Summer only*.

Woodhill House, t (074) 95 41112 (*moderate*). Fresh home cooking. Rooms also.

Sleeping in Ardara
Nesbitt Arms Hotel, t (074) 95 41103 (*inexpensive*). Comfortable rooms and a traditional menu.

The Green Gate, Ardvally, Ardara, t (074) 95 41546 (*inexpensive*). Traditional cottage B&B. Paul Chatenoud charms visitors into a sense of what life must have been like in Donegal a century ago (apart from the bathrooms and central heating). Best seen in the warm months, when you can enjoy the glorious surroundings. *Smokers welcome*.

Drumbarron House, The Diamond, t (074) 95 41200 (*inexpensive*). Bed and breakfast in the town centre.

Campbell's Holiday Hostel, Ardara, t (074) 95 51491, *campbellshostel@eircom.net* (*inexpensive*). Youth hostel.

Day 3A: Up the Coast: The Rosses and Horn Head

Morning: If you travel a few miles on to the next little peninsula of Dunmore Head you will come to **Portnoo** and **Naran**, two popular beaches. There is a fascinating fort near here, built on an island in Doon Lough (beside Naran). It is over two thousand years old and is a very impressive sight – a circular stone fort which spreads over most of the island. It can easily be seen from the lough shore. At the neck of this peninsula you go through **Maas**, a small fishing resort, and on north to **Dunglow** and 'The Rosses', as this area is called. The Irish name is *naRosa*, meaning 'Headlands', and although this area is going through a housing boom it is still one of the most charming routes you can take: loughs are scattered through the hilly country, the beaches are lovely and there are islands offshore. You can follow the coast road round to **Bunbeg**, which has an attractive 19th-century harbour

Lunch: In Burtonport or Bunbeg, *see* below.

Afternoon: Continue on round the coast, through Derrybeg and **Gortahork**, from where you cannot help but notice the glorious outlines of the mountains inland: Errigal is cone-shaped, and Muckish means 'pig's back' in Irish. Between Falcarragh and Dunfanaghy is the great granite promontory of **Horn Head**. You can do a complete circuit by taking the little road signposted 'Horn Head Coastal Drive' by the bridge at the top of the main street in **Dunfanaghy**, an attractive village overlooking Sheep Haven with, on the outskirts, the Workhouse Heritage Centre and Art Gallery (*open Mar–Oct Mon–Fri 10–5 weekends 12–5; adm*).

Dinner and Sleeping: In Dunfanaghy, *see* below.

Day 3

Lunch between Burtonport and Bunbeg
Danny Minnies, Teach Killindarra, Annagry, t (074) 95 48201 (*moderate*). Fish platters and *à la carte*.

Lunch in Burtonport
Lobster Pot, t (074) 95 42012 (*inexpensive*). Seafood in a lively pub.
Skippers Tavern, t (074) 95 42234 (*inexpensive*). A quieter pub to eat your seafood.

Lunch in Bunbeg
Bunbeg House, The Harbour, t (074) 95 31305 (*moderate*). Cosy and family-run; healthy snacks and simple vegetarian meals, plus heartier food. Also has accommodation.

Dinner in Dunfanaghy
The Cove, Port na Blagh, t (074) 91 36300, (*moderate*). Stylish, good food in surroundings to match. Wine bar upstairs.

Dinner and Sleeping in Dunfanaghy
The Mill Restaurant, Figart, t (074) 9136985, (*moderate*). Friendly house with comfortable accommodation. Fine cooking with fresh local produce. *Booking essential*.

Sleeping in Dunfanaghy
Arnold's Hotel, t (074) 91 36208, *arnoldshotel@ eircom.net* (*expensive*). This is a fine, old-fashioned hotel, set in a pretty village overlooking Sheep Haven.
Shandon Hotel, Marble Hill Strand, Port-na-Blagh, near Dunfanaghy, t (074) 91 36137 (*moderate*). Large family hotel with leisure centre and fine food.
Rosman House, t (074) 91 36273 (*inexpensive*), Comfortable, spacious rooms in a home with panoramic views.
Corcreggan Mill Hostel, t (074) 91 36507/91 36409, f (074) 91 36902 (*inexpensive*). Basic hostel in a renovated mill and simulated railway station, 1¼ miles out of town. There is also an organic garden.

Day 3B: Into the Mountains (an inland alternative)

Morning: Take the N56 to **Glenties**, a small town at the junction of glens. Take the R250 up one of these glens to **Fintown** (*Baile na Finne*). Just before the village, turn left up the R252 signposted to Dunglow. This corkscrew road brings you into the tiny village of **Doocharry** (*An Duchoraidh*). Across the river, turn right up the Gweebara Valley along a narrow road (R254) towards Churchill. You now enter spectacular scenery seemingly untouched by human life. The deserted road drops down to **Gartan Lough** and then enters the St Colmcille Heritage Area. On the shores of the lake is the **Colmcille Heritage Centre** (*open Easter and May–Sept, Mon–Fri 10.30–6.30, Sun 1–6.30*), which charts the life of St Colmcille who was born on the far shore of the lake. **Churchill**, to the right, is a charming row of cottages with a wonderful view. Go on left around the lake to the turn-off signposted to the **Glebe Gallery** (*open Sat–Thurs 11–5.30; adm*), a plain Georgian house packed with exquisite art. Further along the road is St Colmcille's Cross, and the ruins of St Colmcille's Oratory.

Lunch: In Churchill or Glenveagh.

Afternoon: If you continue along the same road it will bring you back out on to the R251 where you turn left for the unmissable **Glenveagh National Park** (*open Mar–Oct daily 10–6.30*), a beautiful, isolated park with a 19th-century fairytale castle outlined against the mountains on the loughside. Continue along the R251 and turn off to travel behind Muckish Mountain down to the coast at **Falcarragh**. Further north along the coast is the busy, pretty village of **Dunfanaghy**.

Dinner and Sleeping: In Dunfanaghy.

Day 3

Lunch by Gartan Lough
St Colmcille Heritage Centre, Lough Gartan, t (074) 91 37306 (*inexpensive*). Large self-service restaurant. *Open Mon–Fri 10.30–6.30, Sun 1–6.30.*

Lunch in Churchill
Wilkins Bar, t (074) 91 37019, (*inexpensive*). Soup and sandwiches.

Lunch in Glenveagh
The **visitor centre** has a large café and the castle has a tea room serving soup, sandwiches and home-baking.

Dinner in Dunfanaghy
The Cove, Port na Blagh, near Dunfanaghy, t (074) 91 36300, (*moderate*). Stylish, good food in surroundings to match. Wine bar upstairs. *Evening meals served from 7pm.*

Dinner and Sleeping in Dunfanaghy
The Mill Restaurant, Figart, t (074) 9136985, (*moderate*). Friendly house with comfortable accommodation. Fine cooking with fresh local produce. *Booking essential.*

Sleeping in Dunfanaghy
Arnold's Hotel, Sheep Haven, nr Dunfanaghy, t (074) 91 36208, *arnoldshotel@ eircom.net* (*expensive*). This is a fine, old-fashioned hotel, set in a pretty village overlooking Sheep Haven.

Shandon Hotel, Marble Hill Strand, Port-na-Blagh, near Dunfanaghy, t (074) 91 36137 (*moderate*). Large family hotel with leisure centre and fine food.

Rosman House, t (074) 91 36273 (*inexpensive*), Comfortable, spacious rooms in a home with panoramic views.

Corcreggan Mill Hostel, t (074) 91 36507/ t (074) 91 36409, f 91 36902 (*inexpensive*). Basic hostel in a renovated mill and simulated railway station, 1¼ miles out of town. There is also an organic garden.

Day 4: The Fanad Peninsula

Morning: Set off south. At **Creeslough** you can admire a modern church designed by Liam McCormick; its shape echoes the view of Muckish. On the road to **Carrigart** is one of the most romantic castles in Ireland: Doe Castle, set on the water's edge (*undergoing restoration*). Leaving Carrigart, another centre for local crafts, the lough-side road takes you down to Mulroy Bay, a narrow-necked lough bordered by the Fanad Peninsula on the opposite side. Down the road is **Millford**, a pretty town on a hill, and from here you can explore the Fanad Peninsula on the old road, which takes you past the Knockalla range by Kerrykeel. In this isolated land survives a very idiosyncratic spoken Gaelic. The tiny village of **Portsalon** is beautifully situated over Ballymastocker Bay, an immense curve of strand. Just a little way north, along the pretty road to Fanad Head, is the garden of **Ballydaheen** (*open May–Sept Thurs and Sat 10–3; adm*), with a planted walk leading down to interconnecting caves on a small beach; the house shows a definite Japanese influence.

Lunch: In Kerrykeel or Portsalon, *see* below.

Afternoon: A terrific coastal drive, which joins the R247, has been built with fabulous views over Lough Swilly and the Urris Hills. This brings you to **Rathmullan**, nestling in a sheltered plain. It's a charming town with sandy beaches and lovely views, thoguh becoming a little spoiled. The ruined Carmelite friary in the town has a romantic air borne out by its story – to find out, visit the excellent Flight of the Earls Heritage Centre (*open Easter–mid Sept daily; adm*), in the Martello tower by the pier.

Dinner and Sleeping: In Rathmullan or Ramelton, *see* below.

Day 4

Lunch in Kerrykeel
The Village Inn, Portsalon Road, t (074) 91 50062 (*inexpensive*). Good pub food in a warm, friendly atmosphere.

Lunch in Portsalon
Sarah's, t (074) 91 59135 (*moderate–inexpensive*). Good-value plain cooking, especially seafood. There's a great view over the bay.

Dinner in Rathmullan
An Bonnán Buí, Pier Road, t (074) 91 58453 (*moderate*). Small bistro; excellent food with a South American flavour.

Dinner in Ramelton/Rathmelton
The Bridge Bar, t (074) 91 51833 (*moderate*). Cosy seafood restaurant.
Mirabeau Steak House, t (075) 91 51138 (*moderate*). Georgian town house with unpretentious cooking. Steaks, seafood, and plenty of other choices.

Dinner and Sleeping in Rathmullan
Rathmullan House Hotel, t (074) 91 58188, f 91 58200, *www.rathmullan house.com* (*luxury*). 18th-century country house set on the edge of Lough Swilly. Beautiful gardens and excellent food in the dining room – fresh, original cooking with home-grown seasonal vegetables from the walled garden. Very cosy bar with a turf fire, a heated swimming-pool and a sandy beach.
Fort Royal Hotel, t (074) 91 58100, f 91 58103, *www.fortroyalhotel.com* (*luxury*). Another fine period house, with more of a family atmosphere to it.

Sleeping in Ramelton/Rathmelton
Frewin, Letterkenny Road, t (074) 91 51247, *www.accommodationdonegal.net* (*moderate*). Fine, comfortable Victorian house that was once a rectory. Dinner by arrangement. *Open all year*.
Ardeen, t (074) 91 51243 (*inexpensive*). Elegant B&B.

Day 5: Around Inishowen

Morning: One of the most lovely routes in Ireland is the road from Rathmullan to **Ramelton** (Rathmelton) The town is a relatively unspoilt Plantation town built by the Stewart family, famous for its annual festival in July and for its pantomime in February. It is also famous for its thriving bottling industry. American Presbyterians will be interested in the old Meeting House in the Back Lane which is early-18th-century. The town's history is told in the 'Ramelton Story' (*open Mon–Sat 9.30–5.30, Sun 2–5.30*), an audiovisual exhibition in a refurbished warehouse on the Quay.

Lunch: In Ramelton or Buncrana, *see* below.

Afternoon: Follow the southern shores of Lough Swilly and come around on to the **Inishowen Peninsula**, really a kingdom of its own. At **Fahan**, just north of Inch, see the 7th-century St Mura's Cross in the Church of Ireland graveyard. Here in the rectory in 1848, looking across to Inch Top Hill, Cecil F. Alexander wrote 'There is a Green Hill Far Away'. Take the R238 to **Buncrana** and then the coast road to Dunree Head and through the mountains to the spectacular **Mamore Gap**. On the other side of the Gap, past **Clonmany**, are beaches around the Isle of Doagh. This is unspoiled country, full of fuchsia hedges and little whitewashed cottages. In the Church of Ireland graveyard at **Carndonagh** are monuments including the Marigold Stone which has the same ornamentations as St Mura's Cross. **Malin** has a pretty green, and you can drive up to the most northerly tip of Ireland, **Malin Head**. Head back to Derry in the morning via Culdaff, Moville and Cooley.

Dinner and Sleeping: In Carndonagh, Malin or Culdaff, *see* below.

Day 5

Lunch in Ramelton
Mirabeau Steak House, Ramelton, t (075) 91 51138 (*moderate*). Georgian town house with unpretentious cooking.

Lunch in Buncrana
Inishowen Gateway Hotel, Railway Road, t (074) 93 61059 (*inexpensive*). Lunches are served in the bar or restaurant.
Lake of Shadows Hotel, Griana Park, t (074) 93 61005 (*inexpensive*). Bar lunches available.

Dinner in Carndonagh
The Corncrake, Malin Street, t (074) 93 74534 (*moderate*). Fish, meat and poultry, all served with imaginative sauces and accompaniments. *Dinner only*.

Dinner and Sleeping in Culdaff
McGrory's of Culdaff, t (074) 93 79104 (*inexpensive*). Wide-ranging menu of localy sourced meat and seafood, with salads and vegetarian options. Music Wed, Thurs and Sat. Ten rooms also available. *Food served 6.30–9.30*.

Dinner and Sleeping in Malin
Malin Hotel, t (074) 93 70606 (*moderate*). Small but comfortable family-run hotel.

Dinner at Malin Head
Seaview Tavern, t (074) 93 70117 (*inexpensive*). Steaks, roasts, burgers. *Open 10am–9pm*.

Sleeping at Malin Head
The White Strand, t (074) 93 70355 (*inexpensive*). On the untouched and beautiful Inishowen Peninsula, 4 miles from Malin village, a modern bed and breakfast; contact Mrs Haughton. *Open all year*.
Malin Head Hostel, t (074) 93 70309 (*inexpensive*). Clean and comfortable, with an organic garden and orchard available for visitor use.
Sandrock Holiday Hostel, t (074) 93 70289 (*inexpensive*). Overlooking the strand; bunk beds in an en suite dormitory.

Western Ireland

The West

Oliver Cromwell thought of the province of Connacht (*Cuige Chonnacht*), also spelt Connaught, as a Siberia to which he could banish the troublesome Catholic landowners. It was here on the crowded, stony farms that the famine struck the hardest in the 1840s. Today, it seems a wild paradise of mountains, heather and lakes into which the Atlantic makes spectacular entrances with black cliffs, golden beaches and island-studded bays. This is the wild west, which was for centuries remote from Dublin and fashionable values; where in some parts the local people still speak Gaelic, and where they have clung to their own traditions in spite of the past invaders and the more insidious advance of modern life.

Westport

Westport is an attractive 18th-century octagonal planned town, unusual in the west. James Wyatt, the well-known Georgian architect, designed it for the Marquess of Sligo, and included a pretty walk called the Mall which runs beside the River Carrowbeg and is overhung with trees. Westport's history is so tied up with the Browne family of Westport House that many of the streets – John's Row, James Street,

Getting There

Ryanair, bmiBaby, BA and MyTravelLite fly to Knock airport from Stansted or Manchester. There are also three trains daily to and from Dublin to Westport station, **t** (098) 25253.

Getting from the Airport

Knock International Airport is actually south of Charlestown; for information, call **t** (094) 67222. There is no bus direct from Knock Airport. Take a taxi to Charlestown, which is closest, or Knock village, and catch a bus from there.
Bus Eireann, Westport, **t** (098) 25711, *www.buseireann.ie*.

Getting Around

By Bus

You can get around by bus to almost anywhere, but buses are never as frequent or convenient as they might be. There are a number of obscure local lines; as always, the tourist offices are the best source for bus information.
Bus Eireann, Westport, **t** (098) 25711; Ballina, **t** (096) 71800, *www.buseireann.ie*. Day trips to many destinations, including Achill Island, *see* p.84.

Car Hire

Knock
Diplomat Cars, Cahill Duffy, **t** (094) 21288.
Alamo/National Car Rental, **t** (094) 67252, **f** (094) 67374.
Europcar, Murray's Rent a Car, **t** (094) 67221.

Westport
Tim Hastings Ltd, The Fairgreen, **t** (098) 25133.

Tourist Information

Westport: James Street, **t** (098) 25711, **f** (098) 26709, *www.visitmayo.com, westport@ irelandwest.ie, westportheritagecentre@ irelandwest.ie*; open all year.

Clew Bay Heritage Centre runs a guided walk of Westport (*July and Aug Tues and Thurs at 8pm*), starting at the junction of Bridge Street and Shop Street. The tourist office has a booklet with other walks you can follow alone.

Internet Access
Dunnings Cyber Café, The Octagon, **t** (098) 25161, *dunning@aun.ie*.

Festivals

June: Westport Horse and Pony Show, **t** (098) 25616; **Westport International Sea Angling Festival**, **t** (098) 27297.
July: Croagh Patrick Pilgrimage, Westport, **t** (098) 25711. Last Sun of month.
Sept: Westport Horse Fair, **t** (098) 25616; **Westport Arts Festival**, **t** (098) 25711.
Oct: Westport Harbour Seafood Festival, **t** (098) 29000/26534.

Shopping

Crafts and Woollens
Westport Crystal, The Quay, **t** (098) 27780. Handmade crystal.
Foxford Woollen Mills, Bridge Street, **t** (098) 27844. Rugs, pottery and knitwear.
Waterfront Gallery, The Harbour, **t** (098) 28406. Jewellery, glass, pottery, paintings.
Carraig Donn, Bridge Street, **t** (098) 26287. Knitwear and gifts; Aran sweaters a speciality; also at Lodge Road, **t** (098) 25566.

Peter Street – are named after members of the family. In summer the place is overflowing with people attracted by the town's relaxed, lively atmosphere.

The **Holy Trinity Church** on the Newport Road has elaborate internal decoration. This includes a pulpit carved from alabaster which was cargo from a shipwreck washed up on the lands of the Sligo estate in Clew Bay. Down the hill on the shores of Clew Bay is an extension to the town where the old quay warehouses have been renovated to house apartments, an hotel, shops, bars and restaurants.

Delicacies

On Thursday mornings there is a **farmers' market** in the town hall, **t** (098) 26486.

Sports and Activities

Fishing
V. Keogh, The Helm Bar, The Quay, **t** (098) 26194. Sea-fishing.

Golf
Westport Golf Club, **t** (098) 28262. A lovely course by the sea above Croagh Patrick.

Walking
Croagh Patrick Walking Holidays, **t** (098) 26090. Guided hill-walking tours.

Horse Riding
Carraholly Stables, Newport Road, **t** (098) 27057.

Where to Stay

Ardmore Country House Hotel, The Quay, **t** (098) 25994 (*expensive*). Comfortable, recently refurbished country house hotel overlooking Clew Bay.

Olde Railway Hotel, The Mall, **t** (098) 25166, *www.theolderailwayhotel.com* (*expensive*). Central town hotel with car park, garden and a conservatory restaurant.

Wyatt Hotel, The Octagon, **t** (098) 25027, *www.wyatthotel.com* (*moderate*). Stylish hotel in the town centre, with leisure centre.

Adare House, Quay Road, **t** (098) 26102, *adarehouse@eircom.net* (*inexpensive*). Bed and breakfast. Contact Margaret Madigan.

Cillcoman Lodge, Rosbeg, **t** (098) 26379 (*inexpensive*). Bed and breakfast overlooking sea. Contact Mary Mitchell.

Eating Out

The Lemon Peel, The Octagon, **t** (098) 26929 (*expensive*). Modern bistro-style restaurant. Open Tues–Sun from 6pm. No under-12s.

La Bella Vita, High Street, **t** (098) 29771 (*expensive–moderate*). Bistro serving authentic Italian food. Open Tues–Sun 6–10pm.

Quay Cottage, The Harbour, **t** (098) 26412 (*moderate*). Folksy seafood restaurant. Very cosy, with a vegetarian menu. Open Tues–Sat from 6pm for dinner only.

Shebeen Pub and Restaurant, Rosbeg, **t** (098) 24987 (*moderate*). 2.5km out of town overlooking Clew Bay, and specializing in seafood. Open daily 12–9.30pm for bar food; restaurant open Thurs–Sat 6–9pm.

The Urchin, Bridge Street, **t** (098) 27532 (*moderate–inexpensive*). Good Irish food. Open 6–10pm.

Towers Bar and Restaurant, The Quay, **t** (098) 26534 (*inexpensive*). Lively, simple bar, with seafood specialities. Open 12–9.30pm.

JW's Bar, Wyatt Hotel, *see left* (*inexpensive*). Lively bar with good menu.

McCormack's Restaurant, Bridge Street, **t** (098) 25619 (*inexpensive*). Cheerful café with fish, stews and home-baking. Open 10–5; closed Wed and Sun.

O'Malley's Bar and Restaurant, Bridge Street, **t** (098) 27307/8 (*inexpensive*). Quality and quantity of fish, steaks and hamburgers.

Entertainment and Nightlife

Matt Molloy's Bar, **t** (098) 26655. Owned by a member of the Irish folk group The Chieftains; if you can't get in, there will be plenty of other choices in summer.

The West Bar, Bridge Street, **t** (098) 25886.

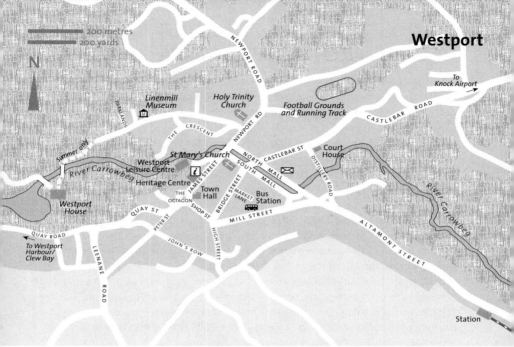

You can walk around one of the few stately homes of the west of Ireland – **Westport House** (**t** *(098) 27766/25430; open Easter–May Sat–Sun 2–5; June daily 1.30–5.30; July–Aug Mon–Fri 11.30–5.30, Sat–Sun 1.30–5.30; 3–23 Sept daily 2–5; adm*). The house is west of the town and is full of old Irish silver, family portraits and lovely furniture, and there is a miniature zoo in the grounds. It was built by Colonel John Browne and his wife, ancestors of the present Marquess of Sligo. He was a Jacobite, and she was the great-great-granddaughter of Granuaile, otherwise known as Grace O'Malley. This part of the coast and the islands off it are associated with the warrior woman who outshone all her male contemporaries in qualities of leadership. A pirate captain, whose symbol was the seahorse, her territory included Clare, Caher, Inishturk and Inishbofin. Her family had been Lords of the Isles for two hundred years, and in the 40 years that it took the Tudors to extend their power to Ireland Granuaile was the mainstay of the rebellion in the west. At the age of 45 she gave birth at sea to her first child, Toby. An hour later, her ship was boarded by Turkish pirates. The battle on the deck was almost lost when she suddenly appeared, wrapped in a blanket, and shot the enemy captain with a blunderbuss. Her men rallied, captured the Turkish ship and hanged the crew. She was also in the habit of mooring her ships by tying them together, passing the main rope through a hole in her castle walls and retiring to bed with the rope wound around her arm, in order to be ready at the first alarm. In her last years she was forced, aged 63, to sail up the Thames to parley with Elizabeth I. Elizabeth offered her a title, but Grace replied that she was a queen in her own right. Finally, they made a deal: Grace would retain some of her old lands, including Clare, and in return she would keep down piracy. People still talk of Grace today, even though she died in 1603.

Day Trips and Overnighters from Westport

The coastline around here is full of little islands and inlets, and just inland to the north is the wild mountain country of the Nephin Beg range.

Clare Island

Clare Island (pop. 140) has more land given over to farming than the other islands, though its higher slopes are covered in heather. It has superb cliffs up to 300ft (91m) high, but even these are overshadowed by the Knockmore Mountain, which drops from 1,550ft (472m) in a few hundred yards to join the cliffs. You could easily spend a couple of days on Clare, although there's not a huge amount to occupy you – or you could just come and have a picnic. As you come into the small stone pier you will see Grace O'Malley's Castle, converted into a coastguard station during the 19th century but now a ruin. The large, square stone tower still dominates the bay. There is a holy well at Toberfelabride, but the gem of Clare is its abbey, which is about 1½ miles (2.4km) west of the harbour. Clare Abbey is a 15th-century church with a tower, and is believed to be a cell of the Cistercian monastery of Abbeyknockmoy in County Galway. The most notable thing about the friary (*always accessible*) is the trace of fresco painting on the plastered ceiling of the vaulted roof; they seldom survive in medieval Irish churches. Grace O'Malley is buried here: on a plain arch leading from the roofless nave to the chancel there is a coat of arms topped by a horse rampant with the words '*Terra Marique potens O'Maille*' ('O'Malley powerful on land and sea'). You can walk to the lighthouse at the north end where there are spectacular views.

Achill Island

Achill is connected to the mainland by a bridge, and because it is one of the easiest islands to reach, it is the most touristy. The island covers 53 square miles (137.25 sq km) and is the largest of the Irish islands.

Keel is a big village with restaurants and craft shops and a large, sandy beach. The west-facing Cliffs of Menawn to the south of Keel have been wrought by the sea and wind into fantastic shapes, which are best viewed from a boat. Particularly note-worthy are the Cathedral Rocks, which are covered in fantastic fretwork. If you walk 3 miles (4.8km) to the end of Menawn Strand, you come to a holy well; and if it is low

Getting There

Two ferry companies make the 15min crossing to Clare Island several times a day, each with bus connections to and from Westport and Roonagh Quay.
The Pirate Queen, tickets available from Westport tourist office, t (098) 28288.
O'Malley's Ferries, James Street, Westport, t (098) 25045.
Chris O'Grady at the Bay View Hotel, *see* below, can organize sea-fishing and boating.

Where to Stay and Eat

Bay View Hotel, Clare Island, t (098) 26307 (*moderate*). Friendly and comfortable. Also pub food during the day and *à la carte* in the evening. *Open 12–4pm and 7–9pm.*
Granuaile House, The Harbour, Clare Island, t (098) 26250 (*inexpensive*).
Sea Breeze, Capnagower, Clare Island, t (098) 25649 (*inexpensive*).
You may prefer to buy a picnic in Supervalu, Shop Street, Westport, before you leave.

Getting There

It is only possible to do an afternoon trip to Achill Island on a Friday. This is a Bus Eireann trip leaving Westport at 3pm, arriving Keel at 4.52pm and departing 6.50pm, arriving at Westport at 8pm. Otherwise you will have to stay overnight.

Tourist Information

Achill: t (098) 45384; *open June–Aug.*
Achill Tourism: t (098) 47353; *open all year.*

Sports and Activities

Watersports

Equipment (sail boards, surfboards, *currachs*, sailing dinghies, canoes, wet suits, buoyancy aids) can be hired from **McDowell's Hotel**, Slievemore Road, Dugort, t (098) 43148, for use on Keel Lake and the sea.

Where to Stay and Eat

McDowell's Hotel, Slievemore, Dugort, Achill Island, t (098) 43148 (*moderate*). Family-run and full of atmosphere. Home cooking. Hire of watersports equipment, *see left.*

Achill Island House, Newtown, Keel, Achill Island, t (098) 43355 (*inexpensive*). Simple, near the beach. Contact Sheila Mangan.

Achill West Coast House, School Road, Dooagh, t (098) 43317 (*inexpensive*). Smoke-free B&B.

The Chalet, t (098) 43157 (*moderate–inexpensive*). Local seafood with a sea view. *Open daily 1–10pm.*

The Beehive, Keel, Achill Island, t (098) 43134 (*inexpensive*). Craft shop café with salads, seafood and home baking. *Open daily 10–6.*

tide you can see the arches and pillars of the rocks clearly. Above, **Mweelin Mountain** rises up. It is an easy climb, if approached from Dookinelly. Keem Bay is a lovely sandy cove obvious from the cliff road, and is a favourite haunt of the basking shark.

Doogort is a little fishing hamlet in the shadow of Slievemore Mountain (2,204ft/672m). The hamlet has a contentious history. In the early 19th century, a Protestant missionary outpost was established here in order to convert the local Catholics. The mission acquired title to the rights of three-fifths of Achill in a short time, and resentment amongst the Achill people ran high. This was intensified when, apparently, soup and bread was given out to islanders during the famine only if they became Protestants. The mission closed down in the late 19th century, but it did help start the first hotel on the island. Along the coast here are the **Seal Caves**; you can hire a boat to get to them and enjoy the superb bathing beaches.

Castlebar

Castlebar is the thriving, busy, administrative centre of Mayo. The town started as a settlement of the de Barrys; it became more important in 1611 when James I granted it a charter, and is remembered for the ignominious scattering of the British garrison in 1798 when the French General Humbert advanced with a motley crowd of French and Irish troops. The event is known today as the 'Races of Castlebar'. John Moore, the first and only president of the Connacht Republic, is buried in the Mall and there is a memorial to 1798 beside his grave. The town has a small green, and you can visit the **Linenhall Arts Centre** in Linenhall Street (*t (094) 23733, www.thelinenhall.com; open Mon–Fri 10–5, Sat 11–5.30*). Refurbished in 2002, it houses a gallery, theatre for drama and music, and a coffee area. There is a bus to the interesting **National Museum of Country Life** (*t 1890 687 386, www.museum.ie; open Tues–Sat 10–5, Sun 2–5*), 4 miles

Getting There

There is a regular daily **bus** service from Westport to Castlebar. **Bus Eireann, t** (098) 25711.

There is also a regular **train** service, **t** (098) 25253.

Tourist Information

Castlebar: **t** (094) 902 1207; *open May–Sept.*

Festivals

May–June: Castlebar International Blues Festival, t (094) 23111.

Eating Out

Café Rua, New Antrim Street, **t** (094) 902 3376 (*inexpensive*). Friendly café with wide range of fresh food and home baking. *Open Tues–Sat 9.30–6.*

The Olive Tree, Newtown Street, **t** (094) 902 3376 (*inexpensive*). Authentic Eastern Mediterranean food. *Open Mon–Sat 9–8, Sun 12–6; kitchen closed Fri 1.15–2.15.*

Flannelly's, Ellison Street, **t** (094) 902 2905 (*inexpensive*). Adequate pub food next door to the bus stop.

Lantern Restaurant, Thomas St, **t** (094) 902 3502 (*moderate–inexpensive*). Cantonese, Thai and northern Chinese cooking. *Open Sun–Thurs 6pm–12.30am, Fri–Sat 6pm–1am.*

from town at Thurlough. The museum houses a broad range of objects, photographs and film drawn from the national folklife collection which show the culture and livelihoods of past rural life. The exhibits are in a modern setting in the beautiful grounds of Thurlough Park, and it also has a shop and a café.

Nine miles south of Castlebar is **Ballintubber Abbey**, off the N84 to the east and only easily accessible by car (*t (094) 30934, btuabby@eircom.net; open daily 9am–8pm; donation*). Known as 'the Abbey that Refused to Die', it is the only one founded by an Irish king that has survived intact. The fame of Ballintubber goes even further back to the time of St Patrick, who baptized his converts in a holy well there, and founded a church. In the early 13th century the king of Connacht, Cathal of the Wine-red Hand, built the abbey for the Augustinian order. When the guest house to the abbey was excavated, many burnt stones were found near the stream over which it was built, revealing how the monks had heated their water: by throwing in red-hot stones. There is a pilgrim path from here to **Croagh Patrick**, 20 miles (32km) away.

Knock

Another noted place of pilgrimage is Knock, situated in the Plain of Mayo, 7 miles (11.3km) from the freshwater fishing centre of Claremorris. In 1879 the Virgin Mary, St Joseph and St John appeared here to 14 people. Although it rained heavily on the

Getting There

There is a daily **bus** to Knock from Westport.

Where to Stay and Eat

Belmont Hotel, t (094) 938 8122, **f** 938 8532, *www. belmonthotel.ie, belmonthotel@ eircom.net* (*moderate*). Offers natural health therapy packages, and there is also an award-winning restaurant.

Knock House Hotel, Ballyhaunis Road, **t** (094) 938 8088, **f** 938 8044, *hotel@knock-shrine.ie* (*moderate*). New hotel in parkland.

Carramore House, Airport Road, **t** (094) 938 8149 (*inexpensive*). Bed and breakfast.

Beirnes Restaurant, St John's, **t** (094) 938 8161, (*inexpensive*). Simple dining room serving traditional food. *Open 12–7.*

witnesses, the area around the apparition remained dry. The quiet little village of Knock has today become very commercialized, with chapels, monuments and a huge basilica; holy water comes from chrome taps and there are endless car parks. Over 750,000 visitors and pilgrims visit the shrine annually – it even has its own airport. At **Knock Folk Museum** (*t (094) 88100; open May, June, Sept and Oct daily 1–6; July and Aug daily 10–7*) you can hear the story of the Knock Apparition. The exhibition reflects local customs from the 1870s.

Ballina

Ballina (pronounced 'bally-nah') is a port town on the estuary of the River Moy surrounded by Franciscan abbeys, and is a good place to stay if you are in Ireland for the fishing. You can watch the fishermen wading in the river from the two bridges. It is a shopping centre as well – though these days Ballina is perhaps best known as the home town of former president Mary Robinson. The two main shopping streets form a cruxiform running down to the river. West of Ballina at **Enniscoe**, Castlehill, is the **Mayo North Heritage Centre** (*t (096) 31809; open April–Nov Mon–Fri 9–6, Sat and Sun 1–6*), off the R315 and 2 miles (3km) south of Crossmolina. It is in the outbuildings of Enniscoe House, which is also an attractive and comfortable place to stay (*see* below).

Getting There

There are **buses** to Ballina from Westport.

Tourist Information

Ballina: **t** (096) 70848; *open late Mar–Oct.*

Festivals

July: **Ballina Street Festival**, mid July, with stalls, pageants and music (**t** (096) 70905, *www.ballinastreetfestival@eircom.net*).

Where to Stay

Enniscoe House, Castlehill, near Crossmolina, Ballina, **t** (096) 31112, **f** 31773 (*expensive*). Georgian house set in parklands on the shores of Lough Conn. Grand, spacious rooms are filled with family furniture, with four-poster and half-tester beds in the pretty bedrooms. There are huge log fires and superlative cooking. The grounds include an ornamental garden and an organic garden (*adm*). A heritage centre adjoins the gardens. Boats and ghillies for the lough can easily be arranged.

Quignalegan House, Sligo Road, Ballina, **t** (096) 71644 (*inexpensive*). Family B&B, recommended by readers.

Bartra House Hotel, Pearse Street, Ballina, **t** (096) 22200, **f** 22111 (*moderate*). Comfortable, well-established hotel.

Ridgepool Hotel, Barrett Street, Ballina, **t** (096) 24600, **f** 24602 (*moderate–expensive*). Modern hotel with pleasant rooms overlooking the river.

Eating Out

Dillon's Bar and Restaurant, Dillon Terrace, **t** (096) 72230 (*moderate*). Famous locally for salmon. *Bar food 12–8.30, restaurant open 6–10pm.*

Gaughan's Bar, O'Rahilly Street, **t** (096) 70096 (*inexpensive*). Traditional pub serving home-cooked seasonal food. They serve Guinness at room temperature as well as chilled. *Open for lunch 12.30–4.*

The Broken Jug, O'Rahilly Street, **t** (096) 72379 (*inexpensive*). Reasonable pub grub. Also traditional music. *Open 12.30–4; restaurant open 5–8.30.*

Beckett's Bistro, Ridgepool Hotel, Barrett Street, **t** (096) 24600 (*inexpensive*). Pleasant modern bistro. *Open 12.30–2.30pm.*

Touring from Westport 1: Connemara

Day 1: Louisburgh and Leenane

Morning: Take the R335 west to **Murrisk Abbey**, founded by Tadhg O'Malley in 1457, with a beautiful east window. Nearby **Croagh Patrick** is a sacred mountain where St Patrick spent 40 days and nights in fasting and prayer. The climb offers magnificent views of Clew Bay. The information centre (*open daily in summer*) is at Teach naMiasa, Murrisk, and has a café, craft shop and shower facilities. A little further west, **Louisburgh** is a pretty village near to Clew Bay. The purple-blue mountain ranges give the village a marvellous backdrop, and it has numerous pubs offering traditional music on different nights. The story of Grace O'Malley (*see* p.83), is documented in the Granuaile Centre here (*open May–Oct Mon–Sat 10–7; adm*).

Lunch: In Louisburgh, *see* below.

Afternoon: Continue south on the R335 through **Delphi**. The Erriff River comes tumbling over the Aasleagh Falls at the bridge just north of **Leenane**. This village, situated at the head of Killary Harbour, is a popular base for walking or fishing. The Leenane Cultural Centre is just above the village on the N59; besides acting as an outlet for local knitters, it also has information on local history, places of interest to visit and a Sheep and Wool Museum (*open Mar–Oct daily 10–7*). Leenane featured as the location for the film *The Field*, and you will find references all over the village.

Dinner and Sleeping: In Leenane, *see* below.

Day 1

Lunch in Louisburgh

Durkans Weir House and Restaurant, Chapel Street, t (098) 66140 (*expensive–moderate*). Bar food and a popular seafood restaurant. *Open daily 12–9pm for bar food; restaurant open June–Sept and Dec daily.*

The Weir House, Chapel Street, t (098) 66140 (*inexpensive*). Cosy restaurant serving fish in the evenings and bar food during the day.

Dinner in Leenane

Portfinn Lodge, t (095) 42265 (*expensive–moderate*). Elegant little restaurant with fantastic views over Killary harbour. Exotic dishes such as shark or Patagonian tooth fish, as well as locally caught seafood, venison and pheasant. Some rooms, too.

Blackberry Café, t (095) 42240. Nice little restaurant serving soups, light meals and delicious puds. *Closed Oct–Good Friday.*

Killary Lodge (*moderate*), *see* below. Open to non-residents for lunch and dinner. Good home cooking with fresh local ingredients and views over the lough to the mountains.

Sleeping in Leenane

Delphi Mountain Resort and Spa, t (095) 42987, f 42303, *www.delphiescape.com* (*luxury*). Elegant, 'Zen' new spa and activity centre in a remote setting 8 miles north of Leenane. The restaurant serves local fish, meat and veg from the organic garden. An expensive indulgence. *Closed Dec–Jan.*

Delphi Lodge, on the Louisburgh road, t (095) 42296, *www.delphilodge.ie* (*expensive–moderate*). One-thousand-acre estate, ideal for fly-fishing. Hospitable owner, excellent food and old-fashioned service that has even pleased Prince Charles. Elegant, comfortable rooms. Meals available.

Killary Lodge, t (095) 42276, *www.killary.com* (*inexpensive*). A wonderful hotel for outdoor activities. Also a peaceful place with good food and an informal atmosphere. Set in extensive grounds on the edge of the water 4 miles west of Leenane.

Day 2: The North Connemara Coast

Morning: Connemara is the western portion of County Galway, south of Killary Harbour between Lough Corrib and the Atlantic. The road west from Leenane is set between the dark blue fjord- and stream-scored green hillsides, which give the effect of crushed velvet. Follow the coast road to Renvyle for splendid views. On the south side of the peninsula, on Ballynakill Harbour, is the **Connemara Sea Leisure: Oceans Alive Visitor Centre** with its aquarium, museum and cruises (*open May–Aug daily 10–5; closes earlier in winter; adm*). Take the N59 inland at Letterfrack to splendid **Kylemore Abbey**, now a girls' school and a convent for the Benedictine Nuns of Ypres, who run a restaurant and craft shop and cultivate beautiful gardens (*abbey open daily 9–5.30; gardens Easter–Oct daily 10.30–4.30; adm*).

Lunch: In Kylemore Abbey itself, or Letterfrack, *see* below.

Afternoon: **Letterfrack**, a pretty village founded by the Quakers, has wonderful bays for swimming. Along the Clifden road is the entrance to the **Connemara National Park Visitors' Centre** (*open daily 10–5.30, longer in summer*) where there is a small exhibition, walking trails and a tea shop. Along the coastal road to **Moyard** there are excellent craft shops. Continue on past Moyard to **Cleggan**. In summer and good weather take a boat over to **Inishbofin Island** (45mins) – it has lovely beaches for swimming and an interesting history: in the 7th century St Colman founded a monastery, the remains of which can still be seen.

Dinner and Sleeping: In Cleggan or on Inishbofin Island, *see* below.

Day 2

Lunch in Kylemore Abbey
Tea room (*inexpensive*) serves teas, coffees, home-made cakes and sandwiches. *Open daily 10–5.* **Self-service restaurant** (*inexpensive*) serves hot meals. *Open daily 12–3.* You don't need an entrance ticket to the abbey.

Lunch in Letterfrack
Rosleague Manor Hotel, t (095) 41101, f 41168 (*expensive*). Pretty, first-class hotel over-looking Ballinakill Bay. Delicious food and a friendly atmosphere. *Open to non-residents for lunch (moderate) and dinner May–Sept; Oct–April dinner only.*
Pangur Ban, t (095) 41243 (*moderate*). Cosy restaurant in a cottage on the edge of the village with creative Mediterranean cooking.

Dinner in Cleggan
Oliver's, t (095) 44640 (*moderate*). Friendly, informal pub-restaurant serving seafood, fish, Irish stew, steaks and other hearty fare.

Dinner on Inishbofin Island
The Dolphin Restaurant, Tiddle Quarter, Inishbofin, t (095) 45991. Simple, light lunches (*inexpensive*) and more substantial evening meals (*moderate*).

Sleeping in Cleggan
The Ocean's Wave, Sallerna, Cleggan, t (095) 44775 (*moderate*). Cosy family home just above pretty Sallerna beach. Simple evening meals on request (*inexpensive*).
Harbour House, t (095) 44702 (*inexpensive*). An attractive house run by the O'Malley family on the hill at the edge of the village over-looking the harbour. Bright, comfortable rooms and evening meals on request.

Sleeping on Inishbofin Island
Day's Hotel, t (095) 45809 (*moderate*). Family-run, friendly hotel right on the pier. Children welcome; facilities for divers. Restaurant.
Doonmore Hotel, t (095) 45804 (*moderate*). Simple and clean with good local seafood. Traditional music in summer (*Wed–Sat*).

Day 3: Clifden

Morning: Head southeast on the N59 to **Clifden**, the 'capital' of Connemara and a lively place in summer with its streets chock-a-bloc with restaurants, cafés and even the odd deli. The town sits in a sheltered bay, and if you walk half a mile to the Atlantic shore and gaze out, you are looking straight towards America. It is a well-planned early 19th-century town founded in 1812 by John D'Arcy, and the two spires of the Protestant church and the Catholic cathedral give it a distinctive outline. The wide streets overflow with people speaking Gaelic as well as an English which uses the idioms of Gaelic. There is a lovely road signposted 'Sky Road' which takes you further north round the indented coast. It climbs high above Clifden until it is above **D'Arcy's Castle**, a baronial-style ruin. From here you can see the waves crashing on to the rock islets of Inishturk and Inishbofin, with Clare Island beyond. The road continues into quiet Streamstown Bay, where white Connemara marble is quarried.
Lunch: In Clifden, *see* below.
Afternoon: Travelling around this part of Connemara, you pass by lakes, rivers, forests and mountains where there is little hint of pollution or industry. Even the farm machinery is fairly traditional. At **Dan O'Hara's Homestead Farm**, part of **Connemara Heritage and History Centre**, just off the N59 in Lettershea (*open April–Oct daily 10–6; adm*), you can see a farm run as in the 19th century. For a fabulous view of the unspoilt 'bog' take the 'Bog Road' from Clifden through a wonderful, wild landscape.
Dinner and Sleeping: In Clifden, *see* below.

Day 3

Lunch in Clifden

Mitchell's, Market Street, t (095) 21867 (*inexpensive*). Home-made food in a welcoming, cosy setting. Evening meals also.
Cullen's Bistro, Market Street, t (095) 21983 (*inexpensive*). Bistro and coffee shop. Try the Bailey's cheesecake.
The Connemara Hamper, Lower Market Street, t (095) 21054. Fantastic Irish cheeses, patés, salamis and ham, wines and home-made breads. Sandwiches, wraps and lunch boxes.

Dinner in Clifden

The Signal, Station House Courtyard, t (095) 22946 (*expensive*). In the redeveloped old station, renowned chef Stefan Matz offers a creative take on the freshest of local ingredients (lamb, duck, beef, turbot, sea bass). *Open Wed–Sun and bank hols dinner only.*
The Ardagh Hotel, Ballyconneely Road, t (095) 21384 (*moderate*). Delicious food with a continental flavour; wonderful sunset views.

Off the Square, Main Street, t (095) 22281 (*moderate*). Super fresh fish (including lobster straight from the tank) plus steaks, duck, Irish stew and local lamb.
High Moors, Doneen, Clifden, t (095) 21342 (*moderate*). The Griffens serve dinner in the sitting room of their bungalow on a hill just outside town. Fruit and veg is home-grown and the excellent food is cooked on the Aga. *Open May–Oct for dinner Wed–Sun.*

Sleeping in Clifden

Rock Glen, Ballyconneely Road, t (095) 21035, *www.connemara.net/rockglen-hotel* (*expensive*). Delightful country house hotel.
Dolphin Beach House, Lower Sky Road, Clifden, t (095) 21204, *www.connemara.net/dolphin beachhouse* (*expensive*). Just outside town, in 14 acres with a private beach, great views and delicious food. *Open Easter–Oct.*
The Quay House, Beach Road, t (095) 21369, *www.thequayhouse.com* (*moderate*). Wonderful guest house on the old quay. Stylish rooms furnished with antiques.

Day 4: Beaches and Bays

Morning: Drive down through **Ballinaboy**; four miles south of Clifden is the site where Alcock and Brown came to ground after the first ever transatlantic flight. Head for **Ballyconneely** on the isthmus; the coast road around Mannin Head from here is called the 'brandy and soda road' because of the exhilarating air. Beside the wide Mannin Bay is **Coral Strand**, so called because of the white sand-like debris of a seaweed which looks like coral. Two miles past Ballyconneely are two of the best beaches in Connacht: **Gorteen** and **Dog's Bay**. Or follow signs to **Connemara Golf Course** at Aillebrack Beach, in a spectacular setting between mountains and a pristine white beach, where you could eat lunch in the club house or have a picnic.

Lunch: In Ballyconneely, at Connemara Golf Course or in Roundstone, *see* below.

Afternoon: **Roundstone** is a pleasant 19th-century village. The name is a corruption of the Irish *Cloch na Ron*, which means 'Rock of the Seals'. There is a pretty harbour, which looks across the water to the low-lying islands in Bertraghboy Bay, and a friendly bar, O'Dowd's, where the fishermen contrast starkly with the Dubliners in their smart Aran sweaters. **Errisbeg Mountain** (987ft) towers above the village. It is a short climb, but the views are superb; look out for the flowers and plants, for this is a place beloved of botanists as well as artists. Then head up on the R341 and R342 to **Cashel**, right on Cashel Bay, an inlet of Bertraghboy Bay. It became famous overnight when General de Gaulle spent his holidays there.

Dinner and Sleeping: In Cashel or Recess, to the north, *see* below.

Day 4

Lunch in Ballyconneely
Keogh's Bar (*inexpensive*). Roadside bar with garden serving standard bar food.
Club House at the Connemara Golf Course, Ballyconneely, **t** (095) 23502 (*inexpensive*). Fabulous setting with views over the links to the mountains and the sea. Atlantic seafood chowder plus a few other hot dishes and sandwiches. *Open to non-members.*

Or stock up from the **Connemara Hamper** in Clifden (*see* left) and have a **picnic** on the beach below the golf course.

Lunch in Roundstone
O'Dowds Seafood Bar, t (095) 35809 (*inexpensive*). Perennially popular, old-fashioned and laid-back. Good chowder, mussels, crab claws, beef and Guinness or lamb stew.
Eldon's Hotel, t (095) 35933 (*inexpensive*). Pleasant hotel bar with superior bar food: Connemara fish bake, garlicky stuffed mussels, steak and chips.

Dinner and Sleeping in Cashel
Cashel House Hotel, t (095) 31001, *www.cashel-house-hotel.com* (*expensive*). Very luxurious but cosy house, full of fine furniture and *objets*. Superb tropical garden overlooking a beautiful sea inlet. The dinners served here are excellent.
Zetland House Hotel, Cashel Bay, **t** (095) 31111, *www.zetland.com* (*expensive*). Converted hunting lodge in an isolated setting overlooking the bay. Superb food. Tennis, billiards, etc. Very welcoming.

Sleeping in Recess
Ballynahinch Castle Hotel, Ballinafad, Recess, **t** (095) 31006, *www.ballynahinch-castle.com* (*expensive*). Magnificent setting, overlooking the Owenmore River. A relaxed and informal country house atmosphere.
Lough Inagh Lodge, Inagh Valley, R344 north of Recess, **t** (095) 34706 (*expensive*). Romantically situated shooting lodge on the shores of beautiful Lough Inagh. Log fires, antiques, excellent food, fishing and walks.

Day 5: The Aran Islands

Morning: Start early, and turn left on to an unmarked road just south of Cashel. This will bring you into the **Gaeltacht** region where Gaelic is the first language. Head via **Gortmore**, on a hill above a small lake, onwards to **Screeb** and then south on the R336 to **Costelloe**; from nearby **Rossaveal** (*Ros An Mhil*), at the mouth of Galway Bay, you can catch a boat to **Inishmore** ('Great Island'), the biggest of the three **Aran Islands** in Galway Bay (*check times in advance from Inis Mór Ferries, **t** (091) 566535, or Island Ferries, **t** (091) 568903*); also *see* pp.104–8.

Lunch: On the Aran island of Inishmore, *see* below.

Afternoon: The people and the islands of Aran were described by the playwright John Millington Synge in his notebooks and in his play *Riders to the Sea*. The Aran Islands today are much the same as they were in Synge's time. Most tourists come for the rugged beauty, the sweeping views, and to visit the prehistoric and early monastic ruins. The landscape is similar to that in the Burren in County Clare and is made up of porous limestone. There are four stone forts on Inishmore, all believed to go back as far as the early Celtic period 2,500 years ago. When you get off the steamer you can hire either a bicycle or a sidecar and jarvey to see the sights. The capital, **Kilronan**, has become rather touristy, but the people remain cheerful; **Dún Aonghasa** or Dun Aengus (*open Mar–Oct daily 10–6, Nov–Feb daily 10–4*) is on the south coast, on the summit of a hill which rises straight up from the sea. The site consists of several concentric ramparts forming a semi-circle on the brink of the cliffs.

Dinner and Sleeping: On Inishmore, *see* below.

Day 5

Lunch on Inishmore

Man of Aran Cottage, Kilmurvey Bay, **t** (099) 61286/61301 (*moderate–inexpensive*). A daytime café which serves soup, sandwiches and a lobster lunch. *Open Mar–mid Oct daily, weather permitting.*

An tSean Cheibh ('The Old Pier'), Kilronan, Inishmore, **t** (099) 61228, *oldpier@ireland. com* (*moderate*). Good home baking and fresh fish. Also a good fish and chip shop in the same building. *Open daily May–Oct.*

Dinner on Inishmore

Aran Fisherman Restaurant, Kilronan, **t** (099) 61363/61104 (*expensive–inexpensive*). Set meals. *Open winter 1–9pm, summer 10–10.*

Dun Aengus Restaurant, Kilronan, **t** (099) 61104 (*moderate*). Traditional stone house serving seafood, steaks, international and vegetarian dishes. *Open daily 6–10pm.*

Joe Watty's Pub, Kilronan, **t** (099) 61155 (*inexpensive*). Good chowders. *Summer only.*

Dinner and Sleeping on Inishmore

Johnston–Heron Kilmurvey House, Kilronan, **t** (099) 61218 (*moderate–inexpensive*). A highly recommended place to unwind, an old stone house with friendly owners. 20mins' walk from Dún Aonghasa. Good, simple meals are served.

Man of Aran Cottage, overlooking Kilmurvey Bay, **t** (099) 61301, *manofaran@ eircom.net* (*moderate–inexpensive*). This cottage appeared in the famous film before it became a B&B. The owners are enthusiastic organic gardeners.

Mainistir House Hostel, Kilronan, Inishmore, **t** (099) 61322 (*inexpensive*). Great value accommodation. Multilingual, friendly atmosphere, good music and an excellent restaurant with wonderful vegetarian buffets, but be sure to book and turn up for 8pm, for it disappears fast.

Dun Aengus Hostel, on the beach at Kilmurvey, Kilronan, **t** (099) 61318 (*inexpensive*).

Day 6: Galway City

Morning: From Rossaveal, continue on the R336 east for about 20 miles to **Galway City**, one of the fastest-growing cities in Europe, with a unique mixture of Celtic tradition and cosmopolitan modernity. The city itself is small enough to walk around in a day. The planned 18th-century part centres around Eyre Square, where the gardens are dedicated to John F. Kennedy. The liveliest part of Galway is the medieval centre, with narrow streets winding down from Eyre Square to the river. Shop Street/High Street/Quay Street is the spine of the district, lined with the city's most popular bars, restaurants and shops. Fragments of buildings and mutilated stone merchant houses still exist among the fast-food signs and modern shop fronts; go and seek out the animal carvings and the fine doorways and windows that have survived. *See* also pp.99–104.

Lunch: In Galway City, *see* below.

Afternoon: Galway City has plenty to see to keep you busy all day. The **Church of St Nicholas** in Market Street is rather attractive, and worth a visit for its fine carvings; you may hear the eight bells peal. No.8 Bowling Green, close by, is the **Nora Barnacle House Museum** (*open May–Sept Mon–Sat 10–5; out of season on request; adm*), once the home of James Joyce's wife. You might also visit the **Galway City Museum** (*open Wed–Sun 11–1 and 2–5; adm*) for its displays on Galway history and folk life, or the **Kenny Art Gallery** in the high street.

Dinner and Sleeping: In Galway City, *see* below. In the morning you can head straight back to Knock, about 1½ hours on the N17, to catch your plane, or back to Westport.

Day 6

Lunch in Galway City

The Malt House, High Street, t (091) 567866 (*inexpensive*). Excellent soups and snacks.

McDonagh's Seafood House, 22 Quay Street, t (091) 565001 (*inexpensive*). Excellent eat-in or takeaway fish and chips.

Goya's, 2/3 Kiwan's Lane, t (091) 567010 (*inexpensive*). Famous for its fabulous cakes and baked goods, but now also a café and busy lunch place serving appetising fare.

Dinner in Galway City

The Archway, 3 Victoria Place, t (091) 563693 (*expensive*). Formal, calm restaurant serving very good classic French food – duck *confit*, *foie gras*, rich sauces, *crème brûlée* – in elegant surroundings. *Open Tues–Sat.*

Tigh Neachtain, 17 Cross Street, t (091) 592189 (*moderate–inexpensive*). One of Galway's oldest pubs, unchanged inside since 1894. Traditional music sessions. Dinner is in the restaurant, upstairs.

Nimmos, Long Walk, Spanish Arch, t (091) 561114 (*moderate–inexpensive*). You can either eat more formally upstairs or in the laid-back, rustic bar downstairs (there's not much difference in price) at this popular, buzzing wine bar-restaurant on the river. *Restaurant open Wed–Sun for dinner; wine bar open Tues–Sun dinner.*

Sleeping in Galway City

Great Southern Hotel, Eyre Square, t (091) 564041, *www.greatsouthernhotels.com* (*expensive*). Recently refurbished, rambling Victorian hotel with a rooftop swimming-pool. The restaurant serves good seafood.

Brennan's Yard Hotel, Merchant's Road, t (091) 568166, *www.brennansyardhotel.com* (*expensive–moderate*). Comfortable, friendly service and pretty bedrooms.

Forster Court, Forster Street, t (091) 564111, *www.forstercourthotel.com* (*moderate*). Comfortable new and modern hotel near the station. Good bar and restaurant.

See also pp.101–102.

Touring from Westport 2: Mayo

Day 1: Inlets and Islands

Morning: Take the N59 north then west from Westport through **Newport** to **Mulrany**. On the way are the many tranquil inlets of Clew Bay where nestle **Burrishoole**, a Dominican friary, and **Carrigahowley Castle**, one of the homes of Grace O'Malley. From Mulrany you head on to the Corraun Peninsula, which is a wild knob of land through which you can pass on the way to **Achill Island**; the single-track road is a fine introduction to the Island, with sleepy whitewashed cottages and the smell of burning turf. Achill is connected to the mainland by a bridge. Take the **Atlantic Drive**, signposted as you leave the little hamlet of Achill Sound beside the causeway. You pass a ruined 12th-century church and then a tower house, Kildownet, supposed to have belonged to Grace O'Malley. The road follows the line of the shore round the south tip and passes **Achillbeg Island**, which contains the remains of a hermitage.

Lunch: In Dooega or Keel, on Achill Island, *see* below.

Afternoon: South of **Keel**, stop at the **Cliffs of Menawn**, wrought by the sea into fantastical shapes. Further on, **Keem Bay** is a sandy cove obvious from the road, where you may spot a basking shark. Continue to **Doogort**, a fishing hamlet in the shadow of Slievemore Mountain and a former Protestant missionary outpost dating from the 19th century. On the way, you'll pass **Slievemore deserted village**, on the road between Keel and Dugort on the lower slopes of Slievemore.

Dinner and Sleeping: On Achill or back in Mulrany, *see* below.

Day 1

Lunch in Dooega
Lavelle's Seaside House, t (098) 45116 (*inexpensive*). The end of the Atlantic Drive. Pub meals.

Lunch in Keel
Calvey's Restaurant, t (098) 43158 (*moderate–inexpensive*). Good vegetarian dishes, plus seafood, beef and lamb from their farm.

The Beehive, t (098) 43134 (*inexpensive*). Café/craft shop, salads, seafood and home baking. *Open daily 10–6pm.*

Masterson's, Golden Strand, Dugort, **t** (098) 984 7216 (*inexpensive*). Large quantities of fresh seafood. *Bar food 1–9pm; restaurant from 6.30pm.*

Dinner on Achill
McDowell's Hotel, Slievemore, Dugort, **t** (098) 43148 (*moderate*). Family-run, atmospheric.

Gray's Hotel, Dugort, **t** (098) 43244/43315 (*moderate–inexpensive*). Home cooking. *Dinner served at 7pm.*

Dinner in Mulrany
Carroll's Restaurant, t (098) 36236 (*moderate–inexpensive*). Traditional thatched cottage specializing in fresh local seafood. *Open June–Oct daily 6–10pm; Nov–May Thurs, Fri and Sat only.*

Cowley's Thatched Cottage Restaurant, **t** (098) 36287 (*moderate–inexpensive*). Local seafood, beef and lamb. *Open Mon–Sat 6–10pm, Sun 12.30–4pm.*

Sleeping on Achill Island
McDowell's Hotel, *see* left.

Gray's Hotel, Dugort, **t** (098) 43244/43315 (*moderate*). Traditional, friendly, family-run hotel.

Fuchsia Lodge, Keel, **t** (098) 43350 (*inexpensive*). B&B overlooking Meenawn Cliffs.

Sleeping in Mulrany
Moynish House, t (098) 36116 (*inexpensive*). Small guest house overlooking the strand.

Fern Hill, t (098) 36182 (*inexpensive*). Modern bed and breakfast.

Day 2: The Bogs of Erris

Morning: North from Mulrany the N59 runs through the **National Park** in Ballycroy, one of the largest expanses of peatland in Europe, a unique habitat for flora and fauna. At **Bangor Erris** turn left on to the R313, passing the Geesala Peninsula to the south, to **Belmullet**, one of the loneliest towns in Connacht, though on market day it is surprisingly busy. It stands on a slender piece of land just wide enough to prevent the Mullet from becoming an island.

Lunch: A picnic or lunch in Belmullet town or Carne, *see* below.

Afternoon: Explore the **Mullet Peninsula**. South to Blacksod Bay are the sheltered Blue Flag beaches of Elly Bay and Mullaghroe. Opposite Elly Bay is a sign for beach angling which takes you to the expansive Atlantic strand, seemingly on the edge of the world. Behind Faulmore beach, on the southern tip of the peninsula, lies St Deirbhile's church and holy well. From Blacksod you can hire a boat for sea angling or to take you out to the **Inishkea Islands**, inhabited until 1929 and home to many remains of early-Christian settlements. At Carne is the very popular golf links. West from Belmullet, the Annagh Marsh is an important breeding site for wading birds including the rare red-necked phalarope. In the north of the peninsula, Ballyglass lighthouse provides an interesting view of the Erris coastline with its distinctive hilltop settlements and strip agricultural fields sweeping down to the sea. From the trigonometric point on **Erris Head** the full panorama of the west coast islands and cliffs can be seen.

Dinner and Sleeping: On the Mullet or in Geesala, *see* below.

Day 2

Lunch in Belmullet or Carne

Evelyn's Bar and Restaurant, Carne Golf Club, Carne, t (097) 82123 (*moderate–inexpensive*). Large quantities of simple, fresh produce served overlooking the dunes. *Open 1–5pm.*

Western Strands Hotel, Main Street, Belmullet t (097) 81096 (*inexpensive*). Meat and two veg or seafood platter in the bar. *Open lunch 12.30–2.30.*

An Builin Blasta, Main Street, Belmullet (*inexpensive*). Soup and sandwiches.

Your other option (perhaps the best bet) is to buy a **picnic** before leaving Achill at Sweeney's in Achill Sound.

Dinner on the Mullet

Evelyn's Bar and Restaurant, Carne Golf Club, Carne, t (097) 82123 (*moderate–inexpensive*). Fresh meat and fish in large portions, simple and well cooked. *Open 6–8pm.*

Western Strands Hotel, Main Street, t (097) 81096 (*inexpensive*). *See left. Open for dinner 7–8.45pm.*

Sleeping on the Mullet

Barnagh House, Clogher, t (097) 81187 (*inexpensive*). Friendly, quiet bed and breakfast on the Mullet peninsula, near Elly Bay. Contact Mary Edwards.

Mill House, America Street, Belmullet, t (097) 81181 (*inexpensive*). Bed and breakfast in the middle of town. Contact Eileen Gaughan.

Dinner and Sleeping in Geesala

Teach Iorrais, t (097) 86888, *www.teachiorrais. com* (*moderate*). Recently refurbished and renovated hotel near the strands of the Geesala peninsula. (The Geesala Festival takes place in August, when it might be worth booking in advance.)

Day 3: The North Coast

Morning: Make your way up towards the hamlet of **Pollatomish** (*Poll a' tSomáis*) and take the unnumbered road west of **Barnatra** (*Barr na trá*) on the R314. The little harbour village of **Portacloy** (*Port a' Chloidh*) is surrounded by high cliffs. A visit to the Hackett & Turpin knitwear factory (*open Mon–Fri 10–5, Sat and Sun 2–5*) in **Carrowteige** (*Ceathru Thaidhg*) may secure you a designer bargain. At **Belderrig** start the **Ceide Fields**, where under the blanket bog lies an enclosed farming landscape dating from more than 5,000 years ago – the oldest in Europe. Further along the R314, **Ballycastle** has a rare atmosphere of calm for the villages in the west; the streets are wide and the air smells faintly of turf. The Ballinglen Arts Foundation (*t (096) 43184*) exhibits work by international artists in the Courthouse Gallery.
Lunch: In Ceide Fields or Ballycastle, *see* below.
Afternoon: From Ballycastle take the coast road out of town to **Downpatrick Head** with its impressive cliffs, blowholes and sea-stack, around which birds wheel. Further along the coast is the magnificent Lachan Strand. Back on the R314 to Killala, turn left before crossing the narrow bridge over the Cloonaghmore River to see ruined **Rathfran Abbey**. **Killala** town is very pretty and rather higgledy-piggledy. A few miles upstream is **Rosserk Abbey**, one of the finest Franciscan friaries in the country. Head south for **Ballina** (*see* p.87) or go on to **Crossmolina** to visit **Enniscoe Heritage Centre** (*open April–Nov Mon–Fri 9–6, Sat and Sun 1–6*) with its restored Victorian garden, 2 miles south of the town on the R315.
Dinner and Sleeping: In Ballina or Crossmolina, *see* below.

Day 3

Lunch in Ceide Fields
Ceide Fields Visitor Centre, t (096) 43325, www.heritageireland.ie (*inexpensive*). Soup and salads. *Open June–Sept daily 10–6, Mar–May and Oct–Nov daily 10–5.*

Lunch in Ballycastle
Mary's Cottage Kitchen, Main Street, t (096) 43361 (*inexpensive*). Fresh seafood and home baking. *Open daily 10–6.*

Sleeping in Ballina
Ridgepool Hotel, Barrett Street, t (096) 24600, f 24602 (*expensive–moderate*). Modern hotel with pleasant rooms overlooking the river.
Bartra House Hotel, Pearse Street, t (096) 22200, f 22111 (*moderate*). Cosy, friendly, well-established hotel.
Quay House, The Quay, t (096) 21208 (*inexpensive*). Bed and breakfast on the edge of the Moy harbour. Contact Mrs Peggy Melvin.

Dinner in Ballina
Crockets on the Quay, The Quay, t (096) 75930 (*moderate*). Popular restaurant, with a menu of international flavour. *Dinner 6–10.15.*
Dillon's Bar and Restaurant, Dillon Terrace, t (096) 72230 (*moderate*). Locally famous for salmon. *Bar food 12–8.30, restaurant open 6–10.*
Murphy Bros., Clare Street, t (096) 22702 (*inexpensive*). Good pub food. *Bar open 12.30–8.30; restaurant 6–9.*

Dinner and Sleeping in Crossmolina
Enniscoe House, Castlehill, near Crossmolina, Ballina, t (096) 31112, f 31773 (*expensive*). Georgian house set in parklands on the shores of Lough Conn. Grand, spacious rooms, log fires and superlative cooking. The grounds include an ornamental garden and an organic garden (*adm*). Enniscoe Heritage Centre adjoins the gardens. Boats and ghillies for the lough can be arranged. There are self-catering cottages available also for short lets.

Day 4: Along the River Moy

Morning: Take the N26 south to **Foxford**. The small town is known for salmon-fishing on the River Moy and for the Foxford Woollen Mills. The Foxford Woollen Mills Visitor Centre (*open Mon–Sat 10–6, Sun 2–6*) has tours of the working mill telling the story of the indomitable Mother Agnes who established the mill in 1892. The mill shop sells examples of the rugs, tweed and scarves made there. This is also the birthplace of Admiral Brown, who founded the Argentinian navy. Along the R318 are beaches along the shore of Lough Cullin and then **Pontoon Bridge**, where the Loughs Conn and Cullin connect and fishermen try their luck with the salmon.

Lunch: In Pontoon, *see* below.

Afternoon: Return to Foxford and take the N58 to **Straide**, the birthplace of Michael Davitt (1846–1906), who started the Land League. The Michael Davitt National Memorial Museum (*open Mar–Oct daily 10–6; adm*) here has a large collection of documents and photographs relating to the League. Opposite is a ruined Franciscan abbey, founded in the mid-13th century, which has a wonderful series of sculptures; the *Pietà* is especially good. Continue on towards Castlebar on the N5, visiting the **Museum of Country Life** (*open Tues–Sat 10–5, Sun 2–5*) in Thurlough Park. The modern museum sits alongside the lake in the grounds of the old Thurlough Park House of 1865. The museum houses a broad range of objects, photographs and film drawn from the national folklife collection, which shows the culture and livelihoods of past rural life. Continue on to **Castlebar**, a vibrant shopping centre.

Dinner and Sleeping: In Castlebar, *see* below.

Day 4

Lunch in Pontoon

Pontoon Bridge Hotel, t (094) 925 6120/ 56699, *fishing@pontoonbridge.com* (*expensive– moderate*). Simple three-star hotel, popular with fishermen. Bar food is served in a conservatory overlooking the lake.

Healy's Hotel, t (094) 925 6443 (*moderate*). Quiet place with a lovely setting on the shore of the lough; great for anglers. Good pub food is served in the lounge.

There are also cafés at Foxford Woollen Mill and the Museum of Country Life.

Dinner in Castlebar

An Carraig, Chapel Street, t (094) 902 6159 (*moderate*). Traditional Irish fresh meat and fish. *Open 6–10pm; closed Mon.*

Al Muretto, Tucker Street, t (094) 902 5954 (*moderate–inexpensive*). Cheerful restaurant serving real Italian food. *Open Mon–Sat 12.30–2.30 and 6–11, Sun 1–10.*

Tulsi, Lower Charles Street, t (094) 902 5066 (*inexpensive*). Indian restaurant, in refurbished church, with range of vegetarian options. *Open Mon–Sat 6–11.30, Sun 1–11.*

The Olive Tree, Newtown Street, t (094) 902 3376 (*inexpensive*). Authentic Eastern Mediterranean food. *Open Mon–Sat 9–8, Sun 12–6; kitchen closed Fri 1.15–2.15pm.*

Sleeping in Castlebar

Breaffy House, Breaffy Road, t (094) 902 2033 (*moderate*). Large hotel in parkland.

The Welcome Inn Hotel, New Antrim Street, t (094) 902 2288 (*moderate*). A busy and friendly hotel.

Daly's Hotel, The Mall, t (094) 902 1961 (*moderate–inexpensive*). Old hotel on the green. Charming but rather threadbare.

Silvar, Ballinrobe Road, t (094) 902 2096 (*inexpensive*). Modern house with panoramic view of Croagh Patrick. Contact Mrs. Marion Silke.

Primrose Cottage, Pontoon Road, t (094) 902 1247 (*inexpensive*). Modern B&B.

Day 5: Limestone and Lakes

Morning: Head south on the N84 towards Ballinrobe. Eight miles out of Castlebar turn off to **Ballintubber Abbey** (*open all year*), the only abbey founded by an Irish king that has survived intact (*see* p.86). Nearby, at Mary Moran's Cottage, a crafts and information centre, you can visit the **Celtic Furrow Folklore Exhibition** (*open June–Aug 10–5*). Continue on the N84 south, passing Lough Carra. At Ballinrobe, take the R334 through The Neale and on to **Cong**. Cong was a busy place in Neolithic times; you can see a stone circle off the R345 and the Giant's Grave west of Cong. Cong lies on porous limestone, which creates interesting natural features such as the Pigeon Hole and Kelly's Cave, and also the man-made canal, which remains dry.

Lunch: In Cong.

Afternoon: Cong is a friendly place, with a reconstructed medieval market cross, a lovely ancient abbey and an attractive modern Catholic church with stained glass by Harry Clarke, all down by the tree-lined river. The Quiet Man Cottage (*open Mar–Nov daily 10–5; adm*) was used as a set in the 1951 film with John Wayne. They had to bring electricity to the town to make filming possible. The beautiful and restful grounds of Ashford Castle and Cong Wood can be approached on foot from the abbey. For a scenic drive take the R345 alongside Lough Corrib to Maam and then circle round east to Lough Naffoey, Lough Mask and back to **Clonbur**. Lough Corrib Cruises (*t (094) 954 6029*) visit **Inchagoill Island** monastic site (from Ashford Castle) and offer a pre-dinner 'Traditional Irish Hour Cruise' with music and bar.

Dinner and Sleeping: In Cong or Clonbur. Head back to Westport via Ballinrobe.

Day 5

Lunch in Cong

The Quiet Man Coffee Shop, Main Street, t (094) 954 6034 (*inexpensive*). Pleasant café with soup, sandwiches and home baking. *Open 10.30–5.*

Hungry Monk Café, Abbey Street, t (094) 954 6866 (*inexpensive*). Café with internet access, soup and salads. *Open April–Sept 10–6; Mar–Oct till 5; closed Mon.*

Danagher's, Abbey Street, t (092) 954 5988 (*inexpensive*). Traditional pub food in a lively bar. *Bar food till 9.15pm.*

Dinner and Sleeping in Cong

Ashford Castle, t (094) 954 6003, *www.ashford.ie* (*luxury*). Stay and dine in sumptuous, grand surroundings.

Dolmen House, Drumsheel, t (094) 954 6466 (*inexpensive*). Modern B&B on a hill north of town.

Micilin's Restaurant, Main Street, t (094) 954 6655 (*moderate–inexpensive*). A pretty little restaurant serving traditional food with vegetarian options available. *Open 6–9pm.*

Dinner and Sleeping in Clonbur

Fairhill House, Main Street, t (094) 954 6176 (*moderate*). Recently upgraded hotel with restrained, tasteful interiors and comfortable rooms.

Ballykine House, Cong Road, t (094) 954 6150 (*inexpensive*). Old stone cottage B&B with lakeside and woodland walks around. Contact Mrs Ann Lambe.

John J. Burke and Sons Restaurant, Main Street, t (094) 954 6175 (*moderate–inexpensive*). Large, dining bar with character. Specializes in seafood. *Open lunch 12–6; dinner 6.30–9.*

Galway City

Galway is a bustling city which has been the centre of trade for the whole of Connacht since the 13th century, despite a decline in the 18th and 19th centuries. The wine trade with Spain and the enterprise of its citizens has given it an independence and character which marks it out from the other provincial towns of Ireland. In recent times, that character has become even more pronounced. With new high-tech industries and its growing prominence as a tourist centre, Galway has become the boom town of Ireland, and one of the fastest-growing cities in Europe. The mixture of Celtic tradition and cosmopolitan modernity make it a unique place indeed.

There has always been some sort of settlement here because of the ford on the Corrib River, but it never achieved any importance until the arrival of the Anglo-Normans. The de Burgos built a castle here in 1226. By the end of the 13th century many Welsh and English families had been encouraged to settle here, and they built themselves strong stone walls to keep out the now dispossessed and disgruntled de Burgos and the wild O'Flahertys. There were 14 main families and they became known as the tribes of Galway. Fiercely independent, they created an Anglo-Norman oasis in the middle of hostile Connacht. In 1549 they placed this inscription over the west gate: 'From the fury of the O'Flaherties, good Lord deliver us.' (It is no longer there.) They also put out edicts controlling the presence of the native Irish in the town. An Irish settlement thus grew up on the west side of the Corrib following completely different traditions. They spoke only Gaelic and earned a livelihood through fishing. The settlement is now renowned for the Claddagh Ring, which you will notice on the fingers of many Irish exiles: a circle joined by two hands clasping a heart, often used as a marriage ring. Nowadays the romantic but poverty-stricken Claddagh settlement which appealed to Victorian travellers is gone, and the thatched and whitewashed one-storey cottages have been replaced by a modern housing scheme. The chief tribe of Galway was the Lynch family and there is a colourful story about the Lynch who was mayor in 1493. The tribe had grown prosperous through trading in wine with Spain and Bordeaux; this Lynch had the son of a Spanish merchant staying in his house who aroused the jealousy of Walter, his son. Walter stabbed the young guest to death, but because he was so popular nobody could be found to hang him. So his father, having pronounced the sentence, did the deed himself and, filled with sadness, became a recluse. Near the Church of St Nicholas, in a built-up Gothic doorway on Market Street, there is a tablet commemorating the event, which gave the verb 'to lynch' to the English language.

The City Centre

Galway was an important administrative centre during the days of the British, from the 17th century until Independence. It now has a strong cultural identity, with its own university where courses are followed in Irish and English, a large technical college and vigorous and high-quality theatre, traditional music and song. The city itself is small enough to walk around in a day. The planned 18th-century part centres around **Eyre Square**, which you come into immediately when approaching the city

Getting There and Around

By Air

Galway Airport handles flights to London Luton, Birmingham, Liverpool and Manchester via Aer Arann (*see* **Travel**, pp.6–7). There is a bus connection from the rail/bus station in Galway City that is scheduled to meet flights. **Galway Airport**, Carnmore, t (091) 755569, f 752876, *www.galwayairport.com*.

By Rail

Galway station, Station Rd, t (091) 562730, *www. irishrail.ie*.

By Bus

Buses depart from the train station, right in the centre off Eyre Square. Galway City is one of Bus Eireann's main hubs, and you can get to almost every town in Galway and around. **Galway Bus Information**, t (091) 562000. **Bus Eireann**, t (091) 562000, *www.buseireann. ie*. Also offers day tours around Connemara and the Burren from Galway City in summer.

Car Hire

Windsor Rent-A-Car, Monivea Rd, Ballybrit, Galway, t (091) 770707, f 752 368, *carhire@ windsor-galway.ie*.
Murrays Europcar, 9 Headford Rd, Galway, t (091) 562222, *www.europcar.ie*
Car Rental Ireland, drop offs in Galway City or Galway Airport, t (045) 531066, *www.car-rental-ireland.com*.
Thrifty Car Rental Ireland, pick up from Galway Airport or Galway town, Irish Republic t 1 800 515 800, UK t 0800 973 163.

Bike Hire

Europa Bicycles, Earls Island, Galway City (also arranges tours), t (091) 563355.
Galway Cycle Hire, Victoria Place, Eyre Square, Galway City, t (091) 61600.
Chieften Cycles, Victoria Place, Merchants Road, Galway, t (091) 567454.

Festivals

April: **Cuirt Literary Festival**, Galway Arts Centre, Galway City, t (091) 565886, *www. galwayartscentre.ie*.

May: **Galway Early Music Festival**, Galway City, t (087) 930 5506, *www.galwayearlymusic. com*, *info@galwayearlymusic.com*.
June: **Bloomsday**, Nora Barnacle House, Bowling Green, Galway City, t (091) 564743. Open-air readings from the works of James Joyce, 16 June.
July: **Galway Arts Festival**, t (091) 509700, *www.galwayartsfestival.ie*, *info@gaf.iol.ie*; **Galway Film** *Fleadh*, Town Hall Theatre, Galway City, t (091) 751655, *gafleadh@iol.ie*; **Galway Races**, 2 miles (3.2km) from the city at Ballybrit Racecourse, *www.galwayraces. com* – the most exciting meetings are held at the end of July.
Sept: **Galway Oyster Festival**, Galway City, t (091) 527282. Oyster-opening championship which attracts international participants. The whole affair snowballs into dances, dinners, shows and speeches from local worthies, and maybe a celebrity or two, *www.galwayoyster festival.ie*, t (091) 587992.

Tourist Information

Galway: *Aras Fáilte*, Forster Street, t (091) 537700, *info@irelandwest.ie*; *open all year*.

Shopping

Antiques

Antique shops cluster around Cross Street.
Cobwebs, 7 Quay Lane, t (091) 564388, *www. cobwebs-galway.com*.
Tempo Antiques, 9 Cross Street, t (091) 562282, *www.tempoantiques.com*.
Twice as Nice, 5 Quay Street, t (091) 566332.

Books

Charlie Byrnes Bookshop, Middle Street, t (091) 561766, *www.charliebyrne.com*.
Kenny's Bookshop & Art Galleries, High Street, t (091) 534760, *www.kennys.ie*.

Crafts

Fadu, Middle Street, t (091) 564429. Modern and traditional handmade pottery, wood, wrought iron and slate items.
Meadows & Byrne, Lower Abbeygate Street, t (091) 567776. Irishmade pottery and glassware, also waterproof oiled jackets.

Crystal

Galway Irish Crystal, Merlin Park, t (091) 757311. Heritage tours, a restaurant and showroom.

Delicacies

Goya's Fine Confectionery, 3 Kirwans Lane, t (091) 567010, *www.goyas.ie*.

McCambridge's Grocery, 38 Shop Street, t (091) 562259. Cheese, coffee and preserves.

Sheridan's Cheesemongers, 14–16 Churchyard Lane, t (091) 564829, *www.sheridanscheese mongers.com*. If it's a nice day and you feel like a picnic (on the river by the Spanish Arch, for example), stock up here on the best of Irish and continental cheeses, fantastic hams, salamis, olives and breads, organic fruit and veg...

Jewellery

Claddagh Jewellers, Eyre Square Centre, Eyre Square,, t (091) 563282, or (US only) t 1800 473 3259, *www.claddagh-jewellery.co.uk*.

Markets

Saturday Morning Market, by St Nicholas' Cathedral. Sells cheese, herbs, vegetables, sausages and home-made jams.

Traditional Music

Zhivago's, 5–6 Shop Street, t (091) 564193, *www.musicireland.com*.

Mulligan, 5 Middle Street Court, t (091) 564961. Traditional and folk music.

Tweeds and Knitwear

Galway Woollen Market, 21 High Street, t (091) 562491.

O'Máille's, 16 High Street, t (091) 562696.

Sports and Activities

Fishing

Freeney's, 19 High Street, t (091) 562609.

Duffy's, 5 Mainguard Street, t (091) 562367.

Galway Fishery, Nun's Island, t (091) 562388.

See *www.fishireland.com* (buy Irish salmon licences online).

Golf

Galway Golf Club, Blackrock, Renville, Oranmore, t (091) 790503, *www.gbaygolf.* *com*. 18-hole par 72 championship golf course with breathtaking views of Clare Hills and Aran Islands.

Horse-racing

For details of the Curragh Races contact the tourist office in Galway, t (091) 537700.

Where to Stay

There are B&Bs galore in Salthill, including a large selection on Fr. Griffin Road, within easy walking distance of the centre.

Great Southern Hotel, Eyre Square, t (091) 564041, *www.greatsouthernhotels.com* (*expensive*). Recently refurbished, rambling, Victorian hotel with rooftop swimming-pool. The restaurant serves good seafood.

Brennan's Yard Hotel, Merchant's Road, t (091) 568166, *www.brennansyardhotel.com* (*expensive–moderate*). Comfortable, friendly service and pretty bedrooms.

Ardilaun House Hotel, Taylors Hill, Galway, t 521433 (*expensive–moderate*). Large mansion house converted into attractive hotel with wooded grounds; leisure club with pool, sauna and jacuzzi. Good food.

Galway Harbour Hotel, The Harbour, t 569466, *www.harbour.ie* (*expensive–moderate*). Chic-boutique hotel on the waterfront, with 96 individually-styled rooms .

Forster Court, Forster Street, t (091) 564111, *www.forstercourthotel.com* (*moderate*). Comfortable new and modern hotel near the station. Good bar and restaurant.

Killeen House, Bushypark, t 091 524179, f 528065, *www.killeenhousegalway.com* (*moderate*). Delightful, award-winning guest house, set in beautiful grounds on the edge of Lough Corrib, 4 miles out of town. Catherine Doyle has filled her house with antiques; guest rooms are supremely comfortable and lacking in nothing from a silver tray beautifully laid for morning tea to the Radio Times open at the right page.

Hotel Spanish Arch, Quay St, t 569600, *www.spanisharchhotel.ie* (*moderate–inex-pensive*). With 20 en-suite bedrooms, bar food and live entertainment weekly.

Skeffington Arms Hotel, 28 Eyre Square, t (091) 563173, *www.skeffington.ie* (*moderate*). Small, central,family-run with restaurant.

Barnacle's Quay Street Hostel, 10 Quay Street, t (091) 568644, *www.barnacles.ie/quaystreet* (*inexpensive*). In the centre of the action.

Darcy's B&B, 92 Fr. Griffin Road, t 589505 (*inexpensive*). New and good, with parking.

Eating Out

The Archway, 3 Victoria Place, t (091) 563693 (*expensive*). Formal, calm restaurant serves very good classic French food in elegant surroundings. *Open Tues–Sat.*

Oyster Room, Great Southern Hotel, t (091) 564041 (*expensive*). Good seafood.

Park Room Restaurant, Forster Street, Eyre Square, t (091) 564924 (*expensive*). One of Galway's finest restaurants since 1974.

Skeff Restaurant, Skeffington Arms Hotel, 8 Eyre Square, t (091) 563173 (*moderate*). Carvery lunches, sandwiches and pub food.

Cactus Jack's, Courthouse Lane, Quay St, t (091) 563838, *www.cactus-jacks.net* (*moderate*). Heady Irish-Cajun-TexMex fusion; live music, and they stay open late.

Tigh Neachtain, 17 Cross Street, t (091) 592189 (*moderate–inexpensive*). One of Galway's oldest pubs, unchanged inside since 1894. Traditional music sessions. Dinner is in the restaurant, upstairs.

Nimmos, Long Walk, Spanish Arch, t (091) 561114 (*moderate–inexpensive*). Eat upstairs or in the laid-back, rustic bar downstairs at this popular, buzzing wine bar-restaurant on the river. *Restaurant open Wed–Sun for dinner; wine bar open Tues–Sun dinner*

Goya's, 2–3 Kiwan's Lane, t (091) 567010 (*inexpensive*). Goya's is famous for its fabulous cakes and baked goods, but it has now expanded into a café and busy lunch place.

Da Tang Noodle House, 2 Middle Street, t (091) 561443 (*inexpensive*). The real thing.

Food For Thought, 5 Abbeygate Street, t (091) 565854 (*inexpensive*). Vegetarian restaurant beside a health food shop.

Fat Freddy's, The Halls, Quay Street, t (091) 567279 (*inexpensive*). First-rate pizza and some innovative dishes; always packed.

The Malt House, High Street, t (091) 567866 (*inexpensive*). Excellent soups and snacks.

McDonagh's Seafood House, 22 Quay Street, t (091) 565001, *www.mcdonaghs.net* (*inexpensive*). Eat-in or take-away fish and chips.

McSwiggan's, 3 Eyre Street, t (091) 568917 (*inexpensive*). Seafood and veggie dishes.

Entertainment and Nightlife

Jazz

Blue Note, 3 William St West, t (091) 589116. Beer garden, dance bar and Sunday brunch.

King's Head, 5 High Street, *www.thekingshead.ie*, t (091) 566630. Sunday jazz brunch.

Quays Bar, Quay Street, t (091) 568347.

Theatre

Druid Theatre, Chapel Lane, t (091) 568660, *www.druidtheatre.com*. Produces very exciting and pioneering performances

Taibhdhearc na Gaillimhe, Middle St, t (091) 562024/530291, *www.antaibhdhearc.com*. Interesting Irish-language theatre as well as traditional music and bilingual folk.

Town Hall Theatre, Courthouse Square, t (091) 569777, *www.townhalltheatregalway.com*. Established in the 1880s: drama, concerts and musicals, etc.

Traditional Music

Ballad-singing and traditional music in the local bars. During the summer months try:

The *An Púcán* Bar, 11 Forster Street, t (091) 561528. Nightly; Galway's best-known Irish-language pub.

The Crane Bar, 2 Sea Road, t (091) 587419. Nightly.

Lisheen Bar, Bridge Street, t (091) 563804. Intimate atmosphere; traditional Irish food.

Quays Bar, Quay St, t (091) 568347. Some of the best traditional Irish music in the city.

The *Roisin Dubh*, 8 Dominick Street Upper, t (091) 586540, *www.roisindubh.net*. Happening venue with 450 live gigs a year: from Irish traditional to solos by lead singers from Donovan, The Doors, Led Zeppelin and Thin Lizzy.

The Snug, William Street. Medieval stone-clad pub.

Taaffes, 19a Shop Street, t (091) 564066. Nightly.

Taylor's, 7 Dominick Street Upper, t (091) 587239. Popular and cosy, with wood panelled interior and beer garden.

from the east. The Galway tourist office, *Aras Fáilte*, in Victoria Park, is just a block away, close to the railway and bus station. The **Gardens** in Eyre Square are dedicated to John F. Kennedy, who received the freedom of the city only a few months before his assassination. In the gardens are captured Russian cannons, brought home from the Crimean War by a famous regiment in the British Army, called the Connaught Rangers, as well as a fine steel sculpture by Eamon O'Doherty based on the sails of the Galway 'hookers' or fishing boats and a statue to Padraic O'Conaire (1883–1928), who wrote short stories in Gaelic and pioneered the revival of Gaelic literature.

The liveliest part of Galway is the medieval centre, with narrow streets winding down from Eyre Square to the river. **Shop Street/High Street/Quay Street** is the spine of the district; lined with the city's most popular bars, restaurants and shops, the area jumps day and night. Fragments of buildings and mutilated stone merchant houses still exist among the fast-food signs and modern shop fronts. You have to go and seek out the strange and memorable animal carvings and the fine doorways and windows that have survived. The best example is Lynch's Castle in Shop Street, which now houses a branch of the Allied Irish Bank.

The **Church of St Nicholas** in Market Street is rather attractive, and worth a visit for its fine carvings. You may hear the eight bells peal, which make a lovely sound over the city. A proud tradition exists that Christopher Columbus stopped at the church for Mass on his first voyage to America. No.8 Bowling Green, close by, is the **Nora Barnacle House Museum** (*t (091) 564743, www.norabarnacle.com; open Jun-Aug Mon–Sat; adm*),, once the home of James Joyce's wife. The little museum contains memorabilia of the couple and their links with County Galway. A Saturday market of organic vegetables, German sourdough breads and local cheeses is held in its shadow, with an atmosphere that revives shades of medieval Galway. The modern **Catholic cathedral**, beside the salmon weir on the river, is an imposing hotchpotch of styles and dominates the skyline. It was completed in 1965. The weir is in fact one of the nicest places to go and idle away the hours. Shoals of salmon making their way up to the spawning grounds of Lough Corrib lie in the clear river – the only entrance from the sea to 1,200 miles (1,930km) of lakes.

Elizabeth I confirmed the city's charter in 1579, and appointed the mayor as admiral with jurisdiction over Galway Bay and the Aran Islands. The town was fully walled with 14 towers, but now there is only a fragment left near the quay, called the **Spanish Arch**. The office of mayor, which had been in decline and abolished in 1840, was restored and given statutory recognition in 1937. The mayor's silver sword and great mace dating from the early 17th century are on display in the **Bank of Ireland** (*open banking hours*) at No.19 Eyre Square. The mace, a fine piece of Galway silver, was returned to the city by the Hearst Foundation in the USA in 1961.

Near the Spanish Arch is the **Galway City Museum** (*t (091) 567641; open Mon–Sat 10–1 and 2–5; adm, closed for renovation until 2005*). It has displays on the history of Galway and folk life. The **Kenny Art Gallery** in the high street holds exhibitions of ceramics, sculptures and paintings by contemporary artists. The **Grain Store** on Lower Abbeygate Street shows work in wood and metal. The **University of Galway Gallery** (*t (091) 24411*) also holds occasional exhibitions. The local newspapers, the *Galway*

Advertiser, Connaught Tribune and the *Galway Sentinel* (which is free), as well as the tourist office, will have details of what's on. Good traditional music is played in the city's bars, and the atmosphere can verge on the raucous. Galway City is always a lively place, partly due to the youthfulness of its inhabitants, but the week of the famous **Galway Races**, in late July, the **Arts Festival** (also July) and the **Oyster Festival** in September bring an extra sparkle and sense of enjoyment to the place.

Salthill is a seaside resort which merges with the city. Many local people holiday there or come on day trips. Hotels, fun-parks and bingo halls line the seafront; it's a bit run-down, like many old seaside resorts all over the British Isles, but at night the place lights up as the strip opens up its clubs and discos, catering primarily to the population of Galway City. Children can splash about all day at **Leisureland** (*t (091) 527777, www.galwayleisureland.com; open daily 8–10; adm*), with rides and amusements, or visit the new museum, **Atlantaquaria** (*t (091) 580734*), in the same complex.

Day Trip or Overnighter from Galway City

The Aran Islands

The people and the islands of Aran were described sensitively by the playwright John Millington Synge in his notebooks and in his play *Riders to the Sea*. If you read them, you will long to visit these windswept islands in Galway Bay. Liam O'Flaherty, another great Irish writer, was born here in 1897, two years before Synge first came to the islands. He describes the hard life of the island people in his short stories, *The Landing* and *Going into Exile*. Tim Robinson, a stranger who came and lived on the islands a few years ago, wrote a wonderful book called *Stones of Aran*, well worth searching out in Kenny's bookshop in Galway City. The Aran Islands today are much the same as they were in Synge's time, although in the summer the irritations that tourism always brings diminishes some of their peace, particularly on Inishmore.

There are three Aran Islands: **Inishmore** (*Inis Mór;* 'Great Island'), **Inisheer** (*Inis Óirr;* 'East Island') and **Inishmaan** (*Inis Meáin;* 'Middle Island'). Most tourists come for the rugged beauty, the sweeping views and to visit the prehistoric and early monastic ruins. The landscape is similar to that in the Burren in County Clare and is made up of porous limestone. You will notice as you approach by boat that it is eroding into great steps. Gentian, maidenhair fern, wild roses and saxifrage blossom on the 11,000 acres (4,450ha) which make up the three islands, but only 6 per cent of the land is rated as productive. The soil has been built up over the years with layer upon layer of seaweed, animal manure and sand from the beaches, so that these limestone rocks can support a few cattle, donkeys and rows of potatoes.

The Aran Islands currently have a population of approximately 1,450, with 900 on Inishmore, 300 on Inishmaan and 250 on Inisheer. The young people tend to disappear to the mainland or further for jobs, and seldom come back.

There are seven **stone forts** on the islands; four on Inishmore, two on Inishmaan and one on Inisheer, all believed to go back as far as the early Celtic period 2,500 years ago. Mythology states that they were built by the Fir Bolg after they were defeated by the Tuatha Dé Danaan at the Battle of Moytura. The people who lived on the islands became Christians in the 5th century, converted by St Enda. Monastic schools were set up which became famous over the centuries, and people came from far and wide to study there. In the Middle Ages, the O'Flahertys of Galway and the O'Briens of Clare fought endlessly over the ownership of the islands. The English ended the dispute by building and garrisoning a fort, **Arkin Castle**, in the late 16th century. It is along the shore of the bay as you arrive at Inishmore, and was occupied at various times by Royalists, Cromwellians, Jacobites and Williamites.

Ask locally about the beaches, and about sea-angling, which can be done from a curragh or the cliffs. Every summer evening there are ballad sessions in the pubs.

Inishmore

Inishmore is the largest of the islands, being about 8 miles (12.9km) long. When you get off the steamer you can hire either a bicycle or a sidecar and jarvey to see the sights. The capital, **Kilronan**, has become rather touristy, but the people remain cheerful and courteous. **Ionad Arann** (*t (099) 61355; open June–Aug 10–7; April–May and Sept–Oct 11–5; Nov–Mar by appointment; adm*) is a museum of folk life in Kilronan, with material about the Gaelic League. Kilronan is linked by road to a chain of villages, and if you want to get to a friendly drinking-house after the gruelling voyage, Daly's pub in **Killeany** (*Cill Einne*) is the place. Amongst the fields separated by loose stone walls (the effect is rather maze-like), you will come upon ancient ecclesiastical sites and the forts. The people of Aran, who could be descended from the Fir Bolgs, never bother with gates – they are too expensive to import. Instead, if they are herding livestock through different fields, they take down the stone walls and then calmly build them up again when the animals have got through.

Dún Aonghasa or Dun Aengus (*t (099) 61008; open Mar–Oct daily 10–6; Nov–Feb daily 10–4*) is on the south coast, on the summit of a hill which rises straight up from the sea. It covers some 11 acres (4.5ha) and consists of several concentric ramparts, 18ft high and 13ft deep (5.5m by 4m), which form a semi-circle with the two edges ending on the brink of the cliffs that fall nearly 350ft (107m) to the Atlantic. The approach is designed to cripple you if you do not advance with caution, for outside the middle wall, sharp spars of stone set closely in the ground form a *chevaux de frise*. Be warned that the site is not enclosed and you could quite easily fall from the cliffs.

Dun Eoghanacha, another stone ring-fort, is to the south of the village of Onaght on the northeast coast, and is circular in shape. The fields to the west and south are full of ancient remains. One and a half miles (2.5km) west of Killeany is **Dubh Chathair** – some of which must have disappeared over the steep cliffs, for it was once even larger than Dun Aonghasa. At Kilchorna, Monasterkieran and Teampall an Cheathrair are more evocative ruins. **Monasterkieran**, just northwest of Kilronan, has the ruins of a transitional period church, early cross slabs, an ancient sundial and a holy well. **Kilchorna**, about a mile southwest of Kilronan, has two *clochans*. **Teampall an Cheathrair** ('The Church of the Four Comely Saints') is near the village of Cowrugh. It is a small 15th-century building outside which four flagstones mark the supposed

Getting There

By Air
Aer Arann flies to all three islands, with daily flights (up to 25 times a day in peak season) to all three islands year round from Connemara Airport in Inverin (19 miles west of Galway; shuttle buses connect to the city centre). It takes less than 10mins' actual flying time; rates are twice the cost of the ferry (c. €44) – though their special packages (from c. €69) which include a night's B&B accommodation on the island make it a much better deal. They will also arrange scenic flights for groups.
Aer Arann, Dominick Street, Galway, t (091) 593034, www.aerarannislands.ie.

By Sea
Three companies operate ferries out to all three of the islands; the main port of call is Kilronan on Inishmore.
Inis Mór Ferries, 29 Forster St, t (091) 566535, www.queenofaran2.com. Owned and operated by the islanders themselves, the Queen of Aran II offers a year-round daily service to Inishmore from Rossaveal: sailings start at 10.30am – a shuttle bus departs from 29 Forster St, opposite Galway Tourist Office; tickets available at either, adult ferry return €20, coach return €6.
Island Ferries, 4 Forster St, t (091) 568903, www.aranislandferries.com. Four boats, 2–4 sailings a day year round from Rossaveal to Inishmoor, or 1–2 sailings a day to Inishmaan and Inishmoor (includes a coach connection leaving from Kinlay House, Merchants Rd, Galway 1hr before sailing). Sailings take 40mins. Timetables and bookings from the Galway tourist office, t (091) 537700.
Doolin Ferries, t (091) 567283/567676, www.doolinferries.com. Services to all three islands, June–Sept daily, departing from Galway docks at 10am, and departing from Aran at 5pm; in winter Tues, Thurs and Sat only. Return tickets about €20.

Getting Around

By Minibus
There is now a regular public bus service on Inishmore, leaving from Kilronan, that can take you to most of the villages. Besides these, a number of islanders offer inexpensive minibus tours of the island from Kilronan. For Inishmoor call Noel Malcolm, t (087) 778 2775.

By Bike or Jaunting Car
Look on the pier as the ferry arrives; there is usually no need to book.
Michael Mullens Bicycle Hire, t (099) 61132.
K&M Bicyle Hire, The Pier, Kilronan, t (099) 61303.
Michael Hernan, Inishmore, t (099) 61131. Jaunting cars.

Pony Trekking
Peak season only, t (099) 61371.

Festivals

June–July: Festival of Saints Peter and Paul, Inishmore. Music and curragh races.
June–Aug: Ragus, Irish music, singing and hard shoe dancing, t (099) 61515, Halla Ronain, www.ragustheshow.net.
July: Traditional Echoes in Song and Dance, Inishmore, t (099) 61424, www.irish-culture.ch. A ten-day programme of set/ceili dancing, old Gaelic songs, boat trips, walks.

Tourist Information

Inis Mor / Inishmoor Tourist Office, t (099) 61263, f 61420, www.visitaranislands.com.
Ireland West Tourism: Galway, t (091) 537700. Can book accommodation on the islands.

Shopping

Snámara Craftshop (Islanders' Co-operative), Main St, Kilronan, Inishmore, t (099) 61359.
Inis Meain Knits, Inishmaan, t (099) 73009, inishmeain@iol.ie. Probably the nicest traditional jumpers in the country.
Aran Knitwear Co-op, Inishmore, t (099) 61140. For Aran sweaters.
Aran Knitting, Lurgan Village, Inisheer, t (099) 75101, www.aranknitting.com. Traditional Aran knits with craftshop.
Inis Meain Knitting Factory, Inishmaan, (Islanders' Co-operative), t (099) 73010.

Where to Stay

There are plenty of choices on Inishmore, mostly in and around Kilronan, but nevertheless in summer you'd do well to have a booking before you get on the boat. Some places outside Kilronan send people to meet visitors coming off the ferries.

Paul Williams, Inishmaan, t 0781 840 3210, *www.gmu58.dial.pipex.com, dr.p.williams@ btinternet.com (expensive–moderate)*. One of the oldest traditional thatched cottages on the island; perched on the highest point of Inishmaan.

Johnston–Heron Kilmurvey House, Kilronan, Inishmore, t (099) 61218, f 61397 *(moderate–inexpensive)*. A highly recommended place to unwind, an old stone house with friendly owners. Lies 20mins' walk from Dún Aonghasa. Good, simple meals are served.

Man of Aran Cottage, overlooking Kilmurvey Bay, Inishmore, t (099) 61301, f 61324, *mano-faran@eircom.net (moderate–inexpensive)*. This cottage appeared in the famous film before it became a B&B. The owners are enthusiastic organic gardeners.

Mainistir House Hostel, Kilronan, Inishmore, t (099) 61322 *(inexpensive)*. There are a number of hostels similar to this, with great value accommodation. Multilingual, friendly atmosphere, good music and an excellent vegetarian restaurant.

Dun Aengus Hostel, on the beach at Kilmurvey, Kilronan, Inishmore, t (099) 61318 *(inexpensive)*.

Ard Einne, Kilmurvey, Inishmore, t (099) 61126, *ardeinne@eircom.net (inexpensive)*. Serves fine dinners at reasonable prices and offers bike rentals and tours.

Ard Alainn, Inishmaan, t (099) 73027, f 73027 *(inexpensive)*. Typical Aran B&B farmhouse where you get a fine welcome from Sean and Maura Faherty; close to 'Synge's Chair' with its views of the Atlantic and Connemara coast. All rooms en-suite; *no evening meals*. Three-bedroom self-catering cottage also available.

Tigh Chonghaile, Moore Village, Inishmaan, t (099) 73085 *(inexpensive)*. Open year-round; contact Mrs Conneely.

Ard Mhuire, Inisheer, t (099) 75005 *(inexpensive)*. Tourist board-approved; situated close to the pier and sandy beach. Contact Mrs Una McDonagh.

Radharc na Mara, West Village, Inisheer, t (099) 75024, *maire.searraigh@oceanfree. net (inexpensive)*. B&B, attached to *Radharc Na Mara* hostel, close to pier, beach and pubs. *Open all year*. Contact Ms Maura Sharry.

Radharc An Chlair, Castle Village, Inisheer, t (099) 75019 *(inexpensive)*. A cosy, friendly bungalow with heart-warming cooking.

Tigh Ui Chathain, Formna, Inisheer, t (099) 75090 *(inexpensive)*. Also approved by the tourist board; family home overlooking the Bay.

Inisheer Campsite – Ionad Campala Inis Oirr, t (091) 537777.

Eating Out

Aran Fisherman Restaurant, Kilronan, Inishmore, t (099) 61363/61104 *(expensive–inexpensive)*. Set dinners. *Open winter daily around 1–9pm, summer daily 10–10.*

An tSean Cheibh ('The Old Pier'), Kilronan, Inishmore, t (099) 61228, f 61437, *oldpier@ 02.ie (moderate)*. Good home-baking and fresh fish. Also a good fish and chip shop. *Open daily May–Sept.*

Dun Aengus Restaurant, Kilronan, Inishmore, t (099) 61104 *(moderate)*. Traditional stone house serving seafood, steaks, international and vegetarian dishes. *Open daily 6–10pm.*

Man of Aran Cottage, Kilmurvey Bay, Inishmore, t (099) 61286/61301 *(moderate–inexpensive)*. A daytime café which serves soup, sandwiches and a lobster lunch. *Open Mar–mid Oct daily, weather permitting.*

Joe Watty's Pub, Kilronan, Inishmore, t (099) 61155 *(inexpensive)*. Good chowders. *Open summer time only.*

Mainister House Hostel, Kilronan, Inishmore, t (099) 61322 *(inexpensive)*. Wonderful vegetarian buffets, but be sure to book and turn up for 8pm, for it disappears fast.

Teach Osta, Inishmaan, t (099) 73003 *(inexpensive)*. This is the only pub on the island, and offers good bar food, a thatched roof and conviviality.

Tigh Ned, near the pier, Inisheer, t (099) 75004. Traditional music, nightly during summer.

graves of the saints. **Teampall Bheanain**, just south of Killeany, is 6th-century, only 10ft by 7ft (3m by 2m), and a unique example of an Early Christian church. With the coming of Christianity and St Enda in AD 483, the island became known as Aran of the Saints: at Killeany, 2 miles (3.2km) southeast of Kilronan, there are the graves of 120 of them. All Enda's followers seem to have reached the glorious state of sainthood after living their lives in the narrow confines of *clochans*. The site also contains the remains of a small, early church and the shaft of a finely carved high cross. A few yards to the northwest of the doorway is a flagstone which is said to cover the grave of St Enda.

Inishmaan

Inishmaan is not usually visited by tourists, who tend to go to Inishmore if they're only on a day-trip. If you do go to Inishmaan or Inisheer, see if you can go by *curragh*; it is an exciting experience to drop into the frail-looking craft and leave the security of the mail boat. (*Curraghs* are made of laths and canvas, which is then tarred over.) You can see the huge **Fort of Dun Conor** (*Dun Chonchuir*) from the sound as you approach the shore of Inishmaan. It is in the middle of the coastline and faces out to Inisheer. Its three outer walls have disappeared, with the exception of the remnants of the inner curtain, but the massive fortress wall, built of stones which only a race of giants could lift easily, is almost intact. Nearby is a freshwater spring which never dries up, called **St Chinndheirg's Well**. It is supposed to have curative properties. In the same area is one of the most interesting churches on the island, known as **Cill Cean Fhionnaigh** ('Church of the Fairheaded One'). It is one of the most perfect primitive Irish churches in existence, and there is another holy well here.

Inisheer

As you come through Foul Sound towards Inisheer, you see **O'Brien's Castle** on the rocky hill south of the landing – a 15th-century tower set in a stone ring-fort. Inisheer is the smallest island, only about 2 miles (3.2km) across, but it greets you with a broad, sandy beach. It also boasts a tiny **10th-century church** dedicated to St Gobhnait, the only woman allowed on the three islands when the saintly men ruled these shores. Situated to the southeast of the landing place is the **Church of St Kevin** (*Teampall Chaomham*). This ancient building is threatened by shifting sand, but the locals clear it every year on the saint's feast day, 14 June. It has a Gothic chancel, and an earlier nave. Islanders are still buried in the ground around the church.

Synge wrote this of the men of Inisheer: 'These strange men with receding foreheads, high cheek bones, and ungovernable eyes seem to represent some old type found on these few acres at the extreme border of Europe, where it is only in the wild jests and laughter that they can express their loneliness and desolation'.

Touring from Galway City

You can follow the second Westport tour, starting with a night in Westport (pp.81–3), then Days 1–5, ending back in Galway on Day 6 (p.93).

Dublin and the Southeast

07

The province of Leinster (*Cúige Laighean*) has always had a reputation for wealth, because of its fertile land. Many aristocrats lived on estates here, within a day's ride from Dublin; the city, which is the symbolic centre of the province, grew ever larger as industry and people were attracted to it. The province includes the ancient Kingdom of Meath, and its pre-Christian kings were the most powerful in the land. Each successive wave of invaders since the Vikings has founded towns and built strong castles in this beautiful and varied region. It has a long sea coast, stretching from Dundalk Bay in County Louth to Hook Head in County Wexford. Essential ports and trading places grew up along it, but Dublin, which became the centre of British rule, has always maintained its position as the most important. Today, the population of Dublin and its swelling suburbs is one million and a half, so the farms of the province are engaged in supplying the huge city market with milk, vegetables, cattle and poultry. Brewing and other industrial ventures have grown up in the Greater Dublin area, but the rest of Leinster is comparatively rural.

The southeast coast has a reputation for being sunny, although the climate is fairly similar all over Ireland. Dublin is considered very cold and damp in winter. Tourist facilities are generally very good because restaurants and lodgings have responded to the sophisticated tastes of Dubliners. In fact, most travellers who come to Leinster head straight for Dublin City – a magnet which promises the most fun, history, culture and comfort. They might make a few sallies out into the countryside, perhaps to beautiful Glendalough in County Wicklow, the fascinating Boyne Valley burial grounds, or Tara, the seat of the high kings in County Meath. But Dublin City draws them all back, and the rest of Leinster pales into insignificance. If you arrive in Ireland at Rosslare, in County Wexford, the province gets a fairer chance of being explored. There are many beautiful places in Counties Wexford, Wicklow, Kilkenny and Carlow. On a clear, blustery day it is easy to imagine yourself a million miles from civilization, even though the city is only an hour's drive away.

Dublin City

Dublin has a worldwide reputation for culture, wit, friendliness and beauty, and this image perpetuates itself as the casual Dublin charm works its way into the heart of every visitor. Irish people themselves call it 'dear dirty Dublin', and at first glance you may think that they are right and discount the affection in their voices when they talk about it. For there is no doubt that Dublin can be a bit of a disappointment, and you may ask yourself what on earth all the fuss is about: the rosy-coloured Georgian squares and delicate, perfectly proportioned doorways are jumbled up together with some grotesque adventures into modern architecture. Fast-food signs and partially demolished buildings mingle with expensive and tacky shops, and the housing estates can be depressing. The tall houses north of the Liffey were divided into run-down flats, although many are now being done up and through the doors and windows you catch glimpses of their former glory – elegant staircases and marvellous plasterwork.

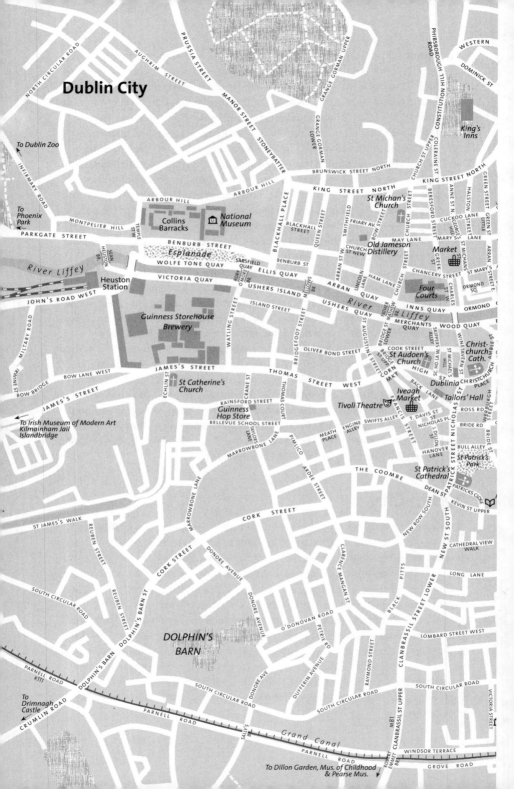

Getting There

By Air

Dublin has the biggest choice of airlines flying from various UK cities and direct from North America; *see* **Travel**, pp.6–9.

Getting from the Airport

Dublin Airport (**t** (01) 814 1111, *www.dublin-airport.com*) is 8 miles from the city.

Dublin Bus runs **Airlink** services (routes 747 and 748) between Dublin Airport, the Central Bus Station (*Busáras*), Connolly and Heuston railway stations and O'Connell Street every 10–15mins Mon–Sat 5.45am to 11.30pm, Sun 7.15am–11.30pm (€4.50). The privately run **Aircoach**, *www.aircoach.ie*, runs every 15mins from early morning to 10.20pm (return €10, single €6), and makes at least 15 stops around the city, mainly outside the bigger hotels.

You can also get the cheaper (€1.45, exact fare required), but slower, **city buses** (routes 16, 16A/B, 41, 41A/B/C, 46A), which circulate between the airport and Eden Quay, outside *Busáras*.

A **taxi** to the centre will cost around €15–20.

By Sea

Dublin Harbour and **Dun Laoghaire** are served by ferries from Holyhead, in North Wales, Mostyn and Liverpool. Contact **Irish Ferries**, **t** 08705 17 17 17 (UK only), **t** 0181 300 400 (Republic of Ireland), *www.irishferries. com*, or **Stena Line**, **t** (01) 204 7777, *www.stena line.ie*. Stena Line also operate a high-speed catamaran service from Dun Laoghaire, which crosses the Irish Sea in 1hr 40mins.

There is also a seasonal service to the Isle of Man with the **Isle of Man Steam Packet Company**, **t** 08705 523 523 (UK only) or **t** 1800 551 743 (Republic of Ireland only), *www. steam-packet.com*.

Getting from the Ports

Buses 7, 7A and 8 run from **Dun Laoghaire** to O'Connell Bridge, which is in the centre of Dublin.

If you arrive at the **Dublin ferry port**, you'll find buses to the bus station and city centre on the Alexandra Road – all buses with *An Lar* ('city centre') signs are going there.

Getting Around

The best and cheapest way of getting around Dublin is by **walking**, because most of the museums, shops and galleries are fairly near to each other. Dublin is a compact city; the central area clusters around the River Liffey and occupies about two square miles. Most of the museums, galleries, theatres, architectural sights and restaurants are within this small area.

The **Liffey** separates the north side from the south. It is spanned by several bridges, the most central being **O'Connell Bridge**. The streets along the River Liffey are called quays, and they change names between bridges. St Stephen's Green, Trinity College, Grafton Street and the Castle area are south of the river. O'Connell Street, Henry Street and Parnell Square are north. Grafton Street and Henry Street are pedestrianized.

Phoenix Park (1,760 acres/712ha) is under 2 miles (3km) from the city centre, to the northwest.

The **Grand Canal** crosses the city and joins the River Liffey, enclosing the southern part of the city centre in a gentle curve.

By Rail

There are two main railway stations in Dublin city: **Heuston**, west of the centre on St John's Road, serves the south, southwest and west of the country, as well as commuter trains to County Kildare. **Connolly Station**, north of the Liffey on Amiens Street, near the bus station, serves Wexford, Sligo and Belfast (where for Derry you must change trains), and has a connection with the main DART line and commuter lines to Maynooth, Mullingar and Longford.

DART (Dublin Area Rapid Transit) electric trains serve 25 suburban stations near the coast from Howth to Bray. A DART day ticket is available from Iarnród Eireann for about €6, but you probably won't need it unless you are doing a lot of exploring in the suburbs.

Iarnród Eireann Travel Centre ('iron road Irish rail'), 35 Lower Abbey Street , Dublin, **t** (01) 836 6222, *www.irishrail.ie*, for all rail information. *Office open Mon–Fri 9–5, phone lines open Mon–Fri 8.30–6, Sat 9–6, Sun 10–6.*

By Bus

Intercity Expressway (long-distance) buses are run by **Bus Eireann** and end up in *Busáras* (the central bus station), at Store Street, on the north side of the Liffey, three streets east of O'Connell Street. Their buses run until about 11.30 or midnight, and are a very convenient way to get around, though you'll find the going slow enough through the centre.

Dublin Bus controls all public bus services in the Greater Dublin Area (which includes the city centre, and parts of Wicklow).

The Travel Centre, *Busáras*, Store Street, Dublin 1, t (01) 836 6111. Information on all services is given here.

Dublin Bus Travel Centre, 59 Upper O'Connell Street, t (01) 873 4222, *www.dublinbus.ie*.

Fares and Passes

Bus **fares** are based on distance, and exact change is required (if you don't have the correct change, you will be given a bus voucher which can only be refunded at the Dublin Bus office on O'Connell St).

To avoid frustration or a heavy pocket full of coins, consider buying a prepaid pass. There are full details of all the passes available online at *www.dublinbus.ie*, but the most useful for tourists are the **Rambler Tickets**, which offer unlimited bus travel and cost €4.50 for 1 day, €8.80 for 3 days, €13.90 for 5 days, and €16.50 for 7 days. Note that these passes don't cover night buses (NiteLink), but they are valid on the Airlink bus from the airport. Passes can be purchased at the Dublin Bus Travel Centre, and at most newsagents. There are **combined rail-and-bus passes** which also include the DART and cost €7.20 for 1 day, €13.30 for 3 days, or €10.70 for a 1-day family ticket.

By Tram (*Luas*)

The first stage in Dublin's new tram system, called the Luas, is expected to open in late 2004. There will be three tram lines, with two (lines A and B) connecting the suburbs with the city centre, and the third (line C) crossing Dublin from Abbey Street to Connolly Station.

By Taxi

Taxis can be found outside hotels and railway stations, and in special taxi parking areas in Central Dublin. There are 24-hour ranks at St Stephen's Green and O'Connell Street; it's often difficult to flag down a cab on the streets. Taxis should always have meters. They charge extra per piece of luggage, per person and at night.

Blue Cabs, t (01) 676 1111.
Metro Cabs, t (01) 668 3333/478 1111/677 2222.
Pony Cabs, t (01) 661 2233.
VIP Taxi and Courier Service, t (01) 478 3333.

By Car

Parking is difficult (and occasionally impossible) in the centre of town, but there is a new computerized system with strategically placed screens telling you which car parks have spaces. The main **car parks** are in Frederick Street and the St Stephen's Green Shopping Centre, and there is metered parking around St Stephen's Green and Merrion Square. On the north side you might find a parking place in the Irish Life Shopping Centre, entrance off Lower Abbey Street. Using your horn is the worst insult.

Car Hire

Most of the major **car hire** chains are represented at the airport, along with a wide choice of local firms.

AVIS, Dublin Airport, t (01) 605 7500, f 605 7565, *www.avis.ie*.

Budget Rent A Car, Dublin Airport t (01) 844 5150, *www.budgetcarrental.ie*.

Dan Dooley/Kenning, 42 Westland Row, Dublin 2, t (01) 677 2723, *www.dan-dooley.ie*.

Hertz Rent-A-Car, Dublin Airport, t (01) 844 5466, *www.hertz.ie*.

Murrays Europcar, Baggot Street Bridge, Dublin 4, t (01) 614 2800; Dublin Airport, t (01) 812 0410, f 812 0428, *www.europcar.ie*.

Bike Hire

It has become increasingly difficult to hire a bicycle in Dublin, as insurance prices have skyrocketed over the last few years.

Belfield Bike Shop, Belfield House, U.C.D., Dublin 4, t (01) 706 1697. Bike rental from €18 per day.

Macdonalds, 38–39 Wexford Street, t (01) 475 2586. Bike rental from €25 per day. Refundable €100 deposit required.

Guided Tours

Signposts have been erected around the city to guide you through the historical sights on foot; there's the Georgian Trail, the Cultural Trail, the Old City Trail and the Rock 'n' Stroll Trail. Contact Dublin Tourism on Suffolk Street, t 1850 230 330, for more details.

If you need more assistance there are guided walking tours on offer, listed below.

Historical Walking Tours of Dublin, t (01) 845 0241, *www.historicalinsights.ie*. Assemble at the front gate of Trinity College. Besides the historical tour, they also runs a series of themed tours in summer which look at a particular aspect of Irish history, from sex to architecture. *April–Sept daily 11, 12 and 3, Oct–Mar Fri, Sat and Sun at 12 noon.*

Old Dublin, t (01) 679 4291. Assemble at Bewley's, Grafton Street or Dublin Writer's Museum, 18 Parnell Square; *call for times.*

The 1916 Rebellion Walking Tour, t (01) 676 2493, *www.1916rising.com*. Departs from the International Bar, 23 Wicklow Street, and takes you around all the sites asociated with this traumatic event. *Mon–Sat 11.30 and 2.20, Sun 1pm. No 2.30 tours during Mar and Oct.*

Revolutionary Dublin 1916–23, t (01) 662 9976. Conducted by Trinity College graduate students; covers the same ground and more. *Daily tours, call for times.*

Zozimus Experience, t (01) 661 8646, *www.zozimus.com*. A creepy but fun tour with a mysterious hooded guide, with ghost stories and a chilling surprise at the end. Departs from the gates of Dublin Castle. *May–Oct 9pm, Nov–April 7pm.*

Besides these normal tours, Dublin can also offer several **pub tours**, where the walking becomes increasingly less steady; there is a charge, and you'll need extra cash for the Guinness.

The Dublin Literary Pub Crawl, 37 Exchequer Street, D2, t (01) 670 5602, f 670 5603/454 5680, *www.dublinpubcrawl.com*. Meets at The Duke pub on Duke Street. Tickets are sold on a first-come-first-served basis. *April–Nov nightly 7.30; Dec–Mar Thurs–Sat 7.30; Sun all year 12 noon and 7.30.*

The Musical Pub Crawl, t (01) 478 0193, *www.musicalpubcrawl.com*. Two knowledgeable musicians lead you through several traditional music bars. Tours leave from upstairs at the Oliver St John Goggarty Pub in Temple Bar. *May–Oct nightly at 7.30, Nov, Feb, Mar and April Thurs–Sat only 7.30. Private tours only in Dec and Jan.*

For a less strenuous way of seeing the sights, **Dublin Bus** offers open-top bus 'hop on-hop off' tours. With these you can get on and off anywhere, and the ticket is good for the entire day. The start is Dublin Bus headquarters (*see* below). Buses run the circuit every 15mins. They also offer full- and half-day tours of North County Dublin, with a stop at Malahide Castle (*daily, 10am from O'Connell Street*), and the southern coast into County Wicklow (*daily, 11 and 2, from O'Connell Street*). **Dublin Bus**: headquarters 59 O'Connell Street (between Henry and Parnell), t (01) 873 4222, *www.dublinbus.ie*.

Festivals and Events

February–March

Six Nations Rugby. Held over two Saturdays at Landsdowne Road; always a good party in the years when the Scots visit.

March

National St Patrick's Day Festival (17th). Celebrations and parades starting on O'Connell Street. Lots of events and music around this date, including a 3-day *fleadh* in Temple Bar: *www.stpatricksday.ie*.

April

Dublin International Film Festival. Held early in the month; highly recommended. Check out the website *www.dubliniff.com*.

May

Heineken Green Energy International Music Festival, t (01) 456 9569, *www.mcd.ie*. A huge event, with past headliners including the Cranberries, Beck and Moloko.

Wicklow Gardens Festival (May–July), t 0404 20070, *www. wicklow.ie*. Open days at private gardens throughout Co. Wicklow.

June

Bloomsday. June 16th is Dublin's own peculiar holiday, the anniversary of the day (in 1904) on which all the action of Joyce's *Ulysses* took place. Various events are held in the places visited by Leopold Bloom – some are scheduled, some aren't. People wear Edwardian costume, make recitations, and some just come along for the pub crawl. The day begins at 8am by the Tower in Sandycove; contact the James Joyce Centre for more information, t (01) 878 8547, *www.jamesjoyce.ie*.

AIB Music in Great Irish Houses. A festival of chamber music, with around 10 evening concerts held in great houses in the Dublin area. Call for information, t (01) 278 1528.

August
Kerrygold Horse Show. International equestrian event in Ballsbridge, t (01) 668 0866.

September
All-Ireland Hurling and Football Finals, t (01) 836 3222.

Dublin Jazz Festival, t (01) 670 3885. Weeklong, held at a number of venues in the city.

Dublin Fringe Theatre Festival, t (01) 872 9433, *www.fringefest.com*.

International Puppetry Festival, t (01) 280 0974.

October
Dublin Theatre Festival, t (01) 877 8439, *www.dublintheatrefestival.com*.

Dublin City Marathon, t (01) 670 7918.

December
Dublin Grand Opera Winter Season, Gaiety Theatre, South King Street, t (01) 677 1717, *www.gaietytheatre.com*.

Tourist Information

The main **Dublin Tourism** office occupies an entire restored church in Suffolk Street; it's all very modern and efficient, but you could be waiting a long time. Just take a number and have a seat. They also change money, and book hotels and theatre tickets. Call their toll-free recorded information line; or try their website, *www.visitdublin.com*.

Dublin Tourism Centre, St Andrew's Church, Suffolk Street (off Grafton Street, near Trinity College), t (01) 605 7700, information line

t 1850 230 330; *open Sept–June Mon–Sat 9.30–5.30; July–Aug Mon–Sat 9.30–6.30, Sun 10.30–3*.

Bord Failté Eireann/Tourism Ireland, Baggot Street Bridge (south of the centre, on the Grand Canal), information line t 1850 230 330, *www.tourismireland.com; open Mon–Fri 9.30–5.15*; also at 14 Upper O'Connell Street (north of the Liffey); *open all year*.

Dublin Airport: *open daily 8am–10pm*.

Dun Laoghaire: New Ferry Terminal; *open daily 8–1*.

Tallaght: The Square; *open daily 8–1*.

Banks and *Bureaux de Change*
Banks are open Monday–Friday 10–4, and on Thursday until 5pm.

Thomas Cook, 51 Grafton Street, t (01) 677 7399.

American Express, 61–63A South William Street, t (01) 617 5588.

Chemists
Both the following are open until 10pm:

O'Connell's, 55 Lower O'Connell Street, D1, t (01) 873 0427.

Leonard's, 106 South Circular Road, D8, t (01) 453 4282.

Emergencies and Health
In an emergency, dial t **999** or t **112**.

St Vincent's University Hospital, Elm Park, D4, t (01) 269 4533.

St James's Hospital, James' Street, D8, t (01) 453 7941.

Dublin Metropolitan Area HQ, t (01) 475 5555/478 1822 and t 1800 666 111. Police (*Garda Siochana*). Tourist Victim Support Centre, Harcourt Square, Dublin 2, t (01) 478 5295, freefone helpline, t 1800 661 771.

Internet Cafés
Central Cyber Café, 6 Grafton Street, D2, t (01) 677 8298, f 677 8299, *www.globalcafe.ie*, *info@centralcafe.ie. Open Mon–Fri 9am–10pm, weekends 10am–9pm*.

Does Not Compute, Unit 2 Pudding Row, Essex Street West, Temple Bar, D8, t (01) 670 4464, f 670 4474, *www.doesnotcompute.ie*, *info@doesnotcompute.ie. Open 24hrs*.

Global Internet Café, 8 Lower O'Connell Street, D1, t (01) 878 0295, f 872 9100, *www. global*

cafe.ie, info@globalcafe.ie. Open Mon–Fri 8am–11pm, Sat 9am–11pm, Sun 10am–11pm.
Internet Exchange Café, 3 Cecilia Street, D2, t (01) 670 3000; 10 Fownes Street, D2, t (01) 635 1680.
Planet Café, 13 St Andrew St, D2, t (01) 670 5183, f 670 5182, *www.irelands-web.ie.*

Post Offices

The **GPO** (General Post Office) is in the centre of O'Connell Street (*open until 8pm*); there are branches in Parnell Street and Summerhill, north of the Liffey, and south of it at Upper Baggot Street, Lower Baggot Street, Clare Street, Earlsfort Terrace, Pearse Street, Merrion Row, Montague Street and South Anne Street.

Telephones

Payphone centres are located in the General Post Office, O'Connell Street, and beside the Gaiety Theatre on South King Street. More and more of these are **cardphones**, the cards for which may be bought in the post office and selected newsagents. The big hotels are other reliable sources for public telephones.

The local dialling code for the whole of County Dublin is **t** (01).

Shopping

The smartest and best shopping is to be found in a small area around **Grafton Street** and the little streets leading off it, just north-east of the river. North of the Liffey, **Henry Street** is the busiest shopping street in Dublin – and generally cheaper than the upmarket Grafton Street area. The flagship of this area is Clery's, on O'Connell Street.

Antiques

The antique shops in Molesworth, South Anne Street and Kildare Street are well thought of and sell top-quality furniture, silver and ornaments. For more junky stuff and bargains try Francis Street, in the Liberties, where there are individual antiques shops and an antiques arcade.
A Star is Born, Clarendon Street. Try here for antique and second-hand items. *Open Saturdays only.*

Iveagh Market, just across the road from the Tivoli Theatre. A fine 19th-century covered market, now very shabby and occupied by second-hand clothes dealers.
Jenny Vander, 50 Drury St, opposite the George's Street Arcade. Also for good second-hand clothes, lovely antique clothing and costume jewellery.

Auctioneers

De Vere's Art Auctions, 35 Kildare Street, D2, t (01) 676 8300, f (01) 676 8305. For mostly Irish paintings.
Herman and Wilkinson, 161 Lower Rathmines Road, D6, t (01) 497 2245. Fortnightly auctions of silver, paintings and furniture.
James Adams and Sons, 26 St Stephen's Green, t (01) 676 0261.

Books

An open-air **book market** is held in Temple Bar Square (*weekends 10am–6pm*), and at the time of writing there are plans afoot to open a **daily market** on Capel Street Bridge.
Cathach Books, 10 Duke Street, t (01) 671 8676. A large, independent bookseller.
Dublin Writers' Museum, 18 Parnell Square, D1, t (01) 872 2077. A good selection of books by and about Irish authors.
Eason & Son, Lower O'Connell Street, t (01) 873 3811. With several other branches in the city.
Fred Hanna's Bookshop, 28–29 Nassau Street, D2, t (01) 677 1255, *www.hannas.ie.* Independent bookseller.
Greene's Bookshop Ltd, 16 Clare Street, D2, t (01) 676 2554, *info@greenesbookshop.com.* For rare and out-of-print books.
Hodges Figgis, 57 Dawson Street, D2.
Waterstone's, 7 Dawson Street, D2.
Winding Stair Books, 40 Lower Ormond Quay, D1, t (01) 873 3292. Has an excellent café and three floors of second-hand books, plus a lovely view.

Clothes

Many of the UK's high street clothing chains – Next, Principles, Marks & Spencer – have set up in Grafton Street. (*See also* 'Department Stores', below.) For something in **Irish tweed**, and for high-quality craft design, head for Nassau Street, at the College Green end of Dawson Street.

Avoca, 11–13 Suffolk St, **t** (01) 677 4215. Beautiful clothes and accessories from Irish designers, as well as gifts, food, ceramics. Great café.

Alias Tom, Duke Street, **t** (01) 671 5443. Designer men's clothes.

A-Wear, 26 Grafton Street, **t** (01) 671 7200 and also at Henry Street, *www.a-wear.ie*. Inexpensive; stocks a diffusion range by Quin and Donnelly. The prices here are very keen and will appeal to all ages.

The Blarney Woollen Mills, 21–3 Nassau Street. Tailored skirts and jackets, soft jersey dresses and jumpers, scarves and luxurious woollen coats, in a good range of colours – from the clear primaries to tweeds full of subtle shades like the Irish countryside, although some of the designs are a little staid.

Cleo, 18 Kildare Street, a little way off Nassau Street, D2, **t** (01) 676 1421, *www.cleo–ltd.com*. A good designer tweed shop.

FX Kelly, 48 Grafton Street, **t** (01) 677 8211. For men's designer clothes.

Kennedy McSharry, 39 Nassau Street, **t** (01) 677 8770. Beautifully tailored suits from Donegal tweed.

Kevin and Howlin, 31 Nassau Street, **t** (01) 677 0257. Tweed heaven – they sell lovely caps, scarves and suits for men.

Se Si Progressive, 11 Fownes St, Temple Bar, **t** (01) 677 4779. Worth a visit for its inexpensive clubby gear, with young designer talent.

Commercial Art Galleries

The following galleries put on shows by Irish artists. You might even decide to invest.

Green on Red, 26 Lombard Street, D2, **t** (01) 671 3414. Contemporary paintings and sculpture.

City Arts Centre, 23 Moss Street, D2, **t** (01) 677 0643. Young emerging artists. The centre also has a pleasant café.

Kerlin Gallery, Anne's Lane, off South Anne Street, D2, **t** (01) 670 9093. Established and new talent – a lovely gallery space.

Oriel Gallery, 17 Clare Street, D2, **t** (01) 676 3410, *www.theoriel.com*. Mostly traditional and figurative early-20th-century.

Rubicon, 10 St Stephen's Green, **t** (01) 670 8055. Mostly contemporary.

Solomon Gallery, Powerscourt Town House Centre, D2, **t** (01) 679 4237, *www.solomon gallery.com*. Pretty pictures – occasionally verges on the twee.

Taylor Galleries, 16 Kildare Street, D2, **t** (01) 676 6055. Established artists.

Crafts

Anthony O'Brien, 14a Ailsbury Road, D4, **t** (01) 260 4064. Pottery.

Designyard, 12 East Essex Street, Temple Bar, **t** (01) 677 8467. In a converted warehouse, this is the new hotspot for designer jewellery, ceramics, furniture and glass.

Irish Georgian Society, 74 Merrion Square, D2, **t** (01) 676 7053. Visit here for historical placemats, books, and so on.

The Kilkenny Shop, 5–6 Nassau Street, **t** (01) 677 7066. Sells excellent glass, pottery, rugs and sweaters.

Tower Craft Design Centre, Pearse Street, D2, **t** (01) 677 5655. Craft-workers produce glass, jewellery, woodcarving, pottery, weaving and other lovely things.

Delicacies

Asia Market, 18 Drury Street, **t** (01) 677 9764. Very good for exotic ingredients.

Bretzel Kosher Bakery, 1A Lennox Street, D8, **t** (01) 475 2724. Just up from Fitzpatrick's, near the Grand Canal, is this famous baker's which doles out treats such as gingerbread men, walnut loaves and *challah*, shiny twisted plaits of bread.

Butler's, 51A Grafton Street, **t** (01) 671 0599. Irish chocolates; not quite as good as the Belgian ones, below.

Caviston's, in the Epicurean Food Hall, Liffey Street Lower, **t** (01) 878 2289. An old-fashioned deli selling fresh fish, Irish cheeses and smoked salmon.

Down to Earth, 73 South Great Georges Street, D2, **t** (01) 671 9702. Health foods.

Fitzpatricks, 40 Camden Street, D8, **t** (01) 475 3996. A cheerful wholefood grocer.

Foodies, Poolbeg Street, D2, **t** 677 9140. Fresh soup, pies and quiches.

Leonidas, Royal Hibernian Way, off Dawson St, **t** (01) 679 5915. Yummy Belgian chocolates.

Magill's, 14 Clarendon Street, **t** (01) 671 3830. A wonderful old-fashioned place smelling of *charcuterie* and sourdough breads.

Patrick Guildbaud, 42 The Liffey Trust, Sheriff Street, D1, **t** 855 5299. French bakery.

Temple Bar Food Market, held every Saturday morning in Meeting House Square. For edible Irish goodies, this is your first stop. Local farmers' organic produce, home-baked breads and pastries, and exotic treats you would have trouble finding elsewhere.

Department Stores

Brown Thomas, 88–95 Grafton Street, t (01) 605 6666. A first-class department store. Always carries Irish designer labels such as Paul Costelloe, Louise Kennedy, John Rocha and Michaelina Stacpoole. The designer room is excellent, as is the Wardrobe department for less expensive options.

Clery's, O'Connell Street, t (01) 878 6000. Famous, old-fashioned, independent department store.

Powerscourt Town House Centre, Design Centre, 59 South William Street, t (01) 679 5718. A must for any serious shopper, this is an innovative shopping mecca that is generally regarded as a showpiece marriage between conservation and commerce. The building is elegantly Georgian, and was constructed over two hundred years ago as a town residence for Lord Powerscourt, an 18th-century nobleman. A glass dome over the old courtyard makes a wonderful space for cafés and restaurants. Small craft shops, fashion shops, antique shops and jewellers have spaces in the old house. Names to look out for include **Emma Stewart Liberty** and **Patrick Flood** (silversmiths) and the **Design Centre**, which sells clothes by up-and-coming and established designers including Mariad Whisker, Louise Kennedy, Lainey Keogh and Deirdre Fitzgerald, who design gorgeous and luxurious knitwear. If you need refuelling, the perfect solution is to order a dessert cake from **Chompy's** or go veggie at **Fresh**.

St Stephen's Green Shopping Centre, on the corner of St Stephen's Green and Grafton Street. This huge glass mall has a wide variety of small shops and a huge **Dunnes** store (something like Marks & Spencer). It also houses the **Crafts Centre of Ireland**, t (01) 475 4526.

The Westbury Centre, near the Powerscourt Centre. Has an Aladdin's cave of a lingerie shop, a leather studio, a good Costa coffee shop and **Angles**, a shop with the best of contemporary Irish jewellery.

Music

Claddagh Records, 2 Cecilia Street, D2, t (01) 677 0262, f 679 3664, *www.claddagh records.com*, *claddagh@crl.ie*. Specialists in traditional Irish music.

Waltons, 69–70 South Great Georges Street, D2, t (01) 475 0661. Irish and world musical instruments.

Street Markets

Cow's Lane Natural Food Market, at Temple Bar. A range of food stalls selling certified organic fruit, fish from the Atlantic Ocean, cheeses, breads and preserves. *Open Saturdays 10–6.*

Dublin Food Co-op, in St Andrew's Centre, 114–16 Pearse Street, D2, t (01) 873 0451. Whole and organic foods, held every Sat.

Moore Street Market. This is the place for fruit and vegetables, although some of the produce is rather suspect, so watch out for the rotten ones. It is also a good place to observe Dublin life. Here the warmly wrapped pram people wait with their wares: in place of a gurgling infant, veteran market-traders, usually women, use prams to carry jewellery, fish, turf, concrete blocks, flowers and evening newspapers. You can buy their vegetables, fruit and the most gaudy of Taiwanese toys. The 'perambulators' are not strictly allowed, as they do not pay rent, unlike the properly established stands; and if the boys in blue appear, they melt away into the crowds. Some of the prams are as old as 70 years, and are still going strong.

Mother Redcap's Market, on Back Lane near Christchurch. Pottery, books and bric-a-brac. Check out the Gallic Kitchen, for delicious pies and cakes, and Ryefield Foods, for farmhouse cheeses.

Sports and Activities

Greyhound Racing

Shelbourne Park, D4, t (01) 668 3502 *www.shelbournepark.com*.

Harold's Cross, D6, t (01) 497 1081.

Hurling and Gaelic Football

The Gaelic Athletic Association's website, *www.gaa.ie*, gives detailed descriptions of the two games and their rules. See them both played in Dublin at Croke Park, Parnell Park and Phoenix Park.

Rugby and Football

See a game at **Landsdowne Road**, one mile south of the city centre, where in February or March you can catch the mighty Six Nations Rugby tournament.

Where to Stay

City Centre: South of the Liffey

Clarence Hotel, 6–8 Wellington Quay, D2, t (01) 407 0800, f 407 0820, *www.the clarence.ie* (*luxury*). Traditional 1930s hotel, owned by rock group U2, with wood panelling, a fashionable bar and friendly staff. At the edge of the Temple Bar area.

Conrad International Dublin, Earlsfort Terrace, D2, t (01) 602 8900, f 676 5424, *www.conrad hotels.com* (*luxury*). Top-of-the-range modern Hilton hotel with excellent facilities.

The Morgan Hotel, 10 Fleet Street, Temple Bar, D2, t (01) 679 3939, f 679 3946, *www.the morgan.com* (*luxury*). Quiet, private accommodation with modern designer elegance, in the heart of Temple Bar. Staff are helpful, friendly and discreet, and continental breakfasts are served in your room. Rooms are also provided with TV, CD/hi-fi, minibar, and tea- and coffee-making.

Shelbourne Hotel, St Stephens's Green, D2, t (01) 663 4500, f 661 6006, *www.shelbourne. com* (*luxury*). Lovely old-fashioned hotel in which the Irish Constitution was drafted. Also has a very elegant drawing room and a gem of a bar.

Westbury, Clarendon Street, off Grafton Street, D2, t (01) 679 1122, f 679 7078, *www. jurysdoyle.com* (*luxury*). Modern hotel, top of the range and conveniently central.

Buswell's Hotel, Molesworth Street, D2, t (01) 614 6500, f 676 2090, *www.buswellshotel. com* (*luxury–expensive*). An old-fashioned, cheerful family hotel. Very central.

Georgian House Hotel, 18 Baggot Street Lower, D2, t (01) 661 8832, or t 1850 320260 (*expensive*). Own phone, TV, telephone, in a Georgian house which has been altered internally to create snug, pastel-coloured rooms. Very central, so you can walk everywhere, but could do with refubishment. Private car park in back garden.

Longfields Hotel, Fitzwilliam Street Lower, D2, t (01) 676 1367 (*expensive*), *www.longfields.ie*. Georgian town house, quiet, intimate, with period furnishings and excellent restaurant.

Number 31, 31 Leeson Close, D2 t (01) 676 5011, f 676 2929, *www.number31.ie* (*expensive–moderate*). Stylish modern décor, comfortable and with a secure car park.

Earl of Kildare Hotel, 47 Kildare Street, D2, t (01) 679 4388 (*moderate*). A good hotel with a perfect location, near Grafton Street and Trinity College.

Barnacle's Temple Bar House, 19 Temple Lane, Temple Bar, D2, t (01) 671 6277, f 671 6591, *www.barnacles.ie* (*inexpensive*). Centrally located hostel with kitchen and laundry facilities. Single, double, quadruple and dorm rooms available.

Brewery Hostel, 21 Thomas Street, D8, t (01) 473 1512 (*inexpensive*). Well-equipped family-run hostel near the Guinness Brewery.

Kinlay House Hostel, 2–12 Lord Edward Street, D2, t (01) 679 6644, f 679 7437, *kinlay. dublin@usitworld.com* (*inexpensive*). Near Christ Church. Big and well-equipped.

City Centre: North of the Liffey

Gresham, Upper O'Connell Street, D1, t (01) 874 6881, f 878 7175, *www.gresham-hotels.com* (*expensive*). Built in the days when a first-class hotel had big bedrooms and huge baths, this still has the atmosphere of the 1920s and '30s. Best bedrooms are at the front. Car parking for residents.

The Morrison Hotel, Ormond Quay, D2, t (01) 887 2400, f 887 2499, *www.morrisonhotel.ie* (*expensive*). Very sleek, minimalist boutique hotel next to the Liffey. The modern, opulent rooms were created by Irish designer John Rocha, and it's a favourite haunt of the fashion pack.

Leeson Inn, 24 Lower Leeson Street, D2, t (01) 662 2002, f 662 1567, *www.iol.ie/leesoninn* (*expensive–moderate*). Stylish, convenient.

Castle Hotel, 3–4 Great Denmark St, D1, t (01) 874 6949, *hotels@indigo.ie* (*moderate*). A Georgian house with attractively furnished rooms; satellite TV and tea- and coffee-making facilities.

Merrion Square Manor, 31 Merrion Square, D2,
t (01) 622 8551, f 662 8556, *www.merrion
squaremanor.com (moderate).* Hotel with
Georgian-style décor.

Anchor Guest House, 49 Lower Gardiner Street
D1, t (01) 878 6913, *www.anchorguest
house.com (moderate–inexpensive).*
Georgian house B&B, conveniently located
near the bus station.

Dublin International Youth Hostel,
61 Mountjoy Street, D7, t (01) 830 1766,
www.irelandyha.org (inexpensive). Central,
clean and friendly.

Isaacs Hostel, 2–5 Frenchman's Lane, D1
(beside the bus station), t (01) 855 6215, f 855
6574, *www.isaacs.ie (inexpensive).* Built as a
wine warehouse on the Liffey in the 1700s,
this is a very clean, central, friendly place,
with excellent restaurant facilities and a
patio garden. Basic dormitory and single
rooms. The restaurant is good value.

Jacob's Inn, 21–28 Talbot Place, D1, t (01) 855
5660, f 855 5664, *www.isaacs.ie (inexpensive).* Modern hostel, near the bus station,
run by the same people as Isaac's Hostel,
above.

Outside the Centre: Dublin City South

Jury's, Pembroke Rd, Ballsbridge, D4, t (01) 660
5000, f 660 5540, *www.jurysdoyle.com
(luxury).* Large, modern chain hotel with
executive wing.

Sachs Hotel, 19 Morehampton Road,
Donnybrook, D4, t (01) 668 0995, f 668 6147
(luxury–expensive). Small, traditional
hotel in a Georgian terrace. Ample parking.

Ariel House, 52 Lansdowne Road, Ballsbridge,
D4, t (01) 668 5512, f 668 5845 *(expensive–
moderate).* A charming Victorian house with
lots of antiques. The bedrooms in the older
part of the house are more individual.
Breakfast is served in the conservatory.

The Schoolhouse Hotel, 2–8 Northumberland
Road, D4, t (01) 667 5014, f 667 5015, *www.
schoolhousehotel.com, school@schoolhouse
hotel.iol.ie (expensive–moderate).* Charming,
friendly hotel set in a converted school, with
a good bar called **The Inkwell.**

Waterloo House, 8–10 Waterloo Road, D4,
t (01) 660 1888, f 667 1955, *waterloohouse@
eircom.net (expensive–moderate).* A small,
friendly hotel in a residential Georgian

street, nearly unchanged by the tacky
elements of the Celtic Tiger and within
walking distance of the city centre.
Breakfasts are carefully prepared and served
in a plush garden dining room by meticulous staff. Perfect for those who require
privacy, cleanliness and efficiency.

McMenamins Townhouse, 74 Marlborough
Road, Donnybrook, D4, t (01) 497 4405, f 496
8585 *(moderate).* A warm welcome awaits
you here, as well as a night's peace, in a residential street not far from University
College Dublin. Your helpful host Padraig
McMenamin knows all about Donnybrook's
history, and his wife Kay serves up excellent
home baking at breakfast. Special breakfasts
are available for vegetarians, and tea-
making facilities are in each room.

Merrion Hall, 56 Merrion Road, Ballsbridge, D4,
t (01) 668 1426, f 668 4280, *merrionhall@
iol.ie (moderate).* Family-run guesthouse
with pretty bedrooms (some with jacuzzis
and four-poster beds), a friendly atmosphere
and a delicious breakfast which includes
home-made yoghurt.

Avalon House, 55 Aungier Street, D2, t (01) 475
0001, *www.avalon-house.ie (inexpensive).*
Old building converted into a modern hostel
with twin, family and dormitory rooms.
Central, clean and efficiently run.

Haddington Lodge, 49 Haddington Road,
Ballsbridge, D4, t (01) 660 0974 *(inexpen-
sive).* Elegant Georgian house; contact
Mrs Egan.

Hilton House, 23 Highfield Road, Rathgar, D6,
t (01) 497 6837 *(inexpensive).* Large Victorian
house in a quiet secluded area; contact
Mr or Mrs Doyle.

Outside the Centre: Dublin City North

Dorchester Guest House, 69 North Circular
Road, D7, t (01) 838 5204 *(inexpensive).* Very
friendly and comfortable B&B in a quiet area
near Phoenix Park, with safe parking.

Eating Out

Dining in Dublin is an extremely popular
occupation, so always make sure you book a
table in advance.

City Centre: South of the Liffey

Luxury

Patrick Guilbaud, Merrion Hotel, 21 Merrion Street Upper, D2, t (01) 676 4192. Excellent classic French cuisine, awarded two Michelin stars, in a modern formal interior.

Expensive

Clarence Hotel Tea Room, 6–8 Wellington Quay, D2, t (01) 407 0800. A fashionable and fun place to eat a set dinner (but not tea). There's an excellent set lunch for €14, or you can push the boat out with a Tasting Menu at €70.

La Stampa, 35 Dawson Street, D2, t (01) 677 8611, *www.lastampa.ie*. Fashionable and graceful brasserie, set in the splendid rooms of the former Guildhall. There's a cheaper, trendy restaurant, Tiger Bec's, in the basement, serving southeast Asian cuisine.

L'Ecrivain, 109 Lower Baggot Street, D2, t (01) 661 1919. Friendly little basement restaurant serving imaginative French food. Popular with local business people and particularly buzzy at lunchtime.

Les Frères Jacques, 74 Dame Street, D2, t (01) 679 4555, *www.lesfreresjacques.com*. Atmospheric and romantic restaurant. French food and friendly staff. Try the lobster ravioli.

Thornton's, 128 St Stephen's Green D8, t (01) 478 7008. First-class modern Irish food in an elegant setting above St Stephen's Green.

Moderate

Avoca Café, inside Avoca Handweavers, 11–13 Suffolk Street, D2, t (01) 672 6019, *info@ avoca.ie*. Excellent café with organic produce used where possible, and tempting baked desserts. *Open Mon–Sat 10–5, Sun 11–5*.

The Chameleon, 1 Lower Fownes Street, D2, t (01) 671 0362. Popular Indonesian restaurant specializing in *Rijsttafel*, with low tables and silk cushions.

The Chilli Club, 1 Anne's Lane, South Anne Street, D2, t (01) 677 3721. Proper Thai cooking by a Thai chef – the lemongrass soups have a real kick, whilst the curries vary in terms of spiciness.

Citron, Fitzwilliam Hotel, St Stephen's Green, D2, t (01) 478 7000. Mediterranean food and fast service within a bright yellow colour scheme. More expensive in the evening.

Chompy's, Powerscourt Town House Centre, South William Street, D2, t (01) 679 4552. American-style deli-restaurant.

Elephant and Castle, 18 Temple Bar, D2, t (01) 679 3121. Burgers, omelettes and really good bumper sandwiches. Always busy, and good for brunch on Sundays.

Good World Chinese Restaurant, 18 South Great Georges Street, D2, t (01) 677 5373. Nice any time, and great for *dim sum* on Sunday.

Imperial, 12A Wicklow Street, D2, t (01) 677 2580. Smart Chinese restaurant with good value set lunches and *dim sum*.

Nico's Restaurant, 53 Dame Street, D2, t (01) 677 3062. Busy and friendly Italian restaurant with a theatrical atmosphere.

Saagar, 16 Harcourt Street, D2, t (01) 475 5060. One of the best Indian restaurants in Ireland, with some innovative dishes as well as the old favourites. *Inexpensive* for lunch.

Yamamori, 71–75 South Great George's Street, D2, t (01) 475 5001. Good Japanese noodle house with an *inexpensive* lunch special.

Inexpensive

Bad Ass Café, 9–11 Crown Alley, Temple Bar, D2, t (01) 671 2596, *www.badasscafe.com*. Diner-style spot for pizza, chops and burgers, famous because Sinead O'Connor used to waitress here. Good set menu for under €15.

Bewley's Café, 78–79 Grafton Street, D2 (also on Westmoreland Street), t (01) 635 5470. Where Dubliners have met, talked and enjoyed delicious coffee and cakes (especially the *barm brack* or almond buns) for generations, although recent remodelling seems to have affected the food and mars what was once a real slice of Dublin life.

Blazing Salads, 42 Drury Street, D2, t (01) 671 9552, *www.blazingsalads.com*. Imaginative and streets ahead of average vegetarian cooking. Excellent soups, salads and homemade desserts. Caters for yeast-/gluten-/sugar-free diets. Organic wine and fresh-pressed vegetable juices.

The Boulevard Café, 27 Exchequer Street, D2, t (01) 679 2131. Handy for shopping day lunches.

Captain America's Cookhouse and Bar, 1st floor, Grafton Court, Grafton Street, D2, t (01)

671 5266. For those who miss burgers and milkshakes. Loud music. Good for kids.

Chez Jules, D'Olier Street, D2, t (01) 677 0499. Another Parisian-style bistro, very informal with chequered tablecloths and a scrubbed wooden floor. Part of a reliable chain.

Cornucopia, Wicklow Street, D2, t (01) 677 7583. Vegetarian restaurant serving wholesome bakes and soups; caters for restricted diets.

Fitzers, in the National Gallery of Art, Merrion Square, t (01) 661 4496. Tempting salads and pasta dishes. Just the place to relax after exploring the gallery.

Gotham Café, 8 South Anne Street, D2, t (01) 679 5266. Pizza, pasta and more. *Open late*.

Govinda's, 4 Aungier Street, D2, t (01) 475 0309. Good vegetarian restaurant serving Indian and wholefood bakes, soups and mild curries.

Irish Film Centre, 6 Eustace Street, D2, t (01) 679 5744. Continental-style café filled with unsurprising salads and fresh breads in their self-service lunch bar.

National Museum Café, Kildare Street, D2, t (01) 602 1269. Simple and tasty. Coddle, salads and cakes.

The Old Stand, 37 Exchequer Street, D2, t (01) 677 7220/677 5849. Famous old pub serving bar food, renowned for its steaks.

Pasta Fresca, 2–4 Chatham Street, D2, t (01) 679 2402. Crowded fresh pasta shop which serves its own produce at a limited number of tables.

Soup Dragon, 168 Capel Street, D1, t (01) 872 3277. Soup kitchen with an ever-changing menu – let the Thai chicken soup or haddock chowder tickle your tastebuds.

The Queen of Tarts, Dame Street, D2, t (01) 670 7499, and also in the City Hall. Excellent pâtisserie and coffee shop.

The Stag's Head, Dame Court, D2, t (01) 679 3701. Boiled bacon and cabbage, Irish stew.

The Stone Wall Café, 187 Exchequer Street, D2, t (01) 672 7323. Pasta and salads during the day, Mediterranean and Asian food at night.

City Centre: North of the Liffey

Chapter One, in the Basement of the Writers' Museum, 18–19 Parnell Square, D1, t (01) 873 2266 (*expensive–moderate*). Smart, atmospheric restaurant with a French and modern Irish menu efficiently delivered to your table.

101 Talbot, 101 Talbot Street, D1, t (01) 874 5011 (*moderate*). Cheerful atmosphere, Mediterranean and eastern-inspired cooking. Good for vegetarians and popular with theatre-going folk.

The Winding Stair, 40 Lower Ormond Quay, D1, t (01) 873 3292 (*inexpensive*). Soup and sandwiches in a charming café-cum-bookshop with a lovely view over the Liffey.

Dublin City South

Locks Restaurant, 1 Windsor Terrace, Portobello, D8, t (01) 454 3391 (*expensive*). This cosy place overlooks the Grand Canal and has an assured and friendly feel to it. Some of the dishes are adventurous and wholesome, with extensive use of organic produce from County Wicklow.

The Old Dublin Restaurant, 90–91 Francis Street, D8, t (01) 454 2028 (*expensive*). A very appealing and well-presented menu which inclines towards the Oriental and east-European – mainly Scandinavian and Russian. They serve lovely *kasha* barley or savoury rice; and vegetarian *satsiv*, which is a crispy version of curried fresh vegetables.

The Orchid Szechuan Restaurant, 120 Pembroke Road, Ballsbridge, D4, t (01) 660 0629 (*expensive*). Excellent Chinese food in this restaurant, recommended by locals.

Satchels Restaurant, in The Schoolhouse Hotel, 2–8 Northumberland Road, D4, t (01) 667 5014, www.schoolhousehotel.com (*expensive*). Good bistro food, served in an impressive beamed hall.

Fitzer's Restaurant, 51 Dawson Street, D4, t (01) 677 1155 (*moderate*). Sassy food from the Pacific rim and the Med, with a small heated terrace. Also at Temple Bar Square, and in the National Gallery, Merrion Square.

The Grey Door, 22/23 Upper Pembroke Street, D4, t (01) 676 3286 (*moderate*). Russian and Scandinavian food.

Kitty O'Shea's Restaurant, 23–25 Grand Canal Street, D4, t (01) 660 8050, www.kittyosheas.com (*moderate*). This deservedly popular spot reopened in 2004.

Marrakesh, 1st Floor, 28 South Anne Street, D2, t (01) 670 5255 (*moderate*). Authentic Moroccan restaurant. Traditional dishes include delicious soups, generous helpings of couscous and a choice of *tagines*.

Roly's Bistro, 7 Ballsbridge Terrace, Ballsbridge, D4, **t** (01) 668 2611 (*moderate*). Lovely interior; a fun, fashionable café atmosphere with food to match. *Advance booking essential.*

Ryan's, 28 Parkgate Street, D8, **t** (01) 671 9352 (*moderate*). Cosy Victorian pub serving fine bar fare, especially the salad plates.

Burdocks, 2 Werburgh Street, D6, **t** (01) 454 0306 (*inexpensive*). Excellent take-away fish and chips to eat in the park.

Entertainment and Nightlife

Listings

In Dublin magazine was started by a group of students, and became so successful that you can now buy it at every news stand. The free newspaper *The Event Guide*, *www. eventguide.ie*, is also great for listings. The *Evening Herald* also contains cinema listings, while the *Irish Mirror* has a Friday supplement that is good for music and nightclubs. Read the *Irish Times* for reviews of plays, concerts and films. Every Saturday it also lists special happenings in Dublin and the provinces.

Good websites for information on city life include *The Dubliner* magazine's stylish website, *www.thedubliner.ie*, and *The Irish Times* website, *www.ireland.com/dublin*, which lists events daily. The official Dublin Tourism website, *www.visitdublin.com*, offers excellent coverage as well.

Bars and Pubs

Dublin's pubs and bars are famous for their warm, convivial atmosphere, their snugs, whiskey, mirrors and food – and, of course, their Guinness.

The Bailey, 2–3 Duke Street, D2, **t** (01) 670 4939. A literary stop-off.

Clarence Hotel Bar, 6–8 Wellington Quay, D2, **t** (01) 407 0800. The Octagon Bar in the Clarence Hotel has friendly staff, and is fashionable with theatre and film people.

Davy Byrnes, 21 Duke Street, D2, **t** (01) 677 5217. Busy with tourists on the literary trail. But they do make good sandwiches.

Dawson Lounge, 25 Dawson Street, D2, **t** (01) 677 5909. Quirky basement bar – famously the smallest bar in Dublin.

Doheny and Nesbitt's, 5 Lower Baggot Street, D2, **t** (01) 676 2945. Victorian décor. Frequented by lawyers and politicians.

The Globe, 11 South Great Georges Street, D2, **t** (01) 671 1220/670 5765. Café popular with the young and beautiful – good sandwiches and cappuccinos at lunchtime.

Grogan's, 15 South William Street, D2, **t** (01) 677 9320. Aspiring writers, artists, etc.

The International Bar, 23 Wicklow Street, D2, **t** (01) 677 9250. Nice in the afternoon; music at night.

Kehoe's Pub, 9 South Anne Street, D2, **t** (01) 677 8312. Authentic and quirky with a good snug.

Long Hall, 51 South Great George's Street, D2, **t** (01) 475 1590. Crammed with knick-knacks and lovely mirrors. Nice barmen.

McDaids, 3 Harry Street, D2, **t** (01) 679 4395. Traditionally a literary haunt; hosts jazz on some nights.

Mulligans, Poolbeg Street, D2, **t** (01) 677 5582. This bar has earned a reputation for high-quality Guinness, and is popular with journalists.

Neary's, 1 Chatham Street, off Grafton Street, D2, **t** (01) 677 7371. Good sandwiches and a theatrical atmosphere.

Palace Bar, 21 Fleet Street, D2, **t** (01) 677 9290. This one was a writers' haunt once upon a time in the 1950s.

Ryan's Bar, 28 Parkgate Street, D7, **t** (01) 677 9352. Well-preserved Victoriana, cosy snugs and very good pub food, especially lunch.

The Shelbourne Hotel, Horseshoe Bar, 27 St Stephen's Green, D2, **t** (01) 663 4500. An elegant spot, and popular with lawyers, politicans and journalists.

Stag's Head, 1 Dame Court, D2, **t** (01) 679 3701. Cosy interior snug with friendly staff; good for sausages, chips and Guinness.

Toner's, 139 Lower Baggot Street, D2, **t** (01) 676 2606. Victorian fittings and a mixed crowd. Nice toasted cheese sandwiches.

Bars with Music

Folk, Jazz and Rock

Bob's Bar, 35–37 East Essex Street, D2, **t** (01) 677 5482. Live music on Sunday nights.

International Bar, 23 Wicklow Street, D2, **t** (01) 677 9250. Four floors, with DJs and live music on Sunday nights.

J. J. Smyth's, 12 Aungier Street, D2, t (01) 475 2565. Mostly jazz.

McDaid's, 3 Harry Street, D2, t (01) 679 4395. Blues upstairs.

O'Dwyers, 7 Lower Mount Street, D2, t (01) 676 1617.

Whelans, 25 Wexford Street, D2, t (01) 478 0766, *www.whelanslive.com*. Music almost every night: indie, rock, bluegrass, country and some styles that you never dreamed existed. Legends like Leo O'Kelly play there.

Traditional Music

Traditional music can be heard on different nights at each venue. Sessions are free, unless a big name is playing. Check in the local newspaper or with the bar. If you wish to learn more about traditional Irish music, pay a visit to *Ceol*, the Irish Traditional Music Centre, at Smithfield Village, Smithfield, D7, t (01) 817 3820, f 817 3821, *www.ceol.ie*, *info@ceol.ie*.

Brazen Head, 20 Lower Bridge Street, D8, t (01) 679 5186. The oldest bar in Dublin. Trad or rock, depending on the night.

The Cobblestone, 77 North King St, D2, t (01) 872 1799. Battered, smoky, labrythine pub with live performances. Good range of beers from the Dublin Brewing Co microbrewery.

Harcourt Hotel, 60 Harcourt Street, D2, t (01) 478 3677, or t 1850 664455. Sessions every night with musicians from all over Ireland.

Hughes, 19 Chancery Street, D7, t (01) 872 6540. One of the best.

Kitty O'Shea's, 23 Upper Grand Canal Street, D4, t (01) 660 8050.

O'Donoghues, 15 Merrion Row, D2, t (01) 676 2807.

O'Shea's Merchants Bar, 12 Lower Bridge Street, D8, t (01) 679 3797. Traditional Irish and ballad music and song; you'll also find set-dancing here.

Mother Redcaps, Back Lane, beside Tailors' Guildhall, Christchurch, D4, t (01) 453 8306. Folk music also. Traditional music on Sundays and Tuesday eves.

The Oliver St John Gogarty, Temple Bar, D2, t (01) 671 1822.

Rumm's, Shelbourne Road, D4, t (01) 667 6422. Pub food and nightly traditional music.

Slattery's, 179 Capel Street, D1, t (01) 874 6844. A very popular place.

Temple Bar, 47 Temple Bar, D2, t (01) 672 5287.

Cinema

Film is extremely popular in Dublin; indeed, the Irish attend the cinema more frequently than any other Europeans. All cinemas are listed in the papers.

Irish Film Centre, 6 Eustace Street, Temple Bar, D2, t (01) 679 3477. Foreign and art-house releases. The spring film festival is organized from here. There is also a café with snacks.

Savoy Cinema, Upper O'Connell Street, D1, t (01) 874 6000. First-runs.

Screen Cinema, D'Olier Street, D2, t (01) 672 5500. Independent, less commercial films.

UGC Cinemas, Parnell Street, D1, t (01) 872 8444. 10-screen, first-run house.

Classical Music and Shows

When big stars of whatever sort come to town, they may appear at the RDS Concert Hall in suburban Ballsbridge; some big rock concerts use the Point Theatre at East Link Bridge, or even the Lansdowne Road Stadium.

Bank of Ireland Arts Centre, Foster Place, D2, t (01) 671 1488. Classical music.

Gaiety Theatre, South King Street, D2, t (01) 677 1717, *www.gaietytheatre.com*. For opera.

Hugh Lane Gallery, Charlemont House, Parnell Square North, D1, t (01) 874 1903, f 872 2182, *www.hughlane.ie*. Another place for classical music; hosts lunchtime concerts.

The National Concert Hall, Earlsfort Terrace, D2, t (01) 475 1666, *www.nch.ie*, *info@nch.ie*. The National Symphony Orchestra is based here, and there is a full schedule of other concerts most of the year, not only classical but jazz, pop and touring shows.

Temple Bar Music Centre, Curved St, Temple Bar, D2, t (01) 670 9202, *www.tbmc.ie*. Music, dance, theatre and art in Temple Bar. It's also the home of the Opera Theatre Company.

Theatre

It is worth spending money on the theatre in Dublin. Things really take off during the **festival** in October, with new plays by Irish authors, some of which have become Broadway hits. The most convenient place to **book tickets** is at the stall in Brown Thomas's in Grafton Street. You can also get them at the tourist offices on Suffolk Street and O'Connell Street, or from the theatres themselves.

Abbey Theatre, Lower Abbey Street, D1, t (01) 878 7222, booking line t (01) 456 9569. The famous theatre founded by the indomitable Lady Gregory and W. B. Yeats. The old building burned down; the new one also houses the **Peacock Theatre**, which concentrates on contemporary playwrights, whereas the Abbey sticks predominently to the old Irish classics. The Abbey has made the Irish turn of phrase famous throughout the world with plays such as *Playboy of the Western World* by J. M. Synge and *Juno and the Paycock* by Sean O'Casey. It can be hard getting tickets, so book ahead.

Andrew's Lane Theatre, 12 St Andrews Lane, t (01) 679 5720. A variety of dramatic fare; adventurous, modern pieces in the **Andrews Lane Studio**.

City Arts Centre, 23 Moss Street, t (01) 677 0643. Exciting productions here too.

Focus Theatre, 6 Pembroke Place, off Pembroke Street, D2, t (01) 676 3071. Fringe theatre.

Gaiety Theatre, South King Street, D2, t (01) 677 1717, *www.gaietytheatre.com*. A splendid, tiered Victorian theatre, showing more traditional plays, and it provides a venue for opera, musicals and pantomime.

Gate Theatre, 1 Cavendish Row, D1, t (01) 874 4045. Stages productions of international and classic dramas; famous names such as Orson Welles and James Mason began their acting careers here.

Olympia Theatre, 72 Dame Street, D2, t (01) 677 7744. Drama, ballet, musical as well as late night concerts.

Project Arts Theatre, 39 East Essex Street, Temple Bar, D2, t (01) 679 6622, booking t 1800 260 027, f 679 2310, *www.project.ie, info@project.ie*. Perhaps some of the most experimental and stimulating theatre in Dublin, with art exhibitions alongside.

Samuel Beckett Centre, Trinity College, t (01) 608 2461, *www.tcd.ie/drama*. Often has exciting lunchtime theatre.

SFX City Theatre, 23 Upper Sherrard Street, D1, t (01) 855 4673, *www.sfx.ie*. Fringe.

Tivoli Theatre, Francis Street, D8, t (01) 453 5998. Stages musicals and plays.

Nightclubs

Dublin has been voted 'hippest city in Europe' by several fashion magazines, in particular for its nightclub scene. This seems extreme, but there is no doubt that Dublin at night can be fun. Most of the clubs stay open until 2–3.30am. They are also by their very nature fairly transient, so do check in advance.

Gaiety Theatre, South King Street, D2, t (01) 677 1717, *www.gaietytheatre.com*. Several levels including jazz, blues and salsa, dance and 60s/70s retro in a relaxed atmosphere. They also have reggae nights.

The Kitchen, East Essex Street, D2, t (01) 677 6635, *www.the-kitchen.com*. U2-owned club, hot, hip and friendly with an open-house music policy – which means anything from hardcore house and techno to drum 'n' bass.

Lillie's Bordello, Adam Court, off Grafton Street, D2, t (01) 679 9204. The longest established of Dublin's currently fashionable clubs, frequented by models, visiting rock stars and other beautiful people. Wide-ranging in age; be prepared to queue. Jazz on Sunday nights.

Klub Zazu, Eustace Street, D2, t (01) 670 7655. Playing classic dance music on two levels – accessible and popular.

The Mean Fiddler, 26 Wexford Street, D2, t (01) 475 8555. A wide choice of live gigs and club nights. Indie, dance, rock and punk.

Olympia, 72 Dame Street, D2, t (01) 677 7744. This club is housed in a delightful old former music hall, and hosts a wide range of music.

Pod, 35 Harcourt Street, D2, t (01) 478 0166, *www.pod.ie*. Serious dance music for late 20- and 30-something posers, tucked beside an old train station. They also run Red Box (next door), see below.

The Red Box, Harcourt Street, D2, t (01) 478 0166. Huge dancefloor with house, techno and disco nights catering to a younger crowd than adjoining Pod.

Ri Ra, Dame Court, D2, t (01) 677 4835. Funky, unpretentious and good for late-night drinking; two floors of music plus a quieter bar upstairs. Strictly Handbag on Monday nights is a classic Dublin night out.

Spirit, 44–47 The Lotts, D1, t (01) 877 9999. The newest of Dublin's hip clubs, Spirit is the current home of the see-and-be-seen crowd. It's the kind of place with a VIP room and a VVIP room.

Modern Dublin was bent on knocking down the past or ignoring it so that it crumbled away on its own, especially during the 1970s. Should you ask about Wood Quay, official indifference reveals itself. Wood Quay was the complete 9th- to 11th-century Danish settlement of houses, walls and quays which was recently excavated, giving great insight into the lives of those first Dubliners. The Dublin City Corporation actually built their ugly modern office block on top of it, despite sustained protests from those who felt the old city should be preserved. On the positive side, the Custom House Quay development, which also houses a financial centre, is a fine attempt at regeneration of the docklands area. And the last few years have seen a quickening of interest in preserving the lovely old buildings of the past. The Dublin Millennium Celebrations in 1988 caused a great sprucing up, and Dubliners took great pride in their city's history and heritage. In 1991 Dublin was European City of Culture, which encouraged more refurbishment. There is still an amount of uncoordinated planning, though: Dublin is threatened with road-widening plans, and what amounts to a motorway has been built, cutting through the city centre.

But you will find that gradually the charm and atmosphere of Dublin – and atmosphere is what it is all about – begins to filter through that first, negative impression. Get up early, explore the ancient medieval streets around Dublin Castle in the morning sunshine, and breakfast at Bewley's Café. Walk down Grafton Street, where noisy, laughing shoppers mingle with some genuine eccentrics. Relax, go with the flow and notice the pleasant things about Dublin which have been there all along.

History

The Greek philosopher Ptolemy mentioned Dublin in AD 140, when it was called Eblana, but it really came to prominence under the **Danes** during the 9th century, because of its importance as a fording place and as a base for maritime expeditions. They established themselves on a section of ground between the River Liffey and Christ Church. The name Dublin comes from the Irish *Dubhlinn*: 'Dark Pool'; although the Irish form in official use at the moment is *Baile Atha Cliath*: 'Town of the Hurdle Ford' – this refers to an ancient river crossing near the present Heuston Station.

The marauding **Vikings** arrived in AD 840 and established a fortress and a settlement along the banks of the Liffey estuary. From a simple base for raiding expeditions, Dublin grew to a prosperous trading port with Europe. The local Gaelic rulers were very keen to grab it for themselves, but it was not until the **Battle of Clontarf** in 1014 that the dominance of the Danes was severely curtailed. They were finally driven out in 1169 by the **Anglo-Normans** under **Strongbow** (Richard de Clare), who took Dublin by storm and executed the Viking leader. The arrival of the Anglo-Norman foreigners began the occupation of Ireland by the **English**, which lasted for seven hundred years. **Dermot MacMurragh**, King of Leinster, invited the invasion by asking Henry II of England for the help of Anglo-Norman mercenaries in his battle for the high kingship of Ireland. They came, and their military campaigns were so successful that they soon controlled not only Wexford and Waterford but also most of Leinster and, of course, Dublin. Once here, the Normans had no intention of leaving. In 1172 Henry II came to Dublin to look over his kingdom, and to curb the powers of his warlike vassal lords.

From then on, Dublin played a dominant role as the centre of English power. The Anglo-Normans fortified themselves with strong castles, and the area surrounding Dublin where they settled was known as **The Pale**. Anything outside was dangerous and barbaric – hence the expression, 'beyond the Pale'. For a short and glorious period in the late 18th century Ireland had its own parliament here, '**Grattan's Parliament**' (1782–1800); the élite who sat within it had many liberal ideas, such as the introduction of Catholic emancipation. One could speculate that the course of Ireland's history might have been happier if this independent parliament had been allowed to develop. A great surge of urban building took place during this time. Grattan was typical of the liberal landowners who wanted legislative reform, and is remembered for his powers of oratory. Unfortunately, the influence of the French Revolution and the growth of the United Irishmen frightened the British Government. The **1798 Rising** was a realization of their worst fears, and the British Parliament resumed direct control of Irish affairs in 1800. This meant that the resident and educated ruling class left Dublin, and took with them much of its dynamism and culture. The struggle for independence from English rule manifested itself in violent episodes and street clashes in the 19th century, with violence becoming more common in the early 20th century. During the **1916 Rising**, buildings and lives were shattered by Nationalists fighting with British troops, which erupted again during the Civil War that followed the peace with England. Many of those buildings, such as the Customs House, the masterpiece of James Gandon (1743–1823), have been restored to their former glory.

It was under the rule of the so-called **Anglo-Irish Ascendency** that Dublin acquired her gracious streets and squares, which amaze one with their variety. Many of the houses were built in small groups by speculators when Dublin was the fashionable place to be – hence the variety. Each door is slightly different and the patterns of the wrought-iron balconies and railings change from house to house. You will not see ironwork like this in London, as most railings were ripped up and melted down during the Second World War.

The size of Dublin increased very slowly during the 19th and early 20th centuries, due in part to the lack of countrywide industrialization, the famine and emigration. The population started to grow in the 1950s with a shift from rural to urban areas; today Dubliners suffer from a lack of housing, inadequate sewage treatment, increasing crime, and a huge traffic problem caused by urban sprawl and the neglect of public transport, which is now being addressed. The population of young people in Ireland, and in Dublin particularly, is high. Greater Dublin has a population of over one million, and plenty of families are living on the dole; some of the suburban housing estates are among the poorest and most troubled in Europe.

Still, since the 1990s booming Dublin has become the power behind the '**Celtic Tiger**' economy. It is a city full of new money and high-tech industries, a city growing outwards in all directions. Tourists pour in, drawn by the city's traditional charms and even more by the continuing worldwide popularity of all things Irish. Changes to the city itself are noticeable. New museums and attractions have appeared, and there is some redevelopment in the city's docklands and around O'Connell Street. Dubliners are showing signs of finally reforming their notorious neglect of the inner city and its historic architecture; a symbol of this is **Temple Bar**, the riverfront area transformed by private initiative into a thriving and attractive entertainment district after the government tried – unsuccessfully – to demolish it. Dublin isn't a city given to grand gestures and showy mega-projects. Its people are cautious and mindful of traditions; they like things to stay as they are.

Throughout the centuries Dublin has produced great writers: Jonathan Swift, Bishop Berkeley, Edmund Burke, Thomas Moore, Sheridan, Le Fanu, Wilde and Goldsmith, to name but a few. Towards the end of the 19th century Dublin became the centre of the Cultural Movement, which resulted in the formation of the **Gaelic League**, which became entangled with the Nationalists' aspirations of the time. How much influence this movement had on the next flurry of great writers it is hard to say, but George Bernard Shaw, George Moore, James Stephens, W. B. Yeats, James Joyce and later Samuel Beckett drew much of their inspiration from the streets of Dublin.

Central Dublin City

Trinity College and Around

The **O'Connell Bridge**, the most important of the bridges that cross the Liffey, is a good spot to get your bearings and begin a tour of Dublin. On the riverbank the monuments of the city line up, the Four Courts on one side, the Custom House on the other. Across the river is the famous O'Connell Street, while, on the southern side, narrow, busy Westmoreland Street invites you into the heart of the city.

The former Parliament House stands where Westmoreland meets College Green, and is nowadays the **Bank of Ireland** (*t (01) 677 2261; open during banking hours Mon–Fri 10–4, Thurs until 5; free guided tours of the House of Lords Tues at 10.30, 11.30 and 1.45 except on bank hols; adm*). The brainchild of Lovat Pearce, who designed it in 1729, it was finished in 1785 by James Gandon, Dublin's most notable architect. It was between these walls that Grattan stunned everybody with his oratory when he demanded constitutional independence from the English Parliament. Later, in 1800, a well-bribed House voted for the Union, and Parliament House became redundant. It is an imposing classical building with Ionic porticoes. Inside you may see the coffered ceiling of the old House of Lords; a Waterford chandelier dating from 1765; and two fine 18th-century tapestries depicting famous Protestant victories, the Battle of the Boyne and the Siege of Derry, as well as the parliament's Golden Mace. The bankers celebrate their trade in the adjacent Bank of Ireland Arts Centre, Foster Place, with **The Story of Banking Museum** (*open Tues–Fri 10–4*).

Just opposite Parliament House is the entrance to **Trinity College**, through Regent House, and during term-time the students are clustered around it, joking, chatting or handing out political leaflets. As you enter through the imposing 1759 façade, you leave bustling Dublin far behind and come upon a giant square, laid out with green lawn and cobbled stone, and surrounded by gracious buildings. Stop to look at the **Museum Building** (which has only a small geological collection) for the stone carving by the O'Shea brothers; they also created the amusing monkeys which play round what used to be the Kildare Street Club on the northeast corner of Kildare Street.

The other buildings in the quadrangle are 18th-century and are described below, but first pass through the peaceful grounds into the second quadrangle, as your main objective will probably be to visit **Trinity College Library** (*t (01) 608 2320, www.tcd.ie/library; open all year Mon–Sat 9.30–4.30, plus Oct–May also Sun 12–4.30; adm*) to take a look at the priceless ***Book of Kells***. The library is on the left of the second quadrangle and dates from 1712. It has been a copyright library since 1801 and contains an enormous number of manuscripts, including the diaries of Wolfe Tone and the manuscripts of John Millington Synge. The library is a fine building and contains the Long Room, which has a barrel-vaulted ceiling and gallery bookcases. The area underneath the Long Room, known as the Colonnades, has been remodelled, and the *Book of Kells* is permanently displayed there. Every day one of the thick vellum pages of the book is turned to present more fantastic and intricate designs. Someone once said that the book was made up of imaginative doodles. The man who copied out the gospels and enlivened them with such 'doodles' was able to draw so perfectly that sections as small as a postage stamp reveal no flaws when magnified. The book is probably 8th-century and comes from an abbey in Kells, County Meath. Have a look, too, at the *Book of Durrow*, the *Book of Armagh* and the *Book of Dimma*, which are also beautifully illuminated.

Next door is the **Berkeley Library** which contains over two million books. It was built in 1967 to designs by Paul Koralek, who also did the skilfully designed **Arts Building**, erected in 1978. An audiovisual show, 'The Dublin Experience' (*t (01) 608 2320; open late May–early Oct daily 10–5, hourly shows; adm*), is held in the Arts Building. It tells the story of the city from its Viking beginnings to the present day.

Trinity College was founded in 1592, in the reign of Elizabeth I. The land on which it was erected had once been occupied by the Augustinian monastery of All Hallows, founded by Dermot MacMurragh in the 12th century. The squares are made up of a mixture of buildings, ranging from early 18th-century to the present day. The red-brick **Rubrics**, beyond the campanile in the middle of the quad, is the oldest bit still standing and dates from *c*. 1700. Oliver Goldsmith had his chambers here, as do modern students and professors. Trinity College has a long and venerable history; so many famous scholars, wits and well-known men of Ireland were educated here. It was freed from its Protestant-only restrictions in 1873, and Catholics were allowed to study here, but Paul Cullen, the Catholic archbishop of the day, threatened any that did with excommunication. The university remained the preserve of the Protestant gentry for some time (although that is far from the case now), but distinguished itself by admitting women students as early as 1903, as well as non-Christians. The **Provost's House** (on the left of the main entrance) is a fine 18th-century mansion. One of its most famous occupants was John Mahaffy (1839–1919) a great scholar and clergyman, as was essential for the fellowship of the college. He was also, in the last year of his life, a knight. His witty dinner talk was legendary, but he could also be very wounding. Apparently he impressed on Oscar Wilde the importance of good social contacts and brilliant conversation, and declared that James Joyce's *Ulysses* was 'the inevitable result of extending university to the wrong sort of people'.

On the right as you enter the first cobbled quadrangle is the **Theatre**, or Examination Hall, which was built between 1779 and 1791 with an Adam-style ceiling and a gilt oak chandelier. On the left is the **Chapel**, built in 1798. Both buildings were designed by William Chambers, the Scottish architect who never actually set foot in Dublin. (*The Theatre and Chapel can be seen on request; ask at the Porter's Lodge.*) Beyond the Chapel is the **Dining Hall**, designed by Richard Cassels in 1743. It was nearly destroyed by fire in 1984 and has now been restored. The quick responses of the staff and students ensured the survival of the portraits and other works of art which now grace its walls again: they formed a human chain to get them safely out. Quite often there is music of some sort in the Junior Common Room, and the **Douglas Hyde Gallery**, in the Arts Building, mounts exhibitions of major Irish artists.

As it passes Trinity College, Westmoreland Street becomes **Grafton Street**, an attractive pedestrian way that is the choice shopping street of Dublin. On its way it passes the ornate **Bewley's Coffee Shop**, a Dublin institution since 1840 – so much so that it has its own museum upstairs (there is another branch on Westmoreland Street). On the side streets west of Grafton, you can find the **Dublin Tourism Centre**, a formidably busy tourist office with the air of an airport terminal, which is housed in an imaginative restoration of the long-abandoned Protestant St Andrew's Church (1860). **Powerscourt Town House** in South William Street, built in 1771, was typical of Georgian town houses of the Ascendency. It has fine rococo and Adamesque plaster-work which has survived in the conversion of the house and surroundings into the **Powerscourt Shopping Centre**. This triumph of enlightened development is a pleasure to visit; it houses a large crafts co-operative and has a variety of restaurants including a very good vegetarian one, called 'Fresh', which is right at the top. Here you can see Ireland's finest boutiques (including the Irish Design Centre) and speciality shops, enclosed under a great glass-roofed courtyard (*see* 'Shopping', p.120). Next to the Centre at 58 South William Street is the **Dublin Civic Museum** (*t (01) 679 4260, www. dublincouncil.ie; open Tues–Sat 10–6, Sun 11–2; adm free*), a collection of old newspapers, cuttings, prints, pictures and coins which build up a clear picture of old Dublin. You can also see some Viking artefacts found in the recent excavations, and Admiral Nelson's head – from the column the IRA blew up in O'Connell Street (*see* p.140).

St Stephen's Green

St Stephen's Green (*open 8am–dusk*), at the top of Grafton Street, is one of the loveliest and best-loved city parks you will ever see. In the middle is a romantic landscaped park with a lake and waterfall, ducks and weeping willows. Every age and type of Dubliner uses it to wander in, and enjoy the trees and flowers. Its cool, green gardens make a perfect setting for a picnic. At the western edge of the green is Henry Moore's graceful monument to W. B. Yeats. Another monument is to Lord Ardilaun – Sir Arthur Guinness, the fellow whose signature is on the bottle. He not only paid for the improvements, but put through a bill in Parliament to purchase the park and open it to the public in the 1880s. Originally the area had been common land; in the

1660s the English fenced it in and converted it into a private residential square. The surviving Anglo-Norman aristocracy, Cromwellian adventurers and the new gentry (mainly composed of those who had profited from the seizure of forfeited lands), then built their grand houses around the square and adjoining streets.

Today, one of Dublin's biggest regrets is her many decades of utter carelessness in looking after her architectural heritage. It is certainly true in the streets around St Stephen's Green. Two of the original houses that survive belong to University College Dublin, an institution founded by the Catholics in the 1860s as a counter to the Protestant Trinity College. **Newman House**, at 85 St Stephen's Green, D12 (*t (01) 716 7422; open June–Aug Tues–Fri for tours at 12, 2, 3 and 4; adm*) is named after Cardinal John Henry Newman, the great theologian of the 19th-century Catholic revival who founded the university. These two buildings contain some of the finest late Baroque and rococo plasterwork in Ireland; poet Gerard Manley Hopkins, who was a professor of Classics at the university, died here after many years' residence. No.85 was built in 1738, designed by Richard Cassels, and it contains the ravishing Apollo room, a master-piece of stucco decoration by the Francini brothers. No.86 was built in 1765 for the MP Richard Chapell Whaley, father of the notorious Buck Whaley, whose memoirs of 18th-century Dublin are still a good read. The house has very good plasterwork by Robert West; the hall is decorated with motifs of musical instruments.

If you are passing the famous Shelbourne Hotel on St Stephen's Green, you may notice a shuttered garden, just to the left of it. The **Huguenot Graveyard** is a secret place. Even Dubliners hardly know it is there. You can peer through the gates and see the mellow gravestones which mark the names of French Huguenots who successfully merged into the Irish way of life after a couple of generations. Ten thousand Huguenots arrived in Ireland to escape persecution for their religous beliefs, between the 1650s and 1700s. They had a great civilizing influence on early 18th-century Dublin, which was then very small and only just beginning to develop its own cultural activities after the turbulence of the 17th century. The Huguenots expanded the wine trade, started silk and poplin industries, and introduced a Horticultural Society, where they used to toast their favourite flowers.

Around Merrion Square

The beautiful Georgian **Merrion Square**, just east of St Stephen's Green, is one of the best-preserved in Dublin, and was the home of many famous literary people and politicians. Sir William and Lady 'Speranza' Wilde (Oscar's parents) lived at No.1; Daniel O'Connell at No.58; W. B. Yeats at Nos.52 and 82; George Russell, known as A. E., at No.84; and Sheridan Le Fanu at No.70. With the Irish Parliament just next door, most of the square's homes have been converted into offices of the government, or inter-ests that like to be close to it. **Leinster House**, on the western edge of the square, was finished in 1745, built to the design of Richard Cassels, who was responsible for so many lovely houses in Ireland – Russborough House in Wicklow, for instance. Leinster House has two different faces, one looking out over Kildare Street and the other on to the pleasant garden of Merrion Square. It was the town house of the dukes of Leinster and was originally known as Kildare House. Leinster House is now the seat of the Irish Parliament, which consists of the *Dáil* ('Lower House', pronounced 'doyle') and the *Seanad* ('Upper House', or 'Senate').

The National Gallery stands just opposite the fountain (*t (01) 661 5133, www.national gallery.ie; open Mon–Wed and Sat 10–5.30, Thurs 10–8.30, Sun 2–5.30; tours on Sat at 3pm and Sun at 2, 3 and 4pm; adm free*). A statue of George Bernard Shaw greets you in the forecourt. He bequeathed one third of his estate to the gallery because he learnt so much from the pictures. Certainly this is one of the most enjoyable, first-class small galleries in the world – although recently extended by the construction of the sleek, ultra-modern Millennium Wing (entrance on Clare Street). There are over two thousand works on view, including a small collection of superb work by Renaissance painters; Spanish, French and Italian 16th- and 17th-century painters; and Dutch Masters. The Irish Room includes some elegant portraits by Lavery, Orpen and many others, work by J. B. Yeats (father of W. B. Yeats) and well-regarded wild and colourful oils by Jack Yeats (brother of W. B. Yeats). Gainsborough is well represented with 10 major works. Upstairs in the Arts Reference Library there is a good collection of Irish watercolours. The gallery restaurant is a good place for lunch or early supper, and the shop selling postcards and art books is also excellent.

The **Irish Architectural Archive** at 73 Merrion Square (south side), a wonderful example of a Georgian town house, opens its reading room to the public (*t (01) 676 3430; open Mon–Fri 10–5; adm free*).

The **National Museum of Ireland**, in a grand Victorian edifice, occupies two sites: most of the block south of Leinster House (*entrance on Kildare Street, t (01) 677 7444, www.museum.ie; open Tues–Sat 10–5, Sun 2–5; adm free*) and Collins Barracks in Benburb Street, D7. It is the treasure house of Ireland, and absolutely vital for anyone who has not yet realized that Ireland between AD 600 and 900 was the most civilized part of northern Europe. It has the finest collection of Celtic ornaments and artefacts in the world, and items recently excavated from the Danish settlement in Wood Quay. The Historical Collection traces the history of Ireland from the 18th to the mid-20th century. In the Antiquities Department you can see the beautiful filigree gold whorl enamelling and design which reached perfection in the Tara Brooch and the Ardagh Chalice. The many beautiful torcs, croziers and decorated shrines on display will leave you amazed at the skill of the craftsmen in those days. Also very interesting are the findings of the Stone and Early Bronze Ages.

Linked to the museum is the **National Library**, which is also in Kildare Street. It has over half a million books and a fascinating collection of Irish-interest source material. There is usually an exhibition on in the entrance hall and the staff are very helpful. The **Genealogical Office** (*t (01) 603 0200; open Mon–Wed 10–8.30, Thurs–Fri 10.30–4.30, Sat 10–12.30; adm free*) is further down the street, in a stately building that was once an Anglo-Irish men's club, and houses a small Heraldic Museum. The **Natural History Museum** on Merrion Street (*t (01) 677 7444; open Tues–Sat 10–5 and Sun 2–5; adm free*) has barely changed in decades; it has a charming, musty atmosphere, with thousands of stuffed birds, fish and animals, and some fascinating elk skeletons. The **Royal Irish Academy**, at 19 Dawson Street (*t (01) 676 2570; open Tues–Fri 9.30–5; adm free*), has one of the largest collections of ancient Irish manuscripts, one of which is on view. **Ely Place** is more melancholy and just a stone's throw away, between Merrion Row and Baggot Street. It was once very grand, but is now wrapped in a gloom which strip-lighting, glimpsed through the elegant windows, does nothing to dispel. **Ely House** is owned by the Knights of Colombanus, a charity organization.

Fitzwilliam Square (1791), two streets south of Merrion Square, is the last of Dublin's residential squares, and contains more well-preserved examples of 18th-century architecture with pretty doors and fanlights above. **Number Twenty Nine**, at 29 Fitzwilliam Street Lower, just off the square (*t (01) 702 6165, www.esb.ie/education; open Tues–Sat 10–5, Sun 2–5; guided tours; adm*), is a charmingly restored Georgian house, furnished in the style of a middle-class family of the period 1790–1820. The house is owned by the ESB, the state electricity company, which restored it as a sort of penance after knocking down much of the rest of the neighbourhood for their unsightly office block in the 1960s.

Walk a street or two northeastwards from Merrion Square and the atmosphere changes rather dramatically. This is Dublin's docklands, a drab patch of abandoned wharves and gas works. Like its London counterpart, this docklands is facing an inevitable recycling into a business centre; a few modest towers and a rash of modern apartment buildings have already appeared, but so far there's little evidence that the transformation will bring any aesthetic improvement. The **Waterways Visitor Centre**, on the basin where the Grand Canal empties into the Liffey (*t (01) 667 7510, www.waterwaysireland.org; open June–Sept daily 9.30–5.30; Oct–May Wed–Sun 12.30–5; adm*) tells the story of the construction and architecture of the waterways, and describes their flora and fauna. The **Grand Canal** marks the extent of the Georgian city south of the Liffey, and the towpath which runs alongside it across the southern edge of the city centre takes you past wildfowl and over humpbacked bridges.

Around Dublin Castle

West of Trinity College and St Stephen's Green, back towards the quays, you will come to an area lacking in governmental glitter and fancy shops – but this is the true heart of the city, where Dublin began under the Vikings a thousand years ago. **Dublin Castle**, on Dame Street (*t (01) 677 7129, www.dublincastle.ie; open Mon–Fri 10–5, Sat, Sun and bank hols 2–5; adm*), long the seat of British rule in Ireland, is well worth a visit, not only because of the place it has in Irish history, but for the beautifully decorated State Apartments and for the Church of the Holy Trinity, designed by Francis Johnston, in the Lower Castle Yard. The various buildings which make up the castle complex are still reminiscent of a fortified city within its own walls. The original medieval walls and towers, begun under King John in 1204, may be gone, but the squares of faded red-brick houses with their elegant Georgian façades are a unity still. Many of the present buildings date from 1688, after the earlier castle was destroyed by fire, with most of the upper yard being built in the mid-18th century. From the 18th century onwards a vice-regal court grew up around the Lord Deputy and his administrators, and there were receptions, balls and levees for the gentry and Dublin merchants. It was far removed from the lives of the ordinary people of Ireland. At that time Dublin Castle was the seat of an alien power, and to the young

Republican activists of the 19th and early 20th century it was understandably a symbol of tyranny. It was handed over to the provisional government of Ireland in 1922, and is used today for rituals such as the inauguration of the President.

The guided tour begins in the upper yard with the **State Apartments**. The lavish decoration, grand chimney pieces and beautiful antique furniture are a feast for the eyes. There is a Throne Room for visiting British monarchs, and a long Portrait Gallery with their pictures. Particularly attractive are the blue and white Wedgwood Room and the Bermingham Tower with its Gothic windows. St Patrick's Hall, site of the inaugurations, has paintings of historical scenes; this leads to the newest – and oldest – attraction in Dublin Castle, the **Undercroft**. Foundations of the original Viking fort and parts of Dublin's first city wall were discovered here during recent excavations.

The **Record Tower** is one of the oldest parts of the castle, though it was substantially rebuilt in 1813. It was from here that, in 1592, Red Hugh O'Donnell, one of the last great Gaelic leaders, managed to escape to the Wicklow Hills. The other blocks in the quadrangle have been refurbished inside and out, but sadly the proportions and original woodwork have been mucked about. **The Church of the Holy Trinity**, also called the Chapel Royal, was designed by Francis Johnston in 1807. The outside is decorated with scores of sculpted heads of Irish saints and historical figures, while the interior has elaborate vaulting, exuberant plasterwork and oak wood carving.

Within the gardens of the castle sits the **Chester Beatty Library** (*t (01) 407 0750, www.cbl.ie; open May–Sept Mon–Fri 10–5, Sat 11–5, Sun 1–5; Oct–April Tues–Fri 10–5, Sat 11–5, Sun 1–5*). Sir Alfred Chester Beatty (1875–1968) was an American mining millionaire and collector who decided to make Dublin his home. The library and its art museum together have one of the finest private collections of oriental manuscripts and miniatures in the world, as well as albums, picture scrolls and jades from the Far East. The highlights are the Korans, the Persian and Turkish paintings, the Chinese jade books and the Japanese and European woodblock prints.

Just outside the castle, facing Dame Street, **City Hall** (*t (01) 672 2204, www.dublin city.ie/cityhall; open Mon–Sat 10–5.15, Sun 2–5; adm to multimedia exhibition, free to City Hall*) occupies a building on Cork Hill, constructed in 1769 as the Royal Exchange. The basement holds a multimedia exhibition called the 'The Story of the Capital', which traces the history of Dublin with a smattering of interactive gizmos. There's also a branch of the excellent Queen of Tarts pâtisserie and café. On the opposite side of the castle, facing Werburgh Street, **St Werburgh's Church** is worth visiting for the massive Geraldine monument and the pulpit, a fine piece of carving, possibly by Grinling Gibbons (*t (01) 478 3710; open by arrangement Mon–Fri 10–4; contribution requested; entrance by the north door, 8 Castle Street*). Lord Edward Fitzgerald of the United Irishmen, and the leader of the 1798 rebellion, is interred in the vault here. This church was for a long time the parish church of Dublin, and, before the Chapel Royal in the Dublin Castle complex was built, British viceroys were sworn in here.

Just across Lord Edward Street is **Christchurch Cathedral** (*t (01) 677 8099, www. cccdub.ie; cathedral open Mon–Fri 9.45–5, Sat and Sun 10–5; Treasures of Christchurch Cathedral exhibition open Mon–Fri 9.45–5, Sat 10–4.45, Sun 10–3.15; adm*). The church was founded by King Sitric and Bishop Donatus in 1038, rebuilt by Strongbow in the

12th century, and heavily restored in the 19th century after part of the walls collapsed – there isn't much solid ground for building in central Dublin. The magnificent stonework and graceful arches are well worth a look, as is the effigy representing Strongbow, who was buried in the church – or at least, part of him was. The crypt is the oldest surviving portion of the building; it used to contain the old punishment stocks, called the 'cat and mouse', but has been recently revamped to house a exhibition called '**The Treasures of Christ Church**', with an occasionally dazzling collection of liturgical plate. Much of the treasure has been lost or sold over the years, but some fine pieces remain, including the 17th-century Royal Plate, bestowed by William and Mary to celebrate the King's victory at the Battle of the Boyne in 1740. The arch which joins the cathedral to the Synod Hall frames a view of Winetavern Street and the River Liffey. The Synod Hall in Christchurch is now home to **Dublinia** (*t (01) 679 4611, www. dublinia.ie; open April–Sept daily 10–5; Oct–Mar Mon–Sat 11–4, Sun 10.30–4; adm*), a multimedia exhibition of medieval Dublin life. with a model of the city as it changed over the centuries, and life-size tableaux. **St Audoen's Church** (*t (01) 677 0088; adm*), in Cornmarket, off High Street (the continuation of Lord Edward Street), is Dublin's only surviving medieval church. The bell tower, restored in the 19th century, has three 15th-century bells. Notice the beautiful Norman font, and make a wish at the lucky stone.

St Patrick's Cathedral (*t (01) 745 4817, www.stpatrickscathedral.ie; open Mar–Oct daily 9–6; Nov–Feb Mon–Fri 9–6, Sat 9–5 and Sun 9–3; adm*), a short distance south in Patrick's Close, marks the site of a holy well that was associated with the saint. The largest church in Ireland, it was founded in 1190 and is Early English in style. It was built outside the city walls, on what was marshy ground, by a powerful Norman bishop who was also a baron, in order to outshine Christchurch (like Christchurch, it is Church of Ireland). In the 14th century it was almost completely rebuilt after a fire, and during the 17th century it suffered terribly from the fighting during the Cromwellian campaign, and was not restored until the 1860s. Benjamin Guinness, the drinks magnate, provided the initiative and funds for this great undertaking. It is an inspiring experience to attend a choir recital here, for its huge dimensions make a perfect auditorium for the song of red-frocked choir boys. It is here that Dean Swift preached his forceful sermons in an effort to rouse some unselfish thoughts in the minds of his wealthy parishioners; over the door of the robing room is his oft-quoted epitaph, 'He lies where furious indignation can no longer rend his heart.' Swift's death mask, chair and pulpit are displayed in Swift Corner, and nearby is the grave of Stella, Swift's pupil and great love. Notice the monument to Richard Boyle, first Earl of Cork, and the monument to the last of the Irish bards, O'Carolan.

Marsh's Library, near the cathedral in St Patrick's Close (*t (01) 454 3511, www.marsh library.ie; open Mon 10–1, Wed–Fri 10–1 and 2–5, Sat 10.30–1; adm*), is the oldest public library in the country. Founded in 1707, it has changed little since, and provides a rare example of an 18th-century library. Dean Swift once owned the copy of Clarendon's *History of the Great Rebellion*, and you can look at his pencilled notes. The entrance is very welcoming, with herbaceous plants softening the stone steps, and a feeling of hallowed learning inside. The library is classical in proportion and has a superb collection of Latin and Greek literature.

Temple Bar

Temple Bar is sold as Dublin's 'left bank' in the brochures; it is, but only if you're rowing upstream. The area is named after Sir William Temple, a provost of Trinity College in the 17th century. It was neglected for a long time and was nearly razed by town planners to build a bus depot. While they were deliberating, artists moved in and rented out studio spaces very cheaply, although now there is a continual battle with property developers, who want to oust the low-rent artistic element, even though the desirability of the area is mainly due to its bohemian atmosphere.

The area is home to various alternative bookshops, bars, clubs and restaurants, and the **Project Arts Centre** on Essex Street, Dublin's new, cutting-edge theatre, which also hosts exhibitions and musical performances. The **Irish Film Centre** (*t (01) 677 8788*), on Eustace Street, shows the classics and arthouse films, and has a film bookshop as well as the National Film Archive. The **Temple Bar Information Centre** (*t (01) 677 2255, www.temple-bar.ie*), also on Eustace Street, can tell you what's going on and provides a free guide to the area. For a live, interactive recreation of Dublin (or 'Dyflin') in the 9th century, visit **Dublin's Viking Adventure** in Essex Street West (*t (01) 679 6040; open Mar–Oct Tues–Sat 10.30–4.30; Nov–Feb Tues–Sat 10–1 and 2–4.30; adm*), with Viking history, archaeological finds and a life-sized longship.

The Guinness Storehouse and the Liberties

Where else but in Dublin would one of the main landmarks of the town be a brewery? In this case, they claim it is the largest one in the world, one that makes fully half of all the beer (stout, really) consumed in Ireland. **The Guinness Storehouse** brewery, at St James's Gate, is just west of the city centre (*t (01) 408 4800, www. guinness-storehouse.com; open daily 9.30–last admission at 5pm; adm very exp*). An informative self-guided tour of the birthplace of Guinness is offered; you can visit a rooftop bar with panoramic views of the city of Dublin and try some of the stuff for free, watch a video of the processes that go into making it, and visit a museum in the old hop-store. The shop sells all sorts of 'black gold' souvenirs to take home with you.

The **Liberties** is the old residential area around the brewery, and many of the workers come from this self-sufficient part of town. It was called 'the Liberties' because it stood outside the jurisdiction of the medieval town, and had its own shops and markets. In the late 17th century, French Huguenots set up a poplin and silk-weaving industry along the river valley (known as the Coombe) of the Poddle, a now-defunct river which used to flow through the Liberties and joined the Liffey at Wood Quay. The area still has great character; despite the new apartments and trendy shops springing up in places, it's very much a working class district, and the people who live in it are the Dubliners of ballad and song. Some families have lived here for many generations. In the late 18th century, faction-fighting was commonplace between the Liberty Boys, or tailors and weavers of the Coombe, and the Ormond Boys, butchers who lived in Ormond Market. Sometimes the fighting would involve up to a thousand men. One landmark of the neighbourhood is **St Catherine's Church** (*no access*) in Thomas Street. This fine 18th-century church has a lovely Roman Doric façade. It is occasionally used for concerts and is owned by the Dublin Corporation.

A few streets west of Guinness and the Liberties is the Kilmainham neighbourhood and the **Royal Hospital and Irish Museum of Modern Art**, on Military Road across from Heuston Station (**t** *(01) 612 9900, www.modernart.ie; open Tues–Sat 10–5.30, Sun 12–5.30; adm free*). The restoration of this wonderful classical building is one of the most exciting things to happen to Dublin in recent years. The Government footed the enormous bill, and has earned much prestige through its role in saving it. The hospital was founded by James Butler, Duke of Ormonde, an able statesman who survived the turbulent times of the Great Rebellion of 1640 and Cromwell's campaigns. He remained loyal to the Stuart kings, and was well rewarded by Charles II on his succession in 1660. The duke was a pragmatist, and was responsible for securing the passing of the Act of Explanation in 1665, which largely approved the Cromwellian land confiscations. But he also did some very charitable works, amongst them the building of this hospital for pensioner soldiers, similar in style to that of the Invalides in Paris. The Royal Hospital is the largest surviving 17th-century building in Ireland and the most fully classical. Arranged around a quadrangle, it includes a Great Hall hung with rich and splendid royal portraits. The chapel has a magnificent Baroque ceiling of plasterwork designs of fruit, flowers and vegetables. The museum has a small permanent collection, mostly of contemporary artists. Temporary exhibitions of new artists and 20th-century greats are held in the long galleries.

Kilmainham Gaol on Inchicore Road, D8, where Parnell, de Valera and the leaders of every Irish revolt from 1798 to 1922 spent time, is now a historical museum (**t** *(01) 453 5984, www.heritageireland.ie; open April–Sept daily 9.30–5; Oct–Mar Mon–Fri 9.30–4, Sun 10–5; adm; guided tour only – it's very busy in summer, so book*). The leaders of the 1916 rising were executed (without trial) in the courtyard. Although rather a grim building, it is nevertheless interesting and quite moving; there is a guided tour, exhibitions and an audiovisual presentation on the prison's history. Kilmainham was used as the prison in the film *In The Name of The Father*, starring Daniel Day Lewis.

North of the Liffey

The broad thoroughfare of **O'Connell Street**, Dublin's Champs-Elysées, has, like its Parisian counterpart, come down in the world a little. After suffering considerable destruction in the Easter Rising, and more in the Civil War, it gradually ceased to be the swanky showcase of the city that it was intended to be. But despite the tatty shop fronts and fast-food signs, it is still one of the most urbane and elegant streets you will find. And, like Paris, Dublin is beginning to pay some attention to its famous boulevard once again; although it has been looking like a building site, a new tree-lined promenade is slowly unfolding and the centrepiece of the project, the controversial **Millennium Spire** (*see* below), already soars high above the traffic.

When O'Connell Street was created in the 18th century, it was purely residential, with a stately mall running up its centre to the Rotunda Hospital. The construction of the Carlisle (now O'Connell) Bridge over the Liffey changed it into a main thoroughfare, and fine department stores, theatres and office blocks replaced the houses. The monuments lining the centre of the street still add glory to it, as do the variety of architectural styles, which you will notice if you lift your eyes above shop level. The (mainly Victorian) statues you see are: Daniel O'Connell (1745–1833), the lawyer who won Catholic emancipation (the street was named after him in 1927; before that it was called Sackville Street); William Smith O'Brien (1803–64), the Nationalist leader; Sir John Gray (1816–75), owner of *The Freeman's Journal* and a Nationalist, who was knighted for organizing Dublin's water supply; James Larkin (1867–1943), the trade union leader; Father Theobald Mathew (1790–1856), who advocated and set up temperance clubs; and Charles Parnell (1846–91), a great parliamentary leader whose career was destroyed by the scandal of his affair with a married woman, Kitty O'Shea.

Lord Nelson, who defeated the French at Trafalgar, used to grace a column outside the GPO, but this was damaged by an IRA explosion in 1966 and subsequently demolished. The **Millennium Spire** (quickly dubbed 'the stiletto in the ghetto' by local wits) finally rose in its place in early 2003, a soaring stainless-steel needle which is supposed to symbolize the city's hopes and aspirations at the dawn of the new millennium. Shooting up high into the sky, it will eventually incorporate fountains at the base and an illuminated section at the top. Most Dubliners are, at the very least, bemused by the hugely expensive monument, and its arrival – too late for the Millennium celebrations – has given the newspapers a lot of fun punning on the point (or lack thereof) of the spire.

Near the site there used to be a very different kind of monument, a modern sculpture of Anna Livia Plurabella, Joyce's eternal feminine personification of both the River Liffey and the women of Dublin, reclining in her fountain – artistic controversy surrounded her as soon as she was put here in 1988, and she was removed in 2001.

The **General Post Office** (*t (01) 705 7000; open Mon–Sat 8–8, Sun and bank hols 10–6.30*), at the centre of the street, is memorable not for its beauty but for the events of 1916, when Pádraig Pearse and his men seized the building on Easter Monday and proclaimed the Irish Republic from its steps. The rebels held out for five days, while the British surrounded the building and shelled it from a gunboat in the Liffey, wrecking it and much of O'Connell Street in the process. In the days that followed, the leaders of the rising, including Pearse and James Connolly, were summarily shot. Inside is a memorial to the 1916 heroes in the form of a bronze statue of the dying Cú Chulainn. The GPO's historical role in the struggle for an independent Ireland has made it a venue for all manner of protest meetings.

Two streets behind, there is a colourful street market on **Moore Street**, while on the other side of O'Connell, on Marlborough Street, the (Catholic) **Pro Cathedral of St Mary** is a Greek Revival Doric temple built between 1815 and 1825; the Catholics would have preferred to build it right on O'Connell Street, but times were still too bigoted for that. There is a lovely sung mass at 11am on Sundays that is a long-standing Dublin tradition; the great tenor John McCormack used to sing in it. Down near the Liffey end of Marlborough Street is the famous **Abbey Theatre**, where the plays of Synge and O'Casey had their premieres – often to the accompaniment of riots, by moral-minded Catholics who packed the house to break up the show. The current grim building replaced the original, which burned down in 1951.

The **Custom House** is just around the corner on the quay, near Butt Bridge. Many consider this the most impressive building in Dublin. A quadrangular building with four decorated faces, it now houses the Customs and Excise and Department of Local Government. It was designed by James Gandon and completed in 1791. Unfortunately, its impact on the waterfront is lessened by a railway bridge which passes in front of it and the new development behind. Gutted by fire in 1921 during the civil war by the Republican side, it has been perfectly restored so that the graceful dome, crowned by the figure of commerce, still rises from the central Doric portico. Inside is a Visitors' Centre (*t (01) 878 2538; open mid Mar–Nov Mon–Fri 10–12.30, Sat and Sun 2–5; Dec–Feb Wed–Fri 10–12.30, Sun 2–5; adm*), with a small museum on Gandon and the history of the building.

Parnell Square

Found at the northern end of O'Connell Street, this square began its life as another of Dublin's residential squares; and in the 18th century it was the most fashionable address in town. Today it is known for its cultural institutions and for the conspicuous landmark of the **Rotunda Hospital**, the first specialized maternity hospital in the world (1752). The Rococo Chapel in the hospital is very sumptuous, with large-scale allegorical figures and curving plasterwork decorated with cherubs and *putti* (*arrangements to view it must be made in writing to the Hospital Secretary, Rotunda Hospital, Parnell Square, D1*). The hospital has always had an unusual connection with the performing arts; its founder staged concerts to finance his project, including the first performance of Handel's *Messiah*. The hospital's auditorium holds the Ambassador Cinema, and another part of the building is home to the Gate Theatre, an important venue for new Irish plays since the 1920s. **The Garden of Remembrance** (*always accessible*), behind the theatre, commemorates Irish freedom. The central feature of the garden is a sculpture of the legendary Children of Lir, by Oísín Kelly.

The **Hugh Lane Gallery of Modern Art** occupies a fine Georgian house at No.1 Parnell Square (*t (01) 874 1903, www.hughlane.ie; open Tues–Thurs 9.30–6, Fri and Sat 9.30–5, Sun 11–5; guided tours Tues 11am, Sun 1.30pm, lunchtime lectures Wed 1.10pm; adm free*). The bulk of the collection was formed by Sir Hugh Lane in the early 20th century (W. B. Yeats wrote a poem about his bequests), and the gallery has a small but wonderful collection of works by well-known artists: portraits of Yeats, Synge and other famous Irish figures and a bust of Lady Gregory by Epstein. The magical stained-glass window by Harry Clarke, 'The Eve of Saint Agnes', is after a poem by John Keats. Within the gallery, the **Francis Bacon Studio** is a complete reconstruction of Bacon's studio at 7 Reece Mews, Kensington, London. The entire contents of the room (right down to the dust) were donated to the gallery after his death.

The **Dublin Writers' Museum**, 18 Parnell Square North (*t (01) 872 2077; open all year Mon–Sat 10–5, Sun 11–5; during June–Aug until 6; adm, combined tickets with the Joyce Museum and Shaw Birthplace available*) is housed in another beautifully restored 18th-century building. The permanent displays introduce you to centuries of Irish literature, illustrated by letters, photographs, first editions and memorabilia. The **Irish Writers Centre**, within the museum, has lectures, readings and workshops. The museum also has a very good bookshop and restaurant. Yet another Georgian house in the area has become the **James Joyce Cultural Centre** (*t (01) 878 8547, www.*

jamesjoyce.ie; open Mon–Sat 9.30–5, Sun 12.30–5; adm), at 35 North Great Georges Street, housing exhibitions, a library, a bookshop and a café.

The Four Courts, St Michan's and the Collins Barracks

At the **Four Courts**, down by Ormond Quay (*t (01) 872 5555; open Mon–Fri 10.30–4.30 exc Aug and Sept*), you get one of the most characteristic views of Dublin. The Four Courts was designed by Gandon, the architect of the Custom House, and completed by Thomas Cooley (1776–84). It was almost completely destroyed in the Civil War of 1921, but it has since been restored. The Law Courts were reinstalled here in 1931. The central block has a Corinthian portico and a copper-green dome, and is flanked by two wings enclosing quadrangles. You may look inside the circular waiting hall under the dome. The **Public Record Office** next door was burnt down completely in 1921, with an irredeemable loss of legal and historical documents.

St Michan's on Church Street, west of the Four Courts, is a 17th-century structure on the site of an 11th-century Danish church. Most people are interested in getting to the vaults (*t (01) 872 4154; open Mar–Oct Mon–Fri 10–12.30 and 2–4.30, Sat 10–12.30; Nov–Mar Mon–Fri 12.30–3.30, Sat 10–12.30; guided tours; adm*), where bodies have lain for centuries without decomposing. Here the air is very dry owing to the absorbent nature of the limestone foundations. The skin of the corpses remains as soft as in life, and even their joints still work. Layers of coffins have collapsed into each other, exposing arms and legs; you can even see a crusader from the Holy Land. The body of Robert Emmet, one of the leaders of the 1798 rebellion, is said to be buried here. The only things that do live down in this curiously warm and fresh atmosphere are spiders, who feed on each other. There are so many types that people come from afar to study them. It is said that a Dublin lad has honourable intentions if he takes his girl there. The interior of the church itself is very fine and plain. A superb wooden carving of a violin intermingled with flowers and fruits decorates the choir gallery, and is supposed to be by Grinling Gibbons. Whoever carved it was a genius, and it is sad that so many people ghoulishly go only to the vaults.

Just around the corner on Bow Street, you can recover from your experience if necessary in the **Old Jameson Distillery** at Smithfield (*t (01) 807 2355; open daily 9.30–6, last tour at 5.30; adm*). Though the big copper tanks are no longer in use, everything is kept as it was for the guided tours. There's also an exhibition on the history of Irish whiskey, a 15-minute film and, most importantly, a generous tasting of all the different Irish whiskies.

A few streets to the west, just north of the Liffey on Benburb Street, stands the **National Museum** at Collins Barracks (*t (01) 677 7444, www.museum.ie; open Tues–Sat 10–5, Sun 2–5; adm free*), an 18-acre site that was known as the Royal Barracks when it was the headquarters of the British military in Ireland. The main building, built in 1701, was restored by the National Museum to hold its collections of decorative arts, including furniture and relics of Irish history. In a sense this is Ireland's Smithsonian, and it holds a little bit of everything, from Etruscan vases to an oar belonging to one of the lifeboats from the *Lusitania*.

Phoenix Park

Phoenix Park is huge, the largest city park in Europe. It is nearly within walking distance of central Dublin (*cross the river northwards and walk west along the quays to Conyngham Road; or catch a bus from O'Connell Street*). The Dubliners are very proud of the park – with good reason. There are sports fields, woodland, small lakes, duck ponds and the Dublin Zoo, and it finds room in its 1,760 acres (712ha) to house *Aras an Uachtarain* (the residence of the President), the residence of the American Ambassador, police headquarters and a hospital.

The name of the park comes from a corruption of the Gaelic *Fionn Uisce*, which means 'Bright Water', from a spring which rises near the Phoenix Column at the Knockmaroon Gate. To English ears the pronunciation of the Gaelic sounded rather like 'phoenix'. The Phoenix Column was put up in 1747 by Lord Chesterfield, who was the viceroy of the time, and who had the impetus and foresight to plant this part of the park with trees. The land was offered by Charles II to one of his mistresses, which illustrates to what degree Dublin, and indeed the whole of Ireland, was up for grabs in the 17th century. Luckily, the Duke of Ormonde (who built Kilmainham Hospital) suggested that it should be granted to the City of Dublin itself. Two hundred years later, in 1882, the Chief Secretary, Lord Frederick Cavendish, and the Under Secretary were murdered by Nationalists in the park.

The park is memorable as a place where cattle still graze and deer can be glimpsed through the trees. It is open to the public at all times, and the **Visitor Centre** (*t (01) 677 0095; open Jan–mid-Mar Sat–Sun 10–5, mid- to end Mar daily 10–5.30; April–Sept daily 10–6; Oct daily 10–5; Nov–Dec Sat–Sun 10–5; adm*), next to a 17th-century tower house, houses a multimedia exhibition on the history of the park over the last 6,000 years. Near the main entrance to the park on Parkgate Street stands the **Wellington Monument**, a 211ft (65m) obelisk completed in 1861. The Duke of Wellington was born in Dublin, though with his lifelong disdain for Ireland and the Irish he did not appreciate being reminded of it. Beyond this lie the **People's Flower Gardens**, and at the northern end is the old **Phoenix Park Race Course**, which is no longer in use. Between lies **Dublin Zoo** (*t (01) 474 8900, www.dublinzoo.ie; open Mar–Sept Mon–Sat 9.30–6, Sun 10.30–6; Oct–Feb Mon–Sat 9.30–dusk, Sun 10.30–dusk; adm exp*), one of the oldest zoos in Europe, set in grounds with artificial lakes. All the usual favourites are in attendance, along with a special Arctic section and a discovery centre for children.

Dublin City Suburbs

Shaw Birthplace, 33 Synge Street, D8, south of the centre near the Grand Canal (*t (01) 475 0854, bus nos.16, 19, 22; open May–Sept Mon–Sat 10–5, Sun 2–6; adm*). It isn't much, this tidy middle-class home where the future genius spent a mildly unhappy childhood, but, restored to what it might have looked like in the 1860s, it is a worthy introduction to the life of Victorian Dublin.

Irish Jewish Museum, 3 Walworth Road, D8, off the South Circular Road (*t (01) 453 1797, bus nos.16, 19, 22; open Oct–April Sun 10.30–2.30; May–Sept Tues, Thurs and Sun*

11–3.30; adm;). Ireland today may have a Jewish population of less than 2,000, but their long and interesting history is recounted in this restored former synagogue.

The **War Memorial Gardens**, Island Bridge, off the South Circular Road (*just before Islandbridge; the gardens are signposted to the left, bus nos.51 and 61; open Mon–Fri 8am–dusk, Sat–Sun 10am–dusk*). Designed by Edwin Lutyens in 1931, this is a very archi-tectural garden. You approach it by formal avenues which centre on the war stone at the heart of the garden. Circles and ovals commemorate the 49,400 Irish soldiers who died in the First World War. There are two sunken gardens, surrounded by terraces, roses, flowers and shrubs.

National Wax Museum, Granby Row, D1 (*t (01) 872 6340, bus nos.11, 13, 16, 22, 22A; open Mon–Sat 10–5.30, Sun 12–5.30; adm*). No big tourist city would be complete without one, and Dublin's is neither more nor less grotesque than the average, except perhaps for the tableau of the apostles reproducing Leonardo da Vinci's *Last Supper*.

Pearse Museum, St Enda's Park, Grange Road, Rathfarnham, D16 (*t (01) 493 4208, bus no.16; open Nov–Jan daily 10–4; Feb–April and Sept–Oct 10–5; May–Aug 10–5.30; adm free, free guided tours available on request*). The poet-patriot ran a Gaelic school here before the 1916 rising.

Dillon Garden, 45 Sandford Road, Ranelagh, D6 (*t (01) 497 1308, www.dillon garden.com; open Mar and July–Aug daily 2–6; April–June and Sept Sun only 2–6; adm*). A lovely city garden with secret areas of light and shade, clematis-draped arches, borders filled with flowers, tubs of sweet-smelling lilies, and wild flowers and roses.

The Casino at **Marino**, north of the city centre off the Malahide Road (*t (01) 833 1618, www.heritageireland.ie; bus nos.20A, 20B, 27, 27B, 42, 42C, 123, or DART to Clontarf Road; open June–Sept daily 10–6; May and Oct daily 10–5; Nov–Mar Sat–Sun 12–4; April Sat–Sun 10–5; adm*). This 18th-century miniature classical temple of three storeys was designed by Sir William Chambers, between 1762 and 1771, for Lord Charlemont (there isn't any gambling – casino means simply 'cottage' in Italian, and fancy ones were a fad among 18th-century aristocrats). It is one of Ireland's architectural gems. The public park nearby was part of Lord Charlemont's estate, the main house being demolished in 1921. It was exceedingly fortunate that this beautiful building did not go the same way. It has recently been restored and opened to the public. So ingenious was the architect that from the outside it only appears to be one storey high. The basement is actually below street level, whilst the ground and first floor are not distinguished in the façade. Inside are splendid inlaid floors, delicate plasterwork ceil-ings and silk-covered walls. Close by is **Croke Park**, the national temple of sport where the all-Ireland hurling and Gaelic football finals are played, and where there is a museum run by the GAA.

National Botanic Gardens, Botanic Road, Glasnevin, D9 (*t (01) 857 0909; open summer Mon–Sat 9–6, Sun 11–6; winter Mon–Sat 10–4.30, Sun 11–4.30; adm free; guided tours available for €2 if you call in advance*). Founded in 1795 by the Royal Dublin Society, the range of beautiful plants and mature trees here make it a wonderful place to walk. There is a magnificent curvilinear glasshouse over 400ft (122m) in length, built and designed by the Dublin ironmaster Richard Turner between 1843 and 1869 (*currently under restoration*). Adjacent to the gardens is the fabulous

Prospect Cemetery, resting place of many famous Dubliners, including Michael Collins, Daniel O'Connell and Charles Stewart Parnell.

Drimnagh Castle, Long Mile Road, Drimnagh, D12, southwest of the centre (*t (01) 450 2530; bus no.56A; open April–Sept Wed, Sat and Sun 12–5; Oct–Mar Wed 12–5, Sun 2–5; adm*). In a quiet suburban neighbourhood, this modest medieval castle, the only one in Ireland with a moat, has an exquisite formal 16th-century garden.

Day Trips and Overnighters from Dublin

Howth

Howth (with the 'o' pronounced as in 'both') comes from the Danish word *hoved*, meaning 'head'. Before the Anglo-Norman family of St Lawrence muscled their way into the area, Howth was a Danish settlement. An important ferry port until superseded by Dun Laoghaire, its harbour today is full of pleasure craft. **Balscadden beach** is sandy and shallow.

Howth Castle still remains in the hands of the St Lawrence family. The public are allowed to walk around the bright **tropical gardens** (*open 8am–sunset, adm free*); in late spring the rhododendrons are a glorious colour. It is said that Grace O'Malley, the famous 16th-century pirate-queen from County Mayo, stopped at Howth to replenish her supplies of food and water and decided to visit the St Lawrences. The family were eating, however, and she was refused admittance. Enraged by this rudeness, she snatched Lord Howth's infant son and heir and sailed away with him to Mayo. She returned the child only on condition that the gates of the castle were always left open at mealtimes, and a place set at the table for the head of the O'Malley clan – a custom that is still kept today.

Getting There

There are regular **DART trains** to Howth station (the line splits at Howth Junction, so be sure to get the right train), or you can take **bus** nos.31 or 31B from Lower Abbey Street. The DART takes about 25mins; the bus can take much longer because of the traffic.

For Donabate and Newbridge House, take the **Suburban Rail** service (hourly, takes 30mins) to Donabate from Connolly or Pearse train stations in the city centre. There is a **bus** service, no.33B, which leaves Eden Quay every 30mins but takes an hour or more, and you may have to change at Swords.

Eating Out

King Sitric, East Pier, Howth, **t** (01) 832 5235 (*luxury*). Famous for seafood. Also has charming rooms if you can't make it home.

Old Schoolhouse Restaurant, Church Road, Swords, **t** 01 840 2846 (*expensive–moderate*). Set in a restored 18th-century stone school building, a delightful restaurant by the river which serves local seafood and other dishes (including wild boar). It's just a few miles from Newbridge House, and in summer you can dine in the garden or conservatory.

The Bloody Stream, Howth, **t** (01) 839 0203 (*moderate*). This cosy pub right underneath Howth DART station does excellent upmarket pub grub, with a slightly smarter restaurant upstairs. It also happens to pour one of the best pints of Guinness in town.

Wright's of Howth, West Pier, Howth, **t** (01) 832 3937 (*inexpensive*). This is a fantastic deli on the seafront, where you can pick up great bread, cheeses and hams for a picnic.

The **National Transport Museum** in Howth Castle Demesne (*t (01) 848 0831 or t (01) 832 0427, www.nationaltransportmuseum.org; open June–Aug Mon–Fri 10–5; Sept–May Sat–Sun only 2–5; adm*) has specimens of everything that ever rolled on an Irish road, from Victorian-era carriages to early trams and fire engines.

Up the neck of the Howth Peninsula stretches the **Velvet Strand**, whilst a mile (1.6km) out to sea is **Ireland's Eye**, a great place for a picnic; you can take a boat out there from the pier in Howth Harbour during the summer months. Its name comes from the corruption of *Inis Eireann*, which means 'Island of Eire'. The old stone church on the island is all that is left of a 6th-century monastery.

Newbridge House

t (01) 843 6534; open April–Sept Tues–Sat 10–1 and 2–5, Sun 2–6; Oct–Mar Sat and Sun 2–5; adm.

At **Donabate** off the N1 is one of the finest and most authentically maintained Georgian manors in Ireland. It was built in 1737 for Charles Cobbe, later Archbishop of Dublin. The authenticity extends to the restored dairy, forge, servants' houses and other buildings, all furnished as they might have been 200 years ago. There is also a working farm, managed according to traditional methods. In the house, the drawing room and its early-Georgian furniture and curios are unique, as is the collection of antique dolls and a doll's house with 14 rooms. There is also a small museum, made up of curiosities brought from all over the world and displayed in specially designed cabinets. Donabate itself is famous for its sand dunes.

Malahide

Malahide is a seaside resort with a long, sandy beach and a wonderful old castle which was the seat of the Talbots from 1185 to 1973. Today, **Malahide Castle** (*t (01) 846 2184/846 2516; open April–Oct Mon–Sat 10–12.45 and 2–5, Sun 11–6; Nov–Mar Mon–Fri 10–5, Sat–Sun 2–5; adm*) is publicly owned, and a part of the National Portrait Collection is housed there. The *Boswell Papers*, which give us such an insight into 18th-century travel, were found here in a croquet box. The castle is made up of three

Getting There

There are regular **DART trains** (journey time 30mins) to Malahide (make sure you are on the right train, as the line splits at Howth Junction). **Bus** no.42 leaves from Talbot St and takes 45mins, unless the traffic is bad.

Tourist Information

Malahide: Malahide Castle, t (01) 845 0490.

Eating Out

Silks, The Mall, Malahide, t (01) 845 3331 (*moderate*). Good Chinese restaurant.

Le Restaurant 12A, 12A New Street, Malahide, t (01) 806 1928 (*expensive*). This elegant little restaurant is perfect for a treat. It serves delicious modern Irish and European cuisine, and does a good-value early evening menu.

Malahide Castle, Malahide, t (01) 846 3027 (*inexpensive*). Soups and snacks.

Old Street Wine Bar, 3 Old Street, Malahide, t (01) 845 1882 (*inexpensive*). Wine by the glass and simple meals, like a traditional Dublin coddle.

different periods, the earliest being a three-storey tower house dating from the 12th century. The façade of the house is flanked by two slender towers built in about 1765. Inside is the only surviving original medieval great hall in Ireland, hung with Talbot family portraits. The display of Irish 18th-century furniture is fascinating, and shows the sophistication of the craftsmanship and artistry existing in Ireland at the time. The grounds are superb, especially the part now known as the **Talbot Botanic Gardens** (*t* *(01)* *816 9910; open May–Sept, daily 2–5; guided tours of Walled Garden Wed at 2; adm*), laid out with thousands of species, many of them exotic plants from the southern hemisphere brought here by Lord Talbot de Malahide between 1948 and 1973.

Also in the grounds is the **Fry Model Railway Museum** (*t* *(01)* *846 3779; open April–Oct Mon–Sat 10–5, Sun 2–6; Oct–Mar Sat and Sun 2–5; adm*). The handmade models were built by Cyril Fry, a railway engineer and draughtsman in the 1930s. They are laid out on a track which passes many miniaturized Dublin landmarks, including Heuston Station and the River Liffey with all its bridges, trams, barges and boats.

A final attraction in the Malahide Castle Demesne is **Tara's Palace and Museum of Childhood**. The Museum of Childhood contains a small collection of antique dolls and toys. Upstairs you'll find Tara's Palace, a magnificent (but still unfinished) doll's house constructed by some of Ireland's best craftsmen, with Castletown House, Leinster House and Carton rebuilt to one-twelfth of their true size.

Dun Laoghaire, Dalkey and Dalkey Island

Dun Laoghaire (pronounced 'Dun Lay-reh' or 'Dun Lyoora', or 'Dun Leary', depending on who's doing the pronouncing) is a terminus for car ferry services from Britain. This Victorian town with its bright terraced houses was traditionally a holiday resort, and is pleasant to stroll around before exploring the wilder delights of the Wicklow Mountains. Dun Laoghaire is named after Laoghaire, who was High King of Ireland when St Patrick converted him in the 5th century. For a time this busy port was called Kingstown, after George IV visited Ireland in 1821, but the name was dropped at the establishment of the Free State. The houses along **Marine Parade** are very handsome, painted different colours, and with intricate ironwork and Regency detail. The two great granite **piers** were built between 1817 and 1859. Both make for an invigorating walk; Sundays are especially good for people-watching. It is an important yachting centre, and the Royal Saint George and Royal Irish Clubs are situated here.

The **National Maritime Museum** is in the Mariner's Church, Haigh Terrace (*closed indefinitely for restoration*). The **Sacred Heart Oratory Dominican Convent**, George's Street, (*access by appointment only*) is a little gem of the Celtic Revival style, decorated by Sister Concepta Lynch in a combination of Celtic and Art Nouveau style.

Marine Parade, laid out with trees and flowers, takes you to the **James Joyce Museum** at the Joyce Tower in Sandycove (*t* *(01)* *280 9265, joycetower@dublintourism. ie; open April–Oct Mon–Sat 10–1 and 2–5, Sun 2–6; adm*). In fact this Martello tower, from the Napoleonic Wars, was rented by Oliver St John Gogarty, whose witty book *As I Walked Down Sackville Street* is a must for all true Hibernian enthusiasts. Joyce

Getting There

There are regular **DART trains** to Dun Laoghaire, which take about 20mins. **Buses** (nos.7, 7A and 8 from O'Connell St) are frequent, but can take up to an hour.

Tourist Information

Dun Laoghaire: New Ferry Terminal, infoline **t** 1850 230330. *Open all year.*

Eating Out

Gresham Royal Marine Hotel, Marine Road, Dun Laoghaire, **t** (01) 280 1911 *(moderate)*. This grand Victorian hotel overlooking the bay is the perfect spot for old-fashioned afternoon tea.

Eagle House, 18 Glasthule Rd, Dun Laoghaire, **t** (01) 280 4740. An excellent, traditional Irish pub serving good bar meals *(inexpensive)*. Upstairs is **Duzy's Café**, a stylish restaurant *(moderate)* with live jazz at weekends.

Outlaws, 62 Upper George Street, Dun Laoghaire, **t** (01) 284 2817 *(inexpensive)*. Cheerful 'Western' themed serving good steaks, chicken and burgers.

Purty Kitchen, Old Dun Laoghaire Road, **t** (01) 284 3576 *(inexpensive)*. Good food with a strong emphasis on seafood and tempting salads; next door they also run a slick barclub, **Coast**, open from 10.30pm Thurs–Sat.

P.D.'s Woodhouse, 1 Coliemore Road, Dalkey, **t** (01) 284 9399 *(moderate)*. Nice friendly atmosphere and oak wood barbecued food.

nosh, 11 Coliemore Rd, Dalkey, **t** (01) 284 0666, *www.nosh.ie (moderate)*. Stylish, minimalist nosh appeals to Dalkey's surprisingly big fashion pack. Simple, tasty food and excellent brunches.

The Queens, 12 Castle Street, Dalkey, **t** (01) 285 8345 *(inexpensive)*. Dalkey's oldest pub, serving good sandwiches and seafood chowder. Pleasant on a sunny day. There are also two restaurants here: **La Romana**, for inexpensive Italian food, or the smarter **Vico** upstairs, for contemporary cuisine in more formal surroundings.

stayed with him for the weekend and used the visit in the opening scene of *Ulysses*. Gogarty ('stately plump Buck Mulligan'), and James Joyce later quarrelled – now their names are perpetually linked. Few people have actually read the whole of *Ulysses*, and for a long time it was banned by the Irish censor for revealing too much of the earthy Dublin character. But the tower is a shrine where visitors can worship and ponder over the collection of Joyceana. Just beside the tower is the Forty Foot Pool, where, in *Ulysses*, Buck Mulligan had a morning dip. Made for the Fortieth Foot infantry regiment, it was traditionally a nude, men-only bathing spot, but now you have to wear a bathing suit after 9am. Aficionados swim here all year round, even on Christmas Day.

Dalkey, adjoining Dun Laoghaire, is a small fishing village where George Bernard Shaw used to stay and admire the skies from Dalkey Hill. In the 15th and 16th centuries it was the main landing place for passengers from England. In the main thoroughfare, Castle Street, are the remains of fortified mansions from that time, plus **Dalkey Castle and Heritage Centre** (*t (01) 285 8366, www.dalkeycastle.com; open April–Dec Mon–Fri 9.30–5, Sat, Sun and bank hols 11–5; Jan–Mar Sat, Sun and bank hols 11–5; adm*), where the history of the castle back to the Middle Ages is described by the area's famous resident author, Hugh Leonard. A boat may be hired from Coliemore Harbour to **Dalkey Island**, where there is a Martello tower and the remains of an ancient church. The Vico road runs along the coast, unfolding beautiful views of Killiney Bay. From the village centre you can walk to **Sorrento Point**, where you get a panoramic view of the distant coastline, the Sugar Loaf Mountains and the sweep of Killiney Bay itself. If you climb **Killiney Hill** you will have an even clearer view.

Drogheda and Brú na Bóinne

Drogheda, the largest town in County Meath, conjures up images of the cruelty of Cromwell, for which he is notorious in Ireland, but it has also been a famous place in Ireland since the Normans settled there in around 1180, and today it is bustling. The old Drogheda Society has adapted some of the buildings of **The Millmount**, an 18th-century military barracks on a motte, as a museum (*t (041) 983 3097, www.millmount. net; open all year Mon–Sat 10–6, last tour 5.30, Sun 2.30–5.30; adm*). It has many interesting exhibits including 18th-century guild banners, a 1912–22 room, information on the old industries of spinning, weaving, brewing and shoe- and rope-making, a folk kitchen and an extensive geological collection. **St Lawrence's Gate**, a twin-towered, four-storey gate stands on the road going to Baltray. It is the best preserved of all the remaining gates in this once-walled town. Off West Street, in the **Church of St Peter**, is the preserved head of St Oliver Plunkett, Archbishop of Armagh, who sadly became caught up in the panic of the 'Popish Plot' fabricated by Titus Oates in 1678. The 'Plot' was a smoke-screen manufactured by powerful men in England to discomfit Charles II and his Catholic heir, James II. Plunkett was canonized in 1975, the first new Irish saint since St Lawrence O'Toole, more than seven hundred years ago.

Brú na Bóinne

The most spectacular ancient site in Ireland is the collection of burial sites known as the 'Palace of the Boyne'. This piece of land is enclosed by the river on three sides. There are at least 15 passage graves from Neolithic times, some of them unexcavated. The three main sites are called Newgrange, Knowth and Dowth. The **Visitors' Centre** (*signposted from N51; t (041) 988 0300, www.heritageireland.ie; open Nov–Feb daily 9.30–5; Mar, April and Oct 9.30–5.30; May and the second half of Sept 9–6.30, June–mid-Sept 9.30–7; adm; last tours begin 1½ hours before closing*) is an attraction in itself, a striking piece of architecture with excellent exhibits. Try to see it after your tour of the 'palace' because it has most of the answers to the questions you will want to ask about the sophistication of the building. And try to avoid going on weekends in

Getting There

Trains to Drogheda run from Dublin (Connolly Station) – Intercity 30mins, other trains 50mins). The **bus** takes 1hr 15 mins.

For Bru na Boinne, get a **bus** from Drogheda bus station headed for Donore, and after 15mins get off at the visitor centre. The last bus back to Drogheda leaves at 4pm.

Tourist Information

Drogheda: t (041) 983 7070; *open June–Sept.*
Bru na Boinne: Bru na Boinne Visitor Centre, Donore, t (041) 988 0305.

Newgrange: t (041) 988 0300; *open all year.*

Eating Out

The Buttergate Restaurant and Wine Bar, Millmount, Drogheda, t (041) 983 4759 (*moderate*). Good, plain food made more sophisticated by imaginative sauces.
Gateway Restaurant, 15 West Street, Drogheda, t (041) 983 8728 (*inexpensive*). Delicious ham and smoked salmon. Self-service lunch.
Borzalino, Mell, Drogheda, t (041) 984 5444 (*inexpensive*). Bright, modern Italian serving decent pizza and pasta dishes.

summer when the place is crowded: it is impossible to appreciate the age or the impressive atmosphere when you are squashed sideways against a sacred stone. Unfortunately, the visit to the actual sites is the most over-bureaucratized tourist experience to be had in Ireland; they'll stick a badge on you with a tour time, load you on a bus to the sites for a guided tour, and haul you back to the Visitors' Centre before you've had time to look around. Newgrange and Knowth have separate tours.

Newgrange, on its hilltop, is visible for miles around. Somebody went to a lot of trouble to bring its sparkling white stones here; the closest place where they are found is in the Wicklow Mountains. Their use as a wall around the sides of a mound is unique to Ireland. Naturally, most of them fell down over the millennia, and restorers in the 1960s and 70s had a long and careful task putting them back into place. The round stones that make such a lovely pattern among the quartz may not be in their original positions; here the restorers had to guess. Originally, to enter, one would have had to climb over the famous decorated slab that lies across the doorway, carved with an undulating pattern of spirals and lozenges. Like everything else at Newgrange, this stone has occasioned all manner of speculations: some see it as a kind of map of the Brú na Bóinne sites, others as an object for religious meditation.

Outside, a few standing stones remain from what was probably an unbroken ring around the mound, its purpose unknown. The tour will take you inside, down the narrow, 6oft (19m) passage that does not quite reach the centre of the mound. At the end is a three-lobed chamber, typical of Neolithic constructions all over Western Europe. Many of the stones in the chamber are carved with designs similar to those at the entrance – beautiful, exasperating designs that show serious intent and meaning, without allowing us to decipher it. Neither can we guess much about what went on here on Newgrange's big day, the winter solstice, when the first rays of the rising sun penetrated the artfully positioned 'roof box' over the entrance and illuminated the entire passage for a few minutes.

Built around 3500–3000 BC, Newgrange is not only one of the most impressive works of the Neolithic age, but one of the oldest, antedating the great circle at Stonehenge by at least a millennium. In its layout it resembles other passage-graves around Europe, notably Gavr'inis, near Carnac in Brittany, and its carved motifs echo those found in the temples of Malta, some of which were built at around the same time. When you visit Newgrange, think of it as, not an isolated peculiarity from long ago, but one of the finest monuments of a culture that stretched around the Atlantic and Mediterranean shores from Malta to Scandinavia – Europe's first great civilization, a world of remarkable achievements that endured for over 3,000 years.

Knowth (open April–Oct), which can be visited on a separate tour from the Brú na Bóinne Visitors' Centre, is approximately the same size as Newgrange and contains a second, smaller passage in addition to the main one. Only part of the site is open to the public while excavations are completed, but you can see the wonderfully lavish kerbstones placed round the mound, decorated with spirals and lozenges. **Dowth**, the third of the great mounds, has a passage made diametrically opposite to the one at Newgrange so that it is illuminated by the midwinter sunset. The archaeologists haven't done much work here yet, and the site is not currently open to the public.

Touring from Dublin 1: North

Day 1: Into the Past

Morning: Take the R154 out of Dublin, past ruins, towers and moats, for **Trim**, the capital of the ancient Kingdom of Meath, which was granted to Hugh de Lacy by Henry II at the time of the Norman Conquest. Imposing **Trim Castle**, the largest Anglo-Norman castle in Ireland, also called King John's Castle (*open Easter–Oct daily 10–6; winter Sat and Sun 10–5; adm*), was built in 1172 by Hugh de Lacy and was at the centre of every battle during the Middle Ages; at one time the future King of England, Henry V, and the Duke of Gloucester were imprisoned here by Richard II.

Lunch: In Trim, *see* below.

Afternoon: Visit the **Hill of Tara**, on a small road off the R154 south of Trim via Kilmessan (*Visitors' Centre open May–Oct daily 10–6; adm; book tours in advance on t (041) 982 4488; free leaflet and plan*). All that is left of Tara is a series of earthworks on a green hill in green fields; the wooden buildings have long disappeared. According to tradition, from the beginning of history Tara was the seat of kings who controlled at least the northern half of the country. It is central to many legends and mentioned in early annals, sagas and genealogies such as the 12th-century *Book of Leinster*. Head north on the N3 to the busy town of **Navan**, which is Norman in origin, where in St Mary's Catholic Church there is a wooden 18th-century carving of Christ.

Dinner and Sleeping: In Kilmessan or Navan, *see* below.

Day 1

Lunch in Trim
Bounty Bar, Bridge Street, **t** (046) 31640 (*inexpensive*). The oldest pub in the county, serving snacks.

The Haggard Inn, Haggard Street, **t** (046) 943 1110 (*inexpensive*). Decent pub grub (including veggie options) in this traditional inn.

Dinner and Sleeping in Kilmessan
The Station House Hotel, **t** (046) 25239, *www.thestationhousehotel.com* (*moderate*). A converted 1850s railway station, which makes for a pleasant stay and also has tasty food: fish, lamb, and beef with herbs and sauces. *Dinner and Sun lunch.*

Seamrog, Tara, **t** (046) 25296 (*moderate–inexpensive*). Mrs Joan Maguire offers B&B right beside the Hill of Tara; her family have owned the nearby café, bookshop and tourist shop for generations.

Dinner in Navan
Hudson's Bistro, 30 Railway Street, **t** (046) 902 9231 (*moderate*). Casual place with international menu. *Dinner only.*

The Loft, Trimgate Street, **t** (046) 71755 (*moderate*). Light evening meals, music and a good atmosphere.

Dunderry Lodge Restaurant, Dunderry, Navan, **t** (046) 31671 (*luxury*). This little restaurant has acquired a tremendous reputation, and Dubliners think nothing of driving out to it for a meal. The restaurant is in converted farm buildings, with good décor, and Mediterranean-influenced food. *Open Tues–Sat for dinner only, also Sun lunch.*

Sleeping in Navan
Ardboyne Hotel, Dublin Road, **t** (046) 23119 (*expensive–moderate*). Modern and friendly, and set in its own grounds.

Newgrange Hotel, Bridge Street, **t** (046) 90 74100, **f** 90 73977, *www.newgrangehotel.ie* (*moderate*). Modern rooms in this classic hotel, with a reasonable restaurant.

Day 2: Seven Wonders

Morning: Take the N51 east from Navan and turn right at Delvin for **Castlepollard**, an attractive 19th-century town with a triangular green. Close by, on the Granard Road (R395), are the beautiful grounds of **Tullynally Castle**, seat of the earls of Longford (*open mid June–July 2–6; gardens open May–Aug 2–6; adm*). Seen from a distance in its romantic setting, Tullynally makes you think of a castle in an illustrated medieval manuscript. Inside the castle is a fine collection of family portraits, furniture and memorabilia. The grounds are beautiful and the castle looks down to Lough Derravaragh. Take the little road east to **Fore**, once an important ecclesiastical centre, situated between Loughs Lene and Bane and freely accessible; stop in at the Seven Wonders Pub and ask them about the 'Seven Wonders of Fore'; they'll send you on a tour of seven sites associated with miracles.

Lunch: In Castlepollard or Fore, *see* below.

Afternoon: Head back to Collinstown and make for Mullingar via **Crookedwood**, at the southern tip of Lough Derravaragh, where the scenery is really charming. On the R394, east of the village, is **St Munna's Church** (*key kept at the house opposite the graveyard*). This fairytale church was built in the 15th century and has a castle-like tower and battlements. **Mullingar**, one of the nicest market towns in Ireland, was a garrison town and has now become a noted angling centre with a busy, brightly painted main street, some excellent pubs and grocery shops.

Dinner and Sleeping: In Crookedwood or Mullingar, *see* below.

Day 2

Lunch in Castlepollard or Fore
Tullynally Castle Tearooms, Tullynally Castle, t (044) 61159. Old-fashioned tea, sandwiches and cakes. *Open June–Aug 2–6pm.*
Fore Abbey Coffee Shop. A friendly spot in the Abbey for a light lunch or coffee break.

Dinner and Sleeping in Crookedwood
Crookedwood House, t (044) 72165, *www.iol. ie/~cwoodhse* (*expensive–moderate*). Cellar restaurant in a converted rectory overlooking a beautiful lough, which has won awards for its plain cooking. It also has eight spacious rooms (*expensive*), and B&B accommodation (*moderate*) in Clonkill House (two miles away). *Dinner only; closed Mon.*

Dinner in Mullingar
Oscar's Restaurant, 21 Oliver Plunkett Street, t (044) 44909 (*moderate*). Bistro-style restaurant, highly recommended by locals.

Open 6–9.30 for dinner every evening, plus Sunday lunch 12.30–2.

Sleeping in Mullingar
Greville Arms Hotel, Pearse Street, t (044) 48563, f 48052, *www.grevillearms. com* (*moderate*). Traditional-style hotel.
Mearescourt House, Rathconrath, Mullingar, t (044) 55112 (*moderate*). Mansion house set in pretty parkland. Good home cooking and comfortable rooms.
Mornington House, Multyfarnham, near Mullingar, t (044) 72191, *www.mornington.ie* (*moderate*). Lovely country house in peaceful grounds, with two dogs. The house is near Lake Derravaragh, to which you can walk. Home-grown vegetables and herbs are served at dinner. *Closed Nov–Mar.*
Woodlands Farm, Streamstown, Mullingar, t (044) 26414 (*inexpensive*). Very typical of Irish farmhouses, Mrs Maxwell's is crammed with holy pictures, is welcoming and has delicious food. There are ponies and donkeys to keep the kids happy. *Closed Oct–Mar.*

Day 3 (optional): Loughside Attractions

If you have a spare day, detour west for Athlone. If not, go straight to the next day.

Morning: Drive south from Mullingar on the N52 to **Tyrellspass**, a very pretty village, laid out as a crescent around the central green in the 18th century by the Countess of Belvedere. The castle, a private residence, was built in the 15th century. Richard Tyrell was a late-16th-century hero. **Belvedere House, Gardens and Park** (*open Nov–April daily 10.30–4.30; May–Aug Mon–Fri 9.30–6, Sat–Sun 10.30–7; Sept–Oct 10.30–6; adm*) lies on the way (4km from Mullingar), on the shores of Lough Ennell.
Lunch: In Tyrellspass, *see* below.

Afternoon: Take the N6 west to **Athlone**, a popular touring centre that straddles the River Shannon and spreads into the lovely Lough Ree. It is a thriving market town, full of good food shops and places where you can have a good jar and listen to traditional or jazz music. One of the most striking buildings in the town is the enormous Roman Catholic Church of St Peter and St Paul, off Grace Road, built in the Roman Renaissance style. On the west bank overlooking the bridge, almost opposite the church, is the 13th-century Athlone Castle (*open May–Sept daily 10–6; adm*). If you want to immerse yourself further in times past, wander into St Mary's Church in Church Street where, frozen into stone statues, Tudor squires kneel with their ladies in perpetual prayer. Or hire a boat at the marina and explore **Hare Island** on Lough Ree, with the ruins of a church founded by St Ciaran in the 6th century.
Dinner and Sleeping: In Glassan or Athlone, *see* below.

Day 3 (optional)

Lunch in Tyrellspass

Tyrellspass Castle, t (044) 23105 (*moderate*). Eat an excellent lunch here.
The Village Inn, t (044) 23171 (*moderate*). A cosy, period town house hotel, part of an elegant crescent around the village green.

Dinner in Glassan

Glassan Village Restaurant, t (090) 285001 (*moderate*). Straightforward but tasty Irish cooking, with seafood a speciality.
Wineport Lakeshore Restaurant, t (090) 285466 (*expensive–moderate*). Modern and elegant restaurant in a sleek cedar and glass building. It has recently added some gorgeous rooms (*expensive*) with heated floors in the bathrooms and fabulous views.

Dinner in Athlone

Conlon's Restaurant, 5–9 Dublingate Street, t (090) 279929 (*moderate*). Relaxed place, which is largely vegetarian. Interesting and imaginative dishes should please even die-hard meat-lovers.
Le Château, St Peters Port, t (090) 294517 (*moderate*). In a converted church.
Left Bank Bistro, Fry Place, t (090) 649 4456 (*inexpensive*). Relaxed, friendly spot serving tasty dishes from Mexican fajitas to Thai curries. And, if you want to tinkle the ivories, the piano is all yours.

Sleeping in Athlone

Castledaly Manor, Castledaly, Moate (5 miles from Athlone), t (090) 281221 (*luxury*). A grand manor house, set in several acres of parkland, with imposing rooms (many with four-poster beds) and a fine restaurant.
The Bastion, 2 Bastion Street, t (090) 649 4954, *www.thebastion.net* (*expensive–moderate*). Charming B&B in an old town-house, with rooms furnished with crisp white cotton and wooden floors.
Riverdale House, Clonown Road, t (0902) 92480 (*moderate–inexpensive*). Welcoming, traditional B&B.

Day 3 or 4: Manuscripts and Old Lace

Morning: From (or back through) Mullingar, the N52 leads northeast to **Kells** in the wooded valley of the Blackwater. The village has a vast wealth of history behind it. The High King of Ireland, Dermot (or Diarmuid) granted this defensive fort to St Columba in AD 550, and the religious centre he established became very important. Today, in the graveyard of the Church of Ireland church of St Columba, you can see a 9th-century round tower in a good state of preservation. St Columba's house, nearby, is a high-roofed oratory with very early barrel-vaulting. There is a replica of the illuminated 8th-century manuscript the *Book of Kells* in the modern Church of Ireland church; the original is in Trinity College, Dublin (*see* p.131). In the town, the main landmark used to be a 10th-century market cross which had been moved there from the graveyard – until a car ran over it in 1996; you can visit it in the Heritage Centre, Headfort Place (*open May–Sept Mon–Sat 10–6, Sun and bank hols 1.30–6; Oct–April Tues–Sat 10–5, Sun and bank hols 10.30–6, last adm 45mins before closing time; adm*). In the 1798 Rising, this cross was used as a gallows.

Lunch: In Kells, *see* below.

Afternoon: Take the R164 north from Kells via Kingscourt to **Carrickmacross** in County Monaghan, a market town famous for its fine handmade lace, appliqué work on tulle, a cottage industry established at the beginning of the 20th century. Examples can be seen in the Lace Co-operative (*open April–Oct*). The Roman Catholic church here has ten splendid windows by the stained-glass artist Harry Clarke.

Dinner and Sleeping: In Carrickmacross, or head 15 miles east to Dundalk, *see* below.

Day 3 or 4

Lunch in Kells

Vanilla Pod, Headfort Place, Headfort Arms Hotel, t (046) 40063, *www.headfortarms. com* (*expensive–moderate*). International menu and a fine reputation. *Sunday lunch only*.

Jack's Railway Bar, Athboy Road, t (046) 40215 (*moderate–inexpensive*). A traditional Irish pub with log fires in winter and a walled garden to sit out and sip a pint in the summer. There are reasonable pub lunches, including a daily carvery.

Dinner and Sleeping in Carrickmacross

Nuremore Hotel, t (042) 9661438, f 966 1853, *www.nuremore-hotel.ie* (*luxury*). Modern hotel in spacious grounds. The award-winning restaurant serves food with French-Irish influences. Popular with golfers, with a fine 18-hole course; also a gym and a big indoor pool.

Shirley Arms, Main Street, t (042) 966 1209, f (042) 966 3299 (*moderate*). Hotel in the town centre.

Dinner and Sleeping in Dundalk

Ballymascanlon Hotel, t (042) 935 8200, f (042) 937 1598, *www.ballymascanlon.com* (*expensive–moderate*). Victorian country house set in an 18-hole parkland golf course, and much favoured by the clergy for ecumenical conferences. In the grounds is a fine example of a portal dolmen, as well as a pool, gym and tennis courts. Families welcome. The restaurant serves Irish and French food.

Cube, 5 Roden Place, t (042) 932 9898, f (042) 935 6656 (*expensive–moderate*). The most fashionable place to eat in Dundalk, with exquisitely presented food to match the exquisitely presented clientele.

Louth Arms, Tallanstown, Dundalk, t/f (042) 937 4290, *www.loutharms.com* (*moderate*). Old-fashioned, friendly inn in a small village 5 miles southeast of Dundalk.

Day 4 or 5: The Cooley Peninsula

Morning: The Cooley Peninsula in the far north of County Louth is one of the most beautiful, untouched places in Ireland. Seek out **Faughart Hill**, signposted a few miles off the Dundalk to Newry Road on the left, where whole of Leinster spreads out below you. This is where Edward Bruce, sent by his brother Robert Bruce, King of Scotland, to make trouble for the Anglo-Normans, was killed in battle in 1318. You can see the Wicklow Hills rippling across the plain to join the Slieve Bloom and the Cooley Hills behind. This part too is touched by myth – Cú Chulainn was born in these heather-coloured hills. In **Faughart** graveyard, there is a shrine to St Brigid, patroness of Ireland and powerful Celtic goddess, christianized and made a saint.

Lunch: In Carlingford, see below.

Afternoon: **Carlingford**, which looks across its lough to the Mourne Mountains, was a place of great strategic importance in medieval times, and is full of castellated buildings; it is said to have possessed 32 'castles' in the days of the Pale. Nowadays, it is nothing more than a little village with a 16th-century arched Tholsel, a Mint, and Taaffe's Castle, attached to a modern house. The ruins of the Anglo-Norman King John's Castle, with arrow slits in the outer walls, are impressive. You can have a marvellous walk across the **Cooley Mountains** (*for information call Dundalk Tourism,* **t** *(042) 35457*) along the slopes of Slieve Foye and Ravensdale Forest. You will find Slieve Foye 2 miles (3.2km) northeast of Carlingford, on the R173 to Omeath.

Dinner and Sleeping: In Carlingford, or head south down the N52 from Dundalk to Ardee, see below.

Day 4 or 5

Lunch in Carlingford

Oystercatcher Bistro, Market Square, **t** (042) 937 3922 (*moderate*). Tasty seafood.

Carlingford Marina Bar & Restaurant, Marina, **t** (042) 937 3073 (*moderate–inexpensive*). Decent food, including soup and sandwich deals at lunchtimes, and fabulous views across the Lough.

Carlingford Arms, Newry Street, **t** (042) 937 3418 (*moderate–inexpensive*). A welcoming traditional pub serving standard pub grub and sturdier fare in the restaurant. Live music at weekends, or whenever the locals feel like a sing-song.

Dinner and Sleeping in Carlingford

Jordan's, Newry Street, **t** (042) 937 3223, **f** 937 3827 (*luxury–moderate*). All rooms have views over the harbour. The restaurant (**Le Brasserie**, *expensive*) offers good, simple cooking using the best of local ingredients, including pig's trotters. An 'early bird' menu is also available.

Ghan House, **t** (042) 937 3682, **f** 937 3772, *www.ghanhouse.com, ghanhouse@eircom. net* (*expensive*). High luxury at this 18th-century B&B manor, with views over the Lough and the Mornes. The renowned restaurant (*expensive*) offers dishes made from local ingredients. There's also a cookery school.

Carlingford Adventure Centre and Holiday Hostel, Tholsel Street, **t** (042) 937 3100 (*inexpensive*), *www.carlingfordadventure.com*. Cheap and basic. *Book well in advance.*

Dinner and Sleeping in Ardee

Red House, **t** (041) 685 3523 (*moderate*). This attractive Georgian house lies in lovely parkland, and is well run by Jim and Linda Connolly, with comfortable rooms. Indoor heated swimming pool and a sauna.

The Gables, Dundalk Road, **t** (041) 685 3789 (*inexpensive*). Offers simple accommodation, with a fine restaurant serving hearty food.

Day 5 or 6: Ancient Sites or Market Towns

Morning: If you haven't visited **Drogheda** and **Brú na Bóinne** as a day trip from Dublin (see pp.149–50), it simply must be seen on this tour. Head straight for the Brú na Bóinne Visitors' Centre in the morning, take the guided tour of the ancient sites, then have lunch in Drogheda and see the town in the afternoon. If you've seen it already, instead have a look around **Ardee**, a very attractive market town, where Cú Chulainn slew his friend Ferdia in a four-day combat to stop the raiding party stealing the Bull of Cooley for Queen Maeve. Ardee was often used by the English as a base for attacking Ulster; that is why you will find two old castles along the main street.

Lunch: In Drogheda, see p.149, or Ardee, see below.

Afternoon: If you're not visiting Drogheda, head for **Slane** on the N2 south of Ardee. Slane once belonged to other Barons of the Pale, the Flemings, who lost out when they supported James II in the 1690s; their lands were forfeited, and a County Donegal family, the Conynghams, were awarded them in their stead. Burton Conyngham built the picture-book Gothic Slane Castle (open 10 Sept–20 Oct daily 12–5; adm), with its fine gates, in the 1780s. Look out for the four Georgian houses in the town arranged in a square. Local legend says they were built for four quarrelling spinster sisters of one of the Conynghams, who detested each other but could not bear to be parted, so he thought of this solution. A few hundred yards outside Slane on the Ardee road (N2) is a very ancient site known as the **Hill of Slane**.

Dinner and Sleeping: In Drogheda or Slane, see below. Dublin is a 20-mile drive south.

Day 5 or 6

Lunch in Ardee

Brian Muldoon & Sons, 1 Bridge Street, t (041) 685 3134 (inexpensive). A traditional pub and restaurant, with a steadfastly old-fashioned menu of steak and prawn cocktails.

Courtyard Restaurant, Smarmore Castle, t (041) 685 7167, f (041) 685 7650 (moderate). Smart café and restaurant attached to a luxury hotel in a beautifully converted medieval castle. Open to non-residents.

Dinner in Drogheda

Tides Bistro, Wellington Quay, t (041) 980 1942 (moderate). An elegant sleekly designed restaurant, serving a range of dishes.

Abbots Bistro, 32 Shop Street, t (041) 30288 (moderate–inexpensive). A simple, charming bistro close to St Patrick's Cathedral.

Dinner in Slane

Poet's Rest, Chapel St, t (041) 24579 (moderate–inexpensive). A traditional, welcoming little spot, with a varied menu of Irish and European dishes and a decent wine list.

Boyles Tea Rooms, Main Street, t (041) 24195 (inexpensive). Home-made soup, sandwiches and afternoon teas. Open daily until 11pm.

Sleeping in Drogheda

Minnamurra House, Dublin Road, t (041) 984 1437 (inexpensive). Very convivial, with Ursula McEntee's children bouncing everywhere.

Westcourt Hotel, West Street, t (041) 98 30965/68 (moderate). A reasonable choice in the town centre, with noisy nightclub.

Sleeping in Slane

Conyngham Arms, t (041) 982 4155 (moderate). Snug hotel, right in the middle of the village with an excellent restaurant.

Slane Farm Hostel, Harlinstown House, Slane, t/f (041) 988 4985, www.slanefarmhostel.ie (inexpensive). For something different, stay at this working farm. Accommodation is in dormitories but they also have family rooms, and everyone mucks in with the farm work.

Touring from Dublin 2: South

Day 1: The Wicklow Way: Nature, Tamed and Wild

Morning: Take the R117 for Enniskerry and the **Powerscourt Estate** (*www.powerscourt. ie; open daily 9.30–dusk; adm*), with one of the finest formal gardens in Ireland. The house was gutted by fire in 1976, but the setting is unforgettable. On the estate is the Powerscourt waterfall, the highest in Ireland. From **Enniskerry**, follow the road through the Scalp, a glacier-formed gap. If you want to glut yourself on forest scenery take the Military Road, which runs through the mountains. One of the most spectacular glens is **Glencree**, which curves from near the base of Sugarloaf Mountain to the foot of the Glendoo Mountain. Through it flows the Glencree River. The wild, beautiful **Sally Gap**, near the source of the River Liffey, is a crossroads, where you can take the Military Road to **Laragh** or the R755 to **Roundwood**.

Lunch: In Laragh or Roundwood, *see* below.

Afternoon: The important Early Christian site of **Glendalough** has overwhelmed people with its peace and isolation for many centuries. It sits high in the hills, with two small lakes cupped in a hollow, a tall round tower and a grey stone church. There are the remains of a famous monastic school founded by St Kevin in the 6th century, and remains of churches spread between the upper and lower lakes, and the little river. A Visitors' Centre (*open daily 9.30–5; adm*) is beside the car park.

Dinner and Sleeping: Wicklow or Rathnew, about 12 miles east on the R763, *see* below.

Day 1

Lunch in Laragh
Mitchell's, t (0404) 45302 (*moderate*). In an old, restored schoolhouse. Wicklow lamb, Irish stew and lovely home-baked cakes. Open for afternoon tea.

Lunch in Roundwood
Roundwood Inn, t (01) 281 8107/t (01) 281 8125 (*expensive*). 17th-century inn. Bar food (*moderate*) – from filling Irish stew to oysters – and *à la carte* in the restaurant. Very large helpings. *Open Tues–Sat 1–2.30 and 7.30–9.30, Sun 1–2.30; booking essential.*

Dinner in Wicklow
The Bakery, Church Street, t (0404) 66770 (*expensive–moderate*). Exposed brickwork and a roaring fire. Good modern Irish cuisine and an inspired dessert list.
The Leitrim Lounge, Leitrim Place, t (0404) 67443. Friendly seafront bar, popular with yachties, with carvery lunches and dinners.

Sleeping in Wicklow
Grand Hotel, Abbey Street, t (0404) 67337, f 69607, www.grandhotel.ie, grandhotel@eircom.net (*moderate*). There are surprisingly few options in Wicklow Town; this modern hotel is comfortable and friendly, but lacks an element of charm.
Lissadell House, Ashdown Lane, t (0404) 67458, lissadellhse@eircom.net (*inexpensive*). A friendly Irish-German couple, the Klaues, have a comfortable house on the outskirts of town.

Dinner and Sleeping in Rathnew
Tinakilly House, t (0404) 69274, f 67806, www.tinakilly.ie (*expensive*). Very stylish Victorian house set in its own gardens, with ambitious *cuisine française* in an elegant dining room (*open 12.30–2 and 7.30–9, reservations essential*).
Hunter's Hotel, t (0404) 40106, f 40338, www.hunters.ie (*moderate*). Attractive old coaching inn, run by the same family for five generations.

Day 2: Through the Vale of Avoca

Morning: The pleasant and resolutely sleepy county town of **Wicklow** overlooks a crescent-shaped shingle bay. Maurice Fitzgerald, a Norman warlord, built the ruined Black Castle on the promontory overlooking the sea at the eastern end of the town. Soon to open is a new museum in the former Wicklow Gaol, dedicated to 1798 and the events of Irish history this grim old building witnessed. The 18th-century Church of Ireland church, off the main street, has a fine carved Romanesque doorway in the south porch. At **Ashford**, a couple of miles north of Wicklow Town on the main Dublin to Wexford road, is **Mount Usher Gardens** (*open 17 Mar–Oct daily 10.30–5.20; adm*), a wonderful example of a naturalized garden on the banks of the River Vartry.
Lunch: In Ashford or nearby Rathnew, *see* below.
Afternoon: South from Ashford on the R752 is **Rathdrum**, which has untouched pubs in Main Street, and enchanting woodland in the Avondale Valley. The 'big' Avondale House (*www.coillte.ie; open Mar–Oct 11–6, last adm 5pm; adm*), south of town, was the birthplace and lifelong home of that great Irishman, Charles Stewart Parnell, who fought for Home Rule and the land rights of the peasants in the 19th century. It is now open as a museum and the estate is a forest park. The scenery continues to be delightful as you travel south through the **Vale of Avoca**. Along the valley road are shops selling the well-known Avoca-weave rugs, which make lovely presents. In **Avoca** village you can visit Avoca Handweavers (*open all year*), the oldest working mill in Ireland, with a justly celebrated café, food hall and gift shop.
Dinner and Sleeping: In Arklow, *see* below.

Day 2

Lunch in Ashford
Ashford House, t (0404) 40481 (*inexpensive*). One of the few lunch options in this small village, Ashford House has a comfortable bar for a snack or some pub grub, and an Oriental restaurant for a hearty lunch.
Chester Beatty's Restaurant, t (0404) 40206, (*moderate–inexpensive*). An unassuming, family-run inn with a reasonable restaurant serving Irish cuisine. The seafood can be particularly good. There are also bar snacks.

Lunch in Rathnew
Tinakilly House, t (0404) 69274 (*expensive*). Ambitious *cuisine française*, *see* Day 1. *Open 12.30–2 and 7.30–9, booking essential.*
Hunter's Hotel, t (0404) 40106 (*moderate*), *see* Day 1. *Open daily 8.30–10, 1–3 and 7.30–9.*

Dinner in Arklow
Kitty's Restaurant & Bar, 56 Main Street, t (0402) 31669, *www.kittysofarklow.com*.

A very popular pub in the town centre, with high-ceilings, dark wooden beams and wooden floors. Upstairs is a sleek restaurant (*expensive*) serving award-winning modern Irish cuisine; and there are simpler dishes available in the bar.
Howard's Dining Room at the Arklow Bay Hotel, t (0402) 32309 (*expensive*). Smart hotel restaurant with open fires and candle light, serving fine contemporary cuisine prepared with local produce. Save room for the desserts.

Sleeping in Arklow
Moneylands Farm, t (0402) 32259, *mland@ eircom.net* (*inexpensive*). Lillie Byrne offers B&B in a Georgian farmhouse, plus three restored self-catering farm buildings.
Plattenstown House, Coolgreany Road, t (0402) 37822, *mcdpr@indigo.ie* (*moderate–inexpensive*). Handsome, traditional 19th-century country house set in extensive gardens and parkland, run by Mrs McDowell. Peaceful and comfortable.

Day 3: Down the East Coast

Morning: Another Danish settlement in the 9th and 10th centuries, **Arklow** is now a popular resort town, as the beaches surrounding it are safe for bathing. The remains of a 12th-century castle stand on the Bluff overlooking the river, and the Maritime Museum in the Old Technical School, St Mary's Road (*open Oct–April Mon–Fri 10–1 and 2–5; May–Sept Sat also; adm*) details this town's surprisingly rich career, which has involved boat-building, fishing – and smuggling. Then take the N11 south to **Enniscorthy**, the most attractive market town in County Wexford. Enniscorthy was one of the hot spots of the 1798 rising, and the town has commemorated it with the National 1798 Visitors' Centre (*open Mon–Sat 9.30–6.30, Sun 11–6.30; adm*) where you can learn the entire story. Wexford County Museum (*open summer Mon–Sat 10–6, Sun 2–6; winter daily 2–5; Dec–Jan Sun 2–6 only; adm*) is in the castle, built by Raymond le Gros.

Lunch: In Enniscorthy, *see* below.

Afternoon: Carry on down the N11 to **Wexford Town**, one of the most atmospheric of all Irish places. The centre of town is a small square called the Bull Ring – a reminder of the Norman pastime of bull-baiting. Some bits of the Norman town walls remain, along with one gate. Off Abbey Street is Selskar Abbey, built in the late 12th century. The 19th-century church stands on the spot where the first treaty between the Anglo-Normans and the Irish was ratified in 1169. Wexford's waterfront is being redeveloped. *See* also pp.162–4.

Dinner and Sleeping: In Wexford, *see* below.

Day 3

Lunch in Enniscorthy

Bagenal Harvey Restaurant, Treacy's Hotel Templeshannon, Enniscorthy, t (054) 37798 (*expensive–inexpensive*). This is a smart restaurant serving excellent fresh seafood from Kilmore Quay. You can dine informally at the traditional Temple Bar pub, also part of the hotel, which has won awards.

The Antique Tavern, Slaney Street, t (054) 33428 (*moderate–inexpensive*). A handsome black and white inn cluttered with all kinds of bric-a-brac, and boasting an unusual rooftop beer garden. There's a good selection of soups and sandwiches at lunchtime.

Dinner in Wexford

Mange 2, 100 South Main Street, t (053) 44033 (*expensive–moderate*). Simply but stylishly furnished with red walls and wooden tables; excellent French-inspired cuisine.

La Dolce Vita, Westgate, t (053) 23935 (*expensive–moderate*). Superb Italian food.

Heavens Above, The Sky and the Ground, 112 South Main Street, t (053) 21273 (*moderate*). A delightful restaurant above a well-loved pub. Excellent food and wine list.

La Riva, Crescent Quay, t (053) 24330 (*moderate*). Bistro-style restaurant serving super seafood, steaks and home-made pasta dishes as you overlook the harbour.

Tim's Tavern, 51 South Main Street, t (053) 23861 (*moderate–inexpensive*). Lovely old-style, intimate restaurant, noted for its traditional Irish cooking as well as French and vegetarian specials. *Children welcome.*

Sleeping in Wexford

Ferrycarrig Hotel, Ferrycarrig Bridge, Wexford, t (053) 20999/20982 (*expensive*). A brand new hotel built on the Slaney estuary. Nice views and good leisure facilities.

Newbay House, near Wexford Town, t (053) 42779 (*moderate*). Log fires and excellent meals in Joan Coyle's 1820s house, only 2 miles from Wexford Town and 20mins from Rosslare. There are lovely gardens.

Day 4: Waterford and Irish Heritage

Morning: About 2½ miles (4km) north of Wexford Town, at Ferrycarrig, is the **Irish National Heritage Park** (*t (053) 20733, www.inhp.com; open Mar–Nov daily 9.30–6.30, but check; adm*). Here you will find reconstructions of life as it was in the past, from 7000 BC to the medieval period. It is a scholarly and exciting exhibition, with full-scale replicas of the dwellings, places of worship, forts and burial grounds over the ages. Then head west on the N25 for **Waterford** for the rest of the day.

Lunch: In Waterford, *see* below.

Afternoon: A quick tour of the city should perhaps start with the Waterford Crystal Glass Factory (*open daily Mar–Dec 8.30–6; Jan–Feb 9–5, tours Nov–Feb Mon–Fri 9–3.15; Mar–Oct daily 8.30–4.15; adm*), a mile or so (2km) west of the city on the Cork Road (N25). Then see a wonderful example in the cut-glass chandelier which hangs in the City Hall in the Mall. Reginald's Tower (*open Easter–May and Oct daily 10–5; June–Sept daily 9.30–6.30; call for winter hours; adm*) guards the end of the Mall by the river. Just down the Quay on Greyfriars Street is the French Church, originally a Franciscan foundation built in 1240; the keys are kept in the adjacent Waterford Museum of Treasures (*open April, May and Sept 9.30–6; June–Aug 9.30–9, Oct–Mar 10–5; adm*). Turn third left after the French Church and you come to St Olaf's Church, founded by the Norsemen in about AD 980. At the end of Greyfriars Street in Cathedral Square is the Church of Ireland Christ Church Cathedral, was built in 1779 and is classical Georgian in style.

Dinner and Sleeping: In Waterford, *see* below.

Day 4

Lunch in Waterford

Haricots Wholefood Restaurant, 11 O'Connell Street, **t** (051) 841299 (*inexpensive*). Home-made soups, and freshly squeezed juice. *Open Mon–Fri 9–8, Sat 9–6*.

The Olde Stand, 45 Michael Street, **t** (051) 879488 (*inexpensive*). Excellent pub food and a good upstairs restaurant.

Dinner in Waterford

The Wine Vault, Lower High Street, **t** (051) 853444, *info@waterfordwinevault.com* (*expensive*). Well-stocked wine bar, perhaps the finest in Ireland, in the cellars of an 18th-century wine merchant. Good nouveau-vegetarian and seafood selection, and substantial entrees. *Dinner only*.

Dwyers Restaurant, 8 Mary Street, **t** (051) 877478 (*moderate*). In a converted barracks, cosy, comfortable ambience and good food.

Poppy's Restaurant, Park Road, **t** (051) 304844, (*moderate*). Fresh local seafood, salads and chargrilled specialities; popular with locals. *Lunch and dinner Tues–Sun*.

Sleeping in Waterford

Granville Hotel, Meagher Quay, **t** (051) 855111/305555, *www.granville-hotel.ie* (*expensive*). Smart, old-world and conveniently central, with rooms overlooking the river.

Brown's Townhouse, 29 South Parade, **t** (051) 870594, *www.brownstownhouse.com* (*moderate*). Victorian house, with TV and tea-making facilities. Breakfast is fresh fruit salad and home-made bread and jams accompanying a full fry-up Convenient for city centre nightlife, and friendly owners.

Dooley's Hotel, 30, The Quay, **t** (051) 873531, *www.dooleys-hotel.ie, hotel@dooleys-hotel.ie* (*moderate*). Old-established, and recently won an award for customer service.

Sion Hill House, Ferrybank, **t** (051) 851558, *sionhill@eircom.net* (*moderate*). Early 19th-century house with lovely gardens covering four acres and spectacular views. Four en-suite bedrooms.

Day 5: Architectural Gems, and a Day at the Races

Morning: Take the N9 and N10 north to old **Kilkenny City**, which is architecturally very interesting. The city takes its name from St Canice, who established a monastery here in the 6th century; the Church of Ireland cathedral now occupies its site off Vicar Street. Visit Rothe House (*open Nov–Mar Mon–Sat 1–5; April–Oct Mon–Sat 10.30–5, Sun 3–5; adm*) on Parliament Street, a unique example of an Irish Tudor merchant's house, built in 1594. On the edge of the town centre, the great fortress of the Ormondes, Kilkenny Castle (*open daily April–May 10.30–5; June–Aug 9.30–7; Sept 10–6.30; Oct–Mar 10.30–12.45 and 2–5; guided tours only; adm*), remains a dominant feature. Across the River Nore, in Lower John Street, is Kilkenny College, a handsome Georgian building where some of Ireland's greatest writers were educated. Many of the pubs in Kilkenny have hand-painted signs.

Lunch: In Kilkenny, *see* below.

Afternoon: Continue north via Carlow. **Kildare Town** with its 13th-century cathedral is on the edge of the Curragh, and is now an important centre for horse-breeding. Green spring grass stretches for miles, the best pasture in the world for building horses' bones, with the blue hills of Dublin on the horizon. The thousand-acre **National Stud** at **Tully** (*t (045) 522963, www.irish-national-stud.ie; open 12 Feb–12 Nov daily 9.30–6; adm for stud and gardens*), just outside Kildare Town on the R415, is open for guided tours in the summer, and there is a horse museum. and a spectacular Japanese Garden symbolizing the life of man from cradle to the grave.

Dinner and Sleeping: In Kildare, or in Athy, 12 miles back towards Carlow, *see* below.

Day 5

Lunch in Kilkenny

Lacken House, Dublin Road, t (056) 776 1085 (*expensive*). Popular, family-run restaurant serving imaginative, perfectly cooked food.

Newpark Hotel, Castlecomer Road, t (056) 776 0500 (*expensive*). Plush restaurant serving Irish and continental food.

Edward Langton's, 69 John Street, t (056) 65133 (*expensive–moderate*). Award-winning, with good pub lunches and dinners.

Kilkenny Castle, t (056) 21450 (*inexpensive*). Restaurant in the old castle kitchen; delicious lunches and teas. *Summer only.*

Dinner and Sleeping in Kildare

Kristiannas Bistro, Market Square, t (045) 522985 (*moderate*). A popular breezy bistro, serving good local dishes and seafood.

Curragh Lodge Hotel, Dublin Street, t (045) 522144. Reasonable hotel and restaurant with plain but well-equipped rooms. Handily located and particularly good for families.

Castle View Farm, Lackaghmore, Kildare, t (045) 521816, *castleviewfarmhouse@ocean free.net*. A pretty whitewashed working dairy farm, 4km from Kildare. Good home cooking – they will cater for children and vegetarians and provide packed lunches.

Dinner and Sleeping in Athy

Tonlegee House and Restaurant, t/f (0507) 31473, *www.tonlegeehouse.com* (*moderate*). Just off the Kilkenny road, outside Athy. An elegant 18th-century country house with en-suite rooms and a restaurant, with dishes made with organic vegetables from their own garden as well as local fish and game.

Ballindrum Farm, t (0507) 26294 (*inexpensive*). Comfortable accommodation on Mr and Mrs Gorman's working farm; good breakfasts and dinner available.

Coursetown House, Stradbally Road, Athy, t (059) 863 1101 (*moderate*). Beautiful, country house set in its own gardens two miles outside Athy. The four welcoming rooms are traditionally decorated and cosy.

Wexford Town

Wexford Town is one of the most atmospheric of all Irish places. It was originally settled by a Celtic Belgic tribe called the Manapii, about 350 BC, and later by the Vikings who gave it the name *Waesfjord*. They ruled from the 9th to the 12th century and built up a flourishing port around the River Slaney and its outlet to the sea. Then the Normans, allies of Dermot McMurragh, captured it and built walls, castles and abbeys in their usual disciplined pattern. Many of the winding streets are so narrow

Getting There

Rosslare Harbour handles passenger and car ferry boats from Fishguard, Pembroke and the French ports of Roscoff and Cherbourg. There's not much of anything in Rosslare Harbour, though you'll find taxis for nearby Wexford (there are only a few, so disembark quickly if you need one), and often Bus Eireann coaches bound for Waterford or Dublin are timed to meet the boats. *See* also **Travel**, p.11.

Getting Around

Bike Hire
Hayes Cycles, 108 South Main Street, t (053) 22462, *hayescycles@eircom.net*.
The Bike Shop, 9 Selskar Street, t (053) 22514.

Tourist Information

Wexford: Crescent Quay, t (053) 23111, *www.wexfordtourism.com; open all year*.

Internet Access
FDYS Training Centre, Frances St, t (053) 23262.
Wexford Library, Redmond Square, t (053) 21637.

Festivals

Spring Music Festival, *Mar–April*. Classical music, t (053) 23923.
Wexford Hooves and Grooves Festival, *July*. With horse-racing and live entertainment.
Wexford Opera Festival, *October*. Contact the Wexford Festival Office, Theatre Royal, t (053) 22400, *info@wexfordopera.com*.

Shopping

Creative Energy, Westgate Heritage Centre, Wexford Town, t (053) 46506. A showcase of decorative arts and crafts designed and produced in Wexford.
Westgate Design, North Main St, t (053) 23787.
Atlantis, Redmond Square, t (053) 22337. Freshly caught fish, sold from a caravan.
Greenacres, 56 North Main Street, t (053) 22975. Good vegetables, wholefoods and a small but very good meat counter.
Rainbow Wholefoods, Walkers Mall, North Main Street, t (053) 24624.

Sports and Activities

Golf
Wexford Golf Club, Mulgannon, Wexford Town, t (053) 42238.

Horse Racing
Wexford Racecourse, Bettyville, Newtown Road, t (053) 42307, *www.WexfordRaces.ie*. Nine days of racing annually.

Walking
Wexford coastal path, from Kilmichael Point to Ballyhack, stretches over 138 miles (221kms) – ask for details from the tourist office.
During the summer evenings a **walking tour** of Wexford Town, led by a local historical society member, departs from Westgate Heritage Centre – details from the tourist office.

Water Sports
Wexford Harbour Boat and Tennis Club, t (053) 22039. For water-skiing and sailing.

that you could shake hands across them. Cromwell left as bloody a reputation behind him here as in Drogheda. He occupied the town in 1649 during his campaign to subdue the 'rebellious Irish', and destroyed many of the churches.

Most people come to Wexford for the **Opera Festival**, held every year in October. Programmes of lesser-known operas are produced with world-famous soloists, an excellent local chorus and the RTE Symphony Orchestra. Its reputation for originality and quality is worldwide. Exhibitions, revues and plays take place at the same time.

Where to Stay

Whites Hotel, George Street, t (053) 22311, *www.whiteshotel.ie* (*moderate*). Central and comfortable; this was the smartest hotel in town for years. It is now largely modern, but incorporates part of an old coaching inn. *Closed until May 2005.*

Ferrycarrig Hotel, Ferrycarrig Bridge, Wexford, t (053) 20999/20982 (*expensive*). A brand new hotel built on the Slaney Estuary. Nice views and good leisure facilities.

Newbay House, near Wexford Town, t (053) 42779 (*moderate*). Log fires, excellent meals and pine/period furnishings in Joan Coyle's 1820s house, only 2 miles (3.2km) from Wexford Town and 20 minutes from Rosslare. There are lovely gardens to stroll in.

Clonard House, Clonard Great, near Wexford, t (053) 47337 (*moderate–inexpensive*). Late-Georgian house with a staircase that curves into the ceiling because the money ran out for the top floor. Kathleen Hayes offers simple, delicious breakfasts, with perfect views and farmland to the sea.

Eating Out

Mange 2, 100 South Main Street, t (053) 44033 (*expensive–moderate*). Simply but stylishly furnished with red walls and wooden tables; excellent French-inspired cuisine.

La Dolce Vita, Westgate, t (053) 23935, (*expensive–moderate*). Superb Italian food, and occasional jazz performances.

Heavens Above, The Sky and the Ground, 112 South Main Street, t (053) 21273, *www.skyandtheground.com* (*moderate*). A delightful restaurant above a well-loved

pub. Excellent food and an enormous wine list make this place a must.

La Riva, Crescent Quay, t (053) 24330, *www.larivawexford.com* (*moderate*). Bistro-style restaurant serving super seafood, steaks and home-made pasta dishes as you overlook the harbour.

Tim's Tavern, 51 South Main Street, t (053) 23861 (*moderate–inexpensive*). A lovely old-style, intimate restaurant, noted for its traditional Irish cooking as well as French and vegetarian specials. *Children are welcome.*

Cappuccinos, 23 North Main Street (*inexpensive*). Very popular lunchtime snack spot, with hot ciabatta sandwiches among the wide-ranging options.

Entertainment and Nightlife

Traditional Music

In Wexford Town it is nearly impossible to stay bored or sober for long.

The Sky and the Ground, South Main Street, t (053) 21273. This was once an old shop and pub in the 1960s, and they've left everything the way it was, including the groceries. Convivial, with a snug and good traditional music played every night Sun–Thurs.

Wren's Nest, Custom House Quay, t (053) 22359.

Mooney's Lounge, 12 Commercial Quay, t (053) 24483. Live entertainment and dancing Thurs–Sun, and sport on plasma screens.

The Centenary Stores, Charlotte Street, t (053) 24424. Old pub, with entertainment most nights in the bar.

The centre of town is a small square called the **Bull Ring** – a reminder of the Norman pastime of bull-baiting, which was held on this spot – and contains a figure of an Irish pikeman, commemorating the Wexford insurgents of 1798. Some bits of the Norman town walls remain, along with one gate, now the **Westgate Heritage Centre** (*t (053) 46506; open June–Aug daily 9–5; Sept–May closed Mon; adm*). Here you can see an audiovisual presentation on the history of Wexford. Near West Gate, off Abbey Street, is **Selskar Abbey**. It was built in the late 12th century, and the remains consist of a square, battlemented tower and a church with a double nave and part of its west gable. The 19th-century **church** (*always accessible*) stands on the spot where the first treaty between the Anglo-Normans and the Irish was ratified in 1169.

Wexford's waterfront is a dowdy, long-neglected part of town that is currently being redeveloped. Notice the **Commodore John Barry Memorial** on Crescent Quay: he was born 10 miles (16km) away at Ballysampson, and is remembered as the father of the US Navy and the first to capture a British ship in the Revolutionary War. A duplicate statue stands in front of Independence Hall in Philadelphia. Lady Wilde (1826–96), mother of Oscar and known as 'Speranza', was born in the Old Rectory, Main Street. Sir Robert McClure (1807–73), who discovered the Northwest Passage in the Arctic, is another famous Wexford son.

There are mud flats close to the town at **Ferrybank**, which were reclaimed from the sea in the 1840s. The **Wexford Wildfowl Reserve** (*t (053) 23129; open mid-April–Sept daily 9–6, Oct–April daily 10–5; guided tours on request; adm free*) provides over 2,500 acres (1,000ha) of mud flats, or 'slobs', for a huge variety of bird life in winter. Vast numbers of Greenland white-fronted geese rest and feed here.

About 2½ miles (4km) north of Wexford Town, at **Ferrycarrig**, is the **Irish National Heritage Park** (*t (053) 20733, www.inhp.com; open Mar–Nov daily 9.30–6.30; adm*). Here you will find reconstructions of life as it was in the past, from 7000 BC to the medieval period. It is a scholarly and exciting exhibition, with full-scale replicas of the dwellings, places of worship, forts and burial grounds over the ages, and contains everything from a prehistoric *crannog* (artificial island) to an incredible Viking ship.

Three miles (4.8km) south of Wexford, near Murntown, is **Johnstown Castle** (*t (053) 42888; open daily 9.30–5.30; adm in summer*). Built in 19th-century Gothic style, it is now a State Agricultural College and visitors can tour round the landscaped gardens and lakes. There are three lakes and a walled garden, as well as the old estate farmyard, now home to the college's **Irish Agricultural Museum** (*t (053) 42888; open all year, Mon–Fri 9–5, also April–Oct, weekends 2–5; adm*).

Day Trips and Overnighters from Wexford

Rosslare and Around

Five miles (8km) north of Rosslare Harbour, the ferry port, and 8 miles south of Wexford, is the resort of **Rosslare**, with 6 miles (9.7km) of curving strand. The coastline beyond, approached from the R736, is well worth travelling around. On **Lady's**

Getting There and Around

Buses go from Wexford Town to Rosslare Harbour to meet the ferries, and **Rosslare** is only a few miles away.

Kilmore Quay is very out of the way, and you may need to take a bus to Rosslare Harbour and then a taxi.

New Ross can be reached from Wexford on the Waterford and Cork bus.

Bike Hire

Quay House Guest House, Kilmore Quay, t (053) 29988.

Tourist Information

New Ross: t (051) 21857; *open mid June–Aug Mon–Sat 10–6.*

Shopping

Butlersland Craft Centre, Butlerstown, New Ross.

Kilmore Quay Country Crafts, Kilmore Quay, t (053) 29885.

Lavery Pottery, John F. Kennedy Park, south of New Ross, t (051) 388544.

Sports and Activities

Fishing

Wexford Boat Charters, Kilmore Quay, t (053) 45888, *wexboats@iol.ie.*

Golf

Rosslare Golf Club, Rosslare Strand, t (053) 32203.

Open Farms

Ballylane Visitor Farm, New Ross (off N25), t (051) 425666. *Open May–Sept daily 10–6; Oct–April Sun and bank hols only.*

Water Sports

Rosslare Watersports Centre, t (053) 32566. Sailboards, canoeing. *Open June–Aug.*

Where to Stay

Rosslare Harbour and the road leading north to Wexford have a huge number of hotels and B&Bs, so you shouldn't have too much trouble finding a place if you get off the ferry in the evening. Even so, in summer it's best to book ahead.

Kilrane House, Kilrane, Rosslare Harbour, t (053) 33135 (*inexpensive*). A comfortable, friendly house run by Mrs Whitehead, only 2mins from Rosslare Harbour.

Creacon Lodge, New Ross, t (051) 421897 (*expensive–moderate*). Situated close to the John F. Kennedy Park, Josephine Flood's cosy house has tiny mullioned windows and creeper climbing up the walls. Restaurant.

Horetown House, Foulksmills, t (051) 565771 (*moderate*). Old fashioned 17th-century manor house in beautiful parkland setting. Mrs Young offers good plain food in the Cellar Restaurant, and facilities include an equestrian centre in the courtyard.

Eating Out

Oyster Restaurant, Strand Road, Rosslare Strand, t (053) 32439 (*moderate*). Scallops and black sole are a speciality.

Galley River Cruising Restaurant, The Quay, New Ross, t (051) 421723 (*expensive*). Six-course meals while you cruise on the river.

Neptune, Ballyhack Harbour, New Ross, t (051) 389284 (*moderate*). Overlooking the harbour. Good value dinner menus. Seafood is their speciality, and you can bring your own wine.

Cedar Lodge Restaurant and Hotel, Carrighbyrne, Newbawn, New Ross, t (051) 428386, f (051) 428222, *www.prideofeire hotels.com* (*inexpensive*). On the main Wexford–New Ross road. Good-quality food, and rooms if you need them.

Island there are ruins of an Augustinian priory and a Norman castle built in 1237; the island is sacred to the Blessed Virgin and is still a favourite place of pilgrimage. Further round the south coast, **Kilmore Quay** is an attractive thatched fishing village where you can get a boat, weather permitting, to the **Saltee Islands**. Nobody lives on the islands, which are verdant with waist-high bracken. Though they are private property and visits are prohibited, boatmen on the Quay will take you out for a trip around them. The puffins and other waterfowl are magnificent. The view from Kilmore Harbour along the headlands looks rather like the 19th-century Dutch-influenced landscapes of the Norwich School of painters. The **Guillemot Maritime Museum** is housed in what was Ireland's last working lightship (*t (051) 561144; open Easter–May and Sept Sat and Sun 12–6, June–Aug daily 12–6; adm*).

New Ross and Around

Near to **Campile**, on the R733 and beside the winding River Barrow, is **Dunbrody Abbey**. This is is one of the most underestimated ruins in Ireland. It was built by the monks of St Mary's, Dublin, in 1182. A vast pile of weathered grey stone, it was suppressed in 1539. The west door is magnificent, and so are the lancet windows over the high altar. It has a tea-room, a small museum, picnic site and a fully grown maze. Close by is **Dunmain House** (*open May–Sept, Tues–Sun, 2–5.30; adm; t (051) 562122*), a 17th-century building that has retained many of its original features; it is covered with slates, quite a common sight as you move further south in Ireland. **Kilmokea Country Manor and Gardens** (*t (051) 388109, www.kilmokea.com; open daily 9–5; guided tours, please ring ahead; adm*), near Campile, is a Georgian rectory with superb grounds. There is a rock garden, an Italian garden, a traditional herbaceous border, a lupin border, wide lawns with topiary hedges and a water garden set in beautiful woodland.

New Ross on the River Barrow has some ancient gabled houses and a medieval feel to it. It was built by Isobel, Strongbow's daughter, and has seen fighting against Cromwell and during the 1798 rebellion. The Kennedy ancestral home (now a ruin) is in nearby **Dunganstown**. In 1848 Jack Kennedy left his family homestead for a new life in America after the dreadful years of the famine. The **Kennedy Centre**, at the Quay in New Ross (*t (051) 425239*), provides genealogical records for those compiling family histories in the area, and the JFK Trust financed the building of the **Dunbrody** (*t (051) 425239, www. dunbrody.com; open April–Sept daily 9–6; Oct–Mar daily 12–5*), a 176ft replica of one of the ships that took emigrants to America during the famine. Early in 1999 the ship left the New Ross docks for its maiden voyage to Boston, and it is now docked here in the town. Also here is the **Berkeley Forest House Costume and Toy Museum** (*t (051) 421361; open May–Sept, Sat only; adm*), which has a collection of rare and delicate dolls and costumes – the lady who runs it makes tiny and exquisite dolls' hats. Just south of New Ross, off the R374, is the **John F. Kennedy Park and Arboretum** (*t (051) 388171; open Oct–Mar daily 10–5; April and Sept daily 10–6.30, May–Aug, until 8; adm*), with marvellous young trees and over 4,500 species of shrubs.

Touring from Wexford

You can follow the second Dublin tour, starting at Day 4 (p.160), with a night in Dublin after Day 5, then Days 1 and 2, ending back in Wexford on Day 3 (p.159).

The Southwest

08

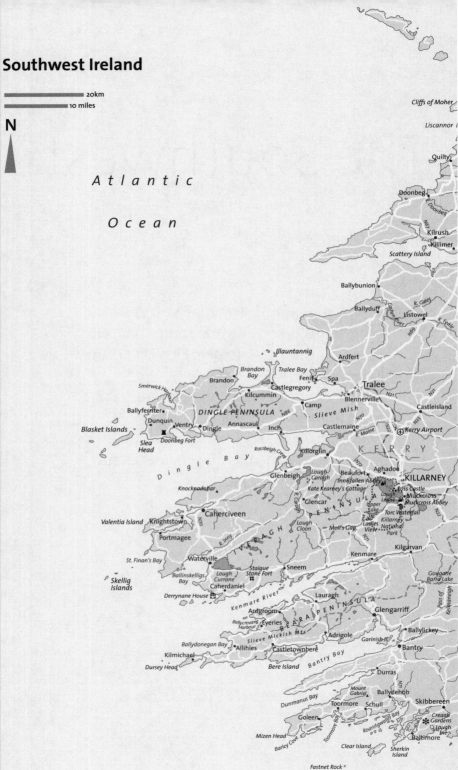

Southwest Ireland

20km
10 miles

N

Atlantic

Ocean

Cliffs of Moher

Liscannor

Quilty

Doonbeg

Kilrush

Killimer

Scattery Island

Ballybunion

Ballyduff

R. Galey

Listowel

R. Feale

Ardfert

Illauntannig

Brandon
Bay

Tralee Bay

Fenit

Spa

Brandon

Castlegregory

Tralee

Smerwick Harbour

Kilcummin

Camp

Blennerville

N21

Castleisland

Ballyferriter

DINGLE PENINSULA

N86

Slieve Mish

N70

Dunquin

Ventry

Dingle

Annascaul

Inch

Castlemaine

R. Maine

Kerry Airport

Blasket Islands

Slea
Head

Doonbeg Fort

Rossbeigh Creek

Killorglin

KERRY

Dingle Bay

Glenbeigh

Lough
Caragh

Beaufort

Aghadoe

KILLARNEY

Knocknadobar

Innisfallen Abbey

Kate Kearney's Cottage

Ross Castle

Glencar

R. Caragh

Muckross

*Upper
Lake*

*Lough
Leane*

Muckross Abbey

Valentia Island

Knightstown

Cahersiveen

N70

IVERAGH

Lough
Cloon

PENINSULA

*Killarney
National
Park*

Torc Waterfall

Ladies
View

Portmagee

R. Inny

Moll's Gap

St. Finan's Bay

Waterville

Kenmare

Kilgarvan

Skellig
Islands

*Ballinskelligs
Bay*

Lough
Currane

Staigue
Stone Fort

Sneem

*Gougane
Barra Lake*

Caherdaniel

*Pass of
Keimaneigh*

Derrynane House

Kenmare River

Lauragh

BEARA PENINSULA

Glengarriff

Ardgroom

*Ballycrovane
Harbour*

Eyeries

Ballylickey

Slieve Mickish Mts

Adrigole

Garinish Is

Bantry

Ballydonegan Bay

Allihies

Castletownbere

Kilmichael

Bere Island

Bantry Bay

Dursey Head

Durras

Mount
Gabriel

Ballydehob

Skibbereen

Dunmanus Bay

Toormore

Schull

*Creagh
Gardens*

Goleen

*Lough
Ine*

Barley Cove

Roaringwater Bay

Baltimore

Mizen Head

Clear Island

*Sherkin
Island*

Fastnet Rock

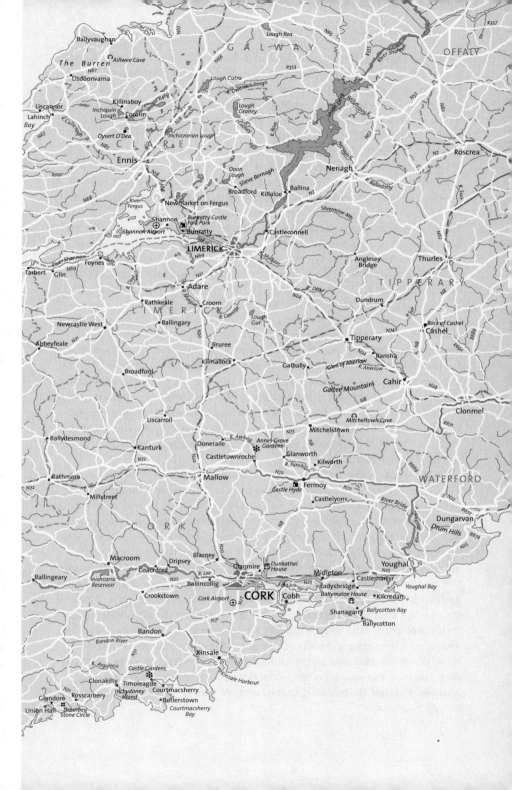

You have chosen well if the southwest of Ireland is your destination. Ireland is the perfect place to take a holiday, and Cork, Kerry and Limerick make up a most beautiful and fascinating region. These counties, which comprise most of the province of Munster, are easily accessible from Shannon, Cork and Kerry airports, and they have all the attractions of this lovely island in abundance. The landscape is varied and unspoilt, and the pace of life is relaxing.

Munster (*Cuige Mumhan*) is the largest province in Ireland and a mixture of everything you consider Irish: the purples of the mountains melt into chessboards of cornfields in which the stooks stand like golden pieces. Houses are whitewashed, glens are deep and the coastline is made ragged by the force of the Atlantic, with sandy bays and rocky cliffs. It is a land of extremes: a large, placid, fertile plain, brooding mountain scenery, luxurious vegetation, and harsh, barren land. The stately River Shannon flows out to sea between County Clare and County Limerick. The extreme southwest coast is swept by westerly gales, distorting trees into twisted shapes. The moonscape of the Burren, the youngest landscape in Europe, contrasts with the softness of Killarney; the dairy-land of the inland valleys contrasts with the thrashing sea around the Dingle and Iveragh Peninsulas.

This is the land of the Mumonians; the 'ster' suffix of Munster is a Scandinavian addition to the more ancient name of Muma. The province as a whole has been described as a little England. The Anglo-Normans certainly had a part in moulding the towns, as did some of the adventurers of Elizabethan times, but Cork City is the creation of lively Irish minds; whether Celts or later arrivals, Cork people think their city ought to be the capital rather than Dublin. There's a sense of separateness about the southwest and this has helped to develop a great local mythological tradition, with mother-goddesses figuring prominently in legend and place names; also strong in the mythological tradition is Donn Forinee, the ancestor-god to whom all the Irish will journey after death.

The history of Ireland has been turbulent, and its telling fraught with prejudice and misunderstanding. But a fascinating thing to do is to approach it through its excellent literary tradition, and travel with your head full of myths, legends and literature.

In the southwest the climate is good and damp, the rainfall varies between 30 inches in parts to as much as 87 inches in Killarney, but the sunshine, when it comes, intensifies the already beautiful colours of the landscape. The roads are usually empty and traffic jams are still an exception. Do not rush, for, if you do, the charm of the countryside and its people will pass you by. The largest concentration of houses and cars is in the energetic and attractive city of Cork; its population is well over 150,000. It is built along the River Lee and the sheltered waters of Cork Harbour, and it stretches up the little hills around. It is a place of exuberant culture and business, and its natives have a great sense of humour about life and the ridiculous. At the other extreme are the wild and beautiful headlands of west Cork, Kerry and Clare, where you can lose yourself in the mountains and on the long white strands. In southwest Ireland, the one thing that is certain is that all the annoyances of everyday life will disappear.

Cork

The name 'Cork' comes from the Gaelic *Corcaigh*, which means 'a marshy place'. Ireland's second city, with a population of 125,000, is built on marshy land on the banks of the River Lee, and has crept up the hills around. Over the years nearly all the islands in this marsh have been reclaimed, their water courses built over and the city walls removed. The river flows in two main channels, crossed by bridges, so that central Cork is actually on an island. It can be confusing if you are driving there for the first time, with its one-way roads and the crossing and recrossing of the river.

Until the Anglo-Norman invasion in 1179, Cork City was largely a Danish stronghold. It was famous from the 7th century for its excellent school under St Finbarr. The Cork citizens were an independent lot, and, although after 1180 English laws were nominally in force, it was really the wealthy merchants who were in charge. In 1492 they took up the cause of the Yorkists and Perkin Warbeck, and went with him to Kent where he was proclaimed Pretender to the English crown – Richard IV, King of England and Lord of Ireland. They lost their charter for that piece of impudence, but Cork continued to be a rebel city (although, rather curiously, it offered no resistance to Oliver Cromwell). William III laid siege to it in 1690 because it stood by James II, and it had to surrender without honour. In the 17th and 18th centuries it grew rapidly with the expansion of the butter trade, and many of the splendid Georgian buildings you can still see were built during this time. By the 19th century it had become a centre for the Fenian movement, which worked for an independent republic. During the War of Independence, 1919–21, the city was badly burned by the Auxiliaries, known as the Black and Tans after the colours of their uniform, and one of Cork's mayors died on hunger strike in an English prison. But Cork is also famous for a more moderate character, Father Theobald Matthew (1790–1856), who persuaded thousands of people to swear off alcohol, though the effect of his temperance drive was ruined by the potato famine and the general misery it brought. Cork still has a reputation for clannish behaviour amongst its businessmen and for independence in the arts and politics, but it would be hard to find a friendlier city to wander around, and you can easily explore it on foot.

City Centre

Cork's business and shopping centre is crowded on to an island between the twin channels of the River Lee, with elegant bridges linking the north and south sides of the city. The city's skyline is still, like Derry's, 19th-century. Cork has spires and gracious wide streets; many of its fine buildings, bridges and quays are of a silvery limestone. **St Patrick's Street** curves close to the river; one side of the street is lined with old buildings, the other by offices, shop fronts and an opera house built since the burning in 1920. Here you will find a statue of Father Matthew. The covered **English Market**, hidden behind the façades of St Patrick's Street, is rather like Smithfield Market in London and displays great pig carcasses and *drisheen* (a type of black pudding which along with tripe is a local delicacy), as well as fresh fish, piles of vegetables, mouth-watering bread and olives of every description. It also has some superb eating places.

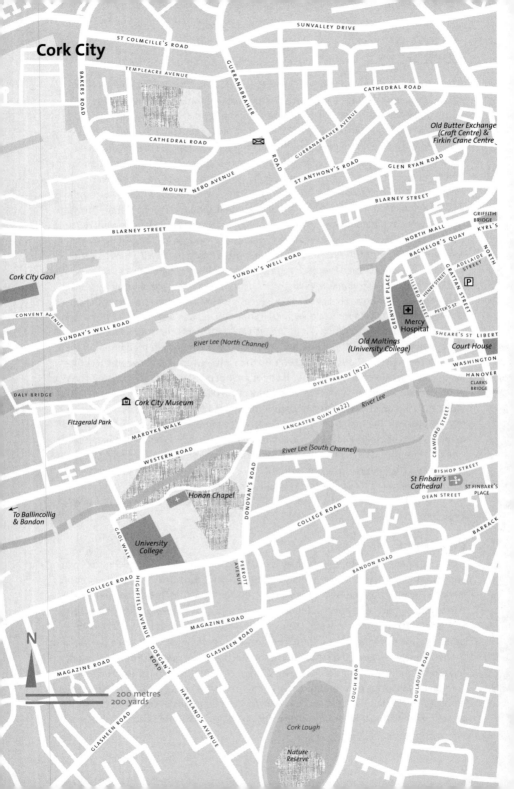

Cork City

SUNVALLEY DRIVE

ST COLMCILLE'S ROAD

TEMPLEACRE AVENUE

BAKERS ROAD

CURRANABRAHER ROAD

CATHEDRAL ROAD

GURRANABRAHER AVENUE

CATHEDRAL ROAD

ST ANTHONY'S ROAD

GLEN RYAN ROAD

Old Butter Exchange
(Craft Centre) &
Firkin Crane Centre

MOUNT NEBO AVENUE

BLARNEY STREET

BLARNEY STREET

GRIFFITH
BRIDGE

KYRL'S

NORTH MALL

BACHELOR'S QUAY

SUNDAY'S WELL ROAD

ADELAIDE
STREET

Cork City Gaol

GRENVILLE PLACE

MILLERD STREET

HENRY STREET

GRATTAN STREET

NORTH
STREET

CONVENT AVENUE

SUNDAY'S WELL ROAD

P

PETER'S ST

River Lee (North Channel)

Mercy
Hospital

SHEARE'S ST

LIBERT

Old Maltings
(University College)

Court House

DALY BRIDGE

Cork City Museum

DYKE PARADE (N22)

WASHINGTON

HANOVER

CLARKS
BRIDGE

Fitzgerald Park

LANCASTER QUAY (N22)

River Lee

CRAWFORD STREET

MARDYKE WALK

River Lee (South Channel)

WESTERN ROAD

BISHOP STREET

St Finbarr's
Cathedral

DONOVAN'S ROAD

ST FINBARR'S
PLACE

Honan Chapel

DEAN STREET

To Ballincollig
& Bandon

COLLEGE ROAD

BARRACK

GAOL WALK

University
College

BANDON ROAD

COLLEGE ROAD

HIGHFIELD AVENUE

PERROTT AVENUE

N

MAGAZINE ROAD

DORGAN'S ROAD

GLASHEEN ROAD

MAGAZINE ROAD

LOUGH ROAD

POULADUFF ROAD

200 metres
200 yards

GLASHEEN ROAD

HARTLAND'S AVENUE

Cork Lough

Nature
Reserve

Getting There

A wide selection of airlines flies to Cork from various UK cities; *see* Travel pp.6–7.
You can also get to Cork by ferry from Fishguard to Rosslare, then a 2hr drive on to Cork, and from March to December there's a direct Swansea–Cork ferry; *see* Travel p.11.

Getting from the Airport

Cork Airport is south of the city on the N27; there is a regular shuttle service from the airport to the bus station on Parnell Place, which takes 20mins and costs €4.
A **taxi** to Cork City centre will cost approximately €15.
Cork Airport, t (021) 431 3131, *www.cork-airport.com.*

Getting Around

Cork is linked to Dublin and other areas by the Irish rail network (*Iarnród Eireann*). **Trains** run from Kent Station, including a suburban service to Fota and Cobh. For all passenger enquiries, bus or train, call **t** (021) 450 6766, *www.irishrail.ie.* Kent Station is 5mins' walk northeast of the city centre on Lower Glanmire Road.
The bus station is centrally located in Parnell Place. Bus Eireann runs both the city and rural services. City centre fares are a flat rate, and a day pass costs approximately €6. Call **t** (021) 450 8188 or use the very helpful travel planner on *www.buseireann.ie.*

Car Hire

Numerous car rental companies operate from both the airport and city locations.
Alamo/National, t (021) 432 0755, *www.carhire.ie.*
Thrifty, t (021) 434 8488, *www.thrifty.ie.*
Murrays, t (021) 491 7300.

Bike Hire

Irish Cycle Hire, Cork train station, **t** (021) 455 1430.
Rothar Cycle Tours, 55 Barrack Street, **t** (021) 431 3133.

Tourist Information

Cork City: Grand Parade, **t** (021) 425 5100, **f** 425 5199, *www.corkkerry.ie; open all year.*

Festivals

Late April–early May: International Choral and Folk Dance Festival.
Mid-June–July: Garden Festival.
Early Sept: Beamish Cork Folk Festival, *www.corkfestival.com.*
Mid-Oct: International Film Festival, *www.corkfilmfest.org.*
End Oct: Cork Jazz Festival, *www.corkjazz festival.com*

Shopping

Cork is great for both dedicated shoppers and those who want to get it all over in a couple of hours. The compact central area, bounded by the north and south channels of the Lee, contain all the interest, though MacCurtain Street to the north is worth a detour. St Patrick's Street contains some high street names and Cork's best department store, Brown Thomas.
Paul Street and the lanes leading off it are good for small quirky shops, as is Oliver Plunkett Street, the other side of St Patrick's Street. Emmet Place has the attraction of the Crawford Art Gallery (and superb café) and a couple of upmarket gift and household stores selling Irish craft items.

Paul Street, north of St Patrick's Street, once the Huguenot quarter, has become the trendy corner of Cork, with cafés, bookshops and buskers in an attractively redesigned pedestrian area. It joins **Cornmarket Street** and its open-air flea market, usually called **Coal Quay**, where you can bargain for trifles and observe the sharp-tongued store owners. Also off Paul Street is **St Peter and St Paul Church**, a Gothic-style building designed by the younger Pugin.

Antiques

The **Flea Market**, Cornmarket Street.
MacCurtain Street. Antiques and bric-a-brac.

Books

The **Mercier Bookshop**, 18 Academy Church Street. A wealth of books of Irish interest, and novels by Irish authors.

Delicacies

The **English Market**, in Cork between St Patrick's Street, Grand Parade and Oliver Plunkett Street; good for food and flowers. **Natural Foods**, 26 Paul Street. For bread.

Gifts and Crafts

Meadows and Byrne, 22 Academy Street. **Marbles and Lennon**, Emmet Place.

Musical Instruments

Crowleys Music Centre, 29 MacCurtain Street. Sells *bodhráns*.

Sports and Activities

Golf

Cork Golf Club, Little Island, t (021) 435 3451, *wwwcorkgolfclub.ie*.
Harbour Point Golf Club, Clash Road, Little Island, t (021) 435 3094, *www.harbourpoint golfclub.com*.

Greyhound Racing

Cork Greyhound Track, Curraheen Park, Bishopstown, t (021) 454 3095, *www.igb.ie*. Wed, Thurs and Sat at 7.30pm.

Water Sports

Royal Cork Yacht Club, Crosshaven, t (021) 483 1023, *www.royalcork.com*.
Cork Water Ski Club, Lower Dripsey, t (021) 733 4605.

Where to Stay

Hayfield Manor, Perrott Avenue, College Road, t (021) 484 5900, f 431 6839, *www. hayfield-manor.ie* (*luxury*). Modern building designed in a traditional style, graciously appointed, with a lovely pool, air-conditioning and various other pampering amenities.

Jury's Hotel, Western Road, t (021) 427 6622, f 427 4477, *www.jurysdoyle.com* (*expensive*). Modern hotel offering sports facilities and a riverside garden.

Gresham Metropole, MacCurtain Street, t (021) 450 8122, f 450 6450, *www. gresham-hotels.com* (*moderate*). Old-fashioned charm and excellent facilities: three pools, two dining areas with great views over the River Lee, and the Met Tavern.

Isaac's, 48 MacCurtain Street, t (021) 450 0011, f 450 6355 (*moderate*). Comfortable hotel with courtyard garden; self-catering apartments also available.

Lotamore House, Tivoli, t (021) 482 2344 (*moderate*). Comfortable bedrooms with en suite baths in a lovely Georgian house 10mins' drive from the city centre.

Killarney Guesthouse, Western Road, t (021) 427 0290, f 427 1010 (*inexpensive*). Charming, comfortable guest house 10mins' walk from the centre. Wonderful breakfasts.

Eating Out

Isaac's Restaurant, 48 MacCurtain Street, t (021) 455 3805 (*expensive*). In a fashionable 18th-century converted warehouse, serving award-winning Irish/Mediterranean fare.

The Ivory Tower, Exchange Buildings, Princes Street, t (021) 427 4665 (*expensive*). In an upstairs restaurant in the heart of the city, perfectly run by its talented chef-patron.

The **South Mall**, to the south of the island, and the adjoining **Grand Parade** have some pretty buildings. The tourist office, on the Grand Parade, offers literary walking tours from June to September on Tuesdays and Thursdays at 7pm, and historical walking tours on Wednesdays at 10am (*walks cost approx. €8*). In Washington Street, east of Grand Parade, is the magnificent Corinthian façade of the 19th-century **Court House**. Just off South Mall is **Holy Trinity Church**, on **Father Matthew Quay**, with a wonderful stained-glass window dedicated to Daniel O'Connell, 'the Great Liberator'.

Bodega/Café Bar Deli, Cornmarket Street, t (021) 427 2878 (*moderate*). An atmospheric old warehouse is now home to this trendy bar and deli. Great salads and an accent on the Mediterranean.

Café Paradiso, 16 Lancaster Quay, Western Road, t (021) 427 7939 (*moderate*). Great organic vegetarian food.

Jacques Restaurant, 9 Phoenix Street, t (021) 427 7387 (*moderate*). Imaginative cooking, with particularly good vegetarian dishes.

Oyster Bar, Market Lane, off St Patrick's Street, t (021) 427 2716 (*moderate*). The atmosphere of a gentlemen's dining room, with white-aproned waitresses. Excellent seafood.

Star Anise, 4 Bridge Street, t (021) 455 1635 (*moderate*). There's an Asian twist to the dishes served here. *Closed Sun and Mon.*

Table 8, 8–9 Carey's Lane, t (021) 427 0725 (*moderate*). In the heart of the city, with a Ballymaloe-trained chef, an international-style menu and the freshest ingredients.

Crawford's Art Gallery Café, Emmet Place, t (021) 427 4415 (*inexpensive*). Run by one of the Allen family of Ballymaloe House fame (*see* p.195), it serves light, original food for lunch or early supper. Particularly good fresh orange juice and gooey cakes.

Eastern Palace, t (021) 427 6967 (*inexpensive*). Chinese restaurant in the English Market; take advantage of their excellent lunch menu. Zesty and imaginative food.

The Gingerbread House, Paul Street Plaza, t (021) 427 6411 (*inexpensive*). Takeaway or eat-in sandwiches, croissants and cakes. Good for early breakfasts.

Gino's, Whinthrop St, t (021) 427 4485 (*inexpensive*). Fabulous pizzas, famous amongst Corkonians. For big appetites.

Quay Co-op, 24 Sullivan's Quay, t (021) 431 7026 (*inexpensive*). Good wholefood vegetarian restaurant, open for lunch and dinner. Also a wholefood shop and bookshop.

Entertainment and Nightlife

Pubs and Clubs

Bodhrán Bar, Oliver Plunkett Street. Specializes in traditional Irish music.

Spailpin Fanach, South Main Street. Also a great venue for traditional music.

City Limits, Coburg Street. Offers different styles of music, plus occasional comedy and disco nights.

The Forum, Grand Parade. Provides a big venue in a converted theatre for traditional and contemporary music.

The Lobby, 1 Union Quay. *The* place to sample a decent pint of Murphy's Stout.

Theatre, Music and Film

Check the *Cork Examiner* and *Evening Echo* for current listings. In the evenings there is plenty to choose from.

Cork Opera House, Emmet Place, t (021) 427 0022, *www.corkoperahouse.ie.* Try to see a production by the **Theatre of the South**. They tend to produce only modern Irish writers' work, which can be very good. The theatre is open for about eight weeks every summer.

Everyman Palace Theatre, MacCurtain Street, t (021) 450 1673. This theatre does not restrict itself in any way – tragedy, farce and comedy, by any author as long as he or she is good. Go prepared for anything and you won't be disappointed.

Kino Cinema, Washington St, t (021) 427 2022. Shows first-run and classic films, catering for all tastes.

Triskel Arts Centre, Tobin Street, off South Main Street, t (021) 427 7300. Hosts a wide range of cultural events – music, drama, exhibitions, film seasons and poetry readings.

Between South Main Street and Grand Parade is the fine 18th-century **Christ Church**, used today to house the archives of the county. At the south end of the Grand Parade is a monument to Ireland's patriot dead, and the tourist office. **Crawford Art Gallery** (*t (021) 427 3377; www.crawfordartgallery.com; open Mon–Sat 10–5*) in Emmet Place has a stunning collection of works by Irish artists such as Sean Keating, Orpen and Walter Osbourne. There are also some very good 18th- and 19th-century paintings – in particular, two magnificent paintings by James Barry, a native of the city, one of which is a self-portrait. The Gallery Café, well known throughout Ireland for its excellence, is just the place for a civilized lunch after the exhausting pastime of art appreciation. Nearby are a couple of excellent craft shops to browse in.

Opposite North Mall, on Cork Island still, the **Old Maltings** buildings have been adapted for the use of the University of Cork. This complex includes a small theatre called **The Granary**. Swans, the symbol of Cork City, are fed near here, so there are often large flocks of them. Close to the Maltings is the large Mercy Hospital, in Prospect Row, off Grenville Place, which incorporates the 1767 **Mayoralty House**, built as the official residence of the Mayor of Cork, with fine rococo interior plasterwork. It was designed by Davis Ducart, a Sardinian whose work can also be seen in the Limerick Customs House.

Follow the river westwards along Dyke Parade and leafy Mardyke Walk, and then cut south across Western Road, and you will come to the Oxbridge-style **University College**, its buildings grouped around a 19th-century Gothic square. There is an important collection of ogham stones here. The only modern building in the complex is the **Boole Library**, opened in 1985, named in honour of George Boole (1815–1864), who was the first professor of mathematics here, and who is credited with working out the principles of modern computer logic.

The Roman Catholic **Honan Chapel** is a period piece of Celtic revivalism, copied from Cormac's Chapel on the Rock of Cashel and adorned with exquisite Irish Revival stained glass. Close to the university is the **Cork City Museum** (*open Mon–Fri 11–1 and 2–5, Sun 3–5, closed Sat; t (021) 427 0679*), a pleasant Georgian house in the gardens of **Fitzgerald Park**, north of the Lee. It is worth visiting for local information and history, particularly on the War of Independence. There are displays of silver, glass and lace and, on the first floor, the Garryduff bird, a tiny wren of exquisite gold filigree from the early Christian period. Bus no.8 from the centre will drop you close by.

Cork is the home of two dark beers that rival Guinness – Murphy's and Beamish. The **Beamish and Crawford Brewery**, South Main Street, (*t (021) 491 1100; www.beamish.ie; tours Tues and Thurs 10.30 and 12 noon*) offers brewery tours throughout the year.

North of the River

'Tis the bells of Shandon
That sounds so grand on
The pleasant waters of the River Lee.
Father Prout

St Patrick's Street leads to St Patrick's Bridge. Once over it, you enter a hilly part of the city. Some of the mostly 19th-century streets here are literally stairs up the steep slopes, and open only to pedestrians. Off Shandon Street, the bell-tower of **St Anne's Church**, the lovely **Tower of Shandon** with its two faces in white limestone and two in red sandstone, topped by a cupola and distinctive salmon weathervane, looks down into the valley. It was nicknamed 'the four-faced liar' because the clock often told a different time on each side, until it was repaired in 1986. The church, which is open daily, was built between 1722 and 1726 to replace the church destroyed during the Williamite siege. The peal of the eight bells, which were made in Gloucestershire in 1750, are dear to every Corkonian heart. You may ring the bells of Shandon for a small fee. **Skiddy's Almshouse**, founded in 1584, stands in the churchyard. In about 1620, the Vintners Company of London settled a perpetual annuity of £24 on 12 widows of Cork.

Down by the river is North Mall, which has some fine 18th-century doorways. The 18th-century **Butter Market** used to be in this area, as was the slaughterhouse for vast numbers of cattle, which were then salted and used as provisions for the British Navy and many European ships before they made the long voyage to America. The **Old Butter Exchange** is now a centre for the Shandon Craft Centre, and beside it is the curiously named **Firkin Crane Centre** (the butter was packed in firkins – oak casks) which is now used as a dance theatre. Nearby, in O'Connell Square, the **Cork Butter Museum** (*t (021) 430 0600; open May–Sept daily 10–1 and 2–5*) tells the important role this commodity played in the city's development in the 18th and 19th centuries.

The Dominican **St Mary's Church** by the River Lee was completed in 1839 and has a magnificent classical façade. It is in a very prominent position, which immediately dates it as post-Catholic Emancipation: Catholic churches built before that time were built away from the main centre of towns and cities. Further north is **St Mary's Pro-Cathedral**, begun in 1808, which has a fine tower.

South of the River

South of the river, between Bishop and Dean Streets, is **St Finbarre's Cathedral**, which was built in the 19th century by wealthy Church of Ireland merchants on the site of the ancient church founded by St Finbarr. Even if you don't have time for much sightseeing, this building and the art gallery are musts. The cathedral's great spires dominate the city, and it has a beautiful west front, with three recessed doors, elaborate carving and a beautiful rose window. The building itself is in the Gothic style of 13th-century France and was built between 1867 and 1879 by a committed medievalist, the English architect William Burgess. His eye for detail was meticulous as well as humorous, and the whole effect is vigorous – a defiant gesture to Catholic Ireland. Also on the south side, off Douglas Street, is the grey limestone tower of **Red Abbey**, a remnant of a 14th-century Augustinian friary. Close by, on Dunbar Street, **South Chapel** was built in 1766 on an inconspicuous site. At this time, the penal laws may have relaxed, but a show of Catholicism was discouraged by the ruling classes. It contains most of its original fittings and furniture, and a sculpture of *The Dead Christ* by John Hogan.

Back on Sullivan's Quay, the **Munster Literature Centre** (*t (021) 431 2955; www.munsterlit.ie*) has gathered together an interesting pictorial exhibition of well known writers from Cork City and County: people such as Elizabeth Bowen, Frank O'Connor, William Trevor and Patricia Lynch (who wrote enchanting children's stories) are all represented. The centre also promotes young poets and writers and is a focus of literary activity in the south.

The Suburbs

The **Church of Christ the King** on Evergreen Road, to the south at Turner's Cross, was designed by an American architect, Barry Byrne, in the 1930s. The carved figure of Christ crucified with his arms spread above the twin entrance doors is very striking.

Riverstown House near **Glanmire**, 3 miles (6km) from the city centre, just off the Cork–Dublin road (*buses hourly to Glanmire from Parnell Place, taking 15mins; t (021) 4382 1205; open May–mid-Sept Wed–Sat 2–6; at other times by appointment; adm*), was built in 1602, and has exquisite plasterwork by the Francini brothers. The brothers were Swiss-Italian stuccodores, who came to Ireland in 1734 and adorned the ceiling of the dining-room with allegorical figures representing Time rescuing Truth from the assaults of Discord and Envy. Dr Browne, the Archbishop of Cork, was responsible for remodelling the original house in the 1730s and it remained in his family until the early 20th century. It has been beautifully restored by its present owners, Mr and Mrs Dooley, with the help of the Irish Georgian Society.

This area is well endowed with large houses overlooking the Lee estuary. One you can visit is **Dunkathel House**, also in Glanmire (*t (021) 482 1014; open May–mid Oct, Wed–Sun 2–6; adm*). It is a fine Georgian Palladian house, well worth visiting if only for afternoon tea. The house was built by a wealthy Cork merchant in 1790, and has a wonderful bifurcated staircase of Bath stone. A permanent display of watercolours by Elizabeth Gubbins, a daughter of the house, is hung on the walls. She was a deaf mute who travelled widely, recording her experiences and the scenery as she went. There is a rare 1880s barrel-organ which is still played for visitors.

Twenty minutes' walk from the city centre via Barrack Street and Bandon Road is the **Lough**, a freshwater lake with wild geese.

The **Cork Heritage Park** (*5 or 6 buses hourly from Parnell Place to Blackrock, 20mins; open May–Sept Mon–Fri 10.30–5.30, Sat and Sun 12–5.30*) in Blackrock illustrates the maritime history of the city and its burning during the War of Independence, as well as the history of a Quaker merchant family, the Pikes, who lived there.

Day Trips and Overnighters from Cork

Blarney

Blarney is five miles (8km) northwest of the city on the R617. This small village has a fame out of all proportion to its size because it is the home of the Blarney Stone: according to legend, whoever kisses this will get the 'gift of the gab'. This magic stone is high up in the ruined keep that is all that is left of **Blarney Castle** (*t (021) 438 5252; www.blarneycastle.ie; open daily 9.30–6; adm*); it is a magnet which attracts almost every visitor to Ireland, so expect to find the place (and the entire town of Blarney) crowded and full of knick-knacks.

In the days of Queen Elizabeth I the castle was held by Dermot MacCarthy, the lord of Blarney, who had the gift of *plamas*, the Irish word for soft, flattering or insincere speech. Elizabeth had asked him to surrender his castle, but he continued to play her

Getting There

There is a regular **bus** service (hourly) from Parnell Place. The journey takes 30mins.

Tourist Information

Blarney: **t** (021) 438 1624; *open in season only.*

Activities

Open Farms

Blarney Woodland Farm, Waterloo Rd, Blarney, **t** (021) 385733. A relaxing river nature trail through lush meadows and woodland.

Golf

Blarney Golf Course, Stone View, Blarney, **t** (021) 438 2455, *www.blarneygolfcourse.com.*

Eating Out

Lemon Tree, Blarney Castle Hotel, **t** (021) 438 5116 (*moderate*). Overlooking the village green, this upmarket hotel restaurant specializes in seasonal fare, offering a tempting Irish international menu.

Blairs Inn, Cloghrow, **t** (021) 438 1470 (*inexpensive*). Just outside Blarney, the wooded riverside setting, great food and family welcome make for a winning combination. A cut above normal pub fare.

along with fair words and no action. In the end the frustrated Queen is supposed to have said, 'This is all Blarney – he says he will do it but never means it at all.' The MacCarthys forfeited their castle in the Williamite wars of 1690, and it was later acquired by the St John Jefferyes family. To kiss the Blarney stone, climb the stone steps up five flights to the parapet, where an attendant will hold your feet while you drop your head down to the stone. The stone is probably a 19th-century invention, and today you can even buy yourself a certificate which guarantees you have kissed it. The castle is well worth seeing for its own sake, as it is one of the largest and finest tower houses in Ireland, built in 1446. The landscaped gardens surrounding it are also superb. You can also visit **Blarney Castle House and Gardens** (*t (021) 438 5252; open June–mid Sept Mon–Sat, 12–6; adm*), a Scottish-style baronial mansion built by Charles Lanyon with a charming garden, ancient yew trees, scattered rocks and a lake. The former mill that is now the huge emporium **Blarney Woollen Mills** (*t (021) 438 5280, www.blarneywoollenmills.ie; open Mon–Sat 9.30–6, Sun 10–6*) is hard to miss. It has an extensive range of Irish products such as glass, pottery, linen and woollens.

Fota Island

Fota House and Estate (*t (021) 481 5543; www.fotawildlife.ie; open all year, summer Mon–Sat 10–5.30, Sun 11–5.30; winter daily 10–4; adm*), over the Belvelly Bridge, is on magical little Fota Island in the River Lee estuary. The arboretum surrounding the house is luxurious and mature, with a collection of semi-tropical and rare shrubs. The restored gardens are now in the care of Duchas, the Heritage Service and the Fota Trust. The house, which is mainly regency in style, was built as a hunting lodge, and

Getting There

Trains run from Cork's Kent Station to Fota approximately hourly, taking 15mins.

Eating Out

The only options for lunch are the charmng tea room in Fota House or the restaurant in the wildlife park – or bring a picnic.

has a splendid neoclassical hallway, but its fine collection of Irish landscape paintings has been transferred to Limerick University Museum. There is also a bee garden and a **wildlife park** (*t (021) 481 2678; open mid-Mar–Oct daily 10–5; Nov–Feb Sat and Sun only 10–4*). The park is an ideal expedition for children as the animals (giraffes, zebras, ostrich, antelope, kangaroos, macaws and lemurs) roam freely – only the cheetahs are in a large pen. The splendid scimitar-horned oryx, extinct in its native North Africa, is being bred here.

Midleton

Midleton is a busy market town approximately 12 miles from Cork, going east on the N25. Its origins date back to the 12th century with the arrival of monks from a Cistercian abbey in County Limerick. **St John the Baptist Church** is thought to be the earliest site and has records dating back to 1302. The **town hall** – the former market house – was built in 1789 and has an attractive clock tower. Also on Main Street, what is now **McDaid's** pub was designed by Pugin and has served time as a hotel and police barracks in the past. An excellent farmers' market enlivens the already bustling town further on Saturday mornings. The **Courtyard Craft and Exhibition Centre** at 8 Main Street is worth a visit; numerous local artisans exhibit, and there is a good restaurant.

Midleton's principal claim to fame, however, is the **Old Midleton Distillery** (*t (021) 461 3594; open Mar–Oct, daily 10–6, rest of the year 11–4; adm*). It is a fine building, self-contained within 11 acres, and you can take a tour around all the major parts – mills, maltings, corn stores, stillhouses and kilns. The water wheel is still in perfect order, and you can see the largest pot-still in the world, with a capacity of more than 30,000 gallons, as well as sample some of the delicious stuff. It stopped being a working distillery in 1975, but there is a mass of information charting the history of Irish whiskey.

Getting There

There is a regular hourly **bus** service from Cork's Parnell Place; the journey takes 30mins.

Tourist Information

Midleton: Jameson Heritage Centre, t (021) 461 3702; *open June–Sept.*

Sports and Activities

Activity Centres

Trabolgan, Midleton, t (021) 466 1551, *www.trabolgan.com*. Indoor jungle safari, outdoor wooden wonderand, sub-tropical pool, adventure sports and pitch and putt. Day or residential visits welcomed.

Golf

East Cork Golf Club, Gurtacrue, Midleton, t (021) 463 1687.
Water Rock Golf Course, t (021) 461 3499, *www.waterrockgolf course.com.*

Eating Out

The Midleton Park Hotel, Old Cork Road, t (021) 463 5100 (*moderate*). Quite luxurious for the price. The décor is beautiful, the atmosphere relaxed and the restaurant food superb.
Old Midleton Distillery, t (021) 461 3394 (*moderate–inexpensive*). Good wholesome Irish dishes and baking.
Finin's, 75 Main St, t (021) 463 1878 (*moderate*). Attractive pub with an excellent restaurant. Steak and duck are the specialities here.

Cobh

Cobh (pronounced 'Cove') is the great harbour of Cork and handles huge ships. In the 18th century, it was a big naval base for the British. Later on, nearly all the transatlantic ships and liners stopped here – it was the last port of call for the *Titanic*, and the destination of the *Lusitania* when it was torpedoed nearby off Old Head. For many thousands of people, it was the embarkation port for the New World of North America and Australia. Despite the industry that surrounds it, Cobh is a rather nice place to stay, near to the city but without its bustle.

The colourful town centre is almost entirely 19th-century and is dominated by the Gothic **St Colman's Cathedral** (*open daily 10–6; adm*), the work of Pugin and Ashlin. It dates from 1868, but it was not completed until 1919, and has a soaring spire and a glorious carillon of some forty bells which can be heard at 9am, 12 noon, 4pm and 6pm. Between 1848 and 1950 two and a half million people emigrated to America and Australia from here, with many a sad scene enacted by the quay. The history of the

Getting There

Cobh is 5 miles (12km) southeast of Cork City on the R624 off the N25. It is served by regular trains from Kent Station; the journey takes 25 minutes.

If you are driving, the shortest and most interesting way to reach it by **car**, if you can find your way through Cork's southern suburbs, is by the little car ferry at Passage West, a five-minute crossing to Carrigaloe, just beside Cobh.

Activities

Fishing
Angling Charters, Kaybille, Carrigaloe, Cobh, t (021) 481 2435. Organizes day or evening trips.

Golf
Cobh Golf Club, Ballywilliam, Cobh, t (021) 481 2399.

Pleasure Cruises
Marine Transport Services, t (021) 481 1485. Daily harbour cruises from Kennedy Pier, departing 12 noon, 2, 3, 4pm daily.

Water Sports
International Sailing Centre, 5 East Beach, Cobh, t (021) 481 1237, *www.sailcork.com*.

Where to Stay

Watersedge Hotel, Yacht Club Quay, t (021) 481 5566, f 481 2011 (*expensive*). A wonderful waterfront location for this three-star hotel with a fine restaurant, **Jacob's Ladder** (*see below*).

Commodore Hotel, t (021) 481 1277 (*moderate*). Old-fashioned seaside hotel.

Rosemount, Bishops Road, t (021) 481 3547 (*inexpensive*). B&B and self-catering overlooking the harbour, within easy walking distance of Cobh centre.

Eating Out

Jacob's Ladder, Watersedge Hotel, Yacht Club Quay, t (021) 481 5566 (*moderate*). Elegant, airy dining area overlooking the harbour. Fresh seafood specialities and good vegetarian options. Also open for morning coffee and afternoon tea.

Robin Hill House, Lake Road, Rushbrooke, t (021) 481 1395, f 481 4680 (*moderate*). A mile or so from Cobh, this Victorian rectory restaurant offers a wide range of Mediterranean-influenced dishes using good Irish produce such as prawns, rabbit and cheeses. There is also an excellent wine selection.

Mansworth's Bar, Midleton Street, t (021) 481 1965 (*inexpensive*). Atmospheric local pub, with bar snacks and tons of history.

port and the story of the emigrants is recorded in the Queenstown Story Exhibition at the **Cobh Heritage Centre** (*t (021) 481 3591; open daily 10–6*), a converted Victorian railway station. A genealogical information centre has been set up here for those with Irish antecedents who may wish to trace them.

The view from the hill above Cobh facing south on to the harbour, peppered with islands (one of which is a prison) and edged with woods, is superb. If you want a stroll, make for the old **churchyard of Clonmel**, a peaceful place where many of the dead from the *Lusitania* are buried. Also buried here is the Reverend Charles Wolfe, 1791–1823, who is remembered for one stirring poem, 'The Burial of Sir John Moore at Corunna', which was extravagantly praised by Byron. Sir John Moore died a hero in the Peninsular Wars, but he was closely connected to Ireland through his role in quelling the 1798 Rebellion. Unlike many of his superiors, he was successful in disarming parts of the south with restraint, and he is remembered for his clemency and humanity; he found the behaviour of his own Irish troops disgraceful.

Not a drum was heard, not a funeral note
As his corse to the ramparts we hurried
Not a soldier discharged his farewell shot
O'er the grave where our hero we buried.

One of the finest public monuments in the country is the **Lusitania Memorial** in Casement Square, sculpted by Jerome Connor (1876–1943), who was born in County Kerry but raised in Massachusetts. It depicts two mourning sailors and, above them, the Angel of Peace.

Crosshaven

Crosshaven, 13 miles (21km) southeast of Cork City, on the Cork Harbour Estuary south across the harbour from Cobh, is a crescent-shaped bay filled with yachts and boats of every description, the playground of the busy Cork businessmen and their families, and home of the Royal Cork Yacht Club. There are delightful beaches at **Myrtleville** and **Robert's Cove** further along the coast.

Kinsale

Kinsale (*Cionn Saile*: 'Tide Head') is 18 miles (29km) southwest of Cork City on the R600. A sheltered port on the Bandon estuary, its fame was established years ago as a quaint seaside town with excellent restaurants and carefully preserved 18th-century buildings, clad often as not with grey slates to keep out the damp, or painted in cheerful colours.

In the last decade, it has become unquestionably the smartest, poshest and most expensive corner of rural Ireland, with music and cinema stars bidding up local property values, and wealthy Cork folk dining out in its restaurants. In recent years it has become known as the gourmet capital of Ireland, and each October there is a Gourmet Festival, which attracts visitors from around the world.

A few far-sighted people restored the dilapidated buildings in the 1960s so that Kinsale avoided the usual fate of a town with a lot of ancient history and decaying

Getting There

There are regular **buses** from Parnell Place in Cork; the journey takes around an hour.

Tourist Information

Kinsale, Pier Road, **t** (021) 477 2234; *open all year*.

Shopping

Kent Gallery, Quayside, **t** (021) 477 4956. Art gallery.
Kinsale Crystal Glass, Market Street. Crafts.
Quay Food Co., Market Quay. Delicacies.
Jagoes Mill Pottery, Farrangalway.
Keane on Ceramics, Pier Road.

Activities

Fishing

The Kinsale Angling Co-op, 1 The Ramparts, Kinsale, **t** (021) 477 4946, *www.kinsale-angling.com.*

Golf

Kinsale Golf Club, Kinsale, **t** (021) 477 2197.
Old Head Golf Links, Kinsale, **t** (021) 477 8444, *www.oldheadgolflinks.com. Open mid-April–Oct.*

Horse Riding

Ballinadee Stables, **t** (021) 477 8152. Ten minutes' drive from Kinsale.

Outdoor Activity Centres

The Kinsale Outdoor Education Centre, Kinsale, **t** (021) 477 2896, *www.oec.ie/kinsale.* Instruction in all watersports.

Pleasure Cruises

Kinsale Harbour Cruises, **t** (021) 477 3188, *www.kinsaleharbourcruises.com.*
Sail Ireland Charters, Kinsale **t** (021) 477 2927. Bare-boat or skippered yachts.

Watersports

Kinsale Dive Centre, Castlepark Marina, Kinsale, **t** (021) 477 4959.
Oysterhaven Centre, Kinsale, **t** (021) 477 0738.

Where to Stay

Blue Haven, **t** (021) 477 2209, *www.bluehaven kinsale.com* (*expensive*). The best hotel in Kinsale: small, cosy and comfortable with excellent food.
Actons Hotel, Pier Road, **t** (021) 477 2135 (*expensive*). Lovely three-star hotel set in beautiful landscaped gardens overlooking the harbour. The hotel has a fitness centre and a good restaurant.
Peryville House, **t** (021) 477 2731 (*expensive*). Sophisticated accommodation, with stunning views and super breakfasts.
Chart House, 6 Denis Quay **t** (021) 477 4568. (*moderate*). A delightful guest house in a 200-year-old property, recently renovated. A very comfortable lodging.
Jim Edwards, Market Quay, **t** (021) 477 2514 (*inexpensive*). B&B rooms above this restaurant in the heart of Kinsale.

Eating Out

Blue Haven, 3 Pearse Street, **t** (021) 477 2209 (*expensive*). Very good restaurant in this cosy hotel in the former Kinsale fish market. Seafood is a speciality, and the steaks are good too.
Max's Wine Bar, Main Street, **t** (021) 477 2443 (*moderate*). Set in an attractive old house, offering a varied menu, with lots of seafood straight from the harbour.
Toddies, Sleaveen House, Eastern Road, **t** (021) 477 7769 (*moderate*). Excellent new restaurant serving the best of modern Irish cuisine. Good wine list too.
Jim Edwards, Market Quay, **t** (021) 477 2514 (*inexpensive*). In the heart of Kinsale, a historic bar with an excellent seafood restaurant.

houses – piecemeal demolition. It can become quite crowded in the summer, and some of the new holiday homes jar the eye a little, but for all that it's still a very agreeable place. There is a lot to see in the area, as well as good quality craft shops, delis, restaurants, antique shops and art galleries.

Kinsale was once an important naval port. In 1601 the Irish joined forces with Spain against the English after the Ulster chieftain Hugh O'Neill called for a national rising and support of the Catholic cause. He met with success at first, and appealed to Spain for help. In September 1601, a Spanish fleet anchored here with 3,500 infantry aboard. They planned to meet with the Gaelic lords O'Neill and Tyrconnell, who were marching south to meet them. In November, the forces of O'Neill met with the forces of Mountjoy, Elizabeth's deputy, who was besieging the Spaniards. Within hours, the Gaelic army had been defeated at the disastrous Battle of Kinsale. This led to what is now called 'The Flight of the Earls', and put an end to the rebellion against Queen Elizabeth I and her reconquest of Ireland. It was the beginning of the end for Gaelic Ireland; anglicization was now inevitable. Although the peasantry still spoke Irish, the language of power was English. Afterwards, Kinsale developed as a shipbuilding port. It declared for Cromwell in 1641, but James II landed and departed from here after his brief and unsuccessful interlude fighting for his throne between 1689 and 1690.

St Multose Church is the oldest building in town, with parts of it dating from the 12th century. Inside, take a look at the Galway slab in the south aisle, and the old town stocks. The churchyard has several interesting 16th-century gravestones which in spring are covered in whitebells and bluebells, and in summer red valerian grows out of crevices in every wall.

Desmond Castle (*t (021) 477 4855; open mid-April–mid-June Tues–Sun 10–6, closed Mon; mid-June–Sept daily 10–6; adm*), a tower house from the 1500s, was once used as a customs house and later as a prison for captured American sailors in the War of Independence, as well as for the French. The castle now accommodates an 'International Museum of Wine' which details the Irish links with some major vineyards in Europe.

There is also the interesting **Kinsale Regional Museum** (*t (021) 477 7929; open daily 10–1 and 2–5.30; adm; town tours for groups over 8 if pre-booked*) in the Dutch-style old courthouse and market building, with a collection of material associated with the life of the town and port through the centuries, especially the Siege and Battle of Kinsale. By the harbour are the ruined remains of King James Fort, built some time after 1600.

A much better example of a military fort can be seen on the opposite shore at Summercove: **Charles Fort** (*t (021) 477 2263; open mid-Mar–Oct daily 10–6; Nov–mid-Mar Sat and Sun 10–5; adm*) was built in the 1670s (in the time of Charles II) as a military stronghold. It is shaped like a star and you can wander round its rather damp nooks and crannies. It was breached by Williamite forces under Marlborough after a 13-day siege. The severe 18th- and 19th-century houses inside were used as barracks for recruit training. The fort was burned by the IRA in 1921. It is possible to walk to Charles Fort: follow the Scilly Walk from the middle of Kinsale, which takes about 45 minutes. Further to the east is the little port of **Oysterhaven**.

Touring from Cork 1: Along the South Coast

Day 1: Villages, Gardens, Forts and Beaches

Morning: Take the N71 southwest from Cork through the market town of **Bandon**, and then turn off left to **Timoleague**, dominated by the ruins of a Franciscan abbey (*always open*) overlooking the mudflats of the estuary, the temporary winter home of birds from the far north. Beside the Argideen River are the Timoleague Castle Gardens (*t (023) 46116; open June–Aug Mon–Sat 11–5.30 by appt, Sun 2–5.30; adm*); the 13th-century castle tower is in ruins, but the 1920s house sits amid landscaped gardens. In the village, the Protestant church has a Harry Clarke window and the Catholic church sports mosaic walls decorated by a maharajah.

Lunch: In Timoleague or Courtmacsherry, *see* below.

Afternoon: Clonakilty, birthplace of Michael Collins, is an attractive place, with traditional hand-painted signs swinging from the pubs and shops. A model railway village (*open daily 11–5; adm*) has been built on the Inchydoney Road. Clonakilty is also famous for its black puddings, which you can buy at Twomey's in Pearse Street. The 10th-century **Lisnagun Ring Fort** (*open 10–5; adm*), a reconstruction, is signposted on the N71, just outside town; or visit the Edwardian gardens at **Lisselan Estate**, 3km east of town (*open mid-Mar–Oct 8–5*). Other attractions include a small stone circle north of the village at **Templebrian**, and a broad beach at **Inchydoney**.

Dinner and Sleeping: In Clonakilty, Butlerstown or Courtmacsherry, *see* below.

Day 1

Lunch in Timoleague
Dillon's Pub, Mill Street, Timoleague, **t** (023) 46390 (*inexpensive*). Continental-style bar/café with good snacks.

Lunch in Courtmacsherry
Lifeboat Inn, t (023) 46835 (*inexpensive*). Busy pub in the heart of the pretty coastal village.

Dinner in Clonakilty
An Sugán, Wolfe Tone Street, **t** (023) 33498 (*moderate–inexpensive*). Excellent quality and range of dishes served in this bistro. The accent is on fish and seafood.

Dinner and Sleeping in Clonakilty
The Lodge, Inchydoney Island, **t** (023) 33143, *www.inchydoneyisland.com* (*moderate*). Luxurious hotel that comes complete with thalassotherapy spa.
O'Donovan's Hotel, 44 Pearse Street, **t** (023) 33250, *www.odonovanshotel.com*

(*moderate*). Plain cooking and pub grub. The bar has a huge Guinness mural and a collection of old bottles. It also has rooms.
Emmet Hotel, Emmet Square, **t** (023) 33394 (*moderate*). Old-fashioned style in a beautiful Georgian hotel set in a quiet square in the heart of town. Good restaurant.

Dinner in Butlerstown
Otto's Creative Catering, Dunworley, **t** (023) 40461 (*moderate*). Inventive cooking. Produce is sourced locally or home-grown, and of the highest quality. Try the roast pheasant or the seafood casserole. *Closed Mon and Tues.*

Sleeping in Butlerstown
Sea Court, t (023) 40151 (*inexpensive*). Beautiful historic house (1760), with fine views of the Seven Heads Peninsula.

Dinner and Sleeping in Courtmacsherry
Travara Lodge, t (023) 46493 (*inexpensive*). Comfortable rooms with views of the bay and good home cooking.

Day 2: West to Baltimore

Morning: Follow the N71 west to **Rosscarbery**, a charming old-fashioned village with a pretty square. It had a famous school of learning founded by St Fachtna in the 6th century, and a medieval Benedictine monastery. The very attractive 17th-century Protestant church is on the site of the old cathedral. From Roury Bridge, the R507 winds to **Drombeg Stone Circle**, with views across pastures and cornfields to the sea. **Glandore** and **Union Hall** are two colourful resort villages on a narrow inlet 5 miles west of Rosscarbery, whose harbours are filled with painted boats. Their grey-steepled Protestant churches add to their prettiness. Glandore is fashionable with the rich; its south-facing seaside houses form a street known as 'Millionaire's Row'.
Lunch: In Glandore or Union Hall, *see* below.

Afternoon: **Skibbereen** is a market town famous for its weekly newspaper, the *Southern Star*. Skibbereen's West Cork Art Centre hosts regular events. For walkers, nearby Lough Ine is Europe's only inland saltwater lake. Three and a half miles south of Skibbereen are the **Creagh Gardens** (*open daily 10–6; adm*), a romantic and informal garden amongst woods. All around Skibbereen is lovely countryside where knuckles and fingers of land reach out into the sea. **Baltimore** is an attractive fishing village perched at the end of one of these fingers; in summer the trawlers are outnumbered by sailing boats and the place is buzzing. You can get a boat for the islands: Sherkin Island is just 10 minutes' crossing.
Dinner and Sleeping: In Skibbereen or Baltimore, *see* below.

Day 2

Lunch in Glandore
The Rectory, t (028) 33072 (*expensive*). Regency house with stunning views over the harbour and excellent food in elegant surroundings.
Haye's Bar, t (023) 33214 (*inexpensive*). Overlooking the harbour; serves delicious home-made dishes and snacks.

Lunch in Union Hall
The Baybery, Glandore Bay, Union Hall, **t** (028) 33605 (*inexpensive*). Serves wholesome food, and has handcrafted pine furniture and pottery for sale. Local seafood is the main speciality.

Dinner in Skibbereen
Liss Ard Lake Lodge, Liss Ard, **t** (028) 40000 (*luxury*). Refined cuisine, Mediterranean to oriental, in a lovely location.
Island Cottage, Heir Island, **t** (028) 38012 (*moderate, plus the boat fee*). Great cooking in an unlikely, remote setting; the only restaurant in County Cork that you need a boat to reach – take the ferry from Cunnamore Pier. *Evenings only.*

Dinner in Baltimore
The Mews, t (028) 20390 (*expensive–moderate*). Impressive contemporary fare.
Custom House Restaurant, t (028) 20200 (*moderate–inexpensive*). Imaginative and excellent dishes, in a seaside setting.

Sleeping in Skibbereen
Bunalun, t (028) 21502 (*inexpensive*). Environmental-award-winning dairy farm 4km from Skibbereen, with a traditional warm welcome and organic home cooking.

Dinner and Sleeping in Baltimore
Casey's, t (028) 20197, *caseys@eircom.net* (*moderate*). The best type of small hotel – welcoming and comfortable, with dramatic views over Roaring Water Bay, great bar and seafood restaurant, and traditional music on Saturdays.

Day 3: Schull, Mizen Head and Bantry

Morning: **Ballydehob** is on the next finger of land, 10 miles from Skibbereen on the N71 and distinguished by a fine 12-arch railway bridge, now defunct. **Schull**, west of Ballydehob on the coast, is a small boating and tourist centre with a deep harbour; ferries run out to Clear Island. Schull has a good selection of craft shops, food shops, restaurants and cafés. It also has a small planetarium (*t (028) 28552/28315 for details of opening times and star shows*). A spectacular road runs from Schull up to **Mount Gabriel**; if you decide to climb it, be careful of the prehistoric copper mines.

Lunch: In Schull, nearby Toormore, or Goleen on the way to Mizen Head, *see* below.

Afternoon: Further on, **Barleycove**, one of the best beaches in the southwest, stretches down to the sheer red sandstone heights of **Mizen Head**. A lighthouse on the islet below is linked to the mainland by a suspension bridge. Many ships have been wrecked here; the old fog signal station, now automatic, has been opened to visitors as the **Mizen Head Signal Station Visitor Centre** (*open April–Oct daily 10.30–5, Nov–Mar weekends only; adm*). From Mizen Head, the R591 goes to **Durras**, from where an amazing route leads over the top of the peninsula down into Bantry.

Bantry has one of the finest views in the world, out over the bay. Don't miss **Bantry House and Gardens** (*t (027) 50047; open Mar–Oct daily 9–6; adm*), built in 1740, one of the most interesting houses in Ireland open to the public. You can go around the house on your own, accompanied by the faint strains of classical music; rare French tapestries, family portraits and china still give the feeling of being used and loved.

Dinner and Sleeping: In Schull or Bantry, *see* below.

Day 3

Lunch in Schull
Adèles, Main Street, t (028) 28865 (*moderate–inexpensive*). Tempting home baking during the day.

Lunch in Toormore
The Altar Restaurant, t (028) 35254 (*moderate*). Very tasty pâté and seafood.

Lunch in Goleen
Heron's Cove Restaurant and B&B, t (028) 35225 (*moderate*). Very good fish and shellfish dishes in a harbour setting.

Dinner in Bantry
Larchwood House, Pearson's Bridge, t (027) 66181 (*moderate*). Good home-cooking in an informal atmosphere.
The Snug, The Quay, t (027) 50057 (*inexpensive*). Eccentric bar opposite the harbour with simple home-cooked dishes.

Dinner in Schull
Adèles, Main Street, t (028) 28865 (*moderate–inexpensive*). Simple but stylish dishes.

Sleeping in Bantry
Bantry House B&B, t (027) 50047 (*moderate*). Converted wing of an interesting country pile, where the plush library, snooker room/bar and extensive gardens are at guests' disposal throughout their stay.
Westlodge Hotel, t (027) 50360, www.westlodgehotel.ie (*moderate*). Scenic location just outside town. Includes fully refurbished leisure centre and gym.
Ardnagashel Lodge, t (027) 51687 (*inexpensive*). Comfortable and modern.
Shangri La, Glengarriff Road, t (027) 50244 (*inexpensive*). Friendly, cosy house.

Sleeping in Schull
Grove House, Colla Road, t (028) 28067 (*moderate*). Overlooking the harbour is this comfortable period guest house. Local produce for breakfast.

Day 4: Mountain Hideaways and Island Idylls

Morning: East from Bantry, **Glengarriff**'s humpy hills and wooded inlets look over limpid water and isles. The village consists of a main street lined with craft shops selling woollens of every description, including soft sheepskins. Walks can be taken in the **Glengarriff Forest**; the tourist office stocks a local walking map. Ilnacullin, alias **Garinish Island** (*closed Sun am; adm*), just off the coast, used to be covered only in rocks, birch, heather and gorse until 1910. Now it is a dream island full of sub-tropical plants, with a formal Italian garden, rock gardens and a marble pool full of goldfish. It is an exceptional place, perfectly structured and full of outstanding plants; well worth the €10-plus return boat fares. Bernard Shaw often stayed here. You will find that there are many boatmen willing to take you out to the island.

Lunch: In Glengarriff, or on Garinish Island, *see* below.

Afternoon: Continue westwards into the **Beara Peninsula** – one of the less touristy parts of the western coasts. The Beara presents rougher, rockier landscapes than its neighbours to the north and south. **Castletownbere**, the only town of any size, is a fishing village built around a deep water harbour where you can get a boat across to **Bere Island**, used by the Irish army for training; it has a pub, shop, splendid restaurant and B&B, and the opportunity for long, peaceful walks. Hungry Hill and Sugarloaf Mountain are very popular with climbers and hill walkers. To the west are the looming Slieve Mickish Mountains with equally lovely views. Just outside Castletownbere is the ruined **Castle of Dunboy** on a small wooded peninsula.

Dinner and Sleeping: In Castletownbere or Bere Island, *see* below.

Day 4

Lunch in Glengarriff
Eccles Hotel, t (027) 63003 (*moderate*). Famous old (1745) hotel with great bar and dining room options for lunch.
Bernard Harrington's, t (027) 63021 (*moderate*). Popular bar, serving good meals, especially salmon.
The Wooden Shoe, Shore, Glengarriff, **t** (027) 63161 (*moderate*). Friendly restaurant on the outskirts of town, with delicious dishes.

Lunch on Garinish Island
There is a small coffee shop on the island with light snacks, otherwise pick up a picnic at the Spar in Glengarriff.

Dinner in Casteltownbere
Old Bank Seafood Restaurant, t (027) 70252 (*moderate*). Characterful house in the heart of town; seafood is a speciality.
MacCarthy's, t (027) 70014 (*inexpensive*). This is a classic Irish pub, with traditional music

and a lively atmosphere. Simple but good bar food is served.

Dinner on Bere Island
Kilty's Café and Restaurant, t (027) 75004 (*moderate*). Traditional Irish fare on offer at this friendly establishment.

Sleeping in Casteltownbere
The Old Presbytery, Brandy Hall House, **t** (027) 70424 (*moderate*). A fine old house set on a small promontory with wonderful sea views.
Realt-na-Mara, t (027) 70101 (*inexpensive*). 1km from Castletownbere, a small, friendly B&B.
Island View House, t (027) 70415 (*moderate*). The name says it all. A bright modern bungalow with stunning views.

Sleeping on Bere Island
Lawrence Cove Lodge, t (027) 75988 (*inexpensive*). Hostel accommodation.
Admirals House, t (027) 75064 (*inexpensive*). Historic naval quarters, now a guest house with dormitory and en suite rooms.

Day 5: Round the Beara Peninsula

Morning: Start early for your final day. At the very tip of the peninsula, **Dursey**, another sparsely inhabited island, is connected to the mainland by a cable car (*Mon–Sat 9–11, 2.30–5 and 7–8; hours vary on Sun*). A road leads through the village of **Kilmichael** and across the middle of the island to a martello tower. Tracks lead around the cliffs to **Dursey Head** which has wonderful views: from here you can see the three rocks in the ocean known as the Bull, the Cow and the Calf. As the road winds around the coast, there is barely a tree to be seen, only beautiful coastal views all the way. **Allihies** village is a tiny place along one street, with a fine hostel and friendly pubs. The next village, **Eyeries**, is painted in strong Mediterranean colours. As you approach **Ardgroom** the seas are calmer, and in the bay you will notice the lines of seaweed-covered ropes and rafts that indicate mussel farming.

Lunch: An early lunch in Allihies, Eyeries or Ardgroom, *see* below.

Afternoon: Head back to Glengarriff via Lauragh and Adrigole and then the R572 as far as Glengarriff. Take the N71 to Ballylickey and turn left here on the R584 through the Pass of Kelmaneigh to **Gougane Barra**, 'the Rock-cleft of Finbarr', a dramatic glacial valley with a shining lake in its hollow into which run silvery streams. In the middle of the lake is a small island, approached by a causeway, where St Finbarr set up his oratory in the 6th century. At the entrance to the causeway are St Finbarr's Well and an ancient cemetery. End the day in the market town of **Macroom** (*see* opposite), from where the N22 will take you back to Cork.

Dinner and Sleeping: In Ballingeary or Macroom, *see* below.

Day 5

Lunch in Allihies
O'Neill's Pub, t (027) 73008 (*inexpensive*). Bar snacks, including good filling sandwiches, available.

Lunch in Eyeries
Causkey's, t (027) 74161 (*inexpensive*). Light snacks available, and there's a fantastic view over Coulagh Bay.

Lunch in Ardgroom
Village Inn, t (027) 74067 (*inexpensive*). Good pub food.

Dinner and Sleeping in Ballingeary
Gougane Barra Hotel, t (026) 47069, *www.gouganebarra.com* (*moderate*). Quiet hotel in a perfect setting on the shores of beautiful Gougane Barra Lake. Restaurant and bar meals are served.

Dinner in Macroom
Don's Bar, Castle Street (*inexpensive*). A traditional Irish pub serving good food until 9pm. There is live music some evenings.

Dinner and Sleeping in Macroom
Castle Hotel, Main Street, t (026) 41074, *www.castlehotel.ie* (*expensive–moderate*). Impressive service, choice and quality in this welcoming hotel, with its own leisure centre and award-winning restaurant. Bar meals are also available at a more moderate price, so there is lots of choice.

Farran House, Farran, Macroom, t (021) 733 1215, *www.farranhouse.com* (*moderate*) Patricia Wiese's elegant country house off the Killarney to Cork road 15mins west of Macroom is set in 12 acres of mature beech woods; the rooms have huge bathrooms.

Mills Inn, Ballyvourney, Macroom, t (026) 45237 (*moderate*). One of Ireland's oldest inns, on the Killarney to Cork road, and full of old-world charm. There is a wide choice of bar meals.

Touring from Cork 2: North and East of Cork

Day 1: Ballincollig, Macroom and North to Kanturk

Morning: Approximately 5 miles west of Cork City on the N22 is **Ballincollig**, where you can visit the 19th-century Royal Gunpowder Mills on the banks of the River Lee (*t (021) 487 4430; open April–Sept daily 10–6; adm*). This factory produced huge quantities of gunpowder for the British army. There is a gallery, craft shop and a pleasant café. The R618 follows the lovely River Lee through **Dripsey** and **Coachford**. Continue on towards Macroom, with a detour to the renovated 19th-century **Bealick Mill** (*open April–Sept Mon–Sat 10–5, Sun 2–6*) just before, with a famine exhibition. **Macroom**, a busy market town on the Sullane river, once belonged to Admiral Sir William Penn, whose son founded Pennsylvania, and it has a small folk museum. This is a gorgeous part of Ireland, lush with bright-flowered pasture.

Lunch: In Macroom, *see below*.

Afternoon: About 25 miles north of Macroom via the R582 and R583 is **Kanturk**, an attractive 18th-century planned town. On the outskirts, Kanturk Castle is a huge building, begun around 1609, but never finished. It is said that the Privy Council ordered the work to stop and the owner, McCarthy, flew into a rage and ordered that the blue glass tiles with which the castle was to be roofed be thrown into the river. A little diversion to the northwest will take you to **Liscarroll**, a remote village with a Norman castle and a donkey sanctuary (*open Mon–Fri 9–4.30 , Sat and Sun 10–5*).

Dinner and Sleeping: In Kanturk, or continue on to Mallow for tomorrow, *see below*.

Day 1

Lunch in Macroom
Castle Hotel, Main Street, t (026) 41074, *www. castlehotel.ie (expensive–moderate)*. Impressive service, choice and quality in this award-winning restaurant. Bar meals are also available at a more moderate price.

T.P. Cotters, 14 Main Street, t (026) 41560 *(moderate)*. Old-fashioned bar serving good food in the heart of town.

Café Muesli, South Square, t (026) 42455 *(inexpensive)*. An interesting variety of vegetarian and Italian cuisine.

Don's Bar, Castle Street *(inexpensive)*. A traditional Irish pub serving good food.

Dinner in Kanturk
The Vintage, O'Brien Street, t (029) 50549 *(moderate)*. Comfortable pub with excellent food from home-made soups to fish dishes and steak.

Sleeping in Kanturk
Assolas Country House, t (029) 50015, *www.assolas.com (expensive)*. This 17th-century house is a superb place to get away from it all, set among mature trees that reach down to the river. Offers tennis, fishing and croquet, and delicious food.

Glenlohane, t (029) 50014, *www.glenlohane. com (expensive)*. Mrs Bolster has rooms in a comfortable Georgian house, set in beautiful parkland.

Dinner and Sleeping in Mallow
Longueville House, t (022) 47156, *www. longuevillehouse.ie (expensive)*. With a maze and the only vineyard in Ireland to be found behind this house, this has long sloping views to the river, with the ruined Callaghan Castle in the front. The food is superlative, and the service attentive.

The Hibernian Hotel, t (022) 21588, *www. hibhotel.com (moderate)*. Delightful old family-run hotel in the town centre.

Day 2: A Land of Poets

Morning: **Mallow** used to be a famous spa where the gentry of Ireland came to take the waters; today it comes alive when the Mallow Races are on, in spring, summer and autumn. The old spa house in Spa Walk is now a private home and the water gushes to waste. The town has pretty 18th-century houses and a timbered, decorated Clock House. Mallow Castle is an impressive ruin of a fortified 16th-century tower house. Catholic St Mary's Church has a Romanesque Revival façade. Davis Street is named after nationalist poet Thomas Davis, who was born in No.72.

Lunch: In Mallow or Doneraile, *see* below.

Afternoon: Take the N20 north and R581 east from Mallow to **Doneraile**. Author Elizabeth Bowen lived near here, and this is also Edmund Spenser country; here the poet wrote most of *The Faerie Queene*. Doneraile Court and Wildlife Park (*open mid April–Oct Mon–Sat 10–8.30, Sun 11–7*) just outside town is a wonderful Georgian house; the beautiful surrounding parkland has nature walks, cascades, and herds of deer in the park. At **Castletownroche** on the N72, notice the pretty Church of Ireland church on a rise above the river, and wander the ruins of Bridgetown Abbey, founded by FitzHugh Roche in the 13th century. To the north of the pretty church is Anne's Grove (*open Easter–end Sept Mon–Sat 10–5, Sun 1–6; adm*) with tranquil woodlands and a walled garden. About 4 miles east is **Glanworth**, a sleepy village dominated by the remains of Roche's castle above the River Funchion, on which stands an 18th-century watermill.

Dinner and Sleeping: In Glanworth, or Fermoy on the N72, *see* below.

Day 2

Lunch in Mallow
Longueville House, t (022) 47156 (*expensive*). Superlative cuisine in generous portions, in a stylish country house hotel.

The White Deer, Bridge Street, **t** (022) 51299 (*moderate*). Next to Mallow Castle grounds, this award-winning pub serves great food, with Irish steak the speciality.

Lunch in Doneraile
St Ledger Arms, t (022) 24405 (*moderate*). Named after the local lords of the manor, an old hostelry serving good pub food.

Dinner and Sleeping in Glanworth
Glanworth Mill, t (025) 38555, *www.glanworth mill.com* (*moderate–inexpensive*). Lovely riverside inn with a café serving delightful soups, salads and wicked desserts at lunchtime; a smarter restaurant attached serves dinner. There are literary bedrooms, including one cut into the cliff face.

Dinner in Fermoy
La Bigoudenne, 28 McCurtain Street, **t** (025) 32832 (*inexpensive*). Quintessentially French bistro, specializing in Breton dishes.

Sleeping in Fermoy
Ballyvolane House, near Fermoy, **t** (025) 36349, *www.ballyvolanehouse.ie* (*expensive*). Run by Mrs Merrie Green and her friendly family. The lovely old Georgian house is set in beautiful grounds, and locally produced vegetables are used in the cooking.

Palm Rise, Barry's Boreen, Duntahane Road, **t** (025) 31386 (*inexpensive*). Friendly modern house half a mile from Fermoy.

Ghillie Cottage, t (025) 32720 (*inexpensive*). Joy Arnold and Doug Lock are the friendly hosts at this charming cottage.

Fuchsia House Hostel, The Square, Kilworth, Fermoy, **t** (025) 27565 (*inexpensive*). Minimalist hostel with almost monastic decoration in a quiet village square three miles north of Fermoy.

Day 3: Fermoy and Mitchelstown

Morning: **Fermoy** used to be a garrison town for the British army. The town, built along both sides of the darkly flowing River Blackwater, has seen more prosperous days and retains an air of shabby gentility; Lord Fermoy is said to have gambled away his Fermoy estates in an evening. The Protestant church, built in 1802, contains some grotesque masks; however, the Catholic church is rather elegant: it was designed by E.W. Pugin in 1867, with an interior by the Pain brothers. Just outside Fermoy, overlooking the river to the west, is one of the most beautiful houses in Ireland, the late-Georgian mansion **Castle Hyde** (*not open to the public*).

Lunch: In Fermoy, *see* below.

Afternoon: The N8 north leads to **Mitchelstown**, famous for butter and cheese, and for its limestone caves (*open daily 10–6; adm*) a further 10 miles (16km) to the north-east on the N8 to Cahir. The Lord of Kingston planned Michelstown in the grand manner with important buildings at the end of vistas; walk through Kingston Square to see 18th-century almshouses and a central chapel. A tree-lined street leads to the Church of Ireland church, designed by G.R. Pain. The old castle (now demolished) was replaced with a Gothic mansion by G.R. Pain in 1823; Mary Wollstonecraft (1759–1797) spent time as a governess here. By the 19th century the land wars were brewing and there was a huge demonstration in Michelstown in 1881, and a riot a few years later. A statue of John Manderville, leader of the agitation for fair rents, and stone crosses to commemorate the dead are in Market Square.

Dinner and Sleeping: In Mitchelstown, Glanworth, or back in Kilworth, *see* below.

Day 3

Lunch in Fermoy
Castlehyde Hotel, t (025) 31865 (*moderate*). Renovated 18th-century house with a courtyard, serving Irish international cuisine, making the most of local produce.
La Bigoudenne, 28 McCurtain Street, t (025) 32832 (*inexpensive*). Quintessentially French bistro, specializing in Breton dishes.
The Fishmarket, MacCurtain Street. Good grocers and deli selling everything you could need for a tasty picnic.

Dinner in Mitchelstown
O'Callaghan's Deli, 19–20 Lower Cork Street, is not to be missed for an afternoon snack.
Paki Fitz's, Cork Street, t (025) 84897 (*moderate*). Recently renovated, this venue offers everything: a café, a three-storey bar serving tasty bar food, and a more sophisticated evening restaurant with an extensive menu. The prices vary depending on where you choose to eat.

Sleeping in Mitchelstown
Castle Park Hotel, Baldwin Street, t (025) 84777 (*moderate*). Plain but comfortable rooms in this central hotel. Unusually for Ireland, this hotel is Bangladeshi-owned, a fact which is reflected in the eclectic menu.
Fir Grove Hotel, Cahir Hill, Mitchelstown, t (025) 24111 (*moderate*). A modern motel-style hotel and restaurant with no frills.

Dinner and Sleeping in Glanworth
Glanworth Mill, t (025) 38555, *www.glanworth mill.com* (*moderate–inexpensive*). Lovely riverside inn with a café serving delightful soups, salads and wicked desserts at lunchtime; a smarter restaurant attached serves dinner. There are literary bedrooms, including one cut into the cliff face.

Sleeping in Kilworth
Fuchsia House Hostel, The Square, Kilworth, Fermoy, t (025) 27565 (*inexpensive*). Minimalist hostel with almost monastic decoration in a quiet village square.

Day 4: Down to the Sea

Morning: Head back down the N8 via Fermoy and then turn left for **Castlelyons**, a quiet and pretty hamlet. Here is the great ruined house of the Barrys, a Norman family, burned down in 1771, and the remains of a 14th-century Franciscan friary. In the graveyard of Kill St Anne is a roofless 15th-century church, and within is the ruin of an 18th-century parish church. The classical Barrymore Mausoleum is impressive.

Lunch: In Castlelyons or Youghal, *see* below.

Afternoon: Take the R626 to Midleton then the N25 east to **Youghal**, an important medieval town which has become one of the most attractive seaside towns in Ireland, with fantastic clean beaches. Visit the 15th-century Church of Ireland collegiate Church of St Mary, built around 1250, rebuilt in 1461 by Thomas, the eighth Earl of Desmond, and restored in 1884. Nearby on Main Street is the ruined 15th century tower house, Tynte's Castle. Large sections of the old town walls still stand, up on the crest of the hill. The old part of town lies at the foot of a steep hill, whilst the new part has grown along the margin of the bay. The main street is spanned by a tower known as the Clock Gate; other buildings of note are the Red House, an early 18th-century Dutch style building, and, on the corner of Church Street, a group of restored medieval almshouses. Youghal's harbour is close by. When you see it, try to imagine it fixed up with picket fences and clapboard siding to look like New Bedford, Massachusetts – that's what John Houston did to it when he filmed *Moby Dick* here in 1954, with Youghal's old salts, housewives and children as extras.

Dinner and Sleeping: In Youghal or Castlemartyr, *see* below.

Day 4

Lunch in Castlelyons
Pedlar's Rock, t (025) 36761 (*inexpensive*). Quaint old pub at the heart of the village, serving bar snacks.
O'Callaghan's Deli, 19–20 Lower Cork Street, Mitchelstown – take a picnic from this fabulous deli before you set off.

Lunch in Youghal
Aherne's Seafood Restaurant, North Main Street, t (024) 92424 (*moderate*). This restaurant is an institution, going back three generations, and is famed for fresh seafood.
Devonshire Arms, Pearse Square, t (024) 92827 (*moderate*). Old-world hotel and award-winning restaurant, with a wide choice of traditional Irish standards.

Dinner in Youghal
Old Imperial Hotel, 27 Main Street, t (024) 92435 (*moderate*). Impressive Mediterranean-style cuisine in the bar.

Ballymakeigh House, on the N25 between Killeagh and Youghal, t (024) 91373 (*moderate*). Large country restaurant serving an excellent choice of local produce, including baked ham with whiskey sauce.

Sleeping in Youghal
Avonmore House, South Abbey, Youghal, t (024) 92617 (*inexpensive*). Elegant old house with beautiful rooms. A good bargain.
Aherne's Accommodation, 163 North Street, t (024) 92424 (*expensive*). Luxurious rooms and self-catering available.
Bay View House, Front Strand, t (024) 92824 (*inexpensive*). Victorian villa over the beach.

Sleeping in Castlemartyr
Old Parochial House, t (021) 466 7454 (*moderate*). Charming period house with elegant rooms and luxurious touches including flowers.
Boulta House, Ballynoe, Couna, t (058) 59247 (*moderate*). Idyllic Georgian farmhouse on a working dairy farm.

Day 5: South of Youghal

Morning: In **Kilcredan**'s 17th-century Church of Ireland church are some fascinating limestone headstones with a variety of imaginative motifs. Sadly, the church has suffered the fate of many of that faith and is now without a roof, and the carved tomb of Sir Robert Tynte has been ravaged by the weather. Two miles northwest at **Ladysbridge**, near Garryvoe, is a grand, fortified house built of the local limestone, called Ightermurragh Castle. Over one of the fireplaces is a Latin inscription which tells that it was built by Edmund Supple and his wife in 1641.

Lunch: In Ballycotton, *see* below.

Afternoon: The R632 from Ladysbridge leads down to **Ballycotton**, a charming fishing village set in a peaceful, unspoiled bay. There is a pretty view out to the Ballycotton Islands, and a bird sanctuary on the extensive marsh by the estuary. Close by is the welcoming **Ballymaloe House** (near Shanagarry), which is now a hotel, famous for its restaurant, cooking school and kitchen/craft shop. The gardens (*open April–Sept daily 11–6; adm*) are new, although laid out within the old grounds, and are designed to resemble a series of 'rooms', including a potager in geometric patterns, a formal fruit garden, a herb garden, a rose garden and herbaceous borders. Just to the south is **Shanagarry**, famous for Stephen Pearce's pottery, and the old home of the father of William Penn, the founder of Pennsylvania. You can buy simple earthenware and glazed pottery from Pearce's studio and tea rooms, or from Ballymaloe House. Make your way back to Cork in the morning via Midleton and the N25.

Dinner and Sleeping: In Ballycotton, Castlemartyr or Midleton, *see* below.

Day 5

Lunch in Ballycotton

Spanish Point Seafood Restaurant, t (021) 464 6177 (*inexpensive*). Seaside restaurant with accommodation.

Also see the hotels below.

Dinner and Sleeping in Ballycotton

Ballymaloe House, t (021) 465 2531, *www. ballymaloe.com* (*expensive*). Beautiful Georgian house near the fishing village of Ballycotton; elegant rooms, friendly service, fabulous food and generous helpings. The whole Allen family are involved in the enterprise – you may be inspired to book into their cookery school. Sea- or river-fishing and horse-riding can be arranged.

Bayview Hotel, t (021) 464 6746 (*expensive*). Medium-sized modernized hotel, in a great location overlooking the sea. A garden path leads from the hotel to the beach. Bar meals and good French-influenced cuisine at **Capricho at the Bayview**.

Dinner in Midleton

The Cross of Cloyne, Cloyne, near Midleton, **t** (021) 465 2401 (*moderate*). Simple surroundings with the freshest of local produce turned into mouthwatering dishes.

Dinner and Sleeping in Midleton

Midleton Park Hotel, Midleton **t** (021) 463 5100 (*expensive*). Quite luxurious for the price. The décor is beautiful, the atmosphere relaxed and the restaurant food superb.

Glenview House, Ballinaclasha, 5km from Midleton, **t** (021) 463 1680 (*moderate*). Pretty 18th-century house in lovely grounds, with tennis and croquet. Good food.

Sleeping in Castlemartyr

Killamuckey House, t (021) 466 7266 (*moderate*). Pedigree dairy and beef farm with an old-world farmhouse; comfortable, spacious rooms and a great breakfast.

The Old Parochial House, t (021) 466 7454 (*moderate*). Elegantly restored Victorian house on the edge of the village.

Killarney (Kerry)

Killarney is a resort town that only began to grow up in the 1750s, when tourism in Kerry first became popular. The town itself is not main the attraction; it is the combination of lakes, woods, mountains and the stunning light and skies in the surrounding countryside which remain beautiful and unspoiled. If you are prepared to walk in the mountains and the National Park away from well-worn tracks, you will find that the luxuriant woods, the soft air, the vivid blue of the lakes and the craggy mountains above will have the same charm for you as they have had for countless travellers since the 18th century. Remember to bring a raincoat, since it nearly always rains, and expect at least one day when the mists will creep over everything.

Killarney town does have one thing to offer sightseers: **St Mary's Cathedral**, built in silvery limestone in the 1840s. It is a very successful early English-style building; austere and graceful, with good stained glass. It was not finished completely until the early 20th century, partly because it served as a refuge for the starving during the famine. You will find it in Cathedral Place, a continuation of New Street. Pugin's fine interior plasterwork was completely destroyed in a bit of post-Vatican II vandalism, except in one small chapel.

Another fine church to visit, in College Street, was built for the Franciscan order by Pugin in the 1860s. Look for the window by Harry Clarke. Facing the church is the **monument** to four Kerry poets who lived in the 17th and 18th centuries. It is worth searching out their poetry in local bookshops; the translations into English are excellent.

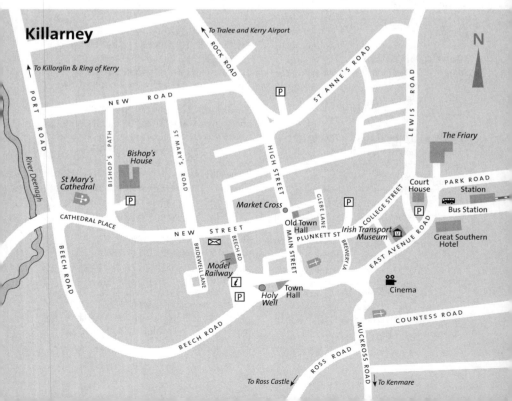

Killarney

Getting There

Ryanair flies daily to Kerry airport from London Stansted. *See* the **Travel** chapter, pp.6–7.

Getting from the Airport

Kerry airport is about 12 miles north of the city on the N23. There is no regular shuttle bus service from the airport. A **taxi** to Killarney city centre will cost approximately €20.
Kerry Airport, t (066) 976 4644, *www. kerryairport.ie*.

Getting Around

Kerry is linked to Dublin by a good rail line from Killarney: **t** (064) 31067. The rail and bus staions are next to each other a few minutes from the centre of town, next to the Great Southern Hotel on Park Road.
Bus Eireann provides a good **bus** service to many parts of the county. In July and August Bus Eireann runs daily coach tours round the Ring of Kerry and the peninsula (from Killarney and Tralee); *see* p.200.
Bus Eireann, Killarney, t (064) 30011.

Car Hire

Murray Europcar, 30 High Street, t (064) 30177, *www.europcar.com*.
National, Kerry Airport, t (021) 432 0755, *www.carhire.ie*.
Randles Irish Car Rental, Kerry Airport, t (064) 31232, *www.irishcarrentals.com*.

By Bike

Killarney Rent-a-Bike, Old Market Lane, Main Street, Killarney, t (064) 32578. Gives out a free map with rentals.
O'Sullivan's Bike Shop, Bishops Lane, New Street, t (064) 31282.
Trailways Outdoor Centre, College Street, t (064) 39929. Also arranges tours and accommodation.

Tourist Information

Killarney: Town Hall, Beech Road (beside town centre car park), t (064) 31633; *open all year*.

Festivals

St Patrick's Week, March (including **Great Parade**, 17 March, and **Roaring 1920s Festival**.
Rally of the Lakes, May.
Killarney Races, May and July.
Regattas, July and August.

Shopping

Crafts

Christy's Irish Store, High Street.
Bricín Craft Shop, 26 High Street.
Frank Lewis Gallery, Bridewell Lane.
Cunningham's Art Gallery, Bishops Lane, off New Road.

Sports and Activities

Golf

Killarney Golf Club, Mahony's Point, t (064) 31034, *www.killarney-golf.com*.

Horse-racing

Look in the local newspapers, or in the back of Tourism Ireland's *Calendar of Events*, available from any tourist office.
Killarney, throughout May and July, t (064) 31125.

Open Farms

Muckross Traditional Farms, t (064) 31440, *see* pp.199–200.

Pleasure Cruises

Killarney Waterbus, t (064) 32638.
Lily of Killarney, t (064) 31068.

Pony-trekking

Killarney Stables, Ballydowney, t (064) 31686.

It is quite fun to wander down some of the old lanes that survive from Victorian times, branching off the main street. There are plenty of banks, shops, craft shops, pubs and restaurants to choose from, but avoid staying in the centre as it gets so

Where to Stay

Great Southern Hotel, t (064) 31262, *www. gshotels.com* (*expensive*). Stylish Victorian hotel with landscaped gardens and impressive facilities, including a choice of dining venues and leisure centre.

Killarney Park Hotel, Kenmare Place, **t** (064) 35555, *www.killarneyparkhotel.ie* (*expensive*). Modern luxury in the heart of Killarney – marble floors, antique furniture, pool and huge suites.

Randles Court Hotel, Muckross Road, **t** (064) 35333, *www.randlescourt.com* (*expensive*). Friendly, family-run manor house hotel.

Coolclogher House, Mill Road, **t** (064) 35996, *coolclogherhouse@eircom.net* (*expensive*). Victorian house in a wonderfully secluded walled estate, with a great conservatory.

West End House Hotel, New Road, **t** (064) 32271, *www.westendhouse.com* (*moderate*). Small period house hotel and restaurant close to the centre of Killarney.

The Holiday Inn, Muckross Road, **t** (064) 33000, *www.holidayinnkillarney.com* (*moderate*). Excellent version of its type – family rooms, pool, gym, good food – in an uninspiring setting on the outskirts.

Castlerosse Hotel and Leisure Centre, **t** (064) 31144, *www.castlerossehotelkillarney.com* (*moderate*). Great lake and mountain views from the self-catering suites or the main hotel, which caters well for disabled guests. Golf packages and an inviting leisure centre offering Swedish massages.

Earls Court House, Muckross Road, **t** (064) 34009, **f** (064) 34366, *www.killarney-earls court.ie* (*moderate*). Comfortable Victorian furnishings, spacious rooms and delicious breakfasts; efficient and friendly service.

Killarney Royal Hotel, College Street, **t** (064) 31853, *www.killarneyroyal.ie* (*moderate*). Boutique town house hotel.

Killeen House Hotel, Aghadoe, Lakes of Killarney, **t** (064) 31711, *www.killeenhouse hotel.com* (*moderate*). Friendly, cosy little hotel up in the hills of Aghadoe, 10 minutes

from Killarney and away from the crowds. A golfer's paradise.

White Gates Hotel, Muckross Road, **t** (064) 31164, *www.whitegates.com* (*moderate*). Lively, with an in-house pub, Kit Flaherty's, hosting traditional music; Irish fare.

Gleann Fia **Country House**, Deerpark, **t** (064) 35035 (*inexpensive*). Recently built, Victorian-style guest house, set in a 30-acre wooded valley a mile from Killarney.

Abbey Lodge, Muckross Road, **t** (064) 34193 (*inexpensive*). Recently opened, a convenient B&B run by the welcoming King family.

Carriglea House, Muckross Road, **t** (064) 31116 (*inexpensive*). Very close to Muckross House and the National Park, so you can avoid the busy centre of town. Comfortable rooms with en suite bathrooms.

Eating Out

The Strawberry Tree, 24 Plunkett Street, **t** (064) 32688 (*expensive*). Easily one of the best restaurants in Killarney.

Foley's Seafood and Steak Restaurant, 23 High Street, **t** (064) 31217 (*moderate*). Serves delicious seafood and lamb, and very good vegetarian dishes.

Gaby's Restaurant, 27 High Street, **t** (064) 32519 (*moderate*). Mediterranean-style café with delicious seafood. Very popular locally with a changing menu dependent upon the day's catch. *Closed lunch and Sun.*

The Laune, 103 New Street, **t** (064) 32772 (*moderate*). Good for lunch; extensive menu.

The Cooperage Restaurant, Old Market Lane, **t** (064) 37716 (*moderate*). Cosy and friendly.

The Old Presbytery, Cathedral Place, **t** (064) 30555 (*moderate*). A newly opened restaurant making its mark on the Kllarney dining scene, with sophisticated dishes and very professional service.

Panis Angelicus, 15 New Street, **t** (064) 39648 (*moderate*). Delicious freshly baked breads and pastries during the day and an extensive, innovative dinner menu with great vegetarian options. *Closed Tues and Wed eve.*

crowded. Those with a mechanical bent might enjoy what claims to be one of the longest **model railways** in the world, on Beech Road (**t** *(064) 34000; adm*) or the **Irish Transport Museum**, Scotts Gardens (**t** *(064) 32638; open April–Oct; adm*).

Expect to be approached by the jarveys (coachmen), who gather with their ponies and traps (jaunting cars) on the street corner as the N71 enters the town; they will guide you around the valley and take you for as long or as short a trip as you want. Be sure to negotiate the price for the ride before you start and be prepared for a certain amount of chat. Most of them have a host of stories about the famous landmarks that have been polished and embroidered ever since Killarney first became a tourist destination. Some of it is tongue-in-cheek, like this hoary old phrase about the constant rain: ''Twasn't rain at all, but just a little perspiration from the mountains.' The jarvey nowadays often carries a mobile phone to check on his next ride.

Day Trips and Overnighters from Killarney

Ross Castle and Innisfallen

Open May–Oct, daily 10–5; adm; 1½mile walk or jaunting car from Killarney.

Ross Castle is 1½ miles southwest of the town centre on a peninsula with pretty, wooded paths to the edge of Lough Leane. Evidence of copper deposits can be seen in the green waters here; these deposits were worked in the Bronze Age and the 18th century. Ross Castle is a fine ruin dating from the 15th century, consisting of a tower house surrounded by a *bawn* (fortified enclosure). The castle was built by the O'Donoghues, and taken by the Cromwellians, one of the last strongholds to fall. It has been restored and there are guided tours with much historical information. On its left is a 17th-century house built by the Brownes, who became earls of Kenmare. From here you can hire a boat to **Innisfallen Isle** (*book in advance during the high season, €3.80–€5 per person*), an isle like a country in miniature, with hills, valleys and dark woods. Holly and other evergreens grow very thickly here. Near the landing stages are the extensive ruins of **Innisfallen Abbey,** founded about AD 600, as a refuge for Christians during the Dark Ages in Europe. The *Annals of Innisfallen*, a chronicle of world and Irish history written between AD 950–1380, are now in the Bodleian Library, Oxford. The monastery lasted until the middle of the 17th century, when the Cromwellian forces took Ross Castle.

Muckross Estate and Abbey

t (064) 31440, www.muckross-house.ie. Open daily 9–5.30; adm, gardens free; for a small extra fee you can visit a traditional working farm within the estate. Take a jaunting car from Killarney.

About three miles south of Killarney is the Muckross Estate on the Kenmare road. Muckross House and Abbey are part of an 11,000-acre estate given to the nation by Mr Bowers Bourne of California and his son-in-law, Senator Arthur Vincent, who had owned the property for 31 years. The estate is now a national park and covers most of the lake district, with walks and drives to all the beauty spots.

Muckross House was built in Tudor style in 1843 by Henry Arthur Herbert, whose family were landlords in this area. On the death of the last MacCarthy, Muckross

The Ring of Kerry

The narrow road that makes up the famous Ring of Kerry is 112 miles (180km) long, and takes about three hours to drive without any detours. If you have hired a car, starting back at Kenmare, you can take the N70 and follow the coiling road south around the coast, stopping to enjoy the views, and perhaps setting off down the tiny R roads to get a better look at St Finan's Bay, Bolus Head and Doulus Head. The Ring ends at Killorglin. The tour we suggest on pp.208–12 does not follow the Ring exactly, but includes many of the sights along it.

Numerous operators offer tours of the Ring of Kerry (*ask at Killarney tourist office, or try **Corcoran's Tours**, 8 College St, t (064) 36666; departs Killarney 10.30am, returning 5pm, with stops for sightseeing, shopping and lunch*). You can also do the Ring of Kerry anticlockwise as a day trip by bus tour in July and August, starting at Killarney on the Killorglin road. The views are equally good. (***Bus Eireann**, leaving Killarney bus station 8.30am, returning 2.15pm, stopping only for 45mins at Waterville; summer only*).

passed to an Anglo-Norman family who eventually became known as Herbert. Queen Victoria stayed here when she visited in 1861. The main rooms are furnished in splendid Victorian style; the rest of the house has been transformed into a museum of Kerry folklore with a craft shop in its basement. You can see a potter, a weaver, a bookbinder and a blacksmith at their trades. A very informative film on the geology and natural beauties of the park is shown every half-hour.

It is worth paying the extra to tour the **traditional farm**, especially if you have children with you; they will love the chickens, pigs, and the little black Kerry cows that give such sweet milk. The gardens around the house are delightful, and here you can see the native Killarney strawberry tree (*Arbutus unedo*), an evergreen with creamy white flowers followed by fruit that resembles strawberries.

Close by, overlooking the Lower Lake, is **Muckross Abbey**, a graceful early English ruin founded in 1448 for the Observatine Franciscans. After being dispossessed by Cromwell in 1652, the Franciscans had to go into hiding, but returned in more tolerant times and set up a boys' school and a new church in Killarney. In fact, this area is a stage set for everything the tourist wishes to see, and the natural beauty of the setting is enhanced by the superb gardens and arboretum. There is a gigantic yew tree in the centre of the cloister. The walks laid out in the park lead you through a mature oak and yew wood and to the very end of the peninsula, to the cliff known as **Eagle Point**, named after the golden eagles that used to be seen here. The path crosses the wooded **Dinis Island** (the Victorian cottage here serves good pizza). You are now 2½ (3.7km) miles from Muckross House, and if you do not want to retrace your steps, you can join the N71 Kenmare road (about a mile away).

Killarney National Park

The area around Killarney is geographically quite spectacular: the underlying rock varies from old red sandstone to limestone, whilst the scooping action of glaciers in the Ice Age created the precipitous mountain corries. Lower down, the indented lakes are softened by oak, holly and arbutus, interspersed with the alien *Rhododendron ponticum*, which splashes mauve among the dark leaves in late spring. The great Macgillycuddy's Reeks rise up to the west of the three famous lakes; to the southwest is the Mangerton Range. The **Upper Lake** is narrow, small and impressive, enclosed by the mountains, and scattered with wooded islands on which cedars of Lebanon stand high amongst the trees. A narrow passage leads into a connecting stretch of water called the Long Range, which flows under the Old Weir Bridge. Here the water rushes over some rapids, giving a frisson of excitement to those on a boat trip. The river then divides at the 'Meeting of the Waters'; the left branch flows into the **Lower Lake**, also called Lough Leane; the right branch empties into **Middle Lake**, known as Muckross Lake. The limestone that underlies the Middle Lake has been worn away by the water into a series of fantastically shaped rocks and cliffs.

A large part of the Killarney Valley is national park land. The valley runs roughly north–south through a break in the Macgillycuddy's Reeks range of mountains, which runs east-west. Lough Leane lies north of the range, and the Middle and Upper Lakes mainly south of it.

The Gap of Dunloe

The Gap of Dunloe is six miles west of Killarney and about eight miles in length, a wild gorge bordered by the dark Macgillycuddy's Reeks, the Purple Mountain and Tomies Mountain. The Macgillycuddy's Reeks include **Carrantuohill**, at 3,414ft (1,040m) the highest mountain in Ireland. Cars are not welcome on the dirt track during the tourist season, as the route is taken up with horse traffic, cyclists and walkers, and the horse traffic on the narrow, unpaved road will not allow you to pass.

A standard **tour** can be booked in town or at the mouth of the Gap (*see* box over-leaf), consisting of a jaunting car ride through the Gap, and then a pleasant boat trip back to town through the lakes. This takes a full day and is idyllic in good weather. Seeing the sights by pony and trap, also known as a jaunting car, can be great fun, and during the trip you are regaled with stories by the jarveys. If the expense of a boat trip down the three lakes does not appeal, you can always hire a bike, walk or catch a bus. There are half-day bus trips, and ponies can be hired to explore the Gap of Dunloe, on the outskirts of Killarney (advisable only for experienced riders).

The mouth of the Gap starts at **Kate Kearney's Cottage** (Kate was a local woman, and reputedly a witch), a convivial refreshment house and coffee shop off the Killorglin road, six miles west of Killarney, and continues through to **Moll's Gap** on the Kenmare road (N71). The journey through the Gap is spectacular, with steep gorges and deep glacial lakes. The Gap is 7 miles long and ends at **Lord Brandon's Cottage**. Here snacks are available and you can take a boat back to Killarney (Ross Castle). A boat trip is the best way to see the lakes; you pass through the Upper Lake first, which is surrounded by oak woodland. The vegetation becomes more luxuriant as the boat descends, passing under the Old Weir Bridge to the Meeting of the Waters where the Upper Lake and Middle (or Muckross) Lake join. The boat trip then continues, sailing past Torc Mountain to the east, into the Lower Lake (Lough Leane). **Innisfallen Island**

Getting Around

There are any number of permutations of the tour options for the Gap of Dunloe and the three lakes. The standard tour – bus from Killarney to Kate Kearney's Cottage, walk or ride through the Gap of Dunloe, then a boat back to Ross Castle and short walk or ride back to Killarney town centre – is widely available and costs around €30. However, you can easily do just part of the tour, e.g, walking or cycling the other way from Killarney to Lord Brandon's Cottage, cycling the whole route, etc. It is advisable, if you are going to want to take a bike on a boat from either Lord Brandon's Cottage or Ross Castle, to book this.

The Killarney tourist office can help with advice on tours and tour operators, or try:
Guided Walks, Richard Claney, t (064) 33471.

Gap of Dunloe Tours, from the little kiosk outside O'Connor's Pub, 7 High Street, t (064) 30200.
O'Donoghue Brothers Boating Tours, Killarney Boating and Tour Centre, Old Weir Lodge, Muckross Road, t (064) 31068.
Destination Killarney, Scott's Gardens, t (064) 32638. Tours of Lough Leane on MV *Pride of the Lakes*.

Eating Out

Snacks are available at Kate Kearney's Cottage and Lord Brandon's Cottage, but on a good day taking a picnic is a good idea – try **Jam** in Killarney High Street for delicious quiches and filled rolls, or **Kathleen's Country Kitchen**, New Road, for good Irish baking.

is passed, where the ruins of the ancient abbey founded in AD 600 can be seen, *see* p.199. The disembarkation point is **Ross Castle**, (*see* p.199) from where you can walk back to town or catch a jaunting car.

If you are not taking the standard tour, however, it's a good idea to approach the Gap from the opposite way to the crowds, especially if you are walking or cycling. Take the main Killarney–Kenmare road (N71); there is plenty to stop for en route. Notice the strawberry tree, or arbutus, growing among ferns and oaks, and the pink saxifrage on the wayside. All of the sights along the way are well signposted. You can stop and take an easy walk up the woodland path to the **Torc Waterfall**, found by following a rough road on the left just before a sign cautioning motorists about deer. The walk is very short, leading you through splendid fir trees to the 60ft (18m) falls. It is also possible to drive there and park. Go back to the main road again (N71) and continue for six miles to **Ladies' View**, which gives you a marvellous view of the Upper Lake. Now turn off right before **Moll's Gap** and right again along the dirt track. You are now close to the Gap of Dunloe. A path leads you along the river to **Lord Brandon's Cottage**, where tour groups coming from the Gap join the boats back to Killarney.

To the west is a continuation of the Gap, the **Black Valley**, a sombre and remote corner of Kerry; nearly the entire population died off during the potato famine and the place counts only a few lonely inhabitants today. Other walks include the **Glen of Cummeenduff** which leads to the heart of the Reeks, or the equally desolate **Glen of Owenreagh**.

Around Lough Leane

If you are interested in seeing a fine example of **ogham stones**, take the main road for Killorglin (R562), past the Dunluce Castle Hotel. Turn right down a hill to a T-junction, and right again, over the bridge and up the hill. A signpost points left to a collection of ogham stones in a wired enclosure high on the bank. This is the best place in Kerry to see the weird ogham writing, the only form that existed in Ireland before the arrival of Christianity. The lateral strokes, incised into the stone and crossing a vertical line, give the name of a man long, long dead.

Dunloe Castle gardens are well worth a visit (*t (064) 44111; open April–Sept; adm by appt or ask at reception*); it is claimed your walk will take you around the world in a botanical sense, such is the variety of plants. The nearby village of **Beaufort** is pretty.

Another fine view of the Killarney lakes and mountains can be seen from **Aghadoe Hill** about 2½ miles from Killarney. It is not at all touristy. In pagan times, the hill was believed to be the birthplace of all beauty, and lovers still meet here. The legend goes that whoever falls in love on Aghadoe Hill will be blessed for a lifetime. From here can be seen the voluptuous pair of hills known as the **Paps of Anu** (Danu), the mother of the gods. James Stephens is said to have remarked jokingly, 'I think those mountains ought to be taught a little modesty.'

Kenmare

This is marvellous walking country, and if that's what you plan to do you might want to spend more than a day or even base yourself in Kenmare, a pretty, colourful 19th-century market town at the head of this long sea inlet. It is an ideal location because two of Ireland's long distance walking routes, the Kerry Way and the Beara Way, converge in the town. During the last week of May, Kenmare is busy with keen walkers taking part in the Walking Festival. For further information on this festival, consult *www.kenmare.com/walking*, which also links to the Caha Mountains Walking Festival that takes place in Glengarriff, Co. Cork, only 30 minutes away. Savour the views of the rolling Kerry Hills, the Macgillycuddy's Reeks, the Caha Mountains on the Cork border and the broad estuary of the River Kenmare.

Leave yourself at least a couple of hours to wander around Kenmare itself, which is full of excellent coffee houses, bars, restaurants, a heritage centre and craft shops. The colours of woven rugs, jerseys and tweeds perfectly echo the beautiful surrounding countryside. Fine silver jewellery and good-quality ceramics are to be found in the many craft shops stocking the work of local artists, and there is a wide range of books of Irish interest to enhance your knowledge of the host country.

It is worth seeking out the small **Neolithic stone circle** along the banks of the River Finnihy. To get there, walk up Market Street; the stone circle is signposted and you'll see it on the right overlooking the river.

Back on the town square and above the tourist office is the **Heritage Centre** (*open April–Sept, Mon–Sat 10–6, also Sun 11–5 in July and Aug; adm*), where inside an exhibition explores the career of Sir William Petty. Another attraction in the Heritage Centre is the **Kenmare Lace and Design Centre** on the square (*t (064) 42636; open Mon–Sat 10–5.30; closed Sun; adm*), where you can look at a display of the locally made point lace and see demonstrations.

During the tourist season there are various operators in town to take you on two-hour-long boat cruises in Kenmare Bay and introduce you to the local marine wildlife.

Getting There

There is an infrequent **bus** service from Killarney to Kenmare – two a day in summer, and afternoon only in winter. The journey takes 45mins.

Tourist Information

Kenmare: beside the Heritage Centre, **t** (064) 41233; *open April–Sept.*

Shopping

Art Galleries
The Iverni Gallery, Henry Street, **t** (064) 41720.

Books
Kenmare Bookshop, Shelbourne Street.

Crafts
Black Abbey Crafts, 28 Main Street. A wide selection of locally made handicrafts.
Cleo's, 2 Shelbourne Street. For quality tweed suits, linen and woven rugs.
Cosy Cottage, Henry Street. Linens, pottery and glassware.
De Barra, Main Street. For traditional Celtic jewellery.
Kenmare Lace and Design Centre, The Square. Sells locally made lace.
Quill's Woollen Market. All manner of woollen goods.
Studio 29, Main Street. Knitwear.

Delicacies
The Pantry, 30 Henry Street, Kenmare. For home-made bread, Capparoe goat's cheese and picnic ingredients.
Jam, Henry Street. Bakery, delicatessen and coffee shop.

Sports and Activities

Fishing
There is excellent deep-sea and brown trout fishing in the **Kenmare River estuary**.
Kenmare Seafari, The Pier, **t** (064) 83171. Fishing and seal-watching trip.

Golf
Kenmare Golf Club, Killowen, **t** (064) 41291.
Ring of Kerry Golf and Country Club, Templenoe, **t** (064) 42000.

Pony-trekking
Dromquinna Stables, **t** (064) 41043.

Tours by Car
ProCar, **t** (064) 42500. Luxury chauffeur-driven tours by bus and car.

Walking
Kenmare Walking Club, **t** (064) 41034. Non-members welcome to join activities.

Water Sports
Kenmare Bay Diving Centre, **t** (064) 42238.
Kenmare Seafari, The Pier, **t** (064) 83171, *www.seafariireland.com*. Guided cruises introducing the local marine life; plus fishing, kayaking and water-skiing.

Where to Stay

Park Hotel, High Street, **t** (064) 41200, *www.parkkenmare.com* (*luxury*). Château-style, award-winning hotel, with every modern comfort in rooms furnished with fine antiques.
Sheen Falls Lodge, **t** (064) 41600, *www.sheenfallslodge.ie* (*luxury*). Set in a beautiful location with sunny, low-key décor. The rooms are elegant, the food is lavish and imaginative and there is even a helipad.

Tralee

Tralee is the chief town and administrative capital of County Kerry, and is invariably jam-packed with cars and shoppers. It is famous outside Ireland for the sentimental Victorian song, 'The Rose of Tralee'. The town was the chief seat of the Desmond

Dromquinna Manor, t (064) 41657, *www. dromquinna.com* (*moderate*). Very comfortable with lovely views over the water and waterskiing and horse-riding nearby.

Lansdowne Arms, William Street, **t** (064) 41368 (*moderate*). Family-run hotel.

Foley's Shamrock, Henry Street, **t** (064) 42162, *www.foleyskenmare.com* (*moderate*). In the heart of town, this refurbished inn has comfortable rooms above a lively bistro serving Irish and international fare.

Darcy's, Main Street, **t** (064) 41589 (*inexpensive*). One of Kenmare's several great restaurants with simple, en suite rooms.

Hawthorne House, Shelbourne Street, **t** (064) 41035 (*inexpensive*). Extremely comfortable, modern house with all bedrooms en suite and lavish, delicious food.

David Cottage, Sneem Road, **t** (064) 41803 (*inexpensive*). Charming stone cottage full of old-world charm.

Muxnaw Lodge, t (064) 41252, *www.muxnaw lodge.com* (*inexpensive*). This attractive house was built in 1801 and overlooks Kenmare Bay, within walking distance of town. There is an all-weather tennis court and good gardens and walks.

The Lake House, Cloonee Tuosist, Kenmare, **t** (064) 84205 (*inexpensive*). Friendly pub and restaurant with accommodation above, run by Mary O'Shea. Highly recommended, especially for its beautiful lakeside setting.

Tara Farm, Tubrid, Kenmare, **t** (064) 41272, *www.tara-farm.com* (*inexpensive*). Fantastic farm B&B 1km out of town, with great views of Kenmare Bay and the mountains.

Eating Out

Park Hotel, High Street, **t** (064) 41200 (*luxury*). Delicious French cuisine in grand surroundings. Ideal for a special occasion.

The Lime Tree, Shelbourne Street, **t** (064) 41225 (*expensive*). Upmarket restaurant, with fish a speciality. An art gallery opens in the evenings at the same establishment.

An Leath Phingin, 35 Main Street, **t** (064) 41559 (*moderate*). The Italian chef, Maria, makes her own pasta and scrumptious sauces. The stone-oven pizzas are also popular.

D'Arcy's Old Bank House, Main Street, **t** (064) 41589 (*moderate*). Well-established local favourite with constantly innovative specialities and colourful décor.

Packies, 35 Henry Street, **t** (064) 41508 (*moderate*). Excellent fish restaurant; unpretentious, skilful cooking with the best ingredients.

Mulcahy's, 16 Henry Street, **t** (064) 42383 (*moderate*). The funky but stylish interior complements the cooking. Fusion is the style here, with lots of delicious combinations using the best of local produce, like Kerry lamb served with an international twist.

P.F. McCarthy's, 14 Main Street, **t** (064) 41516 (*moderate*). An institution in Kenmare, serving great bar food with a French twist. Good salads and craft-brewed beers on offer.

Café Indigo and the Square Pint, The Square, **t** (064) 42356 (*inexpensive*). Very trendy daytime haunt for beautiful young locals and tourists, with an esoteric menu and minimalist décor. The pub below is good for traditional entertainment on summer evenings.

The Horseshoe Bar and Restaurant, 3 Main Street, **t** (064) 41553 (*inexpensive*). Friendly, informal bistro.

The Purple Heather, Henry Street, **t** (064) 41016 (*inexpensive*). Good for lunchtime snacks, home-made soups and seafood. There is a very cosy fire in the bar.

Mickey Ned's, The Square, **t** (064) 40200 (*inexpensive*). This lively and modern pub restaurant serves very good quality food in the heart of Kenmare.

family, but nothing remains of their strong castle. In 1579 the Earl of Desmond was asked to aid the Commissioners of Munster against the Spanish who had landed at Smerwick, but the Desmonds had no love for the English, and that night the representatives of Queen Elizabeth and their entourage were put to death by the Earl's brother. In the following year a ruthless campaign of retribution was waged against the Desmonds. Tralee was threatened and the Earl fired the town rather than leave anything that might be claimed as a prize by the Queen's men. In 1583 the Earl of Desmond, then an old man, was hunted from his hiding place in Glanageenty woods and beheaded. His head was sent in typical Tudor fashion to decorate a spike on London Bridge. The old Dominican priory that the Desmonds founded was completely destroyed by the Elizabethan courtier-soldier Sir Edward Denny, who was granted the town when the Desmond estates were seized.

The town has suffered continually from wars and burnings, and today is largely mid-19th-century in character, although there are some elegant Georgian houses in the centre. The courthouse has a fine Ionic façade, and in Denny Street there is an impressive 1798 memorial of a single man armed with a pike. In Ashe Street the Dominican **Church of the Holy Cross** is by Pugin, built after the monks had managed to re-establish themselves here, long after Sir Edward Denny destroyed their priory. The priory garden contains some ancient carved stones, amongst them the White Knight stone and the Roche slab which date from 1685, proof that the foundation was at least partly in existence in the rein of James II. The interior is very fine, especially the Chapel of the Blessed Virgin, with exquisite mosaics and altar charts by that great artist Michael Healy, who worked in the early 20th century. In Abbey Street there is a modern **church** with a lovely chapel dedicated to the Blessed Virgin Mary, which contains some of Healy's fine stained glass work.

The **Ashe Memorial Hall**, an imposing 19th-century building off Denny Street, is a very fine county museum (**t** *(066) 712 7777; open Mar–Oct daily 10–6, Sun 12–4.30; adm*). The display entitled 'Kerry, The Kingdom' traces the history of Kerry from 5000 BC, and the exhibits include archaeological treasures found in Kerry. There is some fascinating black and white film footage taken during the War of Independence and after, up until 1965. Thomas Ashe, after whom this building is named, was a native of Tralee, and active in the 1916 Uprising and the IRB. He was arrested and imprisoned in Mountjoy Prison, where he went on hunger strike as a protest at being treated as an ordinary convict and not as a political prisoner. After he was roughly force-fed, fluid got into his windpipe and then his lungs, and he died a few hours later. He was a close friend and ally of Michael Collins, who described him as 'a man of no complexes. Doing whatever he did for Ireland and always in a quiet way.' Another attraction is a life-size reconstruction of a street in medieval Tralee – you travel through it in a 'time-car', seeing and smelling what street life was like in the walled Desmond town, so different from the Tralee of today with its supermarket, multi-screen cinema complex and Aquadome fun centre. The **town park** surrounding the museum and tourist office is well maintained with pretty trees and, of course, there is a rose garden, which is at its best during the Rose of Tralee Festival.

Past the rose garden is the headquarters of *Siamsa Tíre*, the National Folk Theatre, which presents performances of song, dance and mime in an idealized version of rural life. During the winter the venue is available to travelling theatres (**t** *(066) 712 3055*). Those with children might carry on around the corner to the **Science Works**, Godfrey Place (**t** *(066) 712 9855*), an interactive science museum.

The **Tralee steam train** (*runs May–Oct, on the hour from Tralee, 11–5; on the half-hour back from Blennerville*), a relic of the old Tralee and Dingle narrow-gauge railway, leaves from Ballyard station (near the Aquadome). The 3km jaunt takes you to **Blennerville Windmill**, the largest in the British Isles, complete with restaurant and craft shops (**t** *(066) 712 1064; open April–Oct, daily 10–6; adm*).

Getting There

There are a few **trains** a day from Killarney to Tralee, taking 40mins.

Tourist Information

Tralee: Ashe Hall, **t** (066) 712 1288, **f** (066) 712 1700; *open all year.*

Shopping

Antiques

15 Princes St, **t** (066) 712 5635. Georgian house with seven rooms furnished with books, prints and antiques for sale.

Art Galleries

The Wellspring, 16 Denny St, **t** (066) 712 1218.

Crafts

Carraig Donn Knitwear, Bridge Street.
Ireland Designs, Denny Street.

Sports and Activities

Donkey Rambles

Slattery's, 1 Russell Street, **t** (066) 712 4088. Hires out a donkey, saddlebags and maps for €30 a day.

Golf

Tralee Golf Club, West Barrow, Ardfert, **t** (066) 713 6379. Links by Arnold Palmer.

Greyhound Racing

Oakview Park, Tralee, **t** (066) 718 0008. *Tues and Fri, 7.50pm.*

Horse-drawn Caravans

Slattery's, 1 Russell Street, **t** (066) 712 9122.

Horse-racing

Look in the local newspapers, or in the back of the free calendar of events available from any tourist office.

Where to Stay

Castlemorris House, Ballymullen, **t** (066) 718 0060 (*inexpensive*). Large 18th-century house in extensive gardens, a short walk from the city centre. With a pleasant drawing room, spacious rooms, welcoming open fires and a friendly atmosphere.
Ashe Townhouse, 15 Denny Street, **t** (066) 712 1003 (*moderate*). Stylish Georgian town-house B&B opposite the public gardens.
Collis Sandes House, Oakpark, **t** (066) 712 8658, *www.colsands.com* (*inexpensive*). Imposing Victorian country house that also features wonderful traditional musical entertainment in the evenings.
Tralee Townhouse, High Street, **t/f** (066) 718 1111 (*inexpensive*). Conveniently located in the city centre.

Eating Out

Restaurant David Norris, Ivy House, Ivy Terrace, **t** (066) 718 5654 (*moderate*). Home-made pasta is just one of the delights of this excellent restaurant.
Restaurant Uno, 14 Princes Street, **t** (066) 718 1950 (*moderate*). Contemporary cuisine with an Italian bent. Good vegetarian options.
Oyster Tavern, The Spa, **t** (066) 713 6102 (*moderate*). An old favourite pub/restaurant serving fine seafood dishes.
Ashes Bar, Upper Camp, **t** (066) 713 0133 (*inexpensive*). Very good seafood platter at lunchtime, with a more elaborate *à la carte* menu in the evening, and traditional music in the summer.

Touring from Killarney

Day 1: The South Coast of the Iveragh Peninsula

Morning: Head southwest out of Killarney via Kenmare, on the N71, for **Sneem**, a quiet village attractively laid out by an 18th-century landlord around a green, through which a river runs. Modern sculptures are positioned around, the most memorable being the modern beehive huts with stained glass panels by James Scanlon, beside the church. About 10 miles west of Sneem, on the N70, a signpost points right to the circular stone **Staigue Fort** (*open Easter–Oct daily 10am–9pm; adm*), isolated at the head of a desolate valley, and between 1,500 and 2,000 years old. Two miles away, the Staigue Fort Hotel has a small exhibition centre about the fort.

Lunch: In Sneem or Caherdaniel, *see* below.

Afternoon: Take the coast road west to **Caherdaniel** and **Derrynane House** (*open May– Sept daily 9–6, Sun 11–6; Oct and April Tues–Sun 1–5;, Nov–Mar Sat–Sun only 1–5; adm*), the home of Daniel O'Connell, 'the Great Liberator', who won Catholic emancipation in 1829. **Derrynane Bay** has one of the most glorious strands in the country. A few miles further round the coast, **Waterville** is the main resort of the Ring of Kerry; palm trees and fuchsia imbue it with a continental air and hotels line the waterfront. The people speak Gaelic (the Munster variety) and **Ballinskelligs Bay** is a favourite place. On the other side of the bay in **Ballinskelligs**, Cill Rialaig Arts Centre, (*t (066) 915 6100*), is a small gallery and tea room associated with an artists' retreat.

Dinner and Sleeping: In Waterville, *see* below.

Day 1

Lunch in Sneem

Parknasilla Great Southern Hotel, t (064) 45122, *www.gshotels.com* (*expensive*). One of Ireland's best hotels, set in 300 acres of subtropical parkland, boasts a fine restaurant. *Book*.

Stone House, t (064) 45188 (*moderate*). Guesthouse producing reasonable Irish food. *Dinner only*.

The Blue Bull, South Square, t (064) 45382 (*inexpensive*). Quality seafood in an old-style building; delicious seafood platters are available.

Lunch in Caherdaniel

The Blind Piper, t (066) 9475126 (*inexpensive*). Good, lively atmosphere in this pretty hamlet.

Dinner in Waterville

Shéilin Seafood Restaurant, t (066) 947 4231 (*moderate*). Charming seafood restaurant, with a cosy atmosphere and the freshest of sea produce.

Dinner and Sleeping in Waterville

Butler Arms Hotel, Waterville, t (066) 947 4144, *www.butlerarms.com* (*expensive*). Intimate, family-run, pleasantly old-fashioned hotel. A lovely place to stay if you like salmon- or trout-fishing. The **Fisherman's Bar** serves good pub fare and is open to non-residents.

Smugglers' Inn, Cliff Road, Waterville, t (066) 947 4330 (*moderate*). Friendy, family-run inn on the beach, with comfortable rooms. The seafood, Kerry lamb and beef are all good here.

Old Cable House, Cable Station, t (066) 947 4233 (*moderate*). Historic B&B in the building where the first transatlantic telegraph cable from Ireland to the USA was started.

Day 2: Out to the Islands

Morning: A trip out to the jagged, rocky **Skellig Islands** will take most of the day and is a high point of any visit to this part of the country. Small Skellig is a nature reserve and boats do not land there. Great Skellig, or Skellig Michael, houses an almost perfect example of an early monastic settlement founded by St Finan, which was in use between the 6th and 12th centuries. The remains still impress with their simplicity – seven beehive huts and oratories which convey something of the indefatigable striving of this community, and the ruins of St Michael's Church. Boats can be hired from Waterville (*mid-Mar–Oct*), and whether you get there will be determined by the weather; the trip can be very rough. Take a waterproof, flat shoes, a picnic and, if you like birdlife, a pair of binoculars. You land to the noisy fury of the seabirds, and approach the monastery up a stairway of about 600 steps, hacked out of stone over a thousand years ago. A waterbus tour is also available May–Sept from the **Skellig Experience Heritage Centre** on Valentia Island (by the bridge from Portmagee) – which is also worth a visit for the background knowledge it gives.

Lunch: A picnic on the Skellig Islands, *see* below.

Late Afternoon: Head round via Portmagee to **Valentia Island** and its quiet harbour village of **Knightstown**. The village was named after the Knight of Kerry, an improving landlord, who opened a slate quarry in 1816 and encouraged the weaving industry; the small museum in the old school house details the natural dyes used. The knight also planted a garden at nearby **Glanleam House** (*open June–Sept 11–7; adm*).

Dinner and Sleeping: In Portmagee, Knightstown or Caherciveen, *see* below.

Day 2

Lunch on the Skellig Islands

Either stock up with a picnic at one of the small supermarkets in Waterville or ask where you have been staying whether they will make you some sandwiches. There are no facilities on Skellig Michael.

Dinner and Sleeping in Portmagee

The Moorings, t (066) 947 7108 (*moderate*). This pub/guesthouse serves good traditional bar food such as seafood chowder and salmon. *Restaurant closed Mon.*

Dinner in Knightstown

Fuchsia Restaurant, t (066) 947 6051. Quayside eatery serving a range of tasty dishes.

Sleeping in Knightstown

Glanleam House, Valentia Island, t (066) 947 6176 (*moderate*). Splendid, sub-tropical gardens surrounding the Knight of Kerry's old home.

Spring Acre, t (066) 947 6141 (*moderate*). Seafront accommodation close to restaurants and pubs. Scenic views.

Valentia Island Sea Sports Guesthouse, t (066) 947 6204 (*moderate*). Right on the pier, great for anglers and divers. Between May and Sept, a pierfront restaurant serves fresh seafood and vegetarian dishes.

Dinner in Caherciveen

QC's Seafood Bar, 3 Main Street, t (066) 947 2244 (*moderate*). Seafood with a Spanish twist – lots of delicious chargrilled dishes.

Sleeping in Caherciveen

Mount Rivers, Carhan Road, t (066) 947 2509 (*inexpensive*). Comfortable rooms with en suite bath in Mrs McKenna's Victorian house.

Sea Breeze, Renard Road, t (066) 947 2609 (*inexpensive*). Friendly, and spectacular views.

O'Shea's B&B, Church Street, t (066) 947 2402 (*inexpensive*). Family-run B&B in a peaceful location.

Day 3: Around Dingle Bay

Morning: Back on the mainland (*car ferry April–Sept from Knightstown*), a theatrical tower (now the heritage centre) guards the bridge and the inlet at **Caherciveen**; from here there is a 3-mile floral walk along the coast. Daniel O'Connell was born here, and the long main street is lined with pubs. Follow the N70 around the peninsula, passing **Knocknadobar**, the holy mountain, and **Kells Bay**. This wildly romantic landscape is peopled with heroes from Ireland's legendary past; Fionn MacCumhaill and the warrior band, the Fianna, hunted these glens, and close by, round **Glenbeigh**, the landscape is rich in memories of Oísin, son of Fionn. The Bog Village Museum (*open Mar–Oct daily 9–6; adm*) just east of Glenbeigh depicts life in the rural 1800s.
Lunch: In Glenbeigh or Killorglin, *see* below.

Afternoon: Back on the N70, the Ring of Kerry ends with attractive **Killorglin**, which grew up around an Anglo-Norman castle (now ruined) on the River Laune, and is famous for its August cattle and horse fair, the Puck Fair. Continue on the N70 to **Castlemaine** beneath the **Slieve Mish Mountains** and then past the vast, beautiful **Strand of Inch** through Annascaul to the fishing port of **Dingle**. Gaily painted houses and busy streets lead you to the harbour, and there is a delightful holiday atmosphere. The choice of restaurants, pub food and traditional music is excellent, but the major attraction is Fungi, a playful bottle-nosed dolphin who wandered into the bay in 1983 and decided to stay. There is a model of him on display at the **Dingle Aquarium** (*www.dingle-oceanworld.ie; open daily 10–6; adm*).
Dinner and Sleeping: In Dingle, *see* below.

Day 3

Lunch in Glenbeigh
Red Fox Inn, t (066) 976 9184 (*moderate*). A welcoming inn, if a little touristy.
Towers Hotel Restaurant, t (066) 976 8212 (*expensive–inexpensive*). Restaurant and bar offering fine dining and cheaper bar meals.

Lunch in Killorglin
Nick's Restaurant and Pub, Lower Bridge Street, **t** (066) 976 1219 (*expensive*). Serves large portions of seafood and steaks.

Dinner in Dingle
Beginish Restaurant, Green Street, **t** (066) 915 1321 (*expensive*). Enthusiastic staff and wonderful seafood; it has a conservatory.
The Chart House, The Mall, Dingle, **t** (066) 915 2255 (*expensive*). Seriously good food.
Armada, Strand Street, Dingle, **t** (066) 915 1505 (*expensive–moderate*). Traditional west coast restaurant with a reputation for quality fare.

The Forge, Holy Ground, **t** (066) 915 2590 (*moderate*). Steaks and seafood.
The Half-door, John Street, **t** (066) 915 1600 (*moderate*). Excellent, imaginative food. Very good value.

Sleeping in Dingle
Doyle's Townhouse, John Street, **t** (066) 915 1174, *www.doylesofdingle.com* (*expensive*). One of the most enjoyable, comfortable places to stay in the country. The rooms are full of individuality, and the sitting-room shelves and tables groan with interesting books over which you can linger by a warm fire. The bar and restaurant next door are famous for their conviviality.
The Captain's House, The Mall, **t** (066) 915 1531 (*moderate*). B&B with a seafaring tradition, plenty of awards adorning the walls and wonderful turf fires.
Greenmount Guesthouse, t (066) 915 1414 (*moderate*). Mrs Curran's guesthouse has been recommended by readers. Enjoy lots of choice for breakfast.

Day 4: Europe's Westernmost Points

Morning: Continue west through **Ventry** and **Slea Head**, looking out for **Doonbeg Fort**, which can be seen from the road. From Slea Head you can see the uninhabited Blasket Islands; the excellent Blasket Centre (*open Easter–Sept daily 10–6; July–Aug daily 10–7; adm*) in **Dunquin** focuses on the islands' story, and you can take a boat trip there from the harbour. This little place became famous after the film *Ryan's Daughter* was filmed here; another unusual attraction is 'The Enchanted Forest', a fairytale museum full of fantasy, fun and friendly bears taking a journey through a mythical forest of the seasons.

Lunch: In Ballyferriter, *see* below.

Afternoon: Back on the mainland again, heading north up round the peninsula, you arrive at **Ballyferriter**, a small village popular because of good beaches. There's a friendly co-operative here that grows parsley to export to France. They are also very keen on preserving their heritage: the Gaelic language, antiquities and beautiful scenery. Their displays on the archaeology, flora and fauna of the area can be seen at the Chorca Dhuibhne Heritage Centre (*open Easter and June–Sept 10.30– 5.30; adm*). East of Ballyferriter, signs point the way to the **Oratory of Gallarus**, the most perfect relic of early Irish architecture. This tiny, inverted, tent-shaped church may go back as far as the 8th century. Continue on east to **Castlegregory**, where you can explore the sandy spit of the peninsula that ends at Rough Point; a trip can be made to **Illauntannig**, one of the Magharee islands, with the remains of an old monastic ruin.

Dinner and Sleeping: In Castlegregory or nearby Camp, *see* below.

Day 4

Lunch in Ballyferriter
Smerwick Harbour Hotel, t (066) 915 6470 (*moderate*). The bar-restaurant inside this hotel specializes in seafood and char-grilled steak.

Dinner in Castlegregory
Ned Natterjack's, t (066) 713 9491 (*moderate*). Cottage-style pub with lots of character. Live music, and good bar menus.
Spillane's, Fahamore Maharees, near Castlegregory, t (066) 713 9125 (*moderate*). Off the beaten track, but this traditional pub is worth the journey: great hospitality and great food.

Dinner in Camp
Cottage Restaurant, t (066) 713 0022 (*moderate*). Bright modern restaurant serving excellent food including good vegetarian dishes.

James Ashe, t (066) 413 0133 (*inexpensive*). Traditional old pub full of character, with a limited menu.

Sleeping in Castlegregory
Aisling House, t (066) 713 9134 (*inexpensive*). Wonderful guesthouse – clean and comfortable, friendly, nice rooms and a delicious breakfast.
Crutch's Hillville House Hotel, Conor Pass Road, t (066) 713 8118 (*moderate*). A truly delightful country house hotel near Fermoyle beach. Generous-sized rooms and home cooking make this a relaxing haven for the night.
The Fuchsia House, West Main Street, t (066) 713 9508 (*moderate*). Comfortable B&B, with excellent breakfasts and home baking.

Sleeping in Camp
Suan Na Mara, Lisnagree, Castlegregory Road, t (066) 713 9258 (*moderate*). An immaculately clean and friendly B&B with its own pitch and putt!

Day 5: The North Kerry Coast

Morning: North Kerry has none of the splendour of Dingle, but rather a quiet charm. **Blennerville** used to be the port for Tralee, although it is now silted up; the shipyard includes a visitor's centre (*open April–Oct daily 10–6; adm*). This was the initial site for the construction of the *Jeanie Johnston*, a replica of an 18th-century passenger ship built from the original plans. Continue north from **Tralee** (*see* p.204), perhaps taking the coast road through the village of **Spa**, once famous for its sulphurous waters, and the R558 to **Fenit**, a small fishing port, from where the coastal views on a bright day are stunning. After a few miles on the R551 you will come to **Ardfert**, a very well-known ecclesiastical site, with its cathedral (*open May–Sept daily 9.30–6.30; guided tours; adm*), a noble Norman building from the 13th century, built on St Brendan's original foundation. Beside it is Temple-na-griffin, a late Gothic ruin.

Lunch: In Fenit or Ardfert, *see* below.

Afternoon: Take the R556 to the northern resort of **Ballybunion**. The golden sand is divided by a black rocky promontory on which perches the dramatic remains of a 14th-century castle. Besides good sea bathing, you can have a relaxing hot seaweed bath right down on the beach (popular with jockeys after the Listowel races). The views of Kerry Head and Loop Head are magnificent and there are bracing walks along the cliffs to Beal Point. The Heritage Centre and Museum at Greenfields on Church Road has relics from the Marconi Station and the Lartigue mono-railway. In the morning, head back to Killarney via Listowel.

Dinner and Sleeping: In Ballybunion or Listowel, *see* below.

Day 5

Lunch in Fenit
The Tankard, Kilfenora, Fenit, t (066) 713 6164 (*moderate*). Dramatic remote shoreside location overlooking the Atlantic. Excellent food.
West End Bar and Restaurant, t (066) 713 6246 (*moderate*). French-influenced fare, making the most of local produce.

Lunch in Ardfert
Kate Browne's Pub, t (066) 34055. Extensive bar menu in a pub with lots of character.

Dinner in Ballybunion
Cliff House Hotel, Cliff Road, t (068) 27777 (*moderate*). A wide selection of dishes.

Dinner in Listowel
Allo's Bar and Bistro, 41 Church Street, t (068) 22880 (*moderate*). Great food – far better than just pub grub.
Listowel Arms Hotel, t (068) 21500 (*moderate*). Famous old hotel with a new restaurant and

bar overlooking the River Feale. Traditional fare such as beef and stout casserole.

Dinner and Sleeping in Ballybunion
Iragh Ti Connor, Main Street, t (068) 27112, raghticonnor@eircom.net (*expensive*). Warm and welcoming, with open fires, a cosy bar, period furniture and walled gardens.
Harty Costello Townhouse, Main Street, t (068) 27129 (*expensive–moderate*). Upmarket inn, serving Ballybunion's golfers. The restaurant offers an extensive seafood menu. *Restaurant closed Sun.*
Teach de Broc, Links Road, t (068) 27581 (*expensive–moderate*). Relaxing guest house next to the famous Ballybunion links.

Sleeping in Listowel
Listowel Arms, The Square, t (068) 21500 (*moderate*). Old-fashioned country hotel and hospitality.
Burntwood House, Ballylongford Road, t (068) 21516 (*inexpensive*). Secluded Georgian house one mile from Listowel.

Limerick (Shannon)

Limerick City boasts the much-lauded Hunt Collection of art treasures, but at first sight has something rather drab about it which it is hard to put your finger on. The city is largely Georgian in character – a grid pattern of streets has been superimposed on to the older town, which followed the curve of the River Shannon. The novelist Kate O'Brien came from the respectable middle class that moulded this city in the 19th century, and she describes it as having 'the grave, grey look of Commerce'.

Yet Limerick is doing its best to forget the hard times of the 1940s–60s, and has recently been given a substantial facelift. It has a reputation for smart clothes shops, and the art school here has produced some talented clothes designers. For a city of its size (52,000), it also has a buzzy nightlife. Previously high levels of unemployment and emigration have significantly decreased recently as new industries have been set up; and the cultural life is healthy, with an excellent arts centre. The city is very proud of its musical heritage, with a strong choral tradition, chamber music and marching bands. Suzanne Murphy, the opera singer, was born here. The people of Limerick are not so proud of the descriptions of their city in Frank McCourt's *Angela's Ashes*, but a walking tour (*daily at 2.30 from the tourist office, Arthurs Quay, t (061) 318106*) points out some of the places mentioned in his grim, exuberant portrait of life in 1930s–40s Limerick. Walking tours of the medieval city (King's Island) leave from St Mary's Action Centre, 44 Nicholas Street (*t (061) 318106, daily at 11am and 2.30pm*).

Like Derry, Limerick is a symbolic city, full of memories, and there is lots to see that reveals Limerick's more ancient past. It was founded in AD 922 by the Norsemen, and has always been an important fording place on the River Shannon; in 1997 the city celebrated the 800th anniversary of its royal charter. More concrete evidence of the past is the massive round tower of King John's Castle, built in 1200, which is on the river guarding Thomond Bridge and is one of the best examples of fortified Norman architecture in the country. The motto of the city is *Urbs antiqua fuit studiisque asperrima belli* ('an ancient city inured to the arts of war'). The history of the city is certainly stirring. In the wars of 1691 it was eventually surrendered to the Williamite Commander Ginkel after a fierce battering from his guns. The siege that preceded the surrender is stored away in the psyche of Irishmen. During the 1690s there were three struggles going on: the struggle of Britain and her Protestant allies to oppose the ascendancy in Europe of Catholic France; the struggle of Britain to subdue Ireland; and the struggle between the Protestant planter families and the Catholic Irish for the leadership of Ireland. The French supplied money and commanders to help Catholic James II wrest his crown back from the Protestant William of Orange. The majority of the Catholic Irish supported the Jacobite cause, and many joined up. It is part of Irish folk memory that the French commander St Ruth and King James were asses, and that the Irish commander Patrick Sarsfield was intelligent, daring and brave. The Irish army had been beaten at the Boyne under St Ruth and had retreated to Limerick, where the walls were said to be paper thin. William began a siege while he waited for the arrival of big guns, but Patrick Sarsfield led a daring raid on the siege train from Dublin and destroyed it. Sarsfield rode through the night with 600 horses into the Clare Hills, forded the Shannon and continued on through the Slievefelim Mountains. Finally, he swooped down on William III's huge consignment of guns and blew them skywards. His action saved Limerick from destruction for a time, when the siege was abandoned. When William did break through the Limerick walls, he sent in 10,000 men to wreak havoc, but the women and children of the city fought alongside their men, and they beat back the invaders. The second siege began the following year, and this time heavy losses were inflicted when the Williamite leader, Ginkel, gained control of Thomond Bridge. The promised help never came, and there was nothing to do but negotiate an honourable treaty. This Sarsfield did, and he agreed to take himself and 10,000 Irish troops off to France, in what became known as 'The Flight of the Wild Geese'. But the terms of the treaty were not carried out and the stone beside Thomond Bridge, where it was supposed to have been signed, is now known as 'The Stone of the Violated Treaty'. In the Roman Catholic Cathedral of St John is the Sarsfield Monument by the sculptor John Lawlor (1820–1901).

Old English Town and its Irish counterpart across the river are the most interesting parts of Limerick to wander in. **English Town**, the old Viking town of Limerick, is on an island formed by the Shannon and what is called the Abbey River (a branch of the Shannon). The Vikings and later the Normans tried to keep the native Irish from living and trading in the city area, so the Irish settled on the other side of the Abbey River – in **Irish Town**. A short circular walk takes you round the main places of interest. One great way to appreciate the beauty of the Shannon is to take a hovercraft trip up and down the river (*enquire at the tourist office, **t** (061) 317522*).

In the city centre is the tourist office and **Arthurs Quay Park**, between the Shannon and the city's sparkling new shopping district. From here, cross the river by Sarsfield Bridge, then turn right up Clancy's Strand, which gives you a good view of the city. This passes the **Treaty Stone**, a block of limestone, and leads to **Thomond Bridge** and the Old Town, passing by King John's Castle. You can visit **King John's Castle** (*t (061) 360788; open mid- April–Oct daily 10–5, Nov–Mar 10.30–4.30; adm*), which has had two floors converted into an interpretative centre with displays of various instruments of early warfare and details of the castle's role in Irish history. The **Limerick Museum** (*t (061) 417826; open Tues–Sat 10–1 and 2.15–5; adm*), now installed in its new home next to the castle, houses an impressive collection of items from the Neolithic, Bronze and Iron Ages, as well as the city's civic treasures, including the famous 'Nail' or pedestal, formerly in the Exchange (now gone, except for a fragment of the façade in Nicholas Street), where the merchants of Limerick used to pay their debts (hence the expression 'paying on the nail').

Walk down Nicholas Street to **St Mary's Cathedral**, the only ancient church building left in the city, built in 1172 by Donal Mor O'Brien, King of Munster. Inside, it has plenty of atmosphere, monuments and impressive furnishings including some superb 15th-century oak misericords (choir stalls) carved into the shapes of fantastic beasts such as the cockatrice and griffin. They are known as mercy seats because, although it looked as if the singers were standing, they could half sit or lean on a ledge. The oak for these and the barrel-vaulted roof came from the Cratloe Woods in County Clare. The cathedral was vandalized by Cromwell's soldiers, although it still has its

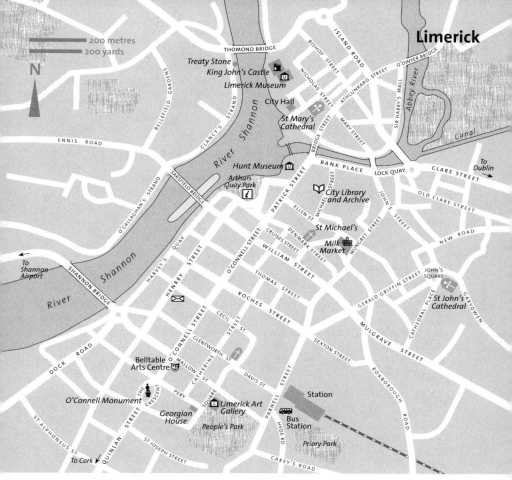

200 metres
200 yards

N

THOMOND BRIDGE

Treaty Stone
King John's Castle
Limerick Museum

City Hall

St Mary's
Cathedral

BELLEFIELD GARDENS

CLANCY'S STRAND

ENNIS ROAD

River Shannon

Hunt Museum

Arthurs
Quay Park

BANK PLACE

LOCK QUAY

CLARE STREET

To
Dublin

OLD CLARE STREET

City Library
and Archive

SARSFIELD BRIDGE

O'CALLAGHAN'S STRAND

PATRICK STREET

ELLEN ST

St Michael's

NEW ROAD

HARVEY'S QUAY

Shannon

To
Shannon
Airport

SHANNON BRIDGE

River

O'CONNELL STREET

HENRY STREET

CRUISES STREET

DENMARK STREET

WILLIAM STREET

Milk
Market

MUNGRET STREET

JOHN'S STREET

THOMAS STREET

ROCHES STREET

GERALD GRIFFIN STREET

JOHN'S
SQUARE

St John's
Cathedral

CECIL STREET

CATHEDRAL PLACE

GLENTWORTH ST

CONNELL STREET

MULGRAVE STREET

SEXTON STREET

ROXBOROUGH ROAD

DOCK ROAD

Belltable
Arts Centre

MALLOW ST

CATHERINE ST

DAVIS ST

PARNELL STREET

Station

O'Connell Monument

THE CRESCENT

PERY STREET

Georgian
House

Limerick Art
Gallery

People's Park

Bus
Station

ST ALPHONSUS ST

QUINLAN ST

ST JOSEPH STREET

HYDE RD

Priory Park

To Cork

CAREY'S ROAD

pre-Reformation limestone high altar. Note the spectacular chandeliers. The Hiberno-Romanesque doorway on the west side is splendid, and the graveyard and garden surrounding the cathedral are charming. In summer a *son et lumière* show about Limerick is put on here (*nightly at 9.15pm*).

A few minutes' walk down Bridge Street and over the little Abbey River brings you to the best thing in Limerick – the Old Custom House in Rutland Street. This restored 18th-century building is now the home of the **Hunt Museum** (*t (061) 312833; open Mon–Sat 10–5, Sun 2–5*) and a rare example of the architecture of Davis Ducart. John Hunt was a noted art historian and Celtic archaeologist who died in the 1970s. He and his wife Gertrude had a remarkable European collection which they gathered over 40 years, containing a hoard of archaeological finds considered the second most important in Ireland. Beyond that, there is 18th-century silver: jewels, including early Christian brooches; paintings (one by Picasso); and Egyptian, Roman, Greek and medieval carved statues and artefacts, including the 9th-century bronze Cashel Bell, the largest in Ireland, found near Cashel town in 1849. As self-portraits go, the one by Robert Fagin with his half-naked wife is rather stunning; so, in a different way, is the

Getting There

Ryanair, British European, BA and Aer Lingus fly to Shannon Airport; see **Travel**, pp.6–7. You can also fly direct from North America, see p.9.

Getting from the Airport

Bus Eireann (**t** (061) 313333) runs a regular **bus** service from Shannon Airport to the bus/train station on Parnell Street; the trip takes 45mins and costs €7. A **taxi** costs around €30.

Shannon Airport offers a variety of duty-free goods and Irish specialities: cut crystal glass, Connemara rugs, Donegal tweed and so on.

Getting Around

By Train and Bus

Limerick City train and bus depots are together on Parnell Street. Bus Eireann runs a **bus** service to Cork, Ennis, Tipperary, Dublin and Waterford. **Bus Eireann, t** (061) 313333.

From Limerick there are **trains** to Dublin, Cork and Clonmel/Waterford/Rosslare.

By Car

Traffic has become one of Limerick City's biggest problems; parking isn't easy either, and most of the centre is a disc parking zone.

Car Hire

Budget, t (903) 27711; Shannon Airport, **t** (061) 471361 *www.budgetcarrental.ie*.

SIXT Irish Car Rentals, t 1850 206088; Shannon Airport, **t** (061) 472649; Ennis Road, Limerick, **t** (061) 206000.

Thrifty Car Rental, t (1800) 515 800; Shannon Airport, **t** (061) 471770 *www.thrifty.ie*.

By Bike

Emerald Alpine, 1 Patrick Street, **t** (061) 416983. Bike hire.

Festivals

Limerick International Band Music Festival, nearest weekend to St Patrick's Day (17 March). Mixture of concert bands, marching bands and street entertainment.

Food Festival, June.

Agricultural Show, August.

Lisdoonvarna Matchmaking Festival, September. Festival with traditional music, dancing and matchmaking.

Sionna, October. Festival of traditional music.

Limerick Racing Festival, December.

Tourist Information

Limerick City: Arthurs Quay, **t** (061) 317522, **f** (061) 317939; *open all year*.

Shannon Airport: **t** (061) 471664; *open all year*.

Shopping

Art Galleries

Belltable Arts Centre, 69 O'Connell Street, **t** (061) 319866.

The Dolmen, Honan's Quay, **t** (061) 417929.

Limerick City Gallery of Art, Carnegie Building, Pery Square, **t** (061) 310633.

Crafts

Convent of the Good Shepherd Sisters, Clare Street. Quality Limerick lace.

Irish Handcrafts, Arthurs Quay and 26 Patrick Street. Woollens and tweeds.

Martin O'Driscoll, Merchant's Quay. Popular gold- and silversmith.

Potato Market, Merchant's Quay.

Fusion, Spring Rice House, Upper Mallow Street, **t** (061) 314511. Collection of works by various artists and craft workers for sale.

Delicacies

The Food Hall, Vintage House, Roches Street. Foodie heaven in the heart of the city, with a particularly good range of cheese.

Quigley's Bakery, 39 Cruises Street. Established since 1890, Some of the best breads and cakes in the city.

The Milk Market. Saturday morning market, a must for picking up fine local produce.

Sports and Activities

Golf

Shannon Golf Club, Shannon Airport, **t** (061) 471849.

Limerick Golf Club, Ballyclough, **t** (061) 414083.

Limerick County Golf and Country Club, Ballyneely, **t** (061) 351881.

Horse-racing
Limerick, four-day meeting, end of December.

Where to Stay

The Castletroy Park, Dublin Road, **t** (061) 335566, **f** 331117, *www.castletroy-park.ie* (*expensive*). Modern four-star hotel with an uninspiring exterior, but the best accommodation in the city and good food.

Jurys Hotel, Ennis Road, **t** (061) 327777, *www.jurysdoyle.com* (*expensive*). Modern and convenient.

Hanratty's Hotel, 5 Glentworth Street, **t** (061) 410999 (*moderate–inexpensive*). Limerick's oldest hotel (1797), pleasant and up to date.

Railway Hotel, Parnell Street, **t** (061) 413653, *www.railway.ie* (*moderate–inexpensive*). Old-fashioned and comfortable family-run hotel.

Alexandra Guest House, 5–6 O'Connell Avenue, **t** (061) 318472, *info@alexandra.iol.ie* (*inexpensive*). Attractive Victorian house with en suite rooms and only 5mins' walk from the city centre.

Mount Gerard, O'Connell Avenue, **t** (061) 314981 (*inexpensive*). Family B&B conveniently close to the city centre.

Trebor, Ennis Road, **t** (061) 454632 (*inexpensive*). Comfortable family home, short walk from city centre. *Closed Nov–Mar.*

Self-catering
Shannon Development Tourist Office, **t** (061) 361555, *www.shannonregiontourism.ie.*

Eating Out

Brulées, corner Henry St/Mallow St, **t** (061) 319931 (*expensive*). Classic dining using the best of Irish produce. Interesting vegetarian dishes also offered.

Tiger Lilies Bistro, 9B Ellen St, **t** (061) 317484 (*expensive–moderate*). Atmospheric renovation of an old warehouse. International menu with lots of good fish dishes.

Pauls, 59 O'Connell St, **t** (061) 316600 (*expensive–moderate*). Classic dishes with seafood, pasta and grilled meat specialities.

Du Cartes at the Hunt Museum, Old Custom House, Rutland St, **t** (061) 312662 (*moderate*). Delightful lunchtime café. *Closed evenings.*

Copper & Spice, 2 Cornmarket Row, **t** (061) 313620 (*moderate*). Fabulous authentic Indian and Thai cuisine including wonderful tandoori dishes.

Locke Bar and Restaurant, 3 Georges Quay, **t** (061) 413733 (*moderate*). Cheery 18th-century pub serving carvery lunches and *à la carte* in the first floor restaurant. Irish fare with a modern twist.

Sorrels, Jurys Hotel, Ennis Road, **t** (061) 327777 (*moderate*). Friendly hotel restaurant.

The Old Quarter, 2 Little Ellen St, **t** (061) 401190 (*moderate*). Art Deco-styled bistro with a wide choice of tempting dishes.

Belltable Arts Centre Café, 69 O'Connell Street, **t** (061) 319866 (*inexpensive*). Tasty lunches and a great choice of cakes. *Daytime only.*

Entertainment and Nightlife

Pubs and Clubs
Anbars, 49-50 Thomas St, **t** (061) 317799. Award-winning Italian influenced restaurant and nightclub.

Brazen Head, O'Connell Street, **t** (061) 417412. Popular pub and eatery, housing an after-hours club called 'Teds'.

Dolan's Pub and Restaurant, 3–4 Dock Road, **t** (061) 314483, *www.dolans.ie*. Lively venue in the old docklands area, with decent pub grub and accommodation. Live gigs by traditional musicians in the Dolan Warehouse.

Thady O'Neills Pub, Ennis Road, **t** (061) 322777. Irish music nightly.

Traditional Music
Belltable Arts Centre, 69 O'Connell Street, **t** (061) 319866. Great live arts centre, with especially good theatre, film and exhibitions during Limerick's many festivals.

Unversity Concert Hall, Limerick University, **t** (061) 331549, *www.uch.ie*. The largest classical concert hall in Ireland.

An Sibín, Royal George Hotel, O'Connell St, **t** (061) 414566. Traditional Irish music.

The Locke, Georges Quay, **t** (061) 413733. Old bar dates back to 1724; relaxed atmosphere.

bronze horse by Leonardo da Vinci. The fascinating and beautiful objects are too numerous to list, but you could easily spend most of a day there, taking a break in the café before going back for more. Around the corner in Michael Street, the **Granary** is a fine example of an 18th-century Georgian warehouse, which has been recently restored as the home of the City Library and Archive.

After the 1760s, when the city walls were dismantled, English and Irish Town merged and Georgian streets and squares were built. **John's Square** has the lofty spire of the Victorian Gothic St John's Cathedral, as well as a number of lovely old buildings of the mid-18th century, some of which have been restored after years of neglect. From here, a walk up Brennan's Row and a right on Sean Heuson Place brings you to the **Milk Market**; scene of a busy farmers' country market on Saturday mornings and an arts and crafts market on Fridays. There are also permanent shops open here.

More fine Georgian streets can be found on the southern edge of the city centre, around the **Crescent**, a development of the early 1800s at the southern end of O'Connell Street, and around **People's Park**. At 2 Pery Square a recently restored **Georgian house** is now open (*t (061) 314130; open Mon–Fri 10–4; adm*). Close to the entrance of the park, off Pery Square, the **Limerick Art Gallery** (*t (061) 310633; open Mon–Fri 10–6, Sat 10–5, Sun 2–5*) has a collection of modern Irish paintings. The beautiful lace shown here is made by the Good Shepherd Sisters in Clare Street, on the Dublin Road. The **Belltable Arts Centre** (*t (061) 319866*) is situated to the southwest and various Irish travelling theatre companies stop off here; it's worth a phone call to find out what's on. There is also a small gallery that shows the work of many local artists and is part of the international EV+A Art Exhibition held around the city.

Three art galleries are housed in the university at Castletroy, Plassey, on the edge of the city, off the main Dublin road (N7); the **National Self-Portrait Collection** is the most worthwhile. The university is also home to the Irish Chamber Orchestra and has a fine concert hall. For those interested in contemporary art, one of the best galleries is **The Dolmen** on Honan's Quay.

Day Trips and Overnighters from Limerick

Bunratty

Just north of the River Shannon, near the airport on the N18, is Bunratty. It's a small village completely dominated by the huge attraction that is Bunratty Castle and the Folk Park which is in the castle grounds. Despite being a very commercial tourist enterprise, both the castle and the folk park are very interesting and well-conceived; it can take a whole day to tour. It is also perfect for inclement weather.

Bunratty Castle (*t (061) 360788; open Sept–May daily 9.30–5.30; June–Aug daily 9–6; last adm to castle 4pm, last adm to Folk Park 4.15pm; adm*) is a splendid tower-house standing beside a small stone bridge over the River Ratty; a perfect, restored example of a Norman-Irish castle keep. The present castle dates from 1460, though it is at least the fourth to have been built on the same spot. It was built by the McNamaras, who were a *sept* of the O'Briens, and it remained an O'Brien stronghold off and on until

Getting There

There is a regular **bus** service from Limerick bus station to Bunratty, taking 20mins.

Shopping

Bunratty Folk Park Gift Shop, Bunratty Castle. Woven clothing, candles and prints.

Bunratty Village Mills, Bunratty. Shopping complex including a Tipperary Crystal shop, a Meadows and Byrne home furnishing store and a restaurant.

The Bunratty Winery, Bunratty (behind Durty Nelly's Bar). Sells a particularly good mead.

Eating Out

Muses Restaurant, Bunratty House Mews, **t** (061) 364082 (*expensive*). In the cellars of an attractive house built in 1846 by a hopeful son waiting to inherit the castle from his father. Seafood and local organic produce feature strongly. *Evenings only.*

Gallagher's of Bunratty, Main Street, **t** (061) 363363 (*moderate*). Charming thatched cottage specializing in local seafood.

Mac's Pub, Bunratty Folk Park, **t** (061) 360788 (*moderate*). Good seafood.

Durty Nelly's, Main Street, **t** (061) 364861 (*inexpensive*). Pub and eating house popular both with locals and visitors.

1712, and played an important part in the struggle between the Anglo-Norman de Clares and the Thomonds. It was then occupied by the parliamentarian Admiral Penn, the father of William Penn who founded Pennsylvania. After years of neglect it was bought by Lord Gort in 1954, who restored it with the help of Tourism Ireland and the Office of Public Works. They have managed to recreate a 15th-century atmosphere, and there is a wonderful collection of 14–17th-century furniture, tapestries and early portraits. The stairs to the upper apartments are narrow and steep, which can make things difficult when the place is crowded, but you get a real feeling of what it was like to be one of the privileged in those times, and the mellow simplicity of the furnishings is very attractive. In the evenings the castle is a memorable setting for medieval-style banquets (*t (061) 360788; nightly at 5.30 and 8.45, booking necessary*).

In the grounds surrounding the castle, the **folk park** (*details as castle*) displays examples of houses from every part of the Shannon region; many of them were re-erected here after being saved from demolition during the Shannon Airport extension. The various types of cottage range from the wealthier small farmer's house, with a small parlour, down to the cabin of a landless labourer. They are all furnished with authentic cottage pieces; one constant is the dresser-cum-henhouse, keeping the fowl snug in the house at night. Patchwork quilts, utensils, ornaments and pictures tell a million stories about life in the olden days, while outside the cottages you can wander around the vegetable patches and hay stooks, and watch the pigs, donkeys, doves and chickens. Inside some of the cottages there are people who can tell you about a lifestyle that has all but disappeared now; you may even get a taste of the scones baking on the open turf fire. You can see butter-making, basket-weaving and all the traditional skills that made people nearly self-sufficient. Village life is depicted, too; the school, the musty-smelling doctor's house with its oil cloth on the floor, the post office selling stamps and sweets and various shops selling crafts and old linens, as well as a bar where you can have a good glass of creamy Guinness. The park's newest addition, Hazelbrook House, built in 1898, was home to the Hughes brothers, who started Ireland's famous HB ice-cream. The Regency walled garden, with its period design and planting, must not be missed either.

Adare

About 10 miles southwest of Limerick, Adare (*Ath Dara*: 'Ford of the Oak Tree') is set in richly timbered land through which the little Maigue river flows. This village has attracted visitors for many years. There is only one wide street, **Main Street**, set on both sides with pretty thatched cottages, many of which house antique shops, craft shops or restaurants. The village is noted for its fine ecclesiastical ruins, but first notice the restored village washing-pool opposite the Trinitarian Abbey, just off Main Street. You can imagine the stories and scandal that might have been exchanged here as the village women washed their clothes. The finest ruin is the **Franciscan Friary**, founded in 1464 by Thomas, Earl of Kildare. (The village belonged to the Kildare branch of the Fitzgeralds or Geraldines.) The friary was attacked and burned by parliamentary forces, but its ruins are beautifully proportioned and can be viewed at a distance from the long narrow bridge of 14 arches (*c.* 1400) on the outskirts of the village, on the N20 going north. If you want to go right up to it, it is in the heart of the Adare Manor Golf Club, so check with the golf club office at the entrance.

The modern village has grown up around the rest of the ecclesiastical buildings. The **Augustinian Priory**, now used as the Church of Ireland church, was founded in 1315 by the Earl of Kildare. It was restored in 1807 by the first Earl of Dunraven; he and his family did much to protect the old buildings, and built the thatched cottages in Main Street in the 1820s. His family, the Dunravens, used to own the Gothic Tudor revival-style manor house whose lush parklands surround the village (now a luxury hotel with formal gardens). The church has carvings of animals and human heads, and gives a good idea of what an Irish medieval church must have looked like.

Desmond Castle, on the banks of the Maigue beside the bridge, was built in the 13th century on the site of an earlier ring fort. It is a fine example of feudal architecture with its square keep, curtain walls, two great halls, kitchen, gallery and stables.

Getting There

There is an hourly **bus** service from Limerick bus station to Adare. It takes only 20mins.

Tourist Information

Adare: Heritage Centre, Main Street, **t** (061) 396666, **f** 396932; *open daily 9–6.*

Eating Out

Adare Manor Hotel, Adare, **t** (061) 396566, *www.adaremanor.com* (*luxury*). Original house of the Earls of Dunraven. Mixture of Victorian, Gothic and Tudor Revival fantasy, with beautiful grounds, horse riding, clay pigeon shooting and an 18-hole golf course designed by Robert Trent Jones. The magnificent **Oak Room** restaurant offers fine dining: classic French cuisine is served, but with a modern Irish twist and the finest of ingredients.

Dunraven Arms Hotel, **t** (061) 396633, *www.dunravenhotel.com* (*expensive*). Old-world hotel, developed from its core – an 18th-century inn. The **Maigue Restaurant** has a delightful formal atmosphere – local beef and salmon are the specialities here. The **Inn Between**, across the road, is a more informal eatery.

The Wild Geese, Rose Cottage, **t** (061) 396451 (*expensive*). Contemporary Irish cooking at its best in a wonderful romantic cottage setting.

O'Coileain, Main Street (*inexpensive*). Traditional pub offering simple food and good conversation.

Getting There

There is a limited **bus** service between Parnell Street Station and Croom. Departures at 8.30am (takes 1½hrs) or noon (takes 30mins), returning at 5pm (takes 30mins).

Eating Out

Croom Mills, t (061) 397130. During the day the **Waterfront Bistro** serves good country fare and home baking. The new **Mill Race** restaurant offers fine dining in the evenings.

Croom

Croom, right in the middle of County Limerick, 12 miles from the city and in a charming position on the Maigue river, is celebrated as the meeting place of the 18th-century Gaelic poets of the Maigue. Fortunately, their poetry is available in translation, since it is unforgettable for its wit and feeling. It is here that the light verse of the 'limerick' was first popularized, to be taken up later by Edward Lear.

An old **castle** of the Geraldines is hidden behind a wall on the southern approach to the village. Croom was frequently attacked by the O'Briens, whose territory it bordered. Their battle cry was '*Lamh laid ir abu*' ('the strong hand forever') and it was always met by the rallying cry of the Geraldines, '*Cromadh abu*' ('Croom forever'). The old **mill** (*open April–Oct 10–5; restaurant and craft shop open all year round*) with its huge water wheel has been restored and once again grinds corn, and its interactive exhibition brings the area's rural past to life.

Cashel

Southeast of Limerick, towards the middle of County Tipperary, is one of the landmarks of Ireland, the **Rock of Cashel** (*t (062) 61437, f 62988; open mid June–mid Sept daily 9–7; mid Sept–mid Mar daily 9–4.30; mid Mar–mid June daily 9–5.30; adm*), a steep outcrop of limestone rising out of the rich agricultural land of the Golden Vale, and crowned with the imposing ecclesiastical ruins of the ancient capital of the kings of Munster. The grouping of the bare, broken buildings against the sky is memorable and worth travelling many miles to see. There is a 12th-century round tower; a small chapel known as Cormac's Chapel; a grand cathedral which was built in the 1230s; and a Vicars' Choral Hall, built around 1420. The Vicars' Choral Hall houses some exhibits including St Patrick's Cross. Outside on the rock is a replica of this cross, which was moved inside to protect it from erosion.

The Rock was the seat of ancient chieftains and later the early Munster kings, and upon this naturally well-defended high place there was very likely a stone fortress or *caiseal*. Legend records that in AD 450 St Patrick came to Cashel to baptize either Corc the Third or his brother and successor, Aengus. During the ceremony Patrick is supposed to have driven the sharp point of his pastoral staff into the king's foot by mistake, and the victim bore the wound without a sign, thinking that such pain was all part of becoming a Christian. From that time onwards, Cashel was also called St Patrick's Rock. Brian Boru, High King of Ireland, was crowned here in 977. In 1101 King Murtagh O'Brien granted the Rock to the Church, for its political importance had declined, and it became the See of the Archbishopric of Munster.

The Rock itself and the buildings are in the care of the Office of Public Works, and the guided tour of 40 minutes or so is very interesting. If you want to walk around on your own, you will find **Cormac's Chapel** on your right as you face the main bulk of the cathedral buildings, in the angle formed by the choir and south transept of the cathedral. It was built in the 1130s by the bishop-king Cormac MacCarthy and is a fascinating building architecturally, in a style described as Hiberno-Romanesque. The most Irish thing about Cormac's Chapel is its steep stone roof. As for the rest – the twin towers, the storeys of blank wall arcading, the high gable over the north doorway and most of the stone-cut decoration – it could be German. Inside is a splendid but broken stone sarcophagus of 11th-century work; the ingenious pattern of ribbons and wild beasts which decorate it was probably reintroduced into Ireland by the Vikings. A gilt copper crozier head was found inside the sarcophagus. The head, which is now preserved in the National Museum in Dublin, is late 13th-century French, and richly ornamented with animal and fish forms in enamel, turquoise and sapphire.

The French and German influences at Cashel are not surprising, for there are documented links between Cashel and the Irish monasteries of Cologne and Ratisbon – before the chapel was built, monks were always travelling to and from the Continent. The fascinating carved-stone heads are a feature of Romanesque architecture, also originating in France. One is reminded of the Celtic head cult, and perhaps both Irish and French carvings derive from ancient Celtic monuments, such as can be seen in Roqueperteuse and Entremont in southern France.

As you enter the complex of buildings through the restored **Vicar's Choral Hall** you will see the Cross of St Patrick, probably of the same date as the sarcophagus. Christ is carved on one side and an ecclesiastic, perhaps St Patrick, on the other. The massive base on which it is set is reputed to be the coronation stone of the Munster Kings. The immense ruins of the cathedral built beside Cormac's chapel date from the second half of the 13th century, and were the scene of two deliberate burnings during the Anglo-Irish wars of the Tudors and Cromwell. In 1686 the cathedral was restored and used by the Church of Ireland, but then it was left to decay until Cashel became a National Monument and everything was tidied up. What remains now is a fine example of austere Irish Gothic architecture with a rather short nave, the end of which is taken up with what is known as **the Castle**, a massive tower built to house the bishops in the 15th century. In marked contrast to Cormac's Chapel, everything about the cathedral is superbly grand and delicate.

The **round tower** is roughly 11th-century. You can see the top of it perfectly if you climb to the top of the Castle, plus a wonderful view of the Golden Vale, the hills to the east and west, and Slievenamon in the south. There is a gap in the hills to the north which is said to correspond exactly to the size of the Rock. Legend tells that the Devil bit off the Rock and spat it on to the plain below, hence the name of the mountain: Devil's Bit. Just below, on the plain, is **Hore Abbey**, built by the Cistercians from Mellifont. It is always accessible if you want to visit it. The Rock looks superb at night, particularly during the summer when it is floodlit.

You should also visit **Cashel Folk Village**, nearby (*t (062) 62525, f 62322; open Mar–Oct daily 10–7*), which recreates an Irish village of a century ago.

Getting There

There's a limited **bus** service from Parnell Street bus station to Cashel (changing at Cahir). The service departs at 8.30am and takes 2½ hours. The return bus leaves at 5.15. This gives you a good chance to see the countryside; or you may decide to stay overnight.

Tourist Information

Cashel: Main Street, **t** (062) 61333; *open April–Sept Mon–Sat 10–6.*

Where to Stay

Cashel Palace Hotel, Main Street, **t** (062) 62707, **f** 61521, *www.cashel-palace.ie, reception@cashel-palace.ie (luxury).* Elegant living in an historic and beautiful 18th-century house(formerly a bishop's residence), just off the main street.
Dundrum House Hotel, Dundrum, **t** (062) 71116 *(expensive).* Elegant three-star hotel and country club situated 7 miles from Cashel. It boasts its own 18-hole golf course and health centre.
Baileys of Cashel, Main Street, **t** (062) 61937 *(moderate).* Beautifully restored Georgian house in the heart of town, with a good restaurant.
Dualla House, t (062) 61487 *(moderate).* Georgian manor house in 300 acres 3 miles from Cashel, offering great tranquillity. Excellent breakfast.

Indaville, south of Main Street on N8, **t** (062) 62075 *(inexpensive).* Friendly and comfortable accommodation from Mrs Murphy in a charming home built in 1729.

Eating Out

Chez Hans, Moor Lane, **t** (062) 61177 *(expensive).* In an old church. Excellent food cooked by Hans, who is German. *Dinner only.*
Cashel Palace Hotel, Main Street, **t** (062) 62707 *(expensive–moderate).* Choose between the formal **Four Seasons Restaurant** and the attractive **Cellar**, where the traditional Irish dishes are a speciality, and rather more affordable.
Legends Restaurant, The Kiln, **t** (062) 61292 *(expensive–moderate).* French and Irish menu offered, and a pre-theatre option served for those attending Brú Ború, next door. *Lunch Sun only, dinner Tues–Sat 6.30–9.30.*
Granny's Kitchen, St Patrick's Rock, **t** (062) 61861 *(inexpensive).* Children and vegetarians welcome in a traditional house. *Open 9.30–8 during summer, for breakfast, lunch and dinner daily.*
Baileys of Cashel, Main Street, **t** (062) 61937 *(inexpensive).* Reasonable lunches and dinners in this guest house.
Spearman's Bakery and Tea Room, 97 Main Street, **t** (061) 61143. Excellent home baking available here 9–6. Soups, sandwiches and a vast range of home-made cakes and pastries. An ideal lunch spot. *Closed Sun.*

Cashel Town is a thriving place with a very good hotel, the Cashel Palace, which was built in gracious Queen Anne style in 1730 and used to be the residence of the Church of Ireland archbishops. The architect was Edward Lovett Pearce (1699–1733), who also built the Irish Houses of Parliament in Dublin. It is worth having at least a coffee there so you can get a glimpse of the panelling and carving. The **GPA Bolton Library** (**t** *(062) 61232; open May–Sept; adm*), in the precincts of the **St John the Baptist Cathedral**, has one of the finest collections of 16th- and 17th-century books in Ireland. There are several on exhibition, but you have to contact the dean if you want to get inside the cathedral. The Roman Catholic **church**, also called after St John the Baptist, is in direct contrast to the simplicity of the cathedral – exotic and full of statues. The shop-fronts in Cashel's main street are very colourful and the plastic age has not made too much impact.

Touring from Limerick

Day 1: Foynes, Glin and Kilrush

Morning: At **Foynes**, Limerick's little port 25 miles west of the city, a very interesting hour can be spent in the radio and weather room of the Flying Boat Museum (*open April–Oct 10–6*); between 1939 and 1945 Foynes was famous as a base for seaplanes crossing the Atlantic. Then take the N69 to **Glin**. Glin Castle (*t (068) 34173; open by appt*) is still the ancestral home of the Knights of Glin; the castle is Georgian Gothic with castellations, and noted for its flying staircase, plasterwork and 18th-century furniture, portraits and landscapes. The gardens are beautifully planned and tended.

Lunch: In Glin or Tarbert, *see* below.

Afternoon: Continue west on the N69 to **Tarbert**, where there is a car ferry over the Shannon into County Clare. Drive on north to **Kilrush**, a busy market town with a marina and a heritage centre that explores the role of the landlords, the Vandeleurs, in shaping the town. In the Vandeleur Walled Garden (*open summer 10–6; winter 10–4; adm*), you can enjoy visiting a recently restored walled garden and 420 acres of woodland. The Catholic church has some Harry Clarke stained glass. About a mile away is the harbour, around Cappagh Pier, and in summer you can take boat trips out to **Scattery Island**, founded in the 6th century, to see its monastic remains. The Scattery Island Centre in Kilrush, on the marina (*open April–Oct daily 9.30–6.30*), offers an introduction before you go.

Dinner and Sleeping: In Kilrush, Kilkee or Donail, *see* below.

Day 1

Lunch in Glin
O'Shaughnessy's Pub (*moderate*). Just outside the castle walls is one of Ireland's finest and most historic pubs. Good bar food.

Lunch in Tarbert
Lanterns Hotel, Coast Road, t (068) 36210 (*moderate*). Modern hotel with restaurant and bar dining options, both of which offer some good vegetarian choices.

Dinner in Kilrush
Kelly's Bar and Restaurant, 26 Henry St, t (065) 905 1811 (*moderate*). A welcoming pub with an extensive range of good quality bar food for a tasty casual supper.

Dinner and Sleeping in Kilrush
Crotty's Bar, t (065) 905 2470 (*inexpensive*). Traditional Irish music in a friendly, cosy traditional bar. The rooms above the bar are a little intimate and can be noisy on music nights, but it's a great place for atmosphere.

Dinner and Sleeping in Kilkee
Halpin's Townhouse Hotel, Erin St, t (065) 905 6032 (*moderate*). A great find – a friendly townhouse hotel in the centre of Kilkee, with a cosy bar and a restaurant for more substantial fare.

Kilkee Bay Hotel, Kilrush Road, t (065) 906 0060 (*moderate*). Modern hotel a few minutes from the blue flag beach. The rooms are fairly spacious, and there is a bistro which serves seafood. The hotel also has a nightclub.

Dinner and Sleeping in Donail
Fortfield Farm, t (065) 905 1457 (*moderate*). Comfortable farm bed and breakfast, a few minutes from the Killimer car ferry. Good views make it worth the trouble to find.

Day 2: The Cliffs of Moher, and Into the Burren

Morning: The N67 takes you on north up the Clare coast through Quilty and Lahinch, after which, take the coast road (R478) and head round through **Liscannor**, with its Holy Well of St Brigid, to the **Cliffs of Moher** – they drop down vertically to the foaming sea. Seabirds somehow manage to rest on the steep slopes; sometimes even peregrines can be seen. On a clear day there is a magnificent view of the Twelve Bens, the mountains of Connemara and the three Aran Islands. O'Brien's Tower, on the cliff edge, was built in 1835 by a local landlord. The R468 leads on to **Lisdoonvarna**, the most important spa in Ireland, with a pump room and baths.

Lunch: In Lisdoonvarna, *see* below.

Afternoon: This district is called the **Burren**, and its 50 square miles are dotted with stone forts, walls and megalithic tombs, which blend perfectly with a landscape strewn with strangely shaped rocks left behind by glaciers. You really have to get out of your car and walk here, for the Burren's appeal is gradual. In late May the place becomes starred with sky-blue gentians, geraniums and orchids. Arctic-alpine mountain avens sprawl lavishly over the rocks and Irish saxifrage tufts cover sea-sprayed boulders. No one has yet been able to explain how such a profusion of different plants came to grow together. On the R480 is the great **dolmen tomb of Poulabrone**, one of the most photographed sites. **Ballyvaughan**, an attractive fishing village on the north edge of the Burren, is set in a green wooded vale, an oasis after the bleached plateaux of limestone, mighty terraces and escarpments to the south.

Dinner and Sleeping: In Ballyvaughan, *see* below.

Day 2

Lunch in Lisdoonvarna

Sheedy's Restaurant, in Sheedy's Country House Hotel, t (065) 707 4026 (*expensive–moderate*). Modern Irish cuisine using the best local produce, including Burren lamb.

Kincora House and Gallery Restaurant, t (065) 707 4470 (*moderate*). Fine restaurant and cosy pub dining on offer here in this atmospheric Victorian hostelry.

Roadside Tavern, Kincora Road, t (065) 707 4494 (*inexpensive*). Wood-panelled pub-cum-smoking-house. Delicious smoked trout, salmon and chowder.

Dinner in Ballyvaughan

Gregan's Castle Hotel, near Ballyvaughan, t (065) 707 7005 (*moderate*). Delicious food all day in the Corkscrew Bar, where the cosy fire and low-beamed ceiling are especially welcoming after a long hike.

Hylands Burren Hotel Bar, t (065) 707 7037 (*moderate*). Fine local seafood and Burren lamb are served in a welcoming bar restaurant – complete with turf fires – located at the harbour.

Aillwee Cave Restaurant, t (065) 707 7036 (*inexpensive*). Eating in a cave is rather a novel experience. Delicious soups, pies and cakes. *Lunch only*.

Monk's Bar, t (065) 707 7059 (*inexpensive*). Delicious mussels and brown bread. Traditional music at night.

Sleeping in Ballyvaughan

Gregan's Castle, near Ballyvaughan, t (065) 707 7005, *www.gregans.ie* (*expensive*). Not actually a castle, but an old manor house, with delicious food and comfortable rooms. Overlooking the Burren, amid green gardens in fantastic contrast to the Burren's moonscape, with views over Galway Bay.

Rusheen Lodge, t (065) 707 7092 (*moderate*). Luxury guesthouse.

Ballyvaughan Lodge, t (065) 707 7292 (*inexpensive*). In the heart of the village, this small guest house offers a great welcome.

Day 3: To Ennis via Dysert O'Dea

Morning: **Aillwee Caves** (*t (065) 707 7036; open daily 10–6; Dec 10–1 only; adm*) are two miles south of Ballyvaughan just off the R480. All over the Burren there are hundreds of caves formed by the underground rivers; these ones date back to two million years BC. Continue south on the R480 and take the R476 to Killinaboy and **Corofin**, where you might stop to visit the Clare Heritage Centre (*open May–Oct daily 10–6*). After Corofin, two miles off the R476, is the famous religious settlement of **Dysert O'Dea**. It was started in the 7th century by St Tola, but he probably lived in a cell of wattle and daub; the present ruin is a much-altered, 12th-century, Hiberno-Romanesque church with a badly reconstructed west doorway that now stands in the south wall. The door is sumptuously carved. Beside the church is the stump of a round tower, and about a hundred yards east is a high cross from the 12th century. Dysert O'Dea Castle (*open May–Sept 10–6; adm*) has a heritage centre and is the start of a short walk around the archaeological remains in its vicinity.

Lunch: In Corofin, *see* below.

Afternoon: Just down the R476 is **Ennis**, the busy and attractive county capital. The streets are narrow and winding, and in the centre is a hideous monument to Daniel O'Connell. Right in the middle of the town is Ennis Friary (*open May–late Sept daily 9.30–6.30; rest of the year key with caretaker*), a substantial ruin rich in sculptures and decorated tombs. There is a small museum (*open Mon–Fri*) in a disused church in Harmony Row with objects associated with famous Clare people.

Dinner and Sleeping: In Ennis, *see* below.

Day 3

Lunch in Corofin

Bofey Quinns Bar and Restaurant, Main Street, t (065) 683 7321 (*moderate*). Hearty home-cooked fare, including good seafood.

The Corofin Arms, Main Street, t (065) 683 7373 (*moderate*). Traditional pub offering good pub fare. Beer garden.

Dinner in Ennis

Hal Pino's Restaurant, 7 High Street, t (065) 684 0011 (*expensive*). Modern first-floor restaurant in the town centre, with fine cuisine and a smart atmosphere.

Town Hall Café, Old Ground Hotel, O'Connell Street, t (065) 682 8127 (*moderate*). Varied bistro-style cuisine served unusually in the old town hall.

The Cloister, Abbey Street, t (065) 682 9521 (*moderate–inexpensive*). Old world bar. Good soups, local cheeses and nutty brown bread during the daytime; at night it becomes more formal as a restaurant.

Cruises Pub and Restaurant, Abbey St, t (065) 684 1800 (*moderate–inexpensive*). Great old pub with open fires. Excellent food, especially steak and seafood.

The **Gíór Irish Music Centre** (Friar's Walk, t (065) 684 3103) is worth checking out for its evening performances.

Sleeping in Ennis

Woodstock Hotel, Shanaway Road, t (065) 684 6600, www.woodstockhotel.com (*luxury*). Luxurious hotel with leisure centre and golf course.

Old Ground Hotel, O'Connell St, t (065) 682 8127 (*expensive*). An ivy-clad manor house in the heart of Ennis. Excellent restaurants.

Queen's Hotel, Abbey Street, t (065) 682 8963, www.irishcourthotels.com (*moderate*). Charming hotel overlooking a 13th-century Franciscan abbey.

Newpark House, Tulla Road, t (065) 682 1233 (*moderate*). Historic (1650) house with comfortable rooms, in a quiet woodland setting. *Closed Oct–Easter*.

Day 4: Deep into the Past

Morning: Take the R462 east out of Ennis towards Lough Derg. Turn south to **Broadford**, a pleasant village, and a little way east is **Killaloe**, which sits on the River Shannon surrounded by the hills of Slieve Bernagh. On the bank of the river is St Flannan's Cathedral, a fine 12th-century building built by Donal O'Brien on the site of an earlier church; it has a magnificent Hiberno-Romanesque door, better than anything of its kind in Ireland, and the view from the top of the tower is superb. Nearby is Thorgrim's Stone, the shaft of a cross bearing a runic and ogham inscription of about AD 1000. In the grounds of the cathedral is St Flannan's Oratory with a lovely high stone roof. The Roman Catholic church standing high above the town is believed by some to be on the site of Kincora, the great palace of Brian Boru. Inside the church are some fine stained-glass windows by Harry Clarke, who worked on many church windows in the early decades of the 20th century. Killaloe is connected to **Ballina** in County Tipperary by an elegant bridge of 13 arches.

Lunch: Lunch early, in Killaloe or Ballina, *see* below.

Afternoon: Make your way across country into the heart of County Tipperary via the R499 and R498 to Thurles and then the N62 and N8. **Cashel Town** is a thriving place that used to be the residence of the Church of Ireland archbishops and was built in gracious Queen Anne style in 1730. But one of the landmarks of Ireland is the **Rock of Cashel**, a steep outcrop of limestone crowned with the imposing ecclesiastical ruins of the ancient capital of the kings of Munster. *See* pp.221–3 for more details.

Dinner and Sleeping: In Cashel, *see* below.

Day 4

Lunch in Killaloe

Kincora Hall Hotel, t (061) 376665 (*moderate*). Overlooking its own marina, this new hotel offers fine bar meals.

Lunch in Ballina

Galloping Hogan's, Cullinagh, t (061) 376162 (*moderate*). Ideal for relaxed *al fresco* dining on tranquil Lough Derg.

Goosers Bar and Eating House, Main Street, t (061) 376791 (*moderate*). Popular award-winning restaurant, with plenty of intimate character and inviting open fires.

Dinner in Cashel

Chez Hans, Moor Lane, t (062) 61177 (*expensive*). In an old church. Excellent food cooked by Hans, who is German. *Dinner only*.

Cashel Palace Hotel, Main Street, t (062) 62707 (*expensive–moderate*). Choose between the formal **Four Seasons Restaurant** and the attractive **Cellar**, where the traditional Irish dishes are a speciality.

Granny's Kitchen, St Patrick's Rock, t (062) 61861 (*inexpensive*). Children and vegetarians welcome in a traditional house. *Open 9.30–8 during summer*.

Sleeping in Cashel

Cashel Palace Hotel, Main Street, t (062) 62707, f 61521, *www.cashel-palace.ie*, reception@cashel-palace.ie (*luxury*). Elegant living in an historic and beautiful 18th-century house, just off the main street.

Baileys of Cashel, Main Street, t (062) 61937 (*moderate*). Beautifully restored Georgian house in the heart of town. Good restaurant.

Dualla House, t (062) 61487 (*moderate*). Georgian manor house in 300 acres 3 miles from Cashel, offering great tranquillity. Excellent breakfast.

Indaville, south of Main Street on N8, t (062) 62075 (*inexpensive*). Friendly and comfortable accommodation from Mrs Murphy in a charming home built in 1729.

Day 5: Through the Glen

Morning: Eight miles south of Cashel at the meeting of the N8 and N24, **Cahir** is the nicest sort of Irish town, on the River Suir, with old-fashioned shops, colourfully painted houses and a wide main square with plenty of space to walk and park. It has a magnificent, fully restored 15th-century castle (*t (052) 41011; open mid-June– mid-Sept daily 9–7.30; rest of year daily 9.30–5; guided tours; adm*) on an island in the river. A visit to the castle is memorable as the guides are so enthusiastic and bring to life the defensive tactics of the powerful Ormonde Butlers, who owned the castle: one's head is set spinning with the ingenuity of the portcullis and the holes for pouring burning oil. The Great Hall and other rooms within the castle are furnished.

Lunch: In Cahir or the Glen of Aherlow, *see* below.

Afternoon: Head northeast from Cahir on the N24 to Bansha and turn left on to the R663, which takes you on a lovely drive through the **Glen of Aherlow**, a lush, colourful river valley between the Galtee Mountains and the Slievenamuck Hills. From Galbally at the other end of the Glen, take the R515 to **Kilmallock**, with a castle, a beautiful 13th-century Dominican priory and a museum (*open daily 1.30–5*).

Bruree, 4 miles to the west on the R518, is where Eamon de Valera grew up; he was born in Manhattan, but his mother sent him back here to be reared by his grandmother. The school he went to is now the De Valera Museum (*open Mon–Fri 10–5, Sat and Sun 2–5; adm*). An old corn mill with a huge millwheel makes a striking image as you enter the village from the west. Limerick is 20 miles north on the N20.

Dinner and Sleeping: In Kilmallock or Bruree, *see* below.

Day 5

Lunch in Cahir
Kilcoran Lodge Hotel, t (052) 41288 (*moderate*). A former hunting lodge in spacious grounds, with a good restaurant.
Cahir House Hotel, The Square, t (052) 42727 (*moderate*). Busy market-square inn with bar and restaurant food.
Crock of Gold, 1 Castle Street, t (052) 41951 (*inexpensive*). Small restaurant above craft shop; handy for snacks and light lunches.

Lunch in the Glen of Aherlow
The Glen Hotel, t (062) 56152 (*moderate*). In a spectacular position sheltered by the wooded Glen of Anerlow. Fine cuisine, if a little old-fashioned.

Dinner in Kilmallock
Bulgaden Castle, t (063) 20001 (*moderate*). Two miles north of Kilmallock, this large 18th-century tavern serves good-value traditional pub food.

Dinner in Charleville
The Four Winds, t (063) 89285 (*moderate*). A great old pub serving wholesome bar meals.

Sleeping in Kilmallock
Ash Hill Stud, t (063) 98035, *www.ashhill.com* (*moderate*). Imposing 18th-century pile with large, comfortable bedrooms, glorious plasterwork and shades of Anglo-Irish splendour – the front door leads straight into the stable yard. Set on a working horse farm; one self-catering apartment also available.
Deebert House, t (063) 98106 (*inexpensive*). Georgian house set in magnificent gardens.

Sleeping in Bruree
Cooleen House, t (063) 90584 (*inexpensive*). Very friendly service and fine, old-fashioned rooms in Mrs McDonoogh's whitewashed Georgian farmhouse.
Ballyteigue House, Rockhill, Bruree, t (063) 90575 (*inexpensive*). Mrs Johnson offers warm hospitality and good food in a splendid Georgian farmhouse.

Old Gods, Heroes and Saints

The Celts

Nobody knows exactly when the first Celts arrived in Ireland; it was some time before 1000 BC, with the last wave of people coming around the 3rd century BC. The Greek chroniclers were the first to name these people, calling them *Keltori*. Celt means 'act of concealment', and it has been suggested that they were called 'hidden people' because of their reluctance to commit their great store of scholarship and knowledge to written records. Kilt, the short male skirt of traditional Celtic dress, may also come from this word.

The Celtic civilization was quite sophisticated, and much of the road-building attributed to the Romans has been found to have been started by the Celts. The Romans frequently built on their foundations. In Ireland, ancient roads are often discovered when bog is cleared.

Ireland's ancient and rich epic story tradition was strictly oral until the Christian era. Even then, it was well into the 7th century before the bulk of it was written down by scribes, who often added to or changed the story to give it some moral Christian interpretation. The reluctance of the Celts to commit their knowledge to writing is directly related to the Druids and their power, because the Druidic religion was the cornerstone of the Celtic world, which stretched from Ireland to the Continent and as far south as Turkey. Irish mythology is therefore concerned with the rest of that Celtic world, and there are relationships with the gods and heroes of Wales, Scotland, Spain and Central Europe.

The *Book of the Dun Cow* and the *Book of Leinster*, the main surviving manuscript sources, date from the late 11th century. Many earlier books were destroyed by the Viking raids, and entire libraries lost. The various sagas and romances that survived have been categorized by scholars into four cycles. First, the **mythological cycle**: the stories that tell of the various invasions of Ireland, from Cesair to the Sons of Milesius. These are largely concerned with the activities of the Túatha Dé Danaan, the pagan gods of Ireland. Next there is the **Ulster Cycle**, or deeds of the Red Branch Knights, which include the tales of Cú Chulainn and the *Táin Bó Cuailgne*. Then there is the **Cycle of Kings**, mainly stories about semi-mythical rulers; and finally the **Fenian Cycle**, which relates the adventures of Fionn MacCumhaill (Finn MacCool) and the warriors of the Fianna. Only qualified story-tellers could recite these sagas and tales under Brehon (Celtic) laws, and they were held in great respect. Several qualities emerge from these sagas and tell us a great deal about the society of Iron Age Ireland, and indeed Europe. The stories are always optimistic, and the Celts had evolved a doctrine of immortality of the soul.

The heroes and gods were interchangeable – there were no hard and fast divisions between gods and mortals. Both had the ability to change shape, and often reappear after the most gruesome deaths. The gods of the Dé Danaan were tall, beautiful and fair, although later, in the popular imagination, they became fairies or the 'little people'. They were intellectual as well as beautiful, but as gullible as mortals, with all our virtues and vices. They loved pleasure, art, nature, games, feasting and heroic single combat. It is difficult to know whether they are heroes and heroines made into gods by their descendants. In the 11th century, Cú Chulainn was the most admired hero, particularly by the élite of society. Then Fionn MacCumhaill took over. He and his band of warriors became very popular with the ordinary people right up to the early 20th century. The English conquests in the 17th century and the resulting destruction and exile of the Irish intelligentsia meant that much knowledge was lost, though the peasantry kept it alive in folklore recited by the *seanachie* or village story-teller. Then, with the famines and vast emigration of the 19th century, the Irish language came under great threat and, with it, the folklore.

The stories were anglicized by antiquarians and scholars at the end of the 18th century and into the 19th century, who did much to record and translate the Irish epic stories into English and to preserve the Gaelic; many were Ulster Presbyterians. Names that should be remembered with honour are William Carleton, Lady Wilde, T. Crofton-Croker, Standish James O'Grady, Lady Gregory and Douglas Hyde. Their writings and records of Irish peasant culture have become standard works.

The question of where Irish myth ends and history begins is impossible to answer. Historical accounts are shot through with allegory, supernatural happenings and fantasy. Nothing at all has changed, as a similar mythical process is applied to modern Irish history.

Directory of the Gods

Amergin: a Son of Milesius. The first Druid of Ireland. There are three poems credited to him in *The Book of Invasions*.

Aonghus Óg: the God of Love, son of Dagda. His palace was by the River Boyne at Newgrange. Also known as Aengus.

Ard Rí: the title of High King.

Badhbha or *Badh*: goddess of battles.

Balor: a god of death, and one of the most formidable Fomorii. His one eye destroyed everything it gazed on. Destroyed by his own grandson, Lugh.

Banba, Fotla and Eire Dé Danaan: sister goddesses who represent the spirit of Ireland, particularly in Irish literature and poetry. It is from the goddess Eire that Ireland takes its modern name.

Bilé: god of life and death. He appears as Cymbeline in Shakespeare's play.

Bran: 'Voyage of Bran'. This is the earliest voyage poem, which describes through beautiful imagery the Island of Joy and the Island of Women. Also, the hound of Fionn MacCumhaill.

Brigid: goddess of healing, fertility and poetry. Her festival is one of the four great festivals of the Celtic world. Also a Christian saint who has become confused in popular folklore with the goddess.

Caílte: cousin of Fionn MacCumhaill. One of the chief Warriors of the Fianna, and a poet. A Christian addition to his story has returned him from the Otherworld to recount to St Patrick the adventures of the Fianna.

Conall Cearnach: son of Amergin, a warrior of the Red Branch, and foster brother and blood cousin of Cú Chulainn. He avenged Cú Chulainn's death by slaying his killers.

Conchobhar MacNessa: king of Ulster during the Red Branch Cycle. He fell in love with Deidre (see below) and died from a magic 'brain ball' which had been lodged in his head seven years before by the Connacht warrior, Cet.

Conn: one of the Sons of Lir, the ocean god, changed into a swan by his jealous step-mother Aoife. Also, Conn of the hundred battles, High King from AD 177 to 212.

Cormac MacArt: High King from AD 254 to 277 and patron of the Fianna, he reigned during the period of Fionn MacCumhaill and his adventures. His daughter was betrothed to Fionn MacCumhaill, but eloped with one of Fionn's warriors, Diarmuid. His son succeeded him and destroyed the Fianna.

Cú Chulainn: the hound of Culann, also called the Hound of Ulster. He has similarities with the Greek hero, Achilles. He was actually called Sétanta until he killed the hound belonging to Culann, a smith god from the Otherworld. He promised to take its place and guarded his fortress at night. He became a great warrior whose battle frenzy was incredible. Women were always falling in love with him, but Emer, his wife, managed to keep him. He is chiefly famous for his single-handed defence of Ulster during the War of the Tain (Bull of Cuailgne) when Ailill and Medb of Connacht invaded (see Medb). He was acknowledged as champion of all Ireland, and forced to slay his best friend, Ferdia, during a combat at a crucial ford. Later Cú Chulainn rejected the love of the goddess of battles, Mórrigan, and his doom was sealed; his enemies finally slew him. During the fatal fight he strapped his body to a pillar stone because he was too weak to stand. But such was his reputation that no one dared to come near him until Mórrigan, in the form of a crow, perched on his shoulder, and finally an otter drank his blood.

Dagha: father of the Gods and patron god of the Druids.

Diarmuid: foster son of the love god, Aonghus Óg, and a member of the Fianna. The goddess of youth put her love spot on him, so that no woman could resist loving him. He eloped with Grainne, who was betrothed to Fionn MacCumhaill, and the Fianna pursued them for 16 years. Eventually the couple made an uneasy peace with Fionn, who went out hunting with Diarmuid on Ben Bulben, where Diarmuid was gored by an enchanted boar who was also his own stepbrother. Fionn had the power to heal him with some enchanted water, but he let it slip through his fingers. Aonghus Óg, the god of love, took Diarmuid's body to his palace and, although he did not restore him to life, sent a soul into his body so that he could talk to him each day.

Deidre: Deidre of the Sorrows was the daughter of an Ulster chieftain. When she was born it was forecast by a Druid that she would be the most beautiful woman in the land, but that, because of her, Ulster would suffer great ruin and death. Her father wanted to put her to death at once, but Conchobhar, the Ulster king, took pity on her and said he would marry her when she grew up. When the time came she did not want to marry such an old man, particularly as she had fallen in love with Naoise, a hero of the Red Branch. They eloped to Scotland. Conchobhar lured them back with false promises, and Naoise and his brothers were killed by Eoghan MacDuracht. Deidre was forced to become Conchobhar's wife. She did not smile for a year, which infuriated her husband. When he asked her who she hated most in the world, she replied, 'you and Eoghan MacDuracht'. The furious Conchobhar then said she must be Eoghan's wife for a year. When she was put in Eoghan's chariot with her hands bound, she somehow managed to fling herself out and dash her head against a rock. A pine tree grew from her grave and touched another pine growing from Naoise's grave, and the two intertwined.

Donn: king of the Otherworld, where the dead go.

Emain Macha: the capital of the kings of Ulster for six centuries, which attained great glory during the time of King Conchobhar and the Red Branch Knights.

Emer: wife of Cú Chulainn. She had the six gifts of womanhood: beauty, chastity, eloquence, needlework, sweet voice and wisdom.

Female champions: in ancient Irish society women had equal rights with men. They could be elected to any office, inherit wealth and hold full ownership under law. Cú Chulainn was instructed in the martial arts by Scáthach, and there was another female warrior in the Fianna called Creidue. Battlefields were always presided over by goddesses of war. Nessa, Queen of Ulster, and Queen Medb of Connacht were great warriors and leaders. Boadicea of Britain was a Celtic warrior queen who died in AD 61, and this tradition survived with Grace O'Malley of County Mayo into the 16th century.

Ferdia: the best friend of Cú Chulainn, killed by him in a great and tragic combat in the battle over the Brown Bull of Cuailgne (or Cooley).

Fergus MacRoth: stepfather of Conchobhar, used by him to deceive Deidre and Naoise and his brothers. He went into voluntary exile to Connacht in a great fury with the king, and fought against Conchobhar and the Red Branch. But he refused to fight against Cú Chulainn, which meant the ultimate defeat of Queen Medb and her armies.

The Fianna: known as the Fenians. A band of warriors guarding the high king of Ireland. Said to have been founded in about 300 BC, they were perhaps a caste of the military élite. Fionn MacCumhaill was their greatest leader. In the time of Oscar, his grandson, they destroyed themselves through a conflict between the clans Bascna and Morna. In the 19th century the term was revived as a synonym for Irish Republican Brotherhood, and today it is used as the title for one of the main Irish political parties, Fianna Fail, which means 'Soldiers of Destiny'.

Fintan: the husband of Cesair, the first invader of Ireland. He abandoned her and survived the Great Deluge of the Bible story by turning into a salmon. Also, the Salmon of Knowledge who ate the Nuts of Knowledge before swimming to a pool in the River Boyne, where he was caught by the Druid Finegas. He was given to Fionn MacCumhaill to cook. Fionn burnt his finger on the flesh of the fish as he was turning the spit, sucked his thumb, and acquired the knowledge for himself.

Fionn MacCumhaill: anglicized as Finn MacCool. He was brought up by two wise women, then sent to study under Finegas the Druid. After acquiring the Knowledge of the Salmon, Fintan, he became known as Fionn, the Fair One. He was appointed head of the Fianna by Cormac MacArt, the High King at the time, in place of Goll MacMorna who had killed his father. His exploits are many and magical, and include creating the Giant's Causeway, in Co. Antrim. His two famous hunting hounds were Bran and Sceolan, who were actually his own nephews, the children of his bewitched sister. His son, Oísín, was the child of the goddess Sadb, but he suffered unrequited love for Grainne. In the story of the Battle of Ventry, Fionn overcomes Daire Donn, the King of the World. He is said not to be dead, but sleeping in a cave, waiting for the call to help Ireland in her hour of need.

Dé Fionnbharr and Oonagh: gods of the Dé Danaan who have degenerated into the king and queen of the Fairies in folklore.

Fionnuala: the daughter of Lir. She and her brothers were transformed into swans by her jealous stepmother, Aoife. The spell was broken with the coming of Christianity, but they were old and senile by then.

Fir Bolg: 'Bagmen'. A race who came to Ireland before the Dé Danaan. They do not take much part in the myths.

Fomorii: a misshapen and violent people, who are the evil gods of Irish myth. Their headquarters seems to have been Tory Island, off the coast of County Donegal. Their leaders include Balor of the Evil Eye, and their power was broken for ever by the Dé Danaan at the second Battle of Moytura, in County Sligo.

Gaul: Celt. Gaulish territory extended over France, Belgium, parts of Switzerland, Bohemia, parts of modern Turkey and parts of Spain.

Geis: a taboo or bond which was usually used by Druids and placed on someone to compel them to obey. Grainne put one on Diarmuid.

Goibhnin: smith god, and god of handicraft and artistry.

Goll MacMorna: leader of the Fianna before Fionn MacCumhaill.

Grainne: anglicized as Grania. Daughter of Cormac MacArt, the high king. She was betrothed to Fionn MacCumhaill but thought him very old, so she put a *geis* on Diarmuid to compel him to elope with her. Eventually he fell in love with her (*see* Diarmuid). After Diarmuid's death, although she had sworn vengeance on Fionn, she allowed herself to be wooed by him and became his wife. The Fianna despised her for this.

Laeg: charioteer to Cú Chulainn.

Lir: ocean god.

Lugh: sun god who slew his grandfather, Balor, and the father of Cú Chulainn by a mortal woman. His godly status was diminished into that of a fairy craftsman, Lugh Chromain, a leprechaun.

Macha: a woman who put a curse called *cest nóiden* on all Ulstermen, so that they would suffer from the pangs of childbirth for five days and four nights in times of Ulster's greatest need. This curse would last nine times nine generations. She did this because her husband boasted to King Conchobhar that she could beat the king's horses in a race, even though she was pregnant. She died in agony as a result.

Medb: anglicized as Maeve. Queen of Connacht, and wife of Ailill. She was famous for her role in the epic tale of the cattle raid of Cuailgne (Cooley), which she started when she found that her possessions were not as great as her husband's. She wanted the Brown Bull of Cuailgne which was in Ulster, to outdo her husband's bull, the White-Horned Bull of Connacht. This had actually started off as a calf in her herd, but had declined to stay in the herd of a woman. She persuaded her husband to join her in the great battle that resulted. The men of the Red Branch were hit by the curse of the *nóiden* (*see* Macha), and none could fight except Cú Chulainn, who was free of the weakness the curse induced and single-handedly fought the Connacht champions. Mebh was killed by Forbai, son of Conchobhar, while bathing in a lake. The bulls over which the great battle had been fought eventually tore each other to pieces.

Milesians: the last group of invaders of Ireland before the historical period. Milesius, a Spanish soldier, was their leader but his sons actually carried out the Conquest of Ireland.

Nessa: mother of Conchobhar. A strong-minded and powerful woman who secured the throne of Ulster for her son.

Niall of the Nine Hostages: High King from AD 379 to 405, and progenitor of the Uí Neill dynasty. There is a confusion of myth and history surrounding him.

Niamh: of the golden hair. A daughter of the sea god Manannán Mac Lir. She asked Oísín to accompany her to the Land of Promise and live there as her lover. After three weeks, he discovered three hundred years had passed.

Nuada of the Silver Hand: the leader of the Dé Danaan gods, who had his hand cut off in the great battle with the Fomorii. It was replaced by the god of healing.

Ogma: god of eloquence and literature, from whom ogham stones were named. These are upright pillars carved with incised lines that read as an alphabet from the bottom upwards. They probably date from AD 300.

Oísín: son of Fionn and Sadh, the daughter of a god, and leading champion of the Fianna. He refused to help his father exact vengeance on Grainne (to whom Fionn was betrothed) and Diarmuid (with whom Grainne eloped), and went with Niamh of the Golden Hair to the Land of Promise. Oísín longed to go back to Ireland, so Niamh gave him a magic horse on which to return, but warned him not to set foot on land, as three hundred years had passed since he was there. He fell from his horse by accident and turned into an old, blind man. A Christian embellishment is that he met St Patrick and told him the stories of the Fianna, and they had long debates about the merits of Christianity. Oísín refused to agree that his Ireland was better off for it. His mood comes through in this anonymous verse from a 16th-century poem translated by Frank O'Connor.

Patrick you chatter too loud
And lift your crozier too high
Your stick would be kindling soon
If my son Osgar stood by.

Oscar or Osgar: son of Oísín. He also refused to help Fionn, his grandfather, against Diarmuid and Grainne. The high king of the time wished to weaken the Fianna and allowed the two clans in it, Morna and Bascna, to quarrel. They fought at the battle of Gabhra. Oscar was killed and the Fianna destroyed.

Partholón: the leader of the third mythical invasion of Ireland. He is supposed to have introduced agriculture to Ireland.

Red Branch: a body of warriors who were the guardians of Ulster during the reign of Conchobhar MacNessa. Their headquarters were at Emain (*Eamhain*) Macha. The Red Branch cycle of tales has been compared to the Iliad in theme. The main stories are made up of the *Táin Bó Cuailgne* (the Brown Bull of Cuailgne or Cooley). Scholars accept that the cycle of stories must have been transmitted orally for nearly a thousand years, providing wonderful descriptions of the remote past.

Irish Saints

Every locality in Ireland has its particular saint. The stories that surround him or her belong to myth and legend, not usually to historical fact. One theory is that all these obscure, miraculous figures are in fact Celtic gods and goddesses who survived under the mantle of sainthood. Included below is a short account of the lives of some of the most famous saints, about whom a few facts are known.

Brendan (*c.* 486–575), Abbot and Navigator

This holy man is remembered for his scholastic foundations, and for the extraordinary journey he made in search of Hy-Brasil, believed to be an island of paradise, which he had seen as a mirage whilst looking out on the Atlantic from the Kerry Mountains. His journey is recounted in the *Navigatio Brendan*, a treasure of every European library during the Middle Ages. The oldest copies are in Latin and date from the 11th century. The account describes a sea voyage that took Brendan and 12 monks to the Orkneys, Wales, Iceland, and to a land where tropical fruits and flowers grew. Descriptions of his voyage have convinced some scholars that he sailed down the east coast of America to Florida. Tim Severin, a modern-day explorer, and 12 others recreated this epic voyage between May 1976 and June 1977. In their leather and wood boat, they proved that the Irish monks could have been the first Europeans to land in America (the boat is at the Lough Gur Interpretative Centre, County Limerick). Christopher Columbus probably read the *Navigatio*, and in Galway there is a strong tradition that he came to the west coast in 1492 to search out traditions about St Brendan. The saint's main foundation was at Clonfert, which became a great scholastic centre. Brendan is buried in Clonfert Cathedral, and he is honoured in St Brendan's Cathedral in Loughrea, County Galway, where the beautiful mosaic floor in the sanctuary depicts his ship and voyage.

St Brigid (died *c.* 525), Abbess of Kildare

Brigid, also known as Bridget, Bride and Brigit, is the most beloved saint in Ireland and is often called Mary of the Gael. Devotion to her spread to Scotland, England and the Continent. Traditions and stories surrounding her describe her generous and warm-hearted acts to the poor, her ability to counsel the rulers of the day, and her great holiness. Her father was a pagan from Leinster and she was fostered by a Druid.

She decided not to marry and founded a religious order with seven other girls. They were the first formal community of nuns and wore simple white dresses. St Brigid has her feast day on 1 February, which is also the date of the pagan festival Imbolg, marking the beginning of spring. She is the patron of poets, scholars, blacksmiths and healers, and is also inevitably linked with Brigid, the pagan goddess of fire and song. There is a tradition that St Brigid's Abbey in Kildare contained a sanctuary with a perpetual fire, tended only by virgins, whose high priestess was regarded as an incarnation and successor of the goddess. The two women are further linked by the fact that Kildare in Irish means 'church of oak', and St Brigid's church was built from a tree held sacred to the Druids. There's a theory that Brigid and her companions accepted the Christian faith, and then transformed the pagan sanctuary into a Christian shrine.

Kildare was a great monastic centre after Brigid's death, and produced the now lost masterpiece, the *Kildare Gospels*. Tradition says that the designs were so beautiful because an angel helped create them. The St Brigid's nuns kept alight the perpetual fire until the suppression of the religious houses during the Reformation. Brigid was buried in Kildare Church, but in AD 835 her remains were moved to Downpatrick in County Down, because of the raids by the Norsemen. She is supposed to share a grave with St Patrick and St Colmcille, but there is no proof of this. In 1283 it is recorded that three Irish knights set out to the Holy Land with her head; they died en route in Lamiar, Portugal, and in a church there her head is enshrined in a chapel to St Brigid. The word 'bride' derives from St Brigid. It is supposed to originate from the Knights of Chivalry, whose patroness she was; they called the girls they married their 'brides'.

St Columban (died 615), Missionary Abbot

Columban, also known as Columbanus, is famous as the great missionary saint. He was born in Leinster and educated at Bangor in County Down under St Comgall, who was famed for his scholarship and piety. Columban set off for Europe with 12 other religious men to preach the gospel and convert the pagans in Gaul (France) and Germany. He founded a monastery at Annegray, which is between Austria and Burgundy, in AD 575, and his rule of austerity attracted many. Lexeuil, a larger monastery, and Fontaines were both established within a few miles of Annegray. When Columban was exiled by the local king, he and his followers founded Bobbio in the Apennines, between Piacenza and Genoa. Bobbio became a great centre of culture and orthodoxy from which monasticism spread. Its great glory was its library, and its books are scattered all over Europe and regarded as treasures.

St Colmcille (*c.* 521–97), Missionary Abbot

Along with St Patrick and St Brigid, Colmcille, also known as Columba and Columcille, is probably the most famous of the Irish saints, a charismatic personality who was a scholar, poet and ruler, and spread the gospel to Iona and hence to Scotland. St Colmcille was a prince of Tyrconnell (County Donegal), and a great-great-grandson of Niall of the Nine Hostages, who had been High King of Ireland. On his mother's side he was descended from the Leinster Kings. He was educated by

St Finian of Movilla, in County Down, and also by Finnian of Clonard and Mobhi of Glasnevin. He studied music and poetry at the Bardic School of Leinster, and the poems he wrote which have survived are delightful. A few are preserved in the Bodleian Library, Oxford. He chose to be a monk, and never to receive episcopal rank. He wrote of his devotion: 'The fire of God's love stays in my heart as a jewel set in gold in a silver vessel.' In AD 545 he built his first church in Derry, the place he loved most. Then he founded Durrow and later Kells, which became very important in the 9th century when the Columban monks of Iona fled from the Vikings and made it their headquarters. In all, Colmcille founded 37 monastic churches in Ireland; he also produced the *Cathach*, a manuscript of the Psalms. At the age of 42 he set out with 12 companions to be an exile for Christ. They sailed to the island of Iona, off the west coast of Scotland, which was part of the Kingdom of Dalriada ruled over by the Irish King Aidan. He converted Brude, King of the Picts, founded two churches in Inverness and helped to keep the peace between the Picts and the Irish colony. The legend that he left Ireland because of a dispute over the copy he made of a psalter of St Finian is very dubious. Apparently the dispute caused a great battle, although the high king of the time, King Diarmuid, tried to settle the dispute and had ruled against Colmcille, saying: 'to every cow its calf, to every book its copy'. The saint is supposed to have punished himself for the deaths he caused by going into exile. Colmcille was famous for his austerity, fasting and vigils; his bed and pillow were of stone. He died at Iona, and his relics were taken to Dunkeld (Scotland) in AD 849.

St Enda of Aran (died *c.* 535), Abbot

Famous as the patriarch of monasticism, he's described as a warrior who left the secular world in middle life. He had succeeded to the kingdom of Oriel, but decided to study for the priesthood. Granted the Aran Islands by his brother-in-law, Aengus, King of Cashel, he is said to have lived a life of great severity, and never had a fire in winter, as he believed that 'hearts so glowing with the love of God' could not feel the cold. He reputedly taught 127 other saints, who are buried close to him on the islands.

St Kevin of Glendalough (died *c.* 618), Abbot

Many stories surround St Kevin, but we know he was one of the many Irish abbots who chose to remain a priest. He lived a solitary, contemplative life in the Glendalough Valley. He played the harp, and the Rule for his monks was in verse. He is supposed to have prayed for so long that a blackbird had time to lay an egg and hatch it on his outstretched hand. His monastery flourished until the 11th century. In the 12th century St Lawrence O'Toole came to Glendalough and modelled his life on St Kevin's, bringing fresh fame to his memory. The foundation was finally destroyed in the 16th century.

St Kieran (*c.* 512–49), Abbot

St Kieran, also known as Ciaran, is remembered for his great foundation of Clonmacnoise, where the ancient chariot road through Ireland crosses the River Shannon . Unlike many Irish abbots he was not of aristocratic blood, for his father was a chariot-maker from County Antrim, and his mother from Kerry. St Kieran attracted craftsmen to his order, and Clonmacnoise grew to be a great monastic school, where, unusually for Ireland, the position of abbot did not become hereditary. Kieran died within a short time of founding the school. Many kings are buried along-side him, for it was believed that he would bring their souls safely to heaven.

St Malachy (1094–1148), Archbishop of Armagh

Malachy is famous as the great reformer of the Irish Church. He persuaded the Pope, Eugenius III, to establish the Archbishops of Ireland separately from those of England. He also ensured that it was no longer possible for important ecclesiastical positions to be held by certain families as a hereditary right. For example, he was appointed Bishop of Armagh, although the See of Armagh was held in lay succession by one family. It was an achievement to separate the family from this post without splitting the Irish Church.

The saint was educated in Armagh and Lismore, County Waterford, and desired only to be an itinerant preacher. His great talents took him instead to be Bishop of Down and Connor, and in 1125 he became Abbot-Bishop of Armagh. He travelled to France, where he made a lasting friendship with Bernard of Clairvaux, the reforming Cistercian. The Pope appointed him papal legate in Ireland, and whilst abroad he made some famous prophecies; one was that there will be the peace of Christ over all Ireland when the palm and the shamrock meet. This is supposed to mean when St Patrick's Day (17 March) occurs on Palm Sunday.

St Patrick (c. 390–461), Bishop and Patron Saint of Ireland

St Patrick was born somewhere between the Severn and the Clyde on the west coast of Britain. As a youth he was captured by Irish slave-traders, and taken to the Antrim coast to work as a farm labourer. Controversy surrounds the details of Patrick's life. Popular tradition credits him with converting the whole of Ireland, but nearly all that can be truly known of him comes from his *Confessio* or autobiography, and other writings. Through these, he is revealed as a simple, sincere and humble man who was full of care for his people; an unlearned man, once a fugitive, who came to trust God completely. Tradition states that after six years of slavery, voices told him he would soon return to his own land, and he escaped. Later, other voices called to him from Ireland, entreating him 'to come and walk once more amongst us'.

It is believed that he spent some time in Gaul (France) and became a priest; perhaps he had some mission conferred on him by the Pope to go and continue the work of Palladius, another missionary bishop who worked among the Christian Irish. It is believed that some confusion has arisen over the achievements of Palladius and Patrick. Patrick, when he returned to Ireland, seems to have been most active in the north, whilst Palladius worked in the south. He made Armagh his primary see, and it has remained the centre of Christianity in Ireland. He organized the church on the lines of territorial sees, and encouraged the laity to become monks or nuns. He was very concerned with abolishing paganism, idolatry and sun-worship, and he preached to the highest and the lowest in the land. Tradition credits him with expelling the snakes from Ireland, and explaining the Trinity by pointing to a shamrock. One of the most famous episodes handed down by popular belief is that of his confrontation with King Laoghaire at Tara, known as the seat of the high kings of Ireland, and the capital of Meath. It was supposedly on Easter Saturday in 432, which that year coincided with a great Druid festival at Tara. No new fire was allowed to be lit until the lighting of the sacred pagan fire by the Druids. St Patrick was camped on the Hill of Slane which looks onto Tara, and his campfire was burning brightly; the Druids warned King Laoghaire that if it was not put out, it would never be extinguished. When Patrick was brought before Laoghaire, his holiness melted the king's hostility and he was invited to stay. Although Laoghaire did not become a Christian, his brother Conal, a prince of the North, became his protector and ally.

Certain places in Ireland are traditionally closely associated with St Patrick, such as Croagh Patrick in County Mayo, where there is an annual pilgrimage to the top of the 2,510ft (765m) mountain on the last Sunday of July; and Downpatrick and Saul in County Down. The cult of St Patrick spread from Ireland to many Irish monasteries in Europe, and in more modern times to North America and Australia, where large communities of Irish emigrants live. The annual procession on 17 March, St Patrick's Day, in New York has become a massive event, where everybody sports a shamrock and drinks green beer. However, quite a few Irish believe St Colmcille should be the patron saint of Ireland, not this mild and humble British missionary.

Oliver Plunkett (1625–81), Archbishop of Armagh and Martyr

This gentle and holy man lived in frightening and turbulent times, when to be a practising Catholic in Ireland was to court trouble. He was born into a noble and wealthy family whose lands extended throughout the Pale. He was sent to study in Rome, and was a brilliant theology and law scholar. He became a priest in 1654 and in 1669 was appointed Archbishop of Armagh. Oliver was one of only two bishops in Ireland at that time, and the whole of the laity was in disorder and neglect. Apart from the hostility of the Protestants, the Catholics themselves were divided by internal squabbles. Oliver confirmed thousands of people, and held a provincial synod. He did much to maintain discipline amongst the clergy, to improve education by founding the Jesuit College in Drogheda, and to promulgate the decrees of the Council of Trent. Oliver managed to remain on good terms with many of the Protestant gentry and clergy, but was eventually outlawed by the British government. The panic caused by the false allegations made by Titus Oates in England about a popish plot was used by Plunkett's enemies, and he was arrested in 1678. He was absurdly charged with plotting to bring in twenty thousand French troops, and levying a charge on his clergy to support an army. No jury could be found to convict him in Ireland, so he was brought to England, where he was convicted of treason for setting up 'a false religion which was the most dishonourable and derogatory to God of all religions and that a greater crime could not be committed against God than for a man to endeavour to propagate that religion'. He was hanged, drawn and quartered at Tyburn in July 1681. His head is in the Oliver Plunkett Church in Drogheda, County Louth, and his body lies at Downside Abbey, Somerset.

Language

The Irish language is the purest of all the Celtic languages; and Ireland is one of the last homes of the prehistoric and medieval European oral tradition. The language was preserved by isolated farming communities, along with many expressions from the dialects of early English settlers. Irish was spoken by the Norman aristocracy, who patronized the Gaelic poets and bards. But with the establishment of an English system of land tenure and an English-speaking nobility, Gaelic became scarce, except in the poorer farming areas. The Famine in the 1840s hit those who lived here very hard; thousands died or emigrated, and spoken Gaelic was severely curtailed. The Gaelic League, founded in 1870, initiated a new interest and pride in the language and became identified with rising nationalism. In 1921 its survival became part of the new State's policy. It was decided that the only way to preserve Gaelic was to protect and stimulate it in the places where it was still a living language.

It is spoken today mostly in the west and around the mountainous coast and islands. These areas form 'the Gaeltacht'. Here, everything is done to promote Irish-speaking, in industry and at home. Centres have been set up for students to learn among the native speakers. There are special grants for people living in Irish-speaking areas, but the boundaries are a little arbitrary. In Galway there's a boundary line through a built-up area, so there's a certain amount of animosity between the two sides of the line, Irish speakers or no. There is also the problem of standardizing Irish, for the different dialects are quite distinct. The modern media tend to iron these out with the adoption of one region's form of words in preference to others. County Donegal seems to get the worst deal, being so much further from the centre of administration, although it has the largest number of native speakers.

One can appreciate all the reasons for promoting Irish, but it is only in the last few generations that the language has become popular. Before, it was left to Douglas Hyde and Lady Gregory to demonstrate the richness of Irish language and myth, and they had the advantage of being far away from the grim realities of hunger and poverty that the Irish speakers knew. Gaelic, like certain foods (usually vegetables), had associations with hunger and poverty, and belonged to a hard past. The cultural coercion of the 1930s had a negative effect on most Irish people. It was only in Ulster that Gaelic speaking and culture kept its appeal in the face of Protestant and official antipathy. Even now, people prefer to use English rather than stay in the Gaeltacht, existing on grants and other government hand-outs. Gaelic is a compulsory subject in schools in the Republic, and there is a certain amount in the newspapers, on TV, radio, sign-posts and street names (with English translations). The use of Gaelic amongst the more intellectual of the middle classes is now on the increase, and this is being reinforced by the establishment of Gaelic-speaking primary schools throughout the country. Irish Gaelic is one of the official languages of the European Union.

The carrying over of Irish idiom into English is very attractive and expressive. J.M. Synge captured this in his play *Riders to the Sea*. In fact, English as spoken by the Irish is in a class of its own. Joyce talked of 'the sacred eloquence of Ireland', and it is true that you could hardly find a more articulate people. Their poetry and prose is superb, and the emotions that their ballads can release is legendary. Great hardship and poverty have not killed the instinctive desire within to explain life with words. The monk who scribbled in the margin of his psalter wrote with oriental simplicity the following poem entitled 'Winter':

My tiding for you: The stag bells
Winter snows, summer is gone.
Wind is high and cold, low the sun,
Short his course, sea running high.
Deep red the bracken, its shape all gone,
The wild goose has raised his wonted cry.
Cold has caught the wings of birds;
season of ice – these are my tidings.

9th century, translation by Kuno Meyer

That hardship brings forth great poetry is a theory strengthened by the school of contemporary northern Irish poets who have become known all over the world: Seamus Heaney, James Simmons, Derek Mahon, Medbh McGuckian. The cutting criticisms of Brian O'Nolan (known as Flann O'Brien), the gentle irony of Frank O'Connor and the furious passion of Sean O'Casey, Patrick Kavanagh, Liam O'Flaherty and John McGahern, to name only a few, have become part of our perception of the Irish spirit since Independence. The list of recent writers could go on and on. One can only urge you to read them. There is a particularly good anthology of short stories edited by Benedict Kiely (Penguin) and an anthology of Irish verse, edited by John Montague (Faber).

Even though the disciplined cadences of the Gaelic bardic order was broken by the imposition of an English nobility in the 17th and 18th centuries, the Irish skill with words has survived, and is as strong as ever. As a visitor to Ireland you will notice this way with words when you have a conversation in a pub, ask the way at a crossroads, or simply chat to the owners of the farmhouse where you spend the night.

The Meaning of Irish Place Names

The original Gaelic place names have been complicated by attempts to give them an English spelling. In the following examples, the Gaelic versions of the prefixes come first, followed by the English meaning.

agh, augh, achadh a field
aglish, eaglais a church
ah, atha, áth a ford
all, ail, aill a cliff
anna, canna, éanarch a marsh

ard, ar, ard a height
as, ess, eas a waterfall
aw, ow, atha a river
bal, bel, béal the mouth (of a river or valley)
bal, balli, bally, baile a town
ballagh, balla, bealach a way or path
bawn, bane, bán white
barn, bearna a gap
beg, beag small
boola, booley, buaile, booleying the movement of cattle from lowland to high pastures (transhumance)
boy, buidhe yellow
bun the foot (of a valley) or mouth (of a river)
caher, cahir, cathair, carraig a rock
cashel, caiseal, caislean a castle
clogh, cloich, cloch a stone
clon, clun, cluain a meadow
derg, dearg red
doo, du, duv, duf, dubh black
dun, dún a fort
dysert, disert hermitage
glas, glen, gleann a valley
illaun, oileán an island
knock, cnoc a hill
ken, kin, can, ceann a headland
kil, kill, cill a church
lis, liss, lios a fort
lough, loch a lake or sea inlet
ma, may, moy, magh a plain
mone, mona, móna turf or bog
monaster, mainistir a monastery
more, mór, mor big or great
owen, avon, abhainn a river
rath a ring-fort
rinn, reen a point
roe, ruadh red
ross, ros a peninsula, a wood
see, suidhe a seat, e.g. Ossian's seat
shan, shane, sean old
slieve, sliabh a mountain
tir, tyr, tír country
tubber, tobrid, tubbrid, tobar a well
tra, traw, tráigh, trá a strand or beach

Some Ulster and Other Expressions

an oul sceach crosspatch
assay attention, as in Hi!
auld flutter guts fussy person
balls of malt whiskey

ballyhooley a telling off (in Cork)
blow-in stranger to the area
boreen country lane
brave commendable, worthy, e.g. a brave wee sort of a girl
bravely could be worse, e.g. business is doing bravely
caution (as in 'He's a caution'), a devil-may-care-type
chawing the rag bickering couple
chick child
cleg horsefly
clever neat, tight-fitting, usually refers to a garment
coul wintry, cold
craic fun, lively chat
cranky bad-tempered
craw thumper a 'holy Mary' or hypocrite
cut insulted, hurt
dead on exactly right
deed passed away, dead
destroyed exhausted
dingle dent, mark with an impression
dip bread fried in a pan
dither slow
doley little fella he's lovely
dulse edible seaweed
eejit fool
fairly excellent, e.g. that wee lad can fairly sing
feed meal
fern foreign
in fiddler's green you're in a big mess
fierce unacceptable, extreme, e.g. it's fierce dear (expensive)
figuresome good at sums
fog feed lavish meal
foostering around fiddling about
guff impertinence, cheek
half sir landlord's son
harp six tumble
he hasn't a titter of wit no sense at all
jar a couple of drinks
lashins plenty
mended improved in health
mizzlin raining gently
mullarkey man
neb nose
nettle drive someone barmy
ni now, this moment
not the full shilling half-witted
oul or auld not young, but can be used about something useful, e.g. my oul car

owlip verbal abuse
palsie walsie great friends
paralytic intoxicated
plamas sweet words
playboy conceited fellow
poless police
put the caibosh on it mess things up
quare memorable, unusual
qurrier or cowboy bad type, rogue
rare to bring up, educate
rightly prospering, e.g. he's doing rightly now
scalded bothered, vexed, badly burned
she's like a corncrake chatterbox
skedaddled ran quickly
skiff slight shower or rain
slainte drinking toast
soft rainy, e.g. it's a grand soft day
spalpeen agricultural labourer
spittin' starting to rain
terrible same use as 'fierce'
themins those persons
thick as a ditch stupid
thundergub loud-voiced person
wean pronounced wain, child
wee little; also in the north means with, e.g. did I see you *wee* that man?
you could trot a mouse on it strong tea

Proverbs and Sayings

Wise, and beautifully expressed with a delightful wry humour, these sayings and proverbs have passed into the English language. They highlight the usual Irish preoccupations with land, God, love, words and drinking, as well as every other subject under the sun. These are just a few examples; for a comprehensive collection read *Gems of Irish Wisdom*, by Padraic O'Farrell.

On God
It's a blessing to be in the Lord's hand as long as he doesn't close his fist.
Fear of God is the beginning of wisdom.
God never closes the door without opening another.
Man proposes, God disposes.

On the Irish Character
The wrath of God has nothing on the wrath of an Irishman outbid for land, horse or woman.

The best way to get an Irishman to refuse to
do something is by ordering it.

The Irish forgive their great men when they
are safely buried.

It is not that the Ulsterman lives in the past...
it is rather that the past lives in him.

Advice

No property – no friends, no rearing – no
manners, no health – no hope!

Never give cherries to pigs, nor advice to a
fool.

Bigots and begrudgers will never bid the past
farewell.

When everybody else is running, that's the
time for you to walk.

You won't be stepped on if you're a live wire.

If you get the name of an early riser you can
sleep till dinner time.

There are finer fish in the sea than have ever
been caught.

You'll never plough a field by turning it over in
your mind.

Don't make a bid till you walk the land.

A man with humour will keep ten men
working.

Do not visit too often or too long.

If you don't own a mount, don't hunt with the
gentry.

You can take a man out of the bog but you
cannot take the bog out of the man.

What is got badly, goes badly.

A watched pot never boils.

Enough is as good as plenty.

Beware of the horse's hoof, the bull's horn and
the Saxon's smile.

Time is the best story-teller.

On Marriage and Love

Play with a woman that has looks,
talk marriage with a woman that
has property.

After the settlement comes love.

A lad's best friend is his mother until he's the
best friend of a lassie.

A pot was never boiled by beauty.

There is no love sincerer than the love of food.
(G. B. Shaw)

It's a great thing to turn up laughing having
been turned down crying.

Though the marriage bed be rusty, the death
bed is still colder.

On Argument and Fighting

Argument is the worst sort of conversation.
(Dean Swift)

There is no war as bitter as a war amongst
friends.

Whisper into the glass when ill is spoken.

If we fought temptation the way we fight
each other we'd be a nation of saints again.

We fought every nation's battles, and the only
ones we did not win were our own.

On Women

It takes a woman to outwit the Devil.

A cranky woman, an infant, or a grievance,
should never be nursed.

A woman in the house is a treasure, a woman
with humour in the house is a blessing.

She who kisses in public often kicks in private.

If she is mean at the table, she will be mean
in bed.

On Drinking

If Holy Water was porter he'd be at Mass every
morning.

It's the first drop that destroys you; there's no
harm at all in the last.

Thirst is a shameless disease, so here's to a
shameless cure.

On the Family

Greed in a family is worse than need.

Poets write about their mothers, undertakers
about their fathers.

A son's stool in his father's home is as steady
as a gable; a father's in his son's, bad luck, is
shaky and unstable.

On Old Age

The older the fiddle, the sweeter the tune.

There is no fool like an old fool.

On Loneliness

The loneliest man is the man who is lonely in
a crowd.

On Bravery

A man who is not afraid of the sea will soon
be drowned. (J. M. Synge)

On Flattery

Soft words butter no turnips, but they won't
harden the heart of a cabbage, either.

Index

Main page references are in **bold**. Page references to maps are in *italics*.

Also available from Cadogan Guides in our European series...

France

France
Dordogne & the Lot
Gascony & the Pyrenees
Brittany
Loire
South of France
Provence
Côte d'Azur
Corsica
Short Breaks in Northern France

Italy

Italy
The Bay of Naples and Southern Italy
Lombardy and the Italian Lakes
Tuscany, Umbria and the Marches
Tuscany
Umbria
Northeast Italy
Italian Riviera and Piemonte
Bologna and Emilia Romagna
Central Italy
Sardinia
Sicily
Rome Venice Florence

Spain

Spain
Andalucía
Northern Spain
Bilbao and the Basque Lands
Granada Seville Córdoba

Greece

Greece
Greek Islands
Athens and Southern Greece
Crete

The UK and Ireland

England
London–Paris
London Markets

Scotland
Scotland's Highlands and Islands

Ireland
Ireland: Southwest Ireland

Other Europe

Portugal
Madeira & Porto Santo
Malta, Gozo & Comino

The City Guide Series

Amsterdam
Barcelona
Bruges
Brussels
Edinburgh
Florence
London
Madrid
Milan
Paris
Prague
Rome
Venice

Flying Visits

Flying Visits France
Flying Visits Italy
Flying Visits Spain
Flying Visits Switzerland
Flying Visits Scandinavia
Flying Visits Germany
Flying Visits Ireland

Cadogan Guides are available from good bookshops, or via **Littlehampton Book Services,** Faraday Close, Durrington, Worthing, West Sussex BN13 3RB, t (01903) 828800, f (01903) 828802; and **The Globe Pequot Press,** 246 Goose Lane, PO Box 480, Guilford, Connecticut 06437–0480, t (800) 458 4500/t (203) 458 4500, t (203) 458 4603.